Create GUI Applications with Python & Qt5

The hands-on guide to making apps with Python

Martin Гitzpatrick

Version 4.0, 2020-12-22

Table of Contents

Introduction

If you want to create GUI applications with Python it can be tricky to know where to start. There are a lot of new concepts you need to understand to get *anything* to work. But, like any coding problem, the first step is learning to approach the problem in the right way. In this book I take you right from the basic principles of GUI development to creating your own, fully functional, desktop apps with PyQt5.

The first edition of this book was released in 2016. Since then it has been updated 4 times, adding and expanding chapters in response to reader feedback. There are more PyQt5 resources available now than when I started, but there is still a shortage of in-depth, practical guides to building complete apps. This book fills that gap!

The book is formatted as a series of chapters exploring different aspects of PyQt5 in turn. They are arranged to put the simpler chapters toward the beginning, but if you have specific requirements for your project, don't be afraid to jump around! Each chapter will guide you through learning the fundamental concepts before taking you through a series of coding examples to gradually explore and learn how to apply the ideas yourself.

You can download source code and resources for all examples in this book from http://www.learnpyqt.com/d/pyqt5-source.zip

It is not possible to give you a *complete* overview of the Qt system in a book of this size, so there are links to external resources—both on the LearnPyQt.com website and elsewhere. If you find yourself thinking "I wonder if I can do *that*?" the best thing you can do is put this book down, then *go and find out!* Just keep regular backups of your code along the way so you always have something to come back to if you royally mess it up.

Throughout this book there are boxes like this, giving info, tips and warnings. All of them can be safely skipped over if you are in a hurry, but reading them will give you a deeper and more rounded knowledge of the Qt framework.

Finally, this book is written to be compatible with Python 3.4+. Python 3 is the future of the language and if you're starting out now is where you should be focusing your efforts. However, many of the examples can be changed with minimal effort to work with Python 2.7.

1. A *very* brief history of the GUI

The **Graphical User Interface** has a long and venerable history dating back as far as the 1960s. Stanford's NLS (oN-Line System) introduced the mouse and windows concepts, first demonstrated publicly in 1968. This was followed by the Xerox PARC Smalltalk system GUI 1973, which is the foundation of most modern general purpose GUIs.

These early systems already had many of the features we take for granted in modern desktop GUIs, including windows, menus, radio buttons, check boxes and later icons. This combination of features—gave us the early acronym used for these types of interfaces: WIMP (windows, icons, menus, pointing device—a mouse).

In 1979 the first commercial system featuring a GUI was released—the PERQ workstation. This spurred a number of other GUI efforts including notably the Apple Lisa (1983), which added the concept of the menu bar and window controls. As well as many other systems from the Atari ST (GEM), Amiga. On UNIX (and later Linux) the X Window System emerged in 1984. The first version of Windows for PC was released in 1985.

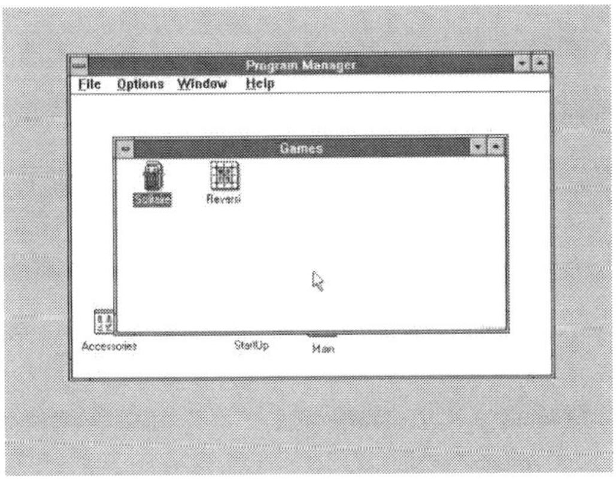

Microsoft Windows 3.1

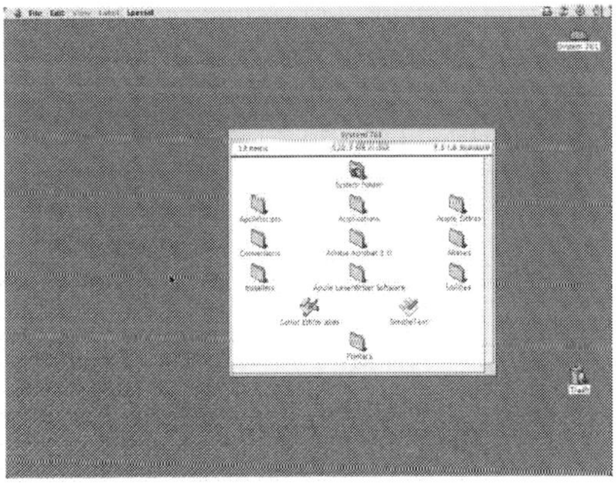

Apple System 7 (Emulated)

Figure 1. The desktop on Microsoft Windows 3.1 (1992) and Apple System 7 (1991)

Early GUIs were not the instant hit we might assume, due to the lack of compatible software at launch and expensive hardware requirements—particularly for home users. Slowly, but steadily, the GUI interface become the preferred way to interact with computers and the

WIMP metaphor became firmly established as the standard. That's not to say there haven't been *attempts* to replace the WIMP metaphor on the desktop. Microsoft Bob (1995), for example, was Microsoft's much maligned attempt to replace the desktop with a house.

Figure 2. Microsoft Bob—Discarding the desktop metaphor for a cartoon house.

There have been no shortage of other GUIs hailed as *revolutionary* in their time, from the launch of Windows 95 (1995) through to Mac OS X (2001), GNOME Shell (2011) and Windows 10 (2015). Each of these overhauled the UIs of their respective desktop systems, often with much fanfare. But fundamentally nothing really changed. These new UIs are still very much WIMP systems and function in exactly the same way as GUIs have since the 1980s.

When the revolution came, it was mobile—the mouse has been replaced by touch, and windows by full-screen apps. But even in a world where we all walk around with smartphones in our pocket, a huge amount of daily work is still done on desktop computers. WIMP has survived 40 years of innovation and looks to survive many more.

2. A bit about Qt

Qt is a free and open-source *widget toolkit* for creating cross-platform GUI applications, allowing applications to target multiple platforms from Windows, macOS, Linux and Android with a single codebase. But Qt is *much more* than a widget toolkit and features built in support for multimedia, databases, vector graphics and MVC interfaces, it is more accurate to think of it as an application development *framework*.

Qt was started by Eirik Chambe-Eng and Haavard Nord in 1991, founding the first Qt company *Trolltech* in 1994. Qt is currently developed by *The Qt Company* and continues to be regularly updated, adding features and extending mobile and cross-platform support.

Qt and PyQt5

PyQt5 is a Python *binding* of the Qt toolkit, developed by *Riverbank Computing*. When you write applications using PyQt5 what you area *really* doing is writing applications in Qt. The PyQt5 library is simply.[1] a wrapper around the C++ Qt library, to allow it to be used in Python.

Because this is a Python interface to a C++ library the naming conventions used within PyQt5 do not adhere to PEP8 standards. Most notably functions and variables are named using `mixedCase` rather than `snake_case`. Whether you adhere to this standard in your own applications is entirely up to you, however I find it helped to follow Python standards for my own code, to help clarify where the PyQt5 code ends and your own begins.

Lastly, while there is PyQt5 specific documentation available, you will often find yourself reading the Qt documentation itself as it is more complete. If you do you will need to translate object syntax and some methods containing Python-reserved function names as follows:

Qt	PyQt5
`Qt::SomeValue`	`Qt.SomeValue`
`object.exec()`	`object.exec_()`
`object.print()`	`object.print_()`

> If you need to convert an entire Qt code example to Python, take a look at Translating C++ Examples to Python.

This book is written to work with the latest version of Qt (and PyQt5). As of writing this is Qt 5.14. However, many of the examples will work fine with earlier and later versions of Qt.

[1] Not really *that* simple.

3. Thank you

This book continues to be expanded and updated in response to reader feedback. Thankyou to the following readers for their contributions, which helped make this edition what it is!

- James Battat, Associate Professor of Physics, Wellesley College
- Alex Bender
- Andries Broekema
- Juan Cabanela
- Richard Hohlfield
- Olivier Girard]
- Cody Jackson, Mentor, Code-a-Mom
- John E Kadwell
- Jeffrey R Kennedy
- Gajendra Khanna
- Bing Xiao Liu
- Alex Lombardi
- Juan Pablo Donayre Quintana
- Guido Tognan

If you have feedback or suggestions for future editions, please get in touch [mailto:martin@learnpyqt.com].

4. Copyright

Basic PyQt5 Features

It's time to take your first steps in creating GUI applications with PyQt5!

In this chapter you will be introduced to the basics of PyQt5 that are the foundations of any application you create. We will develop a simple windowed application on your desktop. We'll add widgets, arrange them using layouts and connect these widgets to functions, allowing you to trigger application behavior from your GUI.

Use the provided code as your guide, but always feel free to experiment. That's the best way to learn how things work.

> Before you get started, you need a working installation of PyQt5. If you don't have one yet, check out Installing PyQt5.

> Don't forget to download the source code that accompanies this book from http://www.learnpyqt.com/d/pyqt5-source.zip

5. My first Application

Let's create our first application! To start create a new Python file — you can call it whatever you like (e.g. `myapp.py`) and save it somewhere accessible. We'll write our simple app in this file.

> We'll be editing within this file as we go along, and you may want to come back to earlier versions of your code, so remember to keep regular backups.

Creating your App

The source code for your very first application is shown below. Type it in verbatim, and be careful not to make mistakes. If you do mess up, Python will let you know what's wrong. If you don't feel like typing it all in, the file is included in the source code with this book.

Listing 1. basic/creating_a_window_1.py

```
from PyQt5.QtWidgets import QApplication, QWidget

# Only needed for access to command line arguments
import sys

# You need one (and only one) QApplication instance per application.
# Pass in sys.argv to allow command line arguments for your app.
# If you know you won't use command line arguments QApplication([])
works too.
app = QApplication(sys.argv)

# Create a Qt widget, which will be our window.
window = QWidget()
window.show()  # IMPORTANT!!!!! Windows are hidden by default.

# Start the event loop.
app.exec_()


# Your application won't reach here until you exit and the event
# loop has stopped.
```

First, launch your application. You can run it from the command line like any other Python script, for example—

```
python MyApp.py
```

Or, for Python 3—

```
python3 MyApp.py
```

From now on, you'll see the following box as a hint to run your application and test it out, along with an indication of what you'll see.

> 🚀 **Run it!** You will now see your window. Qt automatically creates a window with the normal window decorations and you can drag it around and resize it like any window.

What you'll see will depend on what platform you're running this example on. The image below shows the window as displayed on Windows, macOS and Linux (Ubuntu).

Figure 3. Our window, as seen on Windows, macOS and Linux.

Stepping through the code

Let's step through the code line by line, so we understand exactly what is happening.

First, we import the PyQt5 classes that we need for the application. Here we're importing `QApplication`, the application handler and `QWidget`, a basic *empty* GUI widget, both from the `QtWidgets` module.

```
from PyQt5.QtWidgets import QApplication, QWidget
```

The main modules for Qt are `QtWidgets`, `QtGui` and `QtCore`.

> 💡 You could do `from <module> import *` but this kind of global import is generally frowned upon in Python, so we'll avoid it here.

Next we create an instance of `QApplication`, passing in `sys.arg`, which is

Python `list` containing the command line arguments passed to the application.

```
app = QApplication(sys.argv)
```

If you know you won't be using command line arguments to control Qt you can pass in an empty list instead, e.g.

```
app = QApplication([])
```

Next we create an instance of a `QWidget` using the variable name `window`.

```
window = QWidget()
window.show()
```

In Qt *all* top level widgets are windows—that is, they don't have a *parent* and are not nested within another widget or layout. This means you can technically create a window using any widget you like.

> *I can't see my window!*
>
> Widgets *without a parent* are invisible by default. So, after creating the `window` object, we must **always** call `.show()` to make it visible. You can remove the `.show()` and run the app, but you'll have no way to quit it!

> *What is a window?*
>
> - Holds the user-interface of your application
> - Every application needs at least one (...but can have more)
> - Application will (by default) exit when last window is closed

Finally, we call `app.exec_()` to start up the event loop.

What's the event loop?

Before getting the window on the screen, there are a few key concepts to introduce about how applications are organised in the Qt world. If you're already familiar with event loops you can safely skip to the next section.

The core of every Qt Applications is the `QApplication` class. Every application needs one — and only one — `QApplication` object to function. This object holds the **event loop** of your application — the core loop which governs all user interaction with the GUI.

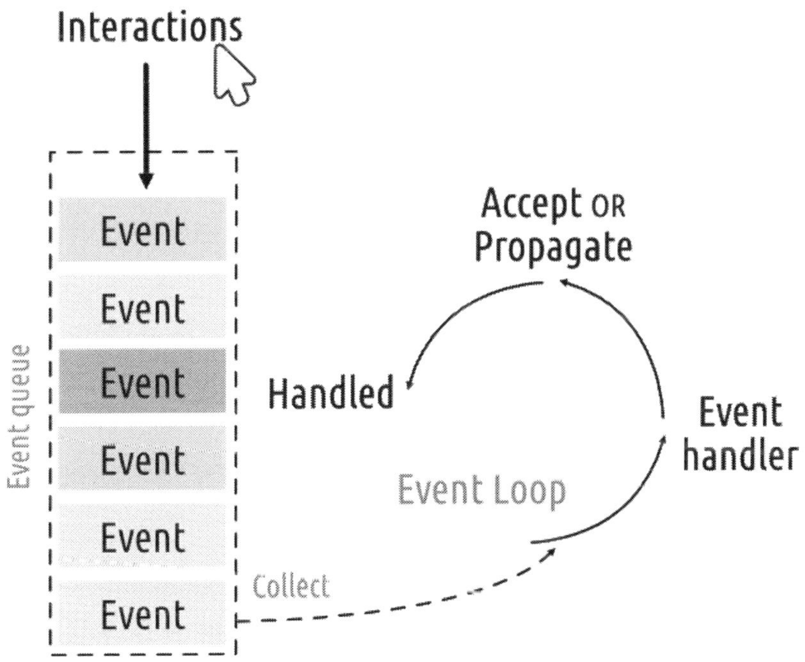

Figure 4. The event loop in Qt.

Each interaction with your application — whether a press of a key, click of a mouse, or mouse movement — generates an *event* which is placed on the *event queue*. In the event loop, the queue is checked on each iteration and if a waiting event is found, the event and control is passed to the specific *event handler* for the event. The event handler deals with the event, then passes control back to the event loop to wait for more events. There is only **one** running event loop per application.

The `QApplication` *class*

- `QApplication` holds the Qt event loop
- One `QApplication` instance required
- You application sits waiting in the event loop until an action is taken
- There is only **one** event loop at any time

The underscore is there because `exec` was a reserved word in Python 2.7. PyQt5 handles this by appending an underscore to the name used in the C++ library. You'll also see `.print_()` methods on widgets for example.

QMainWindow

As we discovered in the last part, in Qt *any* widgets can be windows. For example, if you replace `QtWidget` with `QPushButton`. In the example below, you would get a window with a single push-able button in it.

Listing 2. basic/creating_a_window_2.py

```
from PyQt5.QtWidgets import QApplication, QPushButton
window = QPushButton("Push Me")
window.show()
```

This is neat, but not really very *useful*—it's rare that you need a UI that consists of only a single control! But, as we'll discover later, the ability to nest widgets within other widgets using *layouts* means you can construct complex UIs inside an empty `QWidget`.

But, Qt already has a solution for you—the `QMainWindow`. This is a pre-made widget which provides a lot of standard window features you'll make use of in your apps, including toolbars, menus, a statusbar, dockable widgets and more. We'll look at these advanced features later, but for now, we'll add a simple empty `QMainWindow` to our application.

Listing 3. basic/creating_a_window_3.py

```
from PyQt5.QtWidgets import QApplication, QMainWindow

import sys


app = QApplication(sys.argv)

window = QMainWindow()
window.show()  # IMPORTANT!!!!! Windows are hidden by default.

# Start the event loop.
app.exec_()
```

🚀 **Run it!** You will now see your main window. It looks exactly the same as before!

So our `QMainWindow` isn't very interesting at the moment. We can fix that by adding some content. If you want to create a custom window, the best approach is to subclass `QMainWindow` and then include the setup for the window in the `__init__` block. This allows the window behavior to be self contained. We can add our own subclass of `QMainWindow` — call it `MainWindow` to keep things simple.

Listing 4. basic/creating_a_window_4.py

```
import sys

from PyQt5.QtCore import QSize, Qt
from PyQt5.QtWidgets import QApplication, QMainWindow, QPushButton
①


# Subclass QMainWindow to customize your application's main window
class MainWindow(QMainWindow):
    def __init__(self):
        super().__init__()  ②

        self.setWindowTitle("My App")

        button = QPushButton("Press Me!")

        # Set the central widget of the Window.
        self.setCentralWidget(button)  ③


app = QApplication(sys.argv)

window = MainWindow()
window.show()

app.exec_()
```

① Common Qt widgets are always imported from the `QtWidgets` namespace.

② We must always call the `__init__` method of the `super()` class.

③ Use `.setCentralWidget` to place a widget in the `QMainWindow`.

> When you subclass a Qt class you must **always** call the super `__init__` function to allow Qt to set up the object.

In our `__init__` block we first use `.setWindowTitle()` to change the title of our main window. Then we add our first widget — a `QPushButton` — to the middle of the window. This is one of the basic widgets available in Qt. When creating the button you can pass in the text that you want the button to display.

Finally, we call `.setCentralWidget()` on the window. This is a `QMainWindow` specific function that allows you to set the widget that goes in the middle of the window.

🚀 **Run it!** You will now see your window again, but this time with the `QPushButton` widget in the middle. Pressing the button will do nothing, we'll sort that next.

Figure 5. Our `QMainWindow` *with a single* `QPushButton` *on Windows, macOS and Linux.*

Hungry for widgets?

We'll cover more widgets in detail shortly but if you're impatient and would like to jump ahead you can take a look at the QWidget documentation [http://doc.qt.io/qt-5/widget-classes.html#basic-widget-classes]. Try adding the different widgets to your window!

Sizing windows and widgets

The window is currently freely resizable—if you grab any corner with your mouse you can drag and resize it to any size you want. While it's good to let your users resize your applications, sometimes you may want to place restrictions on minimum or maximum sizes, or lock a window to a fixed size.

In Qt sizes are defined using a `QSize` object. This accepts *width* and *height* parameters in that order. For example, the following will create a *fixed size* window of 400x300 pixels.

Listing 5. basic/creating_a_window_end.py

```
import sys

from PyQt5.QtCore import QSize, Qt
from PyQt5.QtWidgets import QApplication, QMainWindow, QPushButton


# Subclass QMainWindow to customize your application's main window
class MainWindow(QMainWindow):
    def __init__(self):
        super().__init__()

        self.setWindowTitle("My App")

        button = QPushButton("Press Me!")

        self.setFixedSize(QSize(400, 300))  ①

        # Set the central widget of the Window.
        self.setCentralWidget(button)


app = QApplication(sys.argv)

window = MainWindow()
window.show()

app.exec_()
```

① Setting the size on the window.

Run it! You will see a fixed size window—try and resize it, it won't work.

Figure 6. Our fixed-size window, notice that the maximize control is disabled on Windows & Linux. On macOS you can maximize the app to fill the screen, but the central widget will not resize.

As well as `.setFixedSize()` you can also call `.setMinimumSize()` and `.setMaximumSize()` to set the minimum and maximum sizes respectively. Experiment with this yourself!

> You can use these size methods on *any* widget.

In this section we've covered the `QApplication` class, the `QMainWindow` class, the event loop and experimented with adding a simple widget to a window. In the next section we'll take a look at the mechanisms Qt provides for widgets and windows to communicate with one another and your own code.

> Save a copy of your file as `myapp.py` as we'll need it again later.

6. Signals & Slots

So far we've created a window and added a simple *push button* widget to it, but the button doesn't do anything. That's not very useful at all—when you create GUI applications you typically want them to do something! What we need is a way to connect the action of *pressing the button* to making something happen. In Qt, this is provided by *signals* and *slots*.

Signals are notifications emitted by widgets when *something* happens. That something can be any number of things, from pressing a button, to the text of an input box changing, to the text of the window changing. Many signals are initiated by user action, but this is not a rule.

In addition to notifying about something happening, signals can also send data to provide additional context about what happened.

> You can also create your own custom signals, which we'll explore later in Extending Signals.

Slots is the name Qt uses for the receivers of signals. In Python any function (or method) in your application can be used as a slot—simply by connecting the signal to it. If the signal sends data, then the receiving function will receive that data too. Many Qt widgets also have their own built-in slots, meaning you can hook Qt widgets together directly.

Let's take a look at the basics of Qt signals and how you can use them to hook widgets up to make things happen in your apps.

> Load up a fresh copy of `myapp.py` and save it under a new name for this section.

`QPushButton` Signals

Our simple application currently has a `QMainWindow` with a `QPushButton` set as the central widget. Let's start by hooking up this button to a custom Python method. Here we create a simple custom slot named `the_button_was_clicked` which accepts the `clicked` signal from the `QPushButton`.

Listing 6. basic/signals_and_slots_1.py

```
from PyQt5.QtWidgets import QApplication, QMainWindow, QPushButton
①
from PyQt5.QtCore import Qt

import sys


class MainWindow(QMainWindow):
    def __init__(self):
        super().__init__()  ②

        self.setWindowTitle("My App")

        button = QPushButton("Press Me!")
        button.setCheckable(True)
        button.clicked.connect(self.the_button_was_clicked)

        # Set the central widget of the Window.
        self.setCentralWidget(button)

    def the_button_was_clicked(self):
        print("Clicked!")


app = QApplication(sys.argv)

window = MainWindow()
window.show()

app.exec_()
```

Run it! If you click the button you'll see the text "Clicked!" on the console.

Console output

```
Clicked!
Clicked!
Clicked!
Clicked!
```

Receiving data

That's a good start! We've heard already that signals can also send *data* to provide more information about what has just happened. The `.clicked` signal is no exception, also providing a *checked* (or toggled) state for the button. For normal buttons this is always `False`, so our first slot ignored this data. However, we can make our button *checkable* and see the effect.

In the following example, we add a second slot which outputs the *checkstate*.

Listing 7. basic/signals_and_slots_1b.py

```
import sys

from PyQt5.QtCore import Qt
from PyQt5.QtWidgets import QApplication, QMainWindow, QPushButton
①


class MainWindow(QMainWindow):
    def __init__(self):
        super().__init__()  ②

        self.setWindowTitle("My App")

        button = QPushButton("Press Me!")
        button.setCheckable(True)
        button.clicked.connect(self.the_button_was_clicked)
        button.clicked.connect(self.the_button_was_toggled)

        # Set the central widget of the Window.
        self.setCentralWidget(button)

    def the_button_was_clicked(self):
        print("Clicked!")

    def the_button_was_toggled(self, checked):
        print("Checked?", checked)


app = QApplication(sys.argv)

window = MainWindow()
window.show()

app.exec_()
```

🚀 **Run it!** If you press the button you'll see it highlighted as *checked*. Press it again to release it. Look for the *check state* in the console.

Console output

```
Clicked!
Checked? True
Clicked!
Checked? False
Clicked!
Checked? True
Clicked!
Checked? False
Clicked!
Checked? True
```

You can connect as many slots to a signal as you like and can respond to different versions of signals at the same time on your slots.

Storing data

Often it is useful to store the current *state* of a widget in a Python variable. This allows you to work with the values like any other Python variable and without accessing the original widget. You can either store these values as individual variables or use a dictionary if you prefer. In the next example we store the *checked* value of our button in a variable called `button_is_checked` on `self`.

Listing 8. basic/signals_and_slots_1c.py

```
class MainWindow(QMainWindow):
    def __init__(self):
        super().__init__()

        self.button_is_checked = True ①

        self.setWindowTitle("My App")

        button = QPushButton("Press Me!")
        button.setCheckable(True)
        button.clicked.connect(self.the_button_was_toggled)
        button.setChecked(self.button_is_checked) ②

        # Set the central widget of the Window.
        self.setCentralWidget(button)

    def the_button_was_toggled(self, checked):
        self.button_is_checked = checked ③

        print(self.button_is_checked)
```

① Set the default value for our variable.

② Use the default value to set the initial state of the widget.

③ When the widget state changes, update the variable to match.

You can use this same pattern with any PyQt5 widgets. If a widget does not provide a signal that sends the current state, you will need to retrieve the value from the widget directly in your handler. For example, here we're checking the checked state in a *pressed* handler.

Listing 9. basic/signals_and_slots_1d.py

```
class MainWindow(QMainWindow):
    def __init__(self):
        super().__init__()

        self.button_is_checked = True

        self.setWindowTitle("My App")

        self.button = QPushButton("Press Me!")  ①
        self.button.setCheckable(True)
        self.button.released.connect(self.the_button_was_released)
②
        self.button.setChecked(self.button_is_checked)

        # Set the central widget of the Window.
        self.setCentralWidget(self.button)

    def the_button_was_released(self):
        self.button_is_checked = self.button.isChecked()  ③

        print(self.button_is_checked)
```

① We need to keep a reference to the button on `self` so we can access it in our slot.

② The *released* signal fires when the button is released, but does not send the check state.

③ `.isChecked()` returns the check state of the button.

Changing the interface

So far we've seen how to accept signals and print output to the console. But how about making something happen in the interface when we click the button? Let's update our slot method to modify the button, changing the text and disabling the button so it is no longer clickable. We'll also turn off the *checkable* state for now.

Listing 10. basic/signals_and_slots_2.py

```
from PyQt5.QtWidgets import QApplication, QMainWindow, QPushButton
from PyQt5.QtCore import Qt

import sys


class MainWindow(QMainWindow):
    def __init__(self):
        super().__init__()

        self.setWindowTitle("My App")

        self.button = QPushButton("Press Me!")  ①
        self.button.clicked.connect(self.the_button_was_clicked)

        # Set the central widget of the Window.
        self.setCentralWidget(self.button)

    def the_button_was_clicked(self):
        self.button.setText("You already clicked me.")  ②
        self.button.setEnabled(False)  ③

        # Also change the window title.
        self.setWindowTitle("My Oneshot App")


app = QApplication(sys.argv)

window = MainWindow()
window.show()

app.exec_()
```

① We need to be able to access the button in our `the_button_was_clicked` method, so we keep a reference to it on `self`.

② You can change the text of a button by passing a `str` to `.setText()`.

③ To disable a button call `.setEnabled()` with `False`.

> 🚀 **Run it!** If you click the button the text will change and the button will become unclickable.

You're not restricted to changing the button that triggers the signal, you can do *anything you want* in your slot methods. For example, try adding the following line to `the_button_was_clicked` method to also change the window title.

```
self.setWindowTitle("A new window title")
```

Most widgets have their own signals—and the `QMainWindow` we're using for our window is no exception. In the following more complex example, we connect the `.windowTitleChanged` signal on the `QMainWindow` to a custom

In the following example we connect the `.windowTitleChanged` signal on the `QMainWindow` to a method slot `the_window_title_changed`. This slot also receives the new window title.

Listing 11. basic/signals_and_slots_3.py

```
from PyQt5.QtWidgets import QApplication, QMainWindow, QPushButton
from PyQt5.QtCore import Qt

import sys
from random import choice

window_titles = [  ①
    'My App',
    'My App',
    'Still My App',
    'Still My App',
    'What on earth',
    'What on earth',
    'This is surprising',
    'This is surprising',
    'Something went wrong'
]
```

```python
class MainWindow(QMainWindow):
    def __init__(self):
        super().__init__()

        self.n_times_clicked = 0

        self.setWindowTitle("My App")

        self.button = QPushButton("Press Me!")
        self.button.clicked.connect(self.the_button_was_clicked)

        self.windowTitleChanged.connect(self.
the_window_title_changed)  ②

        # Set the central widget of the Window.
        self.setCentralWidget(self.button)

    def the_button_was_clicked(self):
        print("Clicked.")
        new_window_title = choice(window_titles)
        print("Setting title:  %s" % new_window_title)
        self.setWindowTitle(new_window_title) ③

    def the_window_title_changed(self, window_title):
        print("Window title changed: %s" % window_title)  ④

        if window_title == 'Something went wrong':
            self.button.setDisabled(True)




app = QApplication(sys.argv)

window = MainWindow()
window.show()

app.exec_()
```

① A list of window titles we'll select from using `random.choice()`.

② Hook up our custom slot method `the_window_title_changed` to the windows `.windowTitleChanged` signal.

③ Set the window title to the new title.

④ If the new window title equals "Something went wrong" disable the button.

> 🚀 **Run it!** Click the button repeatedly until the title changes to "Something went wrong" and the button will become disabled.

There are a few things to notice in this example.

Firstly, the `windowTitleChanged` signal is not *always* emitted when setting the window title. The signal only fires if the new title is *changed* from the previous one. If you set the same title multiple times, no signal will be fired. It's important to check what conditions signals fire under, to avoid being surprised!

Secondly, notice how we are able to *chain* things together using signals. One thing happening—a button press—can trigger multiple other things to happen in turn. These subsequent effects do not need to know *what* caused them, but simply follow as a consequence of simple rules. This *decoupling* of effects from their triggers is one of the key concepts to understand when building GUI applications. We'll keep coming back to this throughout the book!

In this section we've covered signals and slots. We've demonstrated some simple signals and how to use them to pass data and state around your application. Next we'll look at the widgets which Qt provides for use in your applications—together with the signals they provide.

Connecting widgets together directly

So far we've seen examples of connecting widget signals to Python methods. When a signal is fired from the widget, our Python method is called and receives the data from the signal. But you don't *always* need to use a Python function to handle signals—you can also connect Qt widgets directly to one another.

In the following example, we add a `QLineEdit` widget and a `QLabel` to the window. In the `__init__` for the window we connect our line edit `.textChanged` signal to the `.setText` method on the `QLabel`. Now any time the text changes in the `QLineEdit` the `QLabel` will receive that text to it's `.setText` method.

Listing 12. basic/signals_and_slots_4.py

```
from PyQt5.QtWidgets import QApplication, QMainWindow, QLabel,
QLineEdit, QVBoxLayout, QWidget
from PyQt5.QtCore import Qt

import sys
from random import choice


class MainWindow(QMainWindow):
    def __init__(self):
        super().__init__()

        self.setWindowTitle("My App")

        self.label = QLabel()

        self.input = QLineEdit()
        self.input.textChanged.connect(self.label.setText) ①

        layout = QVBoxLayout() ②
        layout.addWidget(self.input)
        layout.addWidget(self.label)

        container = QWidget()
        container.setLayout(layout)

        # Set the central widget of the Window.
        self.setCentralWidget(container)


app = QApplication(sys.argv)

window = MainWindow()
window.show()

app.exec_()
```

① Note that to connect the input to the label, the input and label must both be defined.

② This code adds the two widgets to a layout, and sets that on the window. We'll cover this in detail in the following chapters, you can ignore it for now.

Run it! Type some text in the upper box, and you'll see it appear immediately on the label.

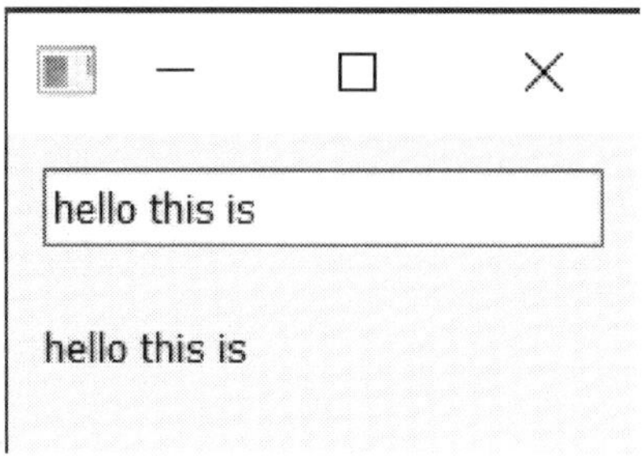

Figure 7. Any text typed in the input immediately appears on the label

Most Qt widgets have *slots* available, to which you can connect any signal that emits the same *type* that it accepts. The widget documentation has the slots for each widget listed under "Public Slots". For example, see QLabel [https://doc.qt.io/qt-5/qlabel.html#public-slots].

7. Widgets

In Qt *widget* is the name given to a component of the UI that the user can interact with. User interfaces are made up of multiple widgets, arranged within the window. Qt comes with a large selection of widgets available, and even allows you to create your own custom widgets.

In the code examples for the book there is a file `basic/widgets_list.py` which you can run to display a collection of widgets in a window. It uses a few complex tricks which we'll cover later, so don't worry about the code just now.

🚀 **Run it!** You will see a window with multiple, interactive, widgets.

Figure 8. The example widgets app shown on Windows, macOS and Linux (Ubuntu).

The widgets shown in the example are given below, from top to bottom.

Widget	What it does
`QCheckbox`	A checkbox
`QComboBox`	A dropdown list box
`QDateEdit`	For editing dates
`QDateTimeEdit`	For editing dates and datetimes
`QDial`	Rotatable dial
`QDoubleSpinbox`	A number spinner for floats
`QFontComboBox`	A list of fonts
`QLCDNumber`	A quite ugly LCD display
`QLabel`	Just a label, not interactive
`QLineEdit`	Enter a line of text
`QProgressBar`	A progress bar
`QPushButton`	A button
`QRadioButton`	A group with only one active choice
`QSlider`	A slider
`QSpinBox`	An integer spinner
`QTimeEdit`	For editing times

There are far more widgets than this, but they don't fit so well! For a full list see the Qt documentation [https://doc.qt.io/qt-5/qtwidgets-module.html]. Here we're going to take a closer look at some of the most useful.

> Load up a fresh copy of `myapp.py` and save it under a new name for this section.

QLabel

We'll start the tour with QLabel, arguably one of the simplest widgets available in the Qt toolbox. This is a simple one-line piece of text that you can position in your application. You can set the text by passing in a string as you create it—

```
widget = QLabel("Hello")
```

Or, by using the .setText() method—

```
widget = QLabel("1") # The label is created with the text 1
widget.setText("2")  # The label now shows 2
```

You can also adjust font parameters, such as the size or alignment of text in the widget.

Listing 13. basic/widgets_1.py

```
import sys

from PyQt5.QtCore import Qt
from PyQt5.QtWidgets import QApplication, QLabel, QMainWindow


class MainWindow(QMainWindow):
    def __init__(self):
        super().__init__()

        self.setWindowTitle("My App")

        widget = QLabel("Hello")
        font = widget.font()  ①
        font.setPointSize(30)
        widget.setFont(font)
        widget.setAlignment(Qt.AlignHCenter | Qt.AlignVCenter)  ②

        self.setCentralWidget(widget)


app = QApplication(sys.argv)

window = MainWindow()
window.show()

app.exec_()
```

① We get the *current* font, using `<widget>.font()`, modify it and then apply it back. This ensures the font face remains in keeping with the desktop conventions.

② The alignment is specified by using a flag from the `Qt.` namespace.

🚀 **Run it!** Adjust the font parameters and see the effect.

Figure 9. A `QLabel` on Windows, macOS and Ubuntu

> The Qt namespace (`Qt.`) is full of all sorts of attributes that you can use to customize and control Qt widgets. We'll cover that in detail later in Enums & the Qt Namespace.

The flags available for horizontal alignment are—

Flag	**Behavior**
`Qt.AlignLeft`	Aligns with the left edge.
`Qt.AlignRight`	Aligns with the right edge.
`Qt.AlignHCenter`	Centers horizontally in the available space.
`Qt.AlignJustify`	Justifies the text in the available space.

The flags available for vertical alignment are—

Flag	**Behavior**
`Qt.AlignTop`	Aligns with the top.
`Qt.AlignBottom`	Aligns with the bottom.
`Qt.AlignVCenter`	Centers vertically in the available space.

You can combine flags together using pipes (|), however note that you can only use one vertical or horizontal alignment flag at a time.

```
align_top_left = Qt.AlignLeft | Qt.AlignTop
```

🚀 **Run it!** Try combining the different alignment flags and seeing the effect on text position.

Qt Flags

Note that you use an **OR** pipe (|) to combine the two flags by convention. The flags are non-overlapping *bitmasks*. e.g. `Qt.AlignLeft` has the binary value `0b0001`, while `Qt.AlignBottom` is `0b0100`. By ORing together we get the value `0b0101` representing 'bottom left'.

We'll take a more detailed look at the `Qt` namespace and Qt flags later in Enums & the Qt Namespace.

Finally, there is also a shorthand flag that centers in both directions simultaneously—

Flag	Behavior
`Qt.AlignCenter`	Centers horizontally **and** vertically

Weirdly, you can also use `QLabel` to display an image using the `.setPixmap()` method. This accepts an *pixmap* (a pixel array), which you can create by passing an image filename to `QPixmap`. In the example files provided with this book you can find a file `otje.jpg` which you can display in your window as follows:

```
widget.setPixmap(QPixmap('otje.jpg'))
```

Figure 10. Otje. What a lovely face.

🚀 **Run it!** Resize the window, and the image will be surrounded by empty space.

By default the image scales while maintaining its aspect ratio. If you want it to stretch and scale to fit the window completely you can set `.setScaledContents(True)` on the `QLabel`.

```
widget.setScaledContents(True)
```

For example—

Listing 14. basic/widgets_2.py

```
import sys

from PyQt5.QtGui import QPixmap
from PyQt5.QtWidgets import QApplication, QLabel, QMainWindow


class MainWindow(QMainWindow):
    def __init__(self):
        super().__init__()

        self.setWindowTitle("My App")

        widget = QLabel("Hello")
        widget.setPixmap(QPixmap("otje.jpg"))
        widget.setScaledContents(True)

        self.setCentralWidget(widget)


app = QApplication(sys.argv)

window = MainWindow()
window.show()

app.exec_()
```

🚀 **Run it!** Resize the window and the picture will deform to fit.

Figure 11. Showing a pixmap with `QLabel` on Windows, macOS and Ubuntu

QCheckBox

The next widget to look at is QCheckBox which, as the name suggests, presents a checkable box to the user. However, as with all Qt widgets there are a number of configurable options to change the widget behaviors.

Listing 15. basic/widgets_3.py

```
import sys

from PyQt5.QtCore import Qt
from PyQt5.QtWidgets import QApplication, QCheckBox, QMainWindow


class MainWindow(QMainWindow):
    def __init__(self):
        super().__init__()

        self.setWindowTitle("My App")

        widget = QCheckBox("This is a checkbox")
        widget.setCheckState(Qt.Checked)

        # For tristate: widget.setCheckState(Qt.PartiallyChecked)
        # Or: widget.setTristate(True)
        widget.stateChanged.connect(self.show_state)

        self.setCentralWidget(widget)

    def show_state(self, s):
        print(s == Qt.Checked)
        print(s)


app = QApplication(sys.argv)

window = MainWindow()
window.show()

app.exec_()
```

🚀 **Run it!** You'll see a checkbox with label text.

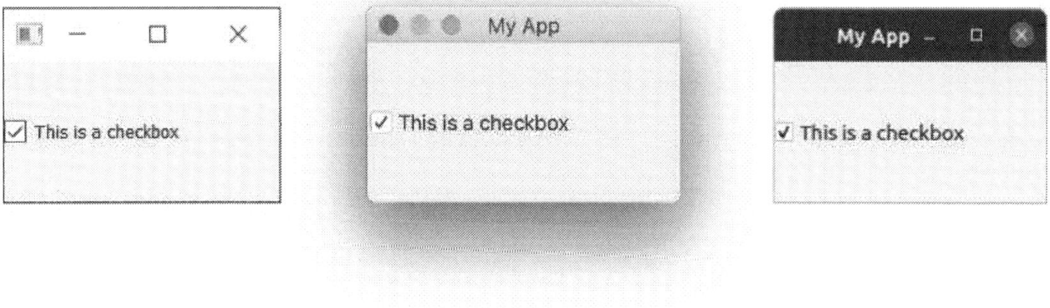

Figure 12. `QCheckBox` *on Windows, macOS and Ubuntu*

You can set a checkbox state programmatically using `.setChecked` or `.setCheckState`. The former accepts either `True` or `False` representing checked or unchecked respectively. However, with `.setCheckState` you also specify a *partially* checked state using a `Qt.` namespace flag—

Flag	**Behavior**
`Qt.Checked`	Item is checked
`Qt.Unchecked`	Item is unchecked
`Qt.PartiallyChecked`	Item is partially checked

A checkbox that supports a partially-checked (`Qt.PartiallyChecked`) state is commonly referred to as 'tri-state', that is being neither on nor off. A checkbox in this state is commonly shown as a greyed out checkbox, and is commonly used in hierarchical checkbox arrangements where sub-items are linked to parent checkboxes.

If you set the value to `Qt.PartiallyChecked` the checkbox will become tri-state—that is have *three* possible states. You can also set a checkbox to be tri-state without setting the current state to partially checked by using `.setTristate(True)`

You may notice that when the script is running the current state number is displayed as an `int` with checked = `2`, unchecked = `0`, and partially checked = 1. You don't need to remember these values, the `Qt.Checked` namespace variable `== 2` for example. This is the value of these state's respective flags. This means you can test state using `state == Qt.Checked`.

QComboBox

The `QComboBox` is a drop down list, closed by default with an arrow to open it. You can select a single item from the list, with the currently selected item being shown as a label on the widget. The combo box is suited to selection of a choice from a long list of options.

> You have probably seen the combo box used for selection of font faces, or size, in word processing applications. Although Qt actually provides a specific font-selection combo box as `QFontComboBox`.

You can add items to a `QComboBox` by passing a list of strings to `.addItems()`. Items will be added in the order they are provided.

Listing 16. basic/widgets_4.py

```
import sys

from PyQt5.QtCore import Qt
from PyQt5.QtWidgets import QApplication, QComboBox, QMainWindow


class MainWindow(QMainWindow):
    def __init__(self):
        super().__init__()

        self.setWindowTitle("My App")

        widget = QComboBox()
        widget.addItems(["One", "Two", "Three"])

        widget.currentIndexChanged.connect(self.index_changed)
        widget.currentTextChanged.connect(self.text_changed)

        self.setCentralWidget(widget)

    def index_changed(self, i):  # i is an int
        print(i)

    def text_changed(self, s):  # s is a str
        print(s)


app = QApplication(sys.argv)

window = MainWindow()
window.show()

app.exec_()
```

Run it! You'll see a combo box with 3 entries. Select one and it will be shown in the box.

Figure 13. `QComboBox` on Windows, macOS and Ubuntu

The `.currentIndexChanged` signal is triggered when the currently selected item is updated, by default passing the index of the selected item in the list. However, when connecting to the signal you can also request an alternative version of the signal by appending `[str]` (think of the signal as a `dict`). This alternative interface instead provides the label of the currently selected item, which is often more useful.

`QComboBox` can also be editable, allowing users to enter values not currently in the list and either have them inserted, or simply used as a value. To make the box editable:

```
widget.setEditable(True)
```

You can also set a flag to determine how the insert is handled. These flags are stored on the `QComboBox` class itself and are listed below—

Flag	Behavior
`QComboBox.NoInsert`	No insert
`QComboBox.InsertAtTop`	Insert as first item
`QComboBox.InsertAtCurrent`	Replace currently selected item
`QComboBox.InsertAtBottom`	Insert after last item
`QComboBox.InsertAfterCurrent`	Insert after current item
`QComboBox.InsertBeforeCurrent`	Insert before current item

Flag	Behavior
`QComboBox.InsertAlphabetically`	Insert in alphabetical order

To use these, apply the flag as follows:

```
widget.setInsertPolicy(QComboBox.InsertAlphabetically)
```

You can also limit the number of items allowed in the box by using `.setMaxCount`, e.g.

```
widget.setMaxCount(10)
```

QListWidget

Next up is QListWidget. This widget is similar to QComboBox, except options are presented as a scrollable list of items. It also supports selection of multiple items at once. A QListWidget offers an currentItemChanged signal which sends the QListItem (the element of the list widget), and a currentTextChanged signal which sends the text of the current item.

Listing 17. basic/widgets_5.py

```
import sys

from PyQt5.QtWidgets import QApplication, QListWidget, QMainWindow


class MainWindow(QMainWindow):
    def __init__(self):
        super().__init__()

        self.setWindowTitle("My App")

        widget = QListWidget()
        widget.addItems(["One", "Two", "Three"])

        # In QListWidget there are two separate signals for the item,
and the str
        widget.currentItemChanged.connect(self.index_changed)
        widget.currentTextChanged.connect(self.text_changed)

        self.setCentralWidget(widget)

    def index_changed(self, i):  # Not an index, i is a QListItem
        print(i.text())

    def text_changed(self, s):  # s is a str
        print(s)

app = QApplication(sys.argv)

window = MainWindow()
window.show()

app.exec_()
```

🚀 **Run it!** You'll see the same three items, now in a list. The selected item (if any) is highlighted.

Figure 14. A `QListWidget` *on Windows, macOS and Ubuntu*

QLineEdit

The QLineEdit widget is a simple single-line text editing box, into which users can type input. These are used for form fields, or settings where there is no restricted list of valid inputs. For example, when entering an email address, or computer name.

Listing 18. basic/widgets_6.py

```python
import sys

from PyQt5.QtCore import Qt
from PyQt5.QtWidgets import QApplication, QLineEdit, QMainWindow


class MainWindow(QMainWindow):
    def __init__(self):
        super().__init__()

        self.setWindowTitle("My App")

        widget = QLineEdit()
        widget.setMaxLength(10)
        widget.setPlaceholderText("Enter your text")

        # widget.setReadOnly(True) # uncomment this to make readonly

        widget.returnPressed.connect(self.return_pressed)
        widget.selectionChanged.connect(self.selection_changed)
        widget.textChanged.connect(self.text_changed)
        widget.textEdited.connect(self.text_edited)

        self.setCentralWidget(widget)

    def return_pressed(self):
        print("Return pressed!")
        self.centralWidget().setText("BOOM!")

    def selection_changed(self):
        print("Selection changed")
        print(self.centralWidget().selectedText())
```

```
    def text_changed(self, s):
        print("Text changed...")
        print(s)

    def text_edited(self, s):
        print("Text edited...")
        print(s)


app = QApplication(sys.argv)

window = MainWindow()
window.show()

app.exec_()
```

🚀 **Run it!** You'll see a simple text entry box, with a hint.

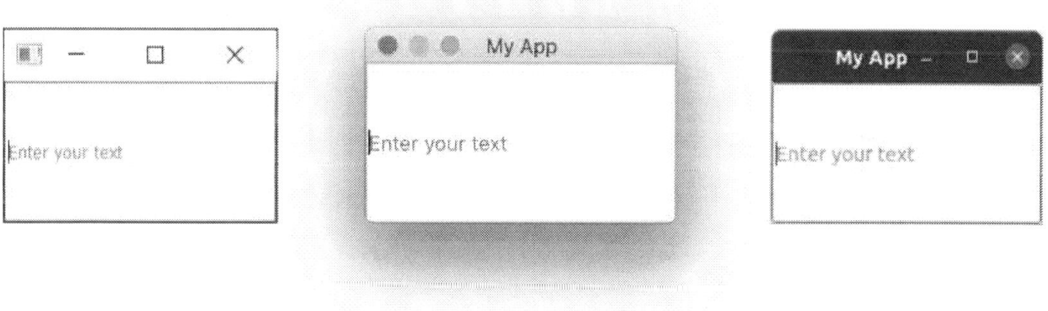

Figure 15. `QLineEdit` *on Windows, macOS and Ubuntu*

As demonstrated in the above code, you can set a maximum length for the text field by using `.setMaxLength`. Placeholder text, which is text shown until something is entered by the user can be added using `.setPlaceholderText`.

The `QLineEdit` has a number of signals available for different editing events including when return is pressed (by the user), when the user selection is changed. There are also two edit signals, one for when the text in the box has been edited and one for when it has been changed. The distinction here is between user edits and programmatic changes. The `textEdited` signal is only sent when the user edits text.

Additionally, it is possible to perform input validation using an *input mask* to define which characters are supported and where. This can be applied to the field as follows:

```
widget.setInputMask('000.000.000.000;_')
```

The above would allow a series of 3-digit numbers separated with periods, and could therefore be used to validate IPv4 addresses.

`QSpinBox` and `QDoubleSpinBox`

`QSpinBox` provides a small numerical input box with arrows to increase and decrease the value. `QSpinBox` supports integers while the related widget `QDoubleSpinBox` supports floats.

Listing 19. basic/widgets_7.py

```python
import sys

from PyQt5.QtCore import Qt
from PyQt5.QtWidgets import QApplication, QMainWindow, QSpinBox


class MainWindow(QMainWindow):
    def __init__(self):
        super().__init__()

        self.setWindowTitle("My App")

        widget = QSpinBox()
        # Or: widget = QDoubleSpinBox()

        widget.setMinimum(-10)
        widget.setMaximum(3)
        # Or: widget.setRange(-10,3)

        widget.setPrefix("$")
        widget.setSuffix("c")
        widget.setSingleStep(3)  # Or e.g. 0.5 for QDoubleSpinBox
        widget.valueChanged.connect(self.value_changed)
        widget.valueChanged[str].connect(self.value_changed_str)

        self.setCentralWidget(widget)

    def value_changed(self, i):
        print(i)

    def value_changed_str(self, s):
        print(s)


app = QApplication(sys.argv)

window = MainWindow()
window.show()

app.exec_()
```

🚀 **Run it!** You'll see a numeric entry box. The value shows pre and post fix units, and is limited to the range +3 to -10.

Figure 16. `QSpinBox` *on Windows, macOS and Ubuntu*

The demonstration code above shows the various features that are available for the widget.

To set the range of acceptable values you can use `setMinimum` and `setMaximum`, or alternatively use `setRange` to set both simultaneously. Annotation of value types is supported with both prefixes and suffixes that can be added to the number, e.g. for currency markers or units using `.setPrefix` and `.setSuffix` respectively.

Clicking on the up and down arrows on the widget will increase or decrease the value in the widget by an amount, which can be set using `.setSingleStep`. Note that this has no effect on the values that are acceptable to the widget.

Both `QSpinBox` and `QDoubleSpinBox` have a `.valueChanged` signal which fires whenever their value is altered. The raw `.valueChanged` signal sends the numeric value (either an `int` or a `float`) while the `str` alternate signal, accessible via `.valueChanged[str]` sends the value as a string, including both the prefix and suffix characters.

QSlider

QSlider provides a slide-bar widget, which functions internally much like a QDoubleSpinBox. Rather than display the current value numerically, it is represented by the position of the slider handle along the length of the widget. This is often useful when providing adjustment between two extremes, but where absolute accuracy is not required. The most common use of this type of widget is for volume controls.

There is an additional .sliderMoved signal that is triggered whenever the slider moves position and a .sliderPressed signal that emits whenever the slider is clicked.

Listing 20. basic/widgets_8.py

```
import sys

from PyQt5.QtCore import Qt
from PyQt5.QtWidgets import QApplication, QMainWindow, QSlider


class MainWindow(QMainWindow):
    def __init__(self):
        super().__init__()

        self.setWindowTitle("My App")

        widget = QSlider()

        widget.setMinimum(-10)
        widget.setMaximum(3)
        # Or: widget.setRange(-10,3)

        widget.setSingleStep(3)

        widget.valueChanged.connect(self.value_changed)
        widget.sliderMoved.connect(self.slider_position)
        widget.sliderPressed.connect(self.slider_pressed)
        widget.sliderReleased.connect(self.slider_released)

        self.setCentralWidget(widget)
```

```
    def value_changed(self, i):
        print(i)

    def slider_position(self, p):
        print("position", p)

    def slider_pressed(self):
        print("Pressed!")

    def slider_released(self):
        print("Released")


app = QApplication(sys.argv)

window = MainWindow()
window.show()

app.exec_()
```

Run it! You'll see a slider widget. Drag the slider to change the value.

Figure 17. `QSlider` on Windows, macOS and Ubuntu. On Windows the handle expands to the size of the widget.

You can also construct a slider with a vertical or horizontal orientation by passing the orientation in as you create it. The orientation flags are defined in the `Qt.` namespace. For example—

```
widget.QSlider(Qt.Vertical)
```

Or—

```
widget.QSlider(Qt.Horizontal)
```

QDial

Finally, the `QDial` is a rotatable widget that functions just like the slider, but appears as an analogue dial. This looks nice, but from a UI perspective is not particularly user friendly. However, they are often used in audio applications as representation of real-world analogue dials.

Listing 21. basic/widgets_9.py

```python
import sys

from PyQt5.QtCore import Qt
from PyQt5.QtWidgets import QApplication, QDial, QMainWindow


class MainWindow(QMainWindow):
    def __init__(self):
        super().__init__()

        self.setWindowTitle("My App")

        widget = QDial()
        widget.setRange(-10, 100)
        widget.setSingleStep(0.5)

        widget.valueChanged.connect(self.value_changed)
        widget.sliderMoved.connect(self.slider_position)
        widget.sliderPressed.connect(self.slider_pressed)
        widget.sliderReleased.connect(self.slider_released)

        self.setCentralWidget(widget)

    def value_changed(self, i):
        print(i)

    def slider_position(self, p):
        print("position", p)

    def slider_pressed(self):
        print("Pressed!")

    def slider_released(self):
```

```
        print("Released")


app = QApplication(sys.argv)

window = MainWindow()
window.show()

app.exec_()
```

🚀 **Run it!** You'll see a dial, rotate it to select a number from the range.

Figure 18. `QDial` *on Windows, macOS and Ubuntu*

The signals are the same as for `QSlider` and retain the same names (e.g. `.sliderMoved`).

This concludes our brief tour through the Qt widgets available in PyQt5. To see the full list of available widgets, including all their signals and attributes, take a look at the Qt documentation [http://doc.qt.io/qt-5/].

`QWidget`

There is a `QWidget` in our demo, but you can't see it. We previously used `QWidget` in our first example to create an empty window. But `QWidget` can also be used as a *container* for other widgets, together with Layouts, to construct windows or compound widgets. We'll cover Creating Custom Widgets in more detail later.

Keep `QWidget` in mind, as you'll be seeing a lot of it!

8. Layouts

So far we've successfully created a window and we've added a widget to it. However, you will usually want to add more than one widget to a window, and have some control over where the widgets you add end up. To arrange widgets together in Qt we use *layouts*. There are 4 basic layouts available in Qt, which are listed in the following table.

Layout	Behavior
`QHBoxLayout`	Linear horizontal layout
`QVBoxLayout`	Linear vertical layout
`QGridLayout`	In indexable grid XxY
`QStackedLayout`	Stacked (z) in front of one another

There are three 2-dimensional layouts available in Qt. The `QVBoxLayout`, `QHBoxLayout` and `QGridLayout`. In addition there is also `QStackedLayout` which allows you to place widgets one on top of the other within the same space, yet showing only one layout at a time.

In this chapter we'll go through each of these layouts in turn, showing how we can use them to position widgets in our applications.

> *Qt Designer*
>
> You can actually design and lay out your interface graphically using the Qt Designer, which we will cover later. Here we're using code, as it's simpler to understand and experiment with the underlying system.

Placeholder widget

> Load up a fresh copy of `myapp.py` and save it under a new name for this section.

To make it easier to visualize the layouts, we'll first create a simple custom widget that displays a solid color of our choosing. This will help to distinguish widgets that we add to the layout. Add the following code to your file as a new class at the top level—

Listing 22. basic/layout_colorwidget.py

```
from PyQt5.QtGui import QColor, QPalette
from PyQt5.QtWidgets import QWidget


class Color(QWidget):
    def __init__(self, color):
        super().__init__()
        self.setAutoFillBackground(True)

        palette = self.palette()
        palette.setColor(QPalette.Window, QColor(color))
        self.setPalette(palette)
```

In this code we subclass `QWidget` to create our own custom widget `Color`. We accept a single parameter when creating the widget — `color` (a `str`). We first set `.setAutoFillBackground` to `True` to tell the widget to automatically fill it's background with the window color. Next we change the widget's `QPalette.Window` color to a new `QColor` described by the value `color` we passed in. Finally we apply this palette back to the widget. The end result is a widget that is filled with a solid color, that we specify when we create it.

If you find the above confusing, don't worry too much! We cover Creating Custom Widgets and Palettes in detail later. For now it's sufficient that you understand that you can create a solid-filled red widget by with the following code—

```
Color('red')
```

First let's test our new `Color` widget by using it to fill the entire window in a single color. Once it's complete we can add it to the main window using `.setCentralWidget` and we get a solid red window.

Listing 23. basic/layout_1.py

```python
import sys

from PyQt5.QtCore import Qt
from PyQt5.QtWidgets import QApplication, QMainWindow

from layout_colorwidget import Color


class MainWindow(QMainWindow):
    def __init__(self):
        super().__init__()

        self.setWindowTitle("My App")

        widget = Color("red")
        self.setCentralWidget(widget)


app = QApplication(sys.argv)

window = MainWindow()
window.show()

app.exec_()
```

🚀 **Run it!** The window will appear, filled completely with the color red. Notice how the widget expands to fill all the available space.

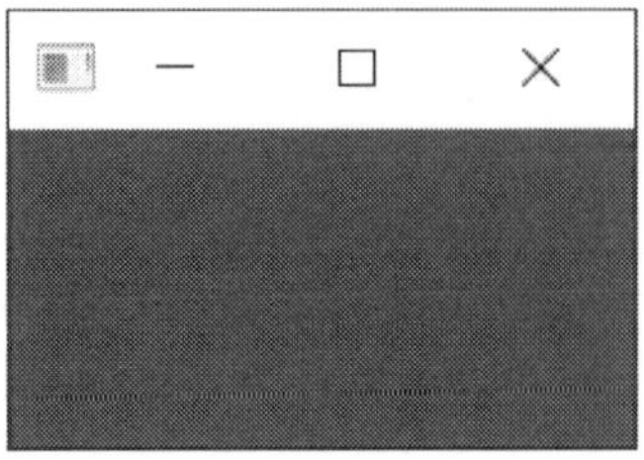

Figure 19. Our `Color` widget, filled with solid red color.

Next we'll look at each of the available Qt layouts in turn. Note that to add our layouts to the window we will need a dummy `QWidget` to hold the layout.

`QVBoxLayout` vertically arranged widgets

With `QVBoxLayout` you arrange widgets one above the other linearly. Adding a widget adds it to the bottom of the column.

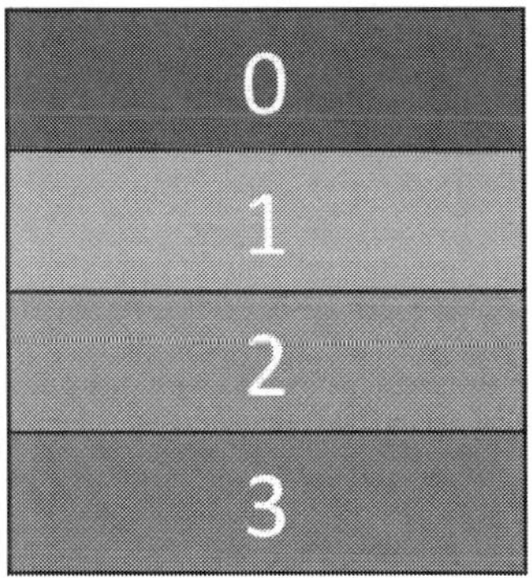

Figure 20. A QVBoxLayout, filled from top to bottom.

Lets add our widget to a layout. Note that in order to add a layout to the `QMainWindow` we need to apply it to a dummy `QWidget`. This allows us to then use `.setCentralWidget` to apply the widget (and the layout) to the window. Our colored widgets will arrange themselves in the layout, contained within the `QWidget` in the window. First we just add the red widget as before.

Listing 24. basic/layout_2a.py

```python
import sys

from PyQt5.QtCore import Qt
from PyQt5.QtWidgets import QApplication, QMainWindow, QVBoxLayout,
QWidget

from layout_colorwidget import Color


class MainWindow(QMainWindow):
    def __init__(self):
        super().__init__()

        self.setWindowTitle("My App")

        layout = QVBoxLayout()

        layout.addWidget(Color("red"))

        widget = QWidget()
        widget.setLayout(layout)
        self.setCentralWidget(widget)


app = QApplication(sys.argv)

window = MainWindow()
window.show()

app.exec_()
```

🚀 **Run it!** Notice the border now visible around the red widget. This is the layout spacing — we'll see how to adjust that later.

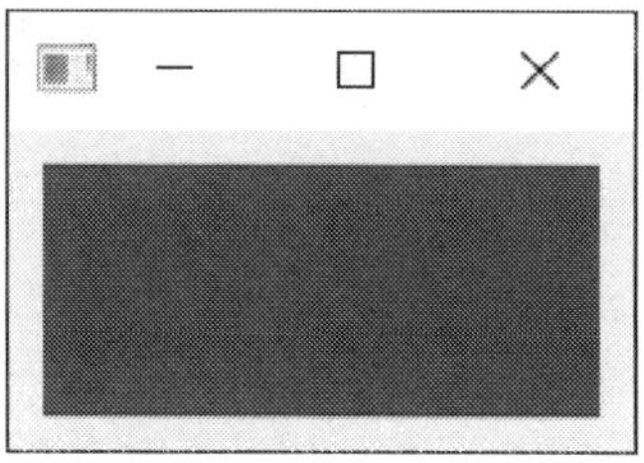

Figure 21. Our `Color` widget, in a layout.

Next add a few more colored widgets to the layout:

Listing 25. basic/layout_2b.py

```
import sys

from PyQt5.QtCore import Qt
from PyQt5.QtWidgets import QApplication, QMainWindow, QVBoxLayout,
QWidget

from layout_colorwidget import Color


class MainWindow(QMainWindow):
    def __init__(self):
        super().__init__()

        self.setWindowTitle("My App")

        layout = QVBoxLayout()

        layout.addWidget(Color("red"))
        layout.addWidget(Color("green"))
        layout.addWidget(Color("blue"))

        widget = QWidget()
        widget.setLayout(layout)
        self.setCentralWidget(widget)


app = QApplication(sys.argv)

window = MainWindow()
window.show()

app.exec_()
```

As we add widgets they line themselves up vertically in the order they are added.

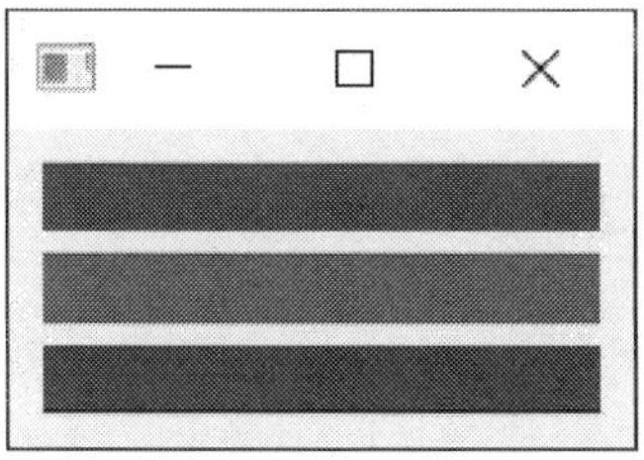

Figure 22. Three `Color` *widgets arranged vertically in a* `QVBoxLayout`.

`QHBoxLayout` horizontally arranged widgets

`QHBoxLayout` is the same, except moving horizontally. Adding a widget adds it to the right hand side.

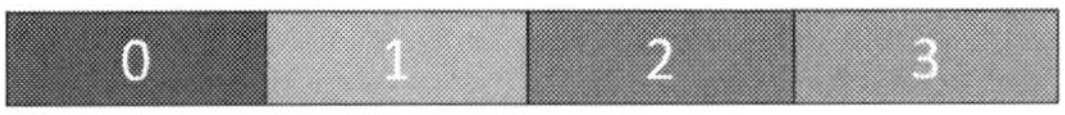

Figure 23. A QHBoxLayout, filled from left to right.

To use it we can simply change the `QVBoxLayout` to a `QHBoxLayout`. The boxes now flow left to right.

Listing 26. basic/layout_3.py

```
import sys

from PyQt5.QtCore import Qt
from PyQt5.QtWidgets import QApplication, QHBoxLayout, QLabel,
QMainWindow, QWidget

from layout_colorwidget import Color


class MainWindow(QMainWindow):
    def __init__(self):
        super().__init__()

        self.setWindowTitle("My App")

        layout = QHBoxLayout()

        layout.addWidget(Color("red"))
        layout.addWidget(Color("green"))
        layout.addWidget(Color("blue"))

        widget = QWidget()
        widget.setLayout(layout)
        self.setCentralWidget(widget)


app = QApplication(sys.argv)

window = MainWindow()
window.show()

app.exec_()
```

Run it! The widgets should arrange themselves horizontally.

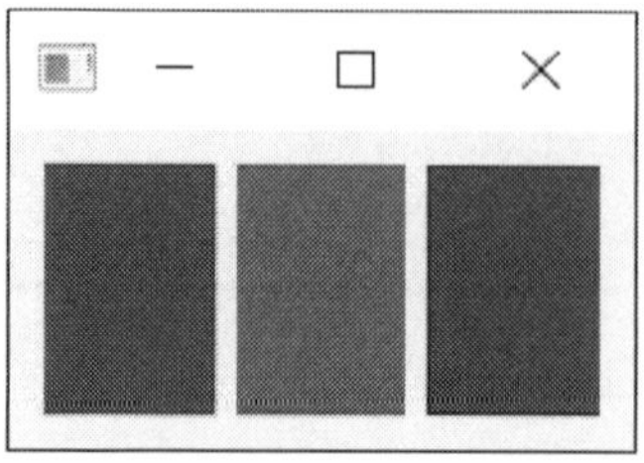

Figure 24. Three `Color` *widgets arranged horizontally in a* `QHBoxLayout`.

Nesting layouts

For more complex layouts you can nest layouts inside one another using `.addLayout` on a layout. Below we add a `QVBoxLayout` into the main `QHBoxLayout`. If we add some widgets to the `QVBoxLayout`, they'll be arranged vertically in the first slot of the parent layout.

Listing 27. basic/layout_4.py

```
import sys

from PyQt5.QtCore import Qt
from PyQt5.QtWidgets import (
    QApplication,
    QHBoxLayout,
    QLabel,
    QMainWindow,
    QVBoxLayout,
    QWidget,
)

from layout_colorwidget import Color


class MainWindow(QMainWindow):
    def __init__(self):
        super().__init__()

        self.setWindowTitle("My App")

        layout1 = QHBoxLayout()
        layout2 = QVBoxLayout()
        layout3 = QVBoxLayout()

        layout2.addWidget(Color("red"))
        layout2.addWidget(Color("yellow"))
        layout2.addWidget(Color("purple"))

        layout1.addLayout(layout2)

        layout1.addWidget(Color("green"))
```

```
        layout3.addWidget(Color("red"))
        layout3.addWidget(Color("purple"))

        layout1.addLayout(layout3)

        widget = QWidget()
        widget.setLayout(layout1)
        self.setCentralWidget(widget)


app = QApplication(sys.argv)

window = MainWindow()
window.show()

app.exec_()
```

🚀 **Run it!** The widgets should arrange themselves in 3 columns horizontally, with the first column also containing 3 widgets stacked vertically. Experiment!

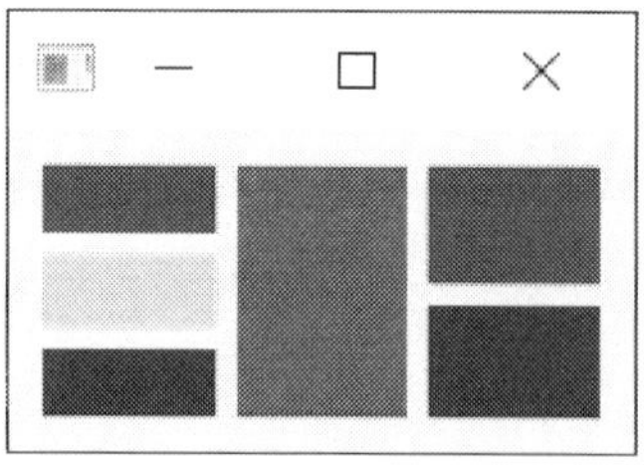

Figure 25. Nested `QHBoxLayout` *and* `QVBoxLayout` *layouts.*

You can set the spacing around the layout using `.setContentMargins` or set the spacing between elements using `.setSpacing`.

```
layout1.setContentsMargins(0,0,0,0)
layout1.setSpacing(20)
```

The following code shows the combination of nested widgets and layout margins and spacing.

Listing 28. basic/layout_5.py

```
import sys

from PyQt5.QtCore import Qt
from PyQt5.QtWidgets import (
    QApplication,
    QHBoxLayout,
    QLabel,
    QMainWindow,
    QVBoxLayout,
    QWidget,
)

from layout_colorwidget import Color


class MainWindow(QMainWindow):
    def __init__(self):
        super().__init__()

        self.setWindowTitle("My App")

        layout1 = QHBoxLayout()
        layout2 = QVBoxLayout()
        layout3 = QVBoxLayout()

        layout1.setContentsMargins(0, 0, 0, 0)
        layout1.setSpacing(20)

        layout2.addWidget(Color("red"))
        layout2.addWidget(Color("yellow"))
        layout2.addWidget(Color("purple"))

        layout1.addLayout(layout2)

        layout1.addWidget(Color("green"))

        layout3.addWidget(Color("red"))
        layout3.addWidget(Color("purple"))

        layout1.addLayout(layout3)
```

```
        widget = QWidget()
        widget.setLayout(layout1)
        self.setCentralWidget(widget)


app = QApplication(sys.argv)

window = MainWindow()
window.show()

app.exec_()
```

Run it! You should see the effects of spacing and margins. Experiment with the numbers until you get a feel for them.

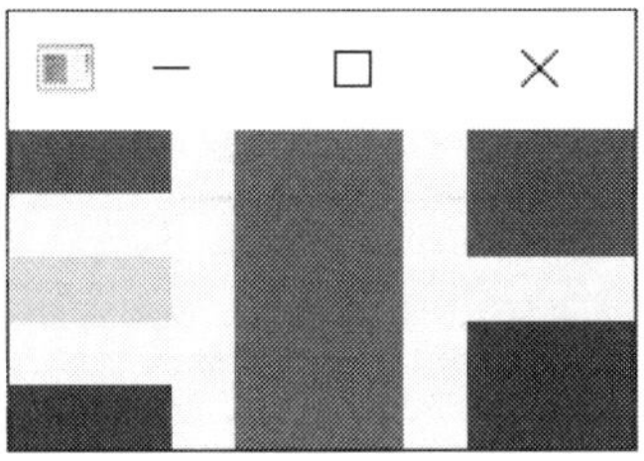

Figure 26. Nested `QHBoxLayout` *and* `QVBoxLayout` *layouts with spacing and margins around the widgets.*

`QGridLayout` widgets arranged in a grid

As useful as they are, if you try and using `QVBoxLayout` and `QHBoxLayout` for laying out multiple elements, e.g. for a form, you'll find it very difficult to ensure differently sized widgets line up. The solution to this is `QGridLayout`.

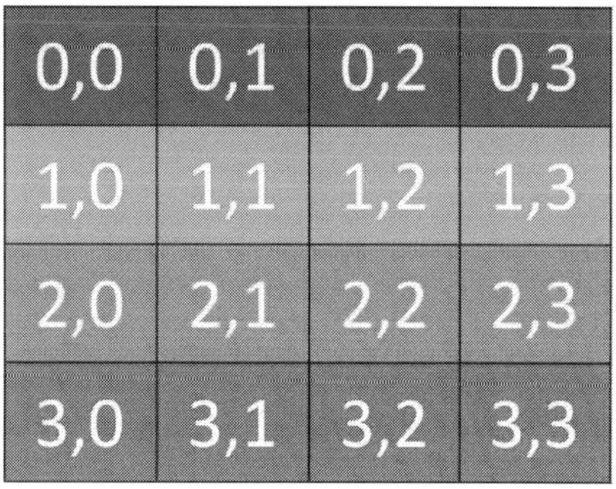

Figure 27. A QGridLayout showing the grid positions for each location.

`QGridLayout` allows you to position items specifically in a grid. You specify row and column positions for each widget. You can skip elements, and they will be left empty.

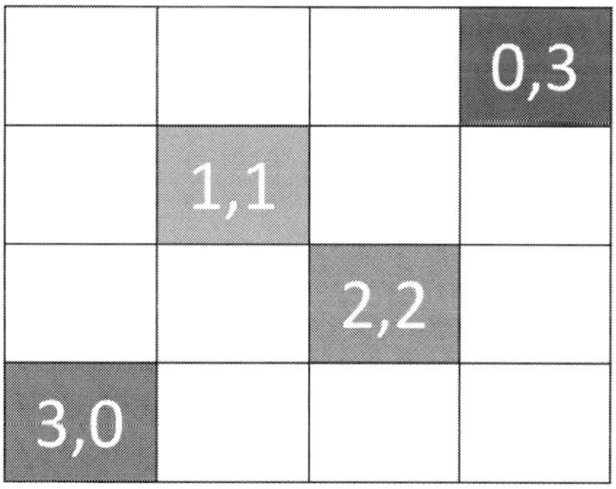

Figure 28. A QGridLayout with unfilled slots.

Listing 29. basic/layout_6.py

```python
import sys

from PyQt5.QtCore import Qt
from PyQt5.QtWidgets import QApplication, QGridLayout, QLabel,
QMainWindow, QWidget

from layout_colorwidget import Color


class MainWindow(QMainWindow):
    def __init__(self):
        super().__init__()

        self.setWindowTitle("My App")

        layout = QGridLayout()

        layout.addWidget(Color("red"), 0, 0)
        layout.addWidget(Color("green"), 1, 0)
        layout.addWidget(Color("blue"), 1, 1)
        layout.addWidget(Color("purple"), 2, 1)

        widget = QWidget()
        widget.setLayout(layout)
        self.setCentralWidget(widget)


app = QApplication(sys.argv)

window = MainWindow()
window.show()

app.exec_()
```

🚀 **Run it!** You should see the widgets arranged in a grid, aligned despite missing entries.

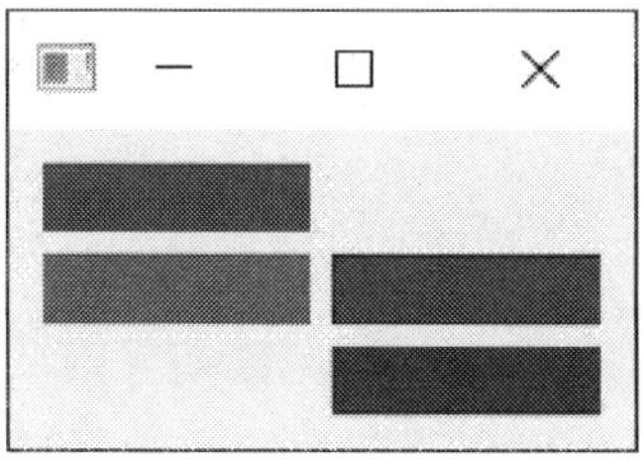

Figure 29. Four `Color` *widgets in a* `QGridLayout`.

`QStackedLayout` multiple widgets in the same space

The final layout we'll cover is the `QStackedLayout`. As described, this layout allows you to position elements directly in front of one another. You can then select which widget you want to show. You could use this for drawing layers in a graphics application, or for imitating a tabbed interface. Note there is also `QStackedWidget` which is a container widget that works in exactly the same way. This is useful if you want to add a stack directly to a `QMainWindow` with `.setCentralWidget`.

Figure 30. QStackedLayout — in use only the uppermost widget is visible, which is by default the first widget added to the layout.

Figure 31. QStackedLayout, with the 2nd (1) widget selected and brought to the front

Listing 30. basic/layout_7.py

```
import sys

from PyQt5.QtCore import Qt
from PyQt5.QtWidgets import QApplication, QLabel, QMainWindow,
QStackedLayout, QWidget

from layout_colorwidget import Color


class MainWindow(QMainWindow):
    def __init__(self):
        super().__init__()

        self.setWindowTitle("My App")

        layout = QStackedLayout()

        layout.addWidget(Color("red"))
        layout.addWidget(Color("green"))
        layout.addWidget(Color("blue"))
        layout.addWidget(Color("yellow"))

        layout.setCurrentIndex(3)

        widget = QWidget()
        widget.setLayout(layout)
        self.setCentralWidget(widget)


app = QApplication(sys.argv)

window = MainWindow()
window.show()

app.exec_()
```

Run it! You will see only the last widget you added.

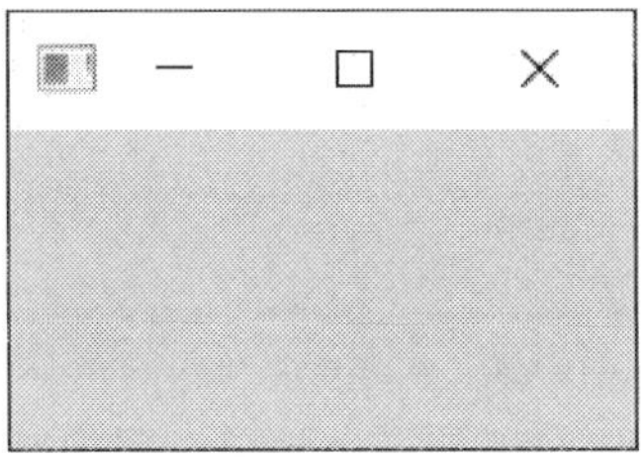

Figure 32. A stack widget, showing one widget only (the last-added widget).

`QStackedWidget` is how tabbed views in applications work. Only one view ('tab') is visible at any one time. You can control which widget to show at any time by using `.setCurrentIndex()` or `.setCurrentWidget()` to set the item by either the index (in order the widgets were added) or by the widget itself.

Below is a short demo using `QStackedLayout` in combination with `QButton` to to provide a tab-like interface to an application—

Listing 31. basic/layout_8.py

```
import sys

from PyQt5.QtCore import Qt
from PyQt5.QtWidgets import (
    QApplication,
    QHBoxLayout,
    QLabel,
    QMainWindow,
    QPushButton,
    QStackedLayout,
    QVBoxLayout,
    QWidget,
)

from layout_colorwidget import Color


class MainWindow(QMainWindow):
    def __init__(self):
        super().__init__()

        self.setWindowTitle("My App")

        pagelayout = QVBoxLayout()
```

```
        button_layout = QHBoxLayout()
        self.stacklayout = QStackedLayout()

        pagelayout.addLayout(button_layout)
        pagelayout.addLayout(self.stacklayout)

        btn = QPushButton("red")
        btn.pressed.connect(self.activate_tab_1)
        button_layout.addWidget(btn)
        self.stacklayout.addWidget(Color("red"))

        btn = QPushButton("green")
        btn.pressed.connect(self.activate_tab_2)
        button_layout.addWidget(btn)
        self.stacklayout.addWidget(Color("green"))

        btn = QPushButton("yellow")
        btn.pressed.connect(self.activate_tab_3)
        button_layout.addWidget(btn)
        self.stacklayout.addWidget(Color("yellow"))

        widget = QWidget()
        widget.setLayout(pagelayout)
        self.setCentralWidget(widget)

    def activate_tab_1(self):
        self.stacklayout.setCurrentIndex(0)

    def activate_tab_2(self):
        self.stacklayout.setCurrentIndex(1)

    def activate_tab_3(self):
        self.stacklayout.setCurrentIndex(2)


app = QApplication(sys.argv)

window = MainWindow()
window.show()

app.exec_()
```

🚀 **Run it!** You'll can now change the visible widget with the button.

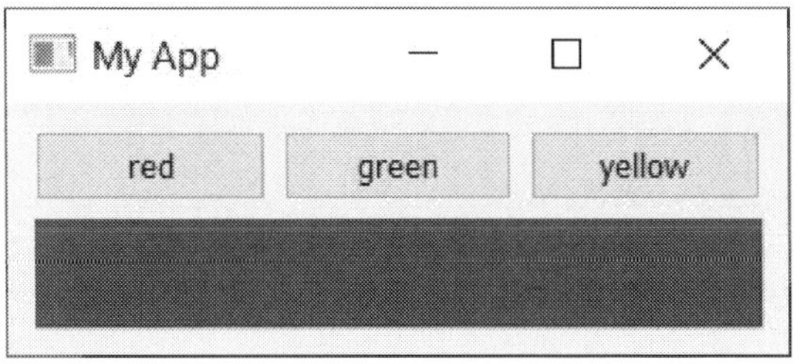

Figure 33. A stack widget, with buttons to control the active widget.

Helpfully, Qt provides a built-in tab widget that provides this kind of layout out of the box - although it's actually a widget, not a layout. Below the tab demo is recreated using `QTabWidget` —

Listing 32. basic/layout_9.py

```python
import sys

from PyQt5.QtCore import Qt
from PyQt5.QtWidgets import (
    QApplication,
    QLabel,
    QMainWindow,
    QPushButton,
    QTabWidget,
    QWidget,
)

from layout_colorwidget import Color


class MainWindow(QMainWindow):
    def __init__(self):
        super().__init__()

        self.setWindowTitle("My App")

        tabs = QTabWidget()
        tabs.setTabPosition(QTabWidget.West)
        tabs.setMovable(True)

        for n, color in enumerate(["red", "green", "blue",
"yellow"]):
            tabs.addTab(Color(color), color)

        self.setCentralWidget(tabs)


app = QApplication(sys.argv)

window = MainWindow()
window.show()

app.exec_()
```

As you can see, it's a little more straightforward — and a bit more attractive!

You can set the position of the tabs using the cardinal directions and toggle whether tabs are moveable with `.setMoveable`.

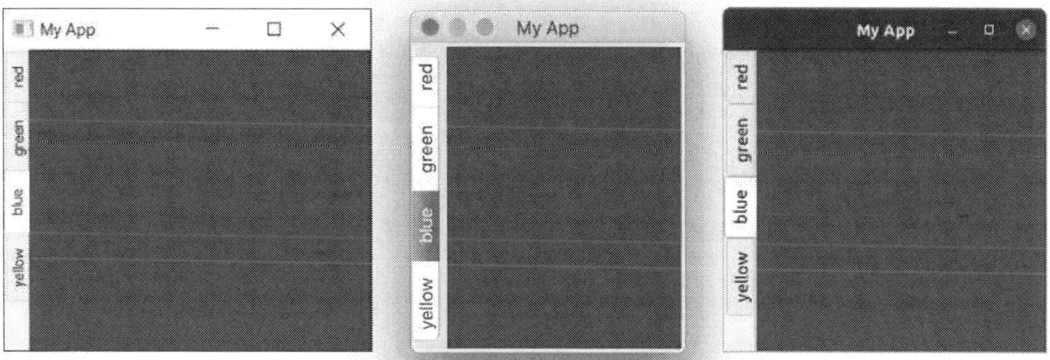

Figure 34. The `QTabWidget` *containing our widgets, with tabs shown on the left (West). Screenshots show Windows, macOS and Ubuntu appearance.*

You'll notice that the macOS tab bar looks quite different to the others—by default on macOS tabs take on a *pill* or *bubble* style. On macOS this is typically used for tabbed configuration panels. For documents, you can turn on *document mode* to give slimline tabs similar to what you see on other platforms. This option has no effect on other platforms.

Listing 33. basic/layout_9b.py

```
        tabs = QTabWidget()
        tabs.setDocumentMode(True)
```

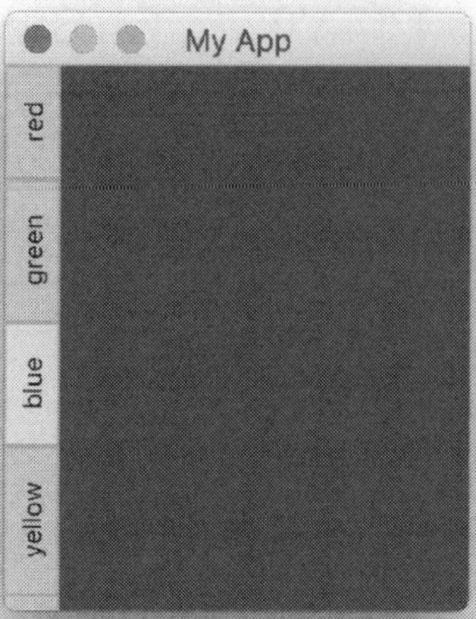

Figure 35. `QTabWidget` with document mode set to `True` on macOS.

9. Actions, Toolbars & Menus

Next we'll look at some of the common user interface elements, that you've probably seen in many other applications — toolbars and menus. We'll also explore the neat system Qt provides for minimising the duplication between different UI areas — `QAction`.

Toolbars

One of the most commonly seen user interface elements is the toolbar. Toolbars are bars of icons and/or text used to perform common tasks within an application, for which accessing via a menu would be cumbersome. They are one of the most common UI features seen in many applications. While some complex applications, particularly in the Microsoft Office suite, have migrated to contextual 'ribbon' interfaces, the standard toolbar is sufficient for the majority of applications you will create.

Figure 36. Standard GUI elements - The toolbar

Qt toolbars support display of icons, text, and can also contain any standard Qt widget. However, for buttons the best approach is to make use of the `QAction` system to place buttons on the toolbar.

Let's start by adding a toolbar to our application.

> Load up a fresh copy of `myapp.py` and save it under a new name for this section.

In Qt toolbars are created from the QToolBar class. To start you create an instance of the class and then call `.addToolbar` on the QMainWindow. Passing a string in as the first parameter to `QToolBar` sets the toolbar's name, which will be used to identify the toolbar in the UI.

Listing 34. basic/toolbars_and_menus_1.py

```
class MainWindow(QMainWindow):
    def __init__(self):
        super().__init__()

        self.setWindowTitle("My App")

        label = QLabel("Hello!")
        label.setAlignment(Qt.AlignCenter)

        self.setCentralWidget(label)

        toolbar = QToolBar("My main toolbar")
        self.addToolBar(toolbar)

    def onMyToolBarButtonClick(self, s):
        print("click", s)
```

Run it! You'll see a thin grey bar at the top of the window. This is your toolbar. Right click and click the name to toggle it off.

Figure 37. A window with a toolbar.

I can't get my toolbar back!?

Unfortunately once you remove a toolbar there is now no place to right click to re-add it. So as a general rule you want to either keep one toolbar un-removeable, or provide an alternative interface to turn toolbars on and off.

Let's make the toolbar a bit more interesting. We could just add a `QButton` widget, but there is a better approach in Qt that gets you some cool features — and that is via `QAction`. `QAction` is a class that provides a way to describe abstract user interfaces. What this means in English, is that you can define multiple interface elements within a single object, unified by the effect that interacting with that element has. For example, it is common to have functions that are represented in the toolbar but also the menu — think of something like Edit→Cut which is present both in the Edit menu but also on the toolbar as a pair of scissors, and also through the keyboard shortcut `Ctrl-X` (`Cmd-X` on macOS).

Without `QAction` you would have to define this in multiple places. But with `QAction` you can define a single `QAction`, defining the triggered action, and then add this action to both the menu and the toolbar. Each `QAction` has names, status messages, icons and signals that you can connect to (and much more).

See the code below for how to add your first `QAction`.

Listing 35. basic/toolbars_and_menus_2.py

```
class MainWindow(QMainWindow):
    def __init__(self):
        super().__init__()

        self.setWindowTitle("My App")

        label = QLabel("Hello!")
        label.setAlignment(Qt.AlignCenter)

        self.setCentralWidget(label)

        toolbar = QToolBar("My main toolbar")
        self.addToolBar(toolbar)

        button_action = QAction("Your button", self)
        button_action.setStatusTip("This is your button")
        button_action.triggered.connect(self.onMyToolBarButtonClick)
        toolbar.addAction(button_action)

    def onMyToolBarButtonClick(self, s):
        print("click", s)
```

To start with we create the function that will accept the signal from the `QAction` so we can see if it is working. Next we define the `QAction` itself. When creating the instance we can pass a label for the action and/or an icon. You must also pass in any `QObject` to act as the parent for the action — here we're passing `self` as a reference to our main window. Strangely for `QAction` the parent element is passed in as the final parameter.

Next, we can opt to set a status tip — this text will be displayed on the status bar once we have one. Finally we connect the `.triggered` signal to the custom function. This signal will fire whenever the `QAction` is 'triggered' (or activated).

🚀 **Run it!** You should see your button with the label that you have defined. Click on it and the our custom function will emit "click" and the status of the button.

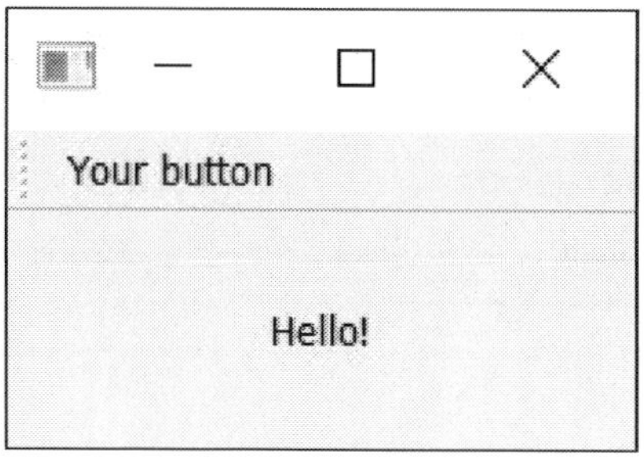

Figure 38. Toolbar showing our `QAction` button.

> *Why is the signal always false?*
>
> The signal passed indicates whether the action is **checked**, and since our button is not checkable — just clickable — it is always false. This is just like the `QPushButton` we saw earlier.

Let's add a statusbar.

We create a status bar object by calling `QStatusBar` and passing the result into `.setStatusBar`. Since we don't need to change the `statusBar` settings we can just pass it in as we create it. We can create and define the status bar in a single line:

Listing 36. basic/toolbars_and_menus_3.py

```
class MainWindow(QMainWindow):
    def __init__(self):
        super().__init__()

        self.setWindowTitle("My App")

        label = QLabel("Hello!")
        label.setAlignment(Qt.AlignCenter)

        self.setCentralWidget(label)

        toolbar = QToolBar("My main toolbar")
        self.addToolBar(toolbar)

        button_action = QAction("Your button", self)
        button_action.setStatusTip("This is your button")
        button_action.triggered.connect(self.onMyToolBarButtonClick)
        toolbar.addAction(button_action)

        self.setStatusBar(QStatusBar(self))

    def onMyToolBarButtonClick(self, s):
        print("click", s)
```

Run it! Hover your mouse over the toolbar button and you will see the status text appear in the status bar at the bottom of the window.

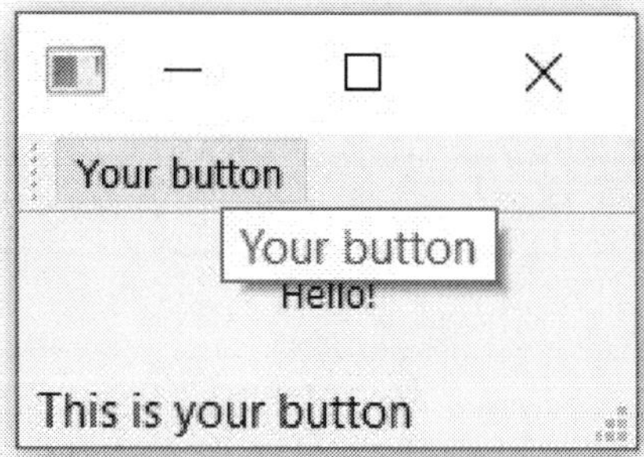

Figure 39. Status bar text is updated as we hover our actions.

Next we're going to turn our QAction toggleable — so clicking will turn it on, clicking again will turn it off. To do this, we simple call `setCheckable(True)` on the `QAction` object.

Listing 37. basic/toolbars_and_menus_4.py

```
class MainWindow(QMainWindow):
    def __init__(self):
        super().__init__()

        self.setWindowTitle("My App")

        label = QLabel("Hello!")
        label.setAlignment(Qt.AlignCenter)

        self.setCentralWidget(label)

        toolbar = QToolBar("My main toolbar")
        self.addToolBar(toolbar)

        button_action = QAction("Your button", self)
        button_action.setStatusTip("This is your button")
        button_action.triggered.connect(self.onMyToolBarButtonClick)
        button_action.setCheckable(True)
        toolbar.addAction(button_action)

        self.setStatusBar(QStatusBar(self))

    def onMyToolBarButtonClick(self, s):
        print("click", s)
```

Run it! Click on the button to see it toggle from checked to unchecked state. Note that custom slot function we create now alternates outputting `True` and `False`.

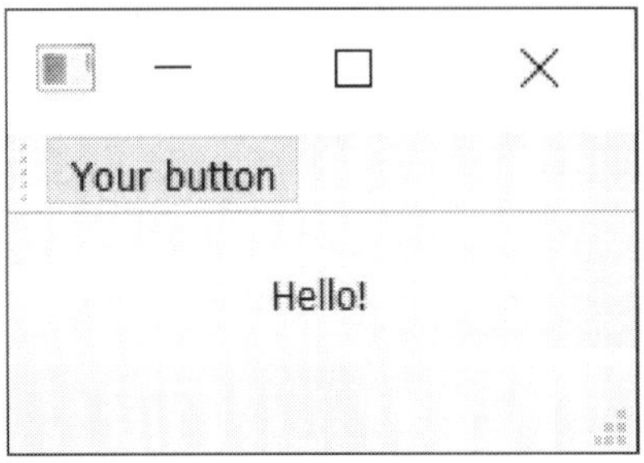

Figure 40. The toolbar button toggled on.

The `.toggled` signal

> There is also a `.toggled` signal, which only emits a signal when the button is toggled. But the effect is identical so it is mostly pointless.

Things look pretty shabby right now — so let's add an icon to our button. For this I recommend you download the fugue icon set [http://p.yusukekamiyamane.com/] by designer Yusuke Kamiyamane. It's a great set of beautiful 16x16 icons that can give your apps a nice professional look. It is freely available with only attribution required when you distribute your application — although I am sure the designer would appreciate some cash too if you have some spare.

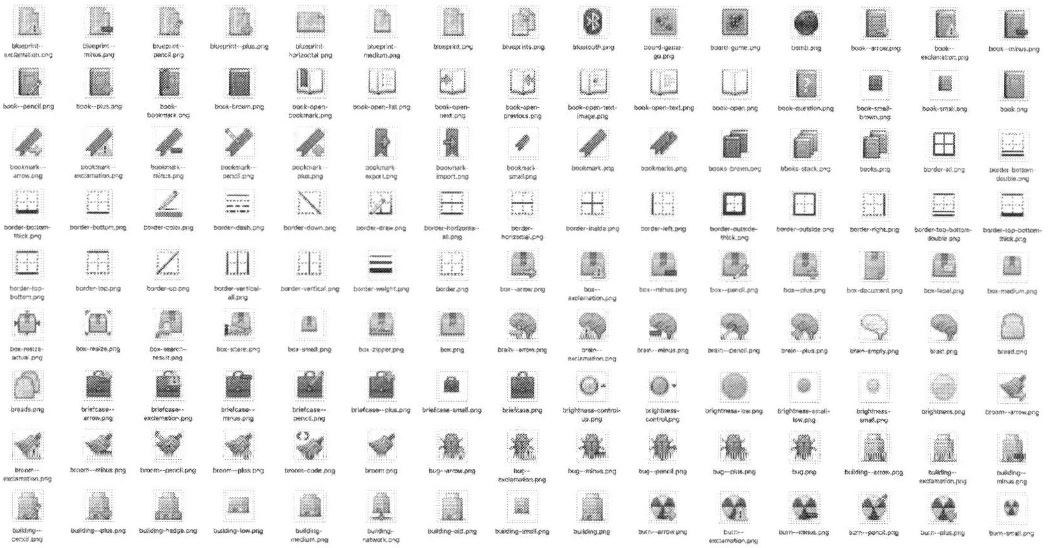

Figure 41. Fugue Icon Set — Yusuke Kamiyamane

Select an image from the set (in the examples here I've selected the file `bug.png`) and copy it into the same folder as your source code. To add the icon to the `QAction` (and therefore the button) we simply pass it in as the first parameter when creating the `QAction`. If the icon is in the same folder as your source code you can just copy it to

You also need to let the toolbar know how large your icons are, otherwise your icon will be surrounded by a lot of padding. You can do this by calling `.setIconSize()` with a `QSize` object.

Listing 38. basic/toolbars_and_menus_5.py

```
class MainWindow(QMainWindow):
    def __init__(self):
        super().__init__()

        self.setWindowTitle("My App")

        label = QLabel("Hello!")
        label.setAlignment(Qt.AlignCenter)

        self.setCentralWidget(label)

        toolbar = QToolBar("My main toolbar")
        toolbar.setIconSize(QSize(16, 16))
        self.addToolBar(toolbar)

        button_action = QAction(QIcon("bug.png"), "Your button",
self)
        button_action.setStatusTip("This is your button")
        button_action.triggered.connect(self.onMyToolBarButtonClick)
        button_action.setCheckable(True)
        toolbar.addAction(button_action)

        self.setStatusBar(QStatusBar(self))

    def onMyToolBarButtonClick(self, s):
        print("click", s)
```

Run it! The QAction is now represented by an icon. Everything should function exactly as it did before.

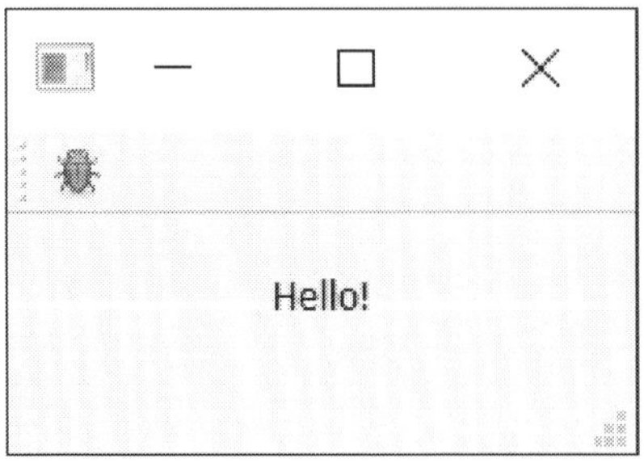

Figure 42. Our action button with an icon.

Note that Qt uses your operating system default settings to determine whether to show an icon, text or an icon and text in the toolbar. But you can override this by using `.setToolButtonStyle`. This slot accepts any of the following flags from the `Qt.` namespace:

Flag	Behavior
`Qt.ToolButtonIconOnly`	Icon only, no text
`Qt.ToolButtonTextOnly`	Text only, no icon
`Qt.ToolButtonTextBesideIcon`	Icon and text, with text beside the icon
`Qt.ToolButtonTextUnderIcon`	Icon and text, with text under the icon
`Qt.ToolButtonIconOnly`	Icon only, no text
`Qt.ToolButtonFollowStyle`	Follow the host desktop style

Which style should I use?

The default value is `Qt.ToolButtonFollowStyle`, meaning that your application will default to following the standard/global setting for the desktop on which the application runs. This is generally recommended to make your application feel as **native** as possible.

Next we'll add a few more bits and bobs to the toolbar. We'll add a second button and a checkbox widget. As mentioned you can literally put any widget in here, so feel free to go crazy.

Listing 39. basic/toolbars_and_menus_6.py

```
class MainWindow(QMainWindow):
    def __init__(self):
        super().__init__()

        self.setWindowTitle("My App")

        label = QLabel("Hello!")
        label.setAlignment(Qt.AlignCenter)

        self.setCentralWidget(label)

        toolbar = QToolBar("My main toolbar")
        toolbar.setIconSize(QSize(16, 16))
        self.addToolBar(toolbar)

        button_action = QAction(QIcon("bug.png"), "Your button",
self)
        button_action.setStatusTip("This is your button")
        button_action.triggered.connect(self.onMyToolBarButtonClick)
        button_action.setCheckable(True)
        toolbar.addAction(button_action)

        toolbar.addSeparator()

        button_action2 = QAction(QIcon("bug.png"), "Your button2",
self)
        button_action2.setStatusTip("This is your button2")
        button_action2.triggered.connect(self.onMyToolBarButtonClick)
        button_action2.setCheckable(True)
        toolbar.addAction(button_action2)

        toolbar.addWidget(QLabel("Hello"))
        toolbar.addWidget(QCheckBox())

        self.setStatusBar(QStatusBar(self))

    def onMyToolBarButtonClick(self, s):
        print("click", s)
```

🚀 **Run it!** Now you see multiple buttons and a checkbox.

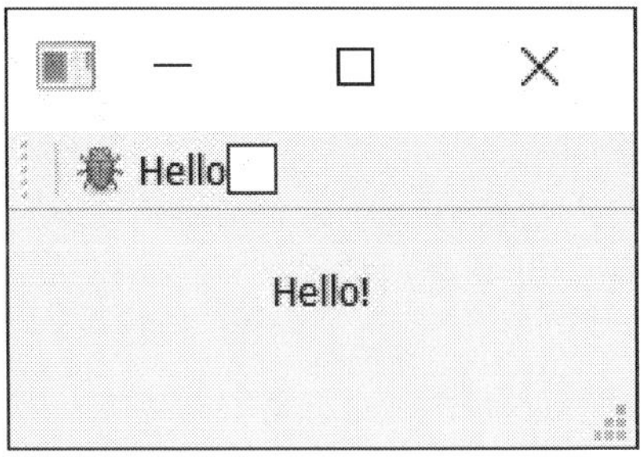

Figure 43. Toolbar with an action and two widgets.

Menus

Menus are another standard component of UIs. Typically they are on the top of the window, or the top of a screen on macOS. They allow access to all standard application functions. A few standard menus exist — for example File, Edit, Help. Menus can be nested to create hierarchical trees of functions and they often support and display keyboard shortcuts for fast access to their functions.

Figure 44. Standard GUI elements - Menus

To create a menu, we create a menubar we call `.menuBar()` on the QMainWindow. We add a menu on our menu bar by calling `.addMenu()`, passing in the name of the menu. I've called it `'&File'`. The ampersand defines a quick key to jump to this menu when pressing Alt.

> *Quick Keys on macOS*
>
> This won't be visible on macOS. Note that this is different to a keyboard shortcut — we'll cover that shortly.

This is where the power of actions comes in to play. We can reuse the already existing QAction to add the same function to the menu. To add an action you call `.addAction` passing in one of our defined actions.

Listing 40. basic/toolbars_and_menus_7.py

```
class MainWindow(QMainWindow):
    def __init__(self):
        super().__init__()

        self.setWindowTitle("My App")

        label = QLabel("Hello!")
        label.setAlignment(Qt.AlignCenter)

        self.setCentralWidget(label)

        toolbar = QToolBar("My main toolbar")
        toolbar.setIconSize(QSize(16, 16))
        self.addToolBar(toolbar)

        button_action = QAction(QIcon("bug.png"), "&Your button",
self)
        button_action.setStatusTip("This is your button")
        button_action.triggered.connect(self.onMyToolBarButtonClick)
        button_action.setCheckable(True)
        toolbar.addAction(button_action)

        toolbar.addSeparator()

        button_action2 = QAction(QIcon("bug.png"), "Your &button2",
self)
        button_action2.setStatusTip("This is your button2")
        button_action2.triggered.connect(self.onMyToolBarButtonClick)
        button_action2.setCheckable(True)
```

```
        toolbar.addAction(button_action2)

        toolbar.addWidget(QLabel("Hello"))
        toolbar.addWidget(QCheckBox())

        self.setStatusBar(QStatusBar(self))

        menu = self.menuBar()

        file_menu = menu.addMenu("&File")
        file_menu.addAction(button_action)

    def onMyToolBarButtonClick(self, s):
        print("click", s)
```

Click the item in the menu and you will notice that it is toggleable — it inherits the features of the QAction.

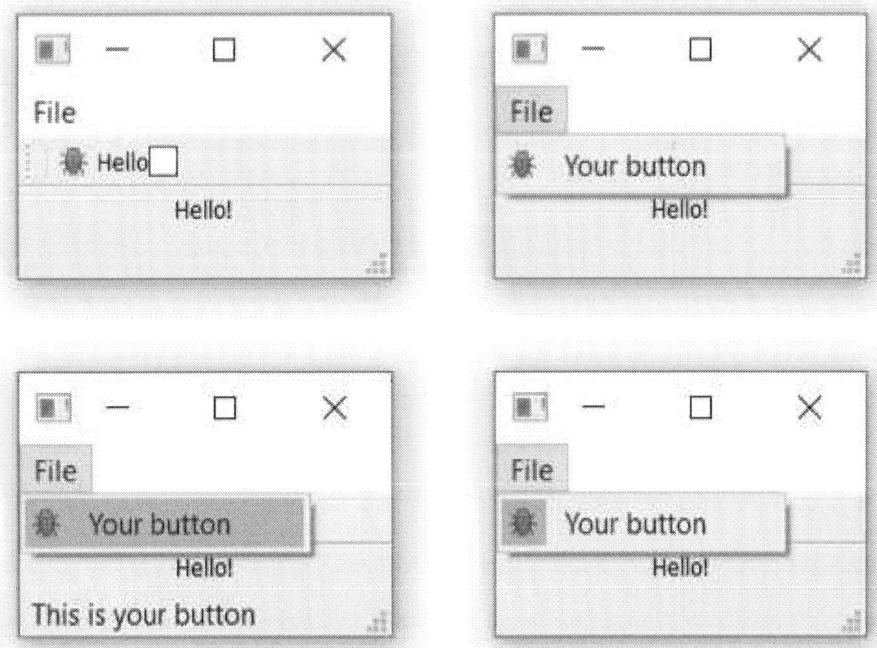

Figure 45. Menu shown on the window—on macOS this will be at the top of the screen.

Let's add some more things to the menu. Here we'll add a separator to the menu, which will appear as a horizontal line in the menu, and then add the second QAction we created.

Listing 41. basic/toolbars_and_menus_8.py

```
class MainWindow(QMainWindow):
    def __init__(self):
        super().__init__()

        self.setWindowTitle("My App")

        label = QLabel("Hello!")
        label.setAlignment(Qt.AlignCenter)

        self.setCentralWidget(label)

        toolbar = QToolBar("My main toolbar")
        toolbar.setIconSize(QSize(16, 16))
        self.addToolBar(toolbar)

        button_action = QAction(QIcon("bug.png"), "&Your button",
self)
        button_action.setStatusTip("This is your button")
        button_action.triggered.connect(self.onMyToolBarButtonClick)
        button_action.setCheckable(True)
        toolbar.addAction(button_action)

        toolbar.addSeparator()

        button_action2 = QAction(QIcon("bug.png"), "Your &button2",
self)
        button_action2.setStatusTip("This is your button2")
        button_action2.triggered.connect(self.onMyToolBarButtonClick)
        button_action2.setCheckable(True)
        toolbar.addAction(button_action2)

        toolbar.addWidget(QLabel("Hello"))
        toolbar.addWidget(QCheckBox())

        self.setStatusBar(QStatusBar(self))

        menu = self.menuBar()

        file_menu = menu.addMenu("&File")
```

```
        file_menu.addAction(button_action)
        file_menu.addSeparator()
        file_menu.addAction(button_action2)

    def onMyToolBarButtonClick(self, s):
        print("click", s)
```

Run it! You should see two menu items with a line between them.

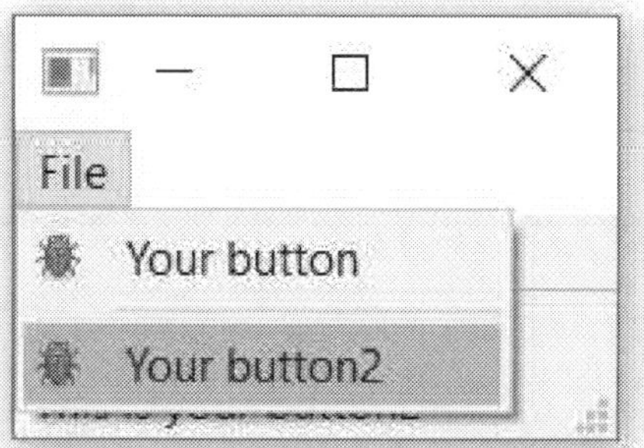

Figure 46. Our actions showing in the menu.

You can also use ampersand to add *accelerator keys* to the menu to allow a single key to be used to jump to a menu item when it is open. Again this doesn't work on macOS.

To add a submenu, you simply create a new menu by calling `addMenu()` on the parent menu. You can then add actions to it as normal. For example:

Listing 42. basic/toolbars_and_menus_9.py

```
class MainWindow(QMainWindow):
    def __init__(self):
        super().__init__()

        self.setWindowTitle("My App")

        label = QLabel("Hello!")
        label.setAlignment(Qt.AlignCenter)
```

```
        self.setCentralWidget(label)

        toolbar = QToolBar("My main toolbar")
        toolbar.setIconSize(QSize(16, 16))
        self.addToolBar(toolbar)

        button_action = QAction(QIcon("bug.png"), "&Your button",
self)
        button_action.setStatusTip("This is your button")
        button_action.triggered.connect(self.onMyToolBarButtonClick)
        button_action.setCheckable(True)
        toolbar.addAction(button_action)

        toolbar.addSeparator()

        button_action2 = QAction(QIcon("bug.png"), "Your &button2",
self)
        button_action2.setStatusTip("This is your button2")
        button_action2.triggered.connect(self.onMyToolBarButtonClick)
        button_action2.setCheckable(True)
        toolbar.addAction(button_action2)

        toolbar.addWidget(QLabel("Hello"))
        toolbar.addWidget(QCheckBox())

        self.setStatusBar(QStatusBar(self))

        menu = self.menuBar()

        file_menu = menu.addMenu("&File")
        file_menu.addAction(button_action)
        file_menu.addSeparator()

        file_submenu = file_menu.addMenu("Submenu")
        file_submenu.addAction(button_action2)

    def onMyToolBarButtonClick(self, s):
        print("click", s)
```

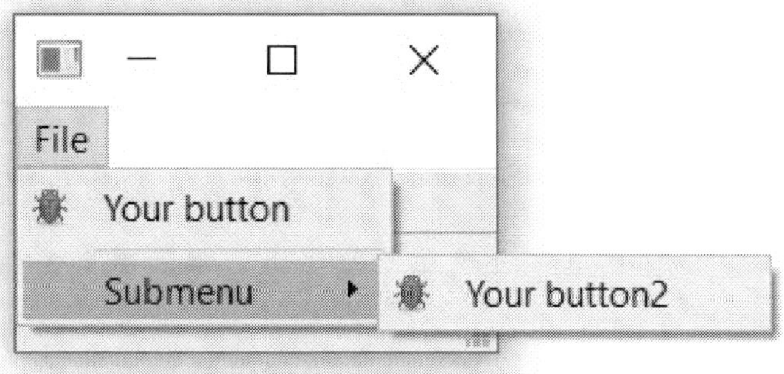

Figure 47. Submenu nested in the File menu.

Finally we'll add a keyboard shortcut to the `QAction`. You define a keyboard shortcut by passing `setKeySequence()` and passing in the key sequence. Any defined key sequences will appear in the menu.

> *Hidden shortcuts*
>
> Note that the keyboard shortcut is associated with the `QAction` and will still work whether or not the `QAction` is added to a menu or a toolbar.

Key sequences can be defined in multiple ways - either by passing as text, using key names from the Qt namespace, or using the defined key sequences from the Qt namespace. Use the latter wherever you can to ensure compliance with the operating system standards.

The completed code, showing the toolbar buttons and menus is shown below.

Listing 43. basic/toolbars_and_menus_end.py

```python
class MainWindow(QMainWindow):
    def __init__(self):
        super().__init__()

        self.setWindowTitle("My App")

        label = QLabel("Hello!")
```

```
        # The `Qt` namespace has a lot of attributes to customize
        # widgets. See: http://doc.qt.io/qt-5/qt.html
        label.setAlignment(Qt.AlignCenter)

        # Set the central widget of the Window. Widget will expand
        # to take up all the space in the window by default.
        self.setCentralWidget(label)

        toolbar = QToolBar("My main toolbar")
        toolbar.setIconSize(QSize(16, 16))
        self.addToolBar(toolbar)

        button_action = QAction(QIcon("bug.png"), "&Your button",
self)
        button_action.setStatusTip("This is your button")
        button_action.triggered.connect(self.onMyToolBarButtonClick)
        button_action.setCheckable(True)
        # You can enter keyboard shortcuts using key names (e.g.
Ctrl+p)
        # Qt.namespace identifiers (e.g. Qt.CTRL + Qt.Key_P)
        # or system agnostic identifiers (e.g. QKeySequence.Print)
        button_action.setShortcut(QKeySequence("Ctrl+p"))
        toolbar.addAction(button_action)

        toolbar.addSeparator()

        button_action2 = QAction(QIcon("bug.png"), "Your &button2",
self)
        button_action2.setStatusTip("This is your button2")
        button_action2.triggered.connect(self.onMyToolBarButtonClick)
        button_action2.setCheckable(True)
        toolbar.addAction(button_action)

        toolbar.addWidget(QLabel("Hello"))
        toolbar.addWidget(QCheckBox())

        self.setStatusBar(QStatusBar(self))

        menu = self.menuBar()

        file_menu = menu.addMenu("&File")
        file_menu.addAction(button_action)
```

```
        file_menu.addSeparator()

        file_submenu = file_menu.addMenu("Submenu")

        file_submenu.addAction(button_action2)

    def onMyToolBarButtonClick(self, s):
        print("click", s)
```

Organising menus & toolbars

If your users can't find your application's actions, they can't use your app to it's full potential. Making actions discoverable is key to creating a user-friendly application. It is a common mistake to try and address this by adding actions *everywhere* and end up overwhelming and confusing your users.

Put common and necessary actions first, making sure they are easy to find and recall. Think of the **File › Save** in most editing applications. Quickly accessible at the top of the File menu and bound with a simple keyboard shortcut `Ctrl` + `S`. If **Save file...** was accessible through **File › Common operations › File operations › Active document › Save** or the shortcut `Ctrl` + `Alt` + `J` users would have a harder time finding it, a harder time using it, and be less **likely** to save their documents.

Arrange actions into logical groups. It is easier to find something among a small number of alternatives, than in a long list. It's even easier to find if it is among similar things.

Figure 48. Grouped toolbars in Qt Designer.

Avoid replicating actions in multiple menus, as this introduces an ambiguity of "do these do the same thing?" even if they have an identical label. Lastly, don't be tempted to simplify menus by hiding/removing entries dynamically. This leads to confusion as users hunt for something that doesn't exist "...it was here a minute ago". Different states should be indicated by disabling menu items or separate windows and dialogs.

✔ DO

- Organize your menus into a logical hierarchy.
- Replicate the *most common* functions onto your toolbars.
- Group toolbar actions logically.
- Disable items in menus when they can't be used.

✘ DON'T

- Add the same action to multiple menus.
- Add all your menu actions onto the toolbar.
- Use different names or icons for the same action in different places.
- Remove items from your menus—disable them instead.

10. Dialogs

Dialogs are useful GUI components that allow you to *communicate* with the user (hence the name dialog). They are commonly used for file Open/Save, settings, preferences, or for functions that do not fit into the main UI of the application. They are small modal (or *blocking*) windows that sit in front of the main application until they are dismissed. Qt actually provides a number of 'special' dialogs for the most common use-cases, allowing you to provide a platform-native experience for a better user experience.

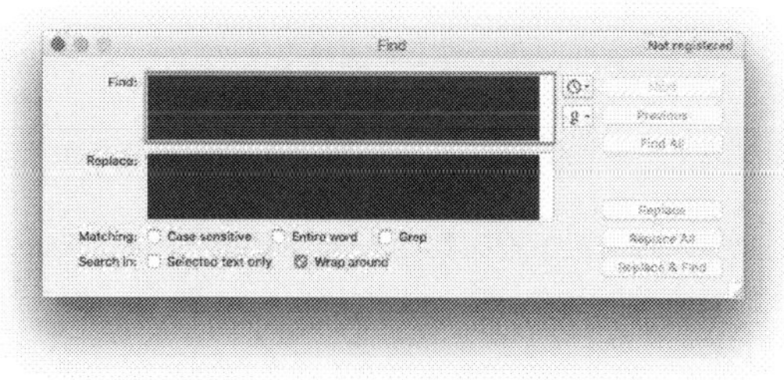

Figure 49. Standard GUI features — A search dialog

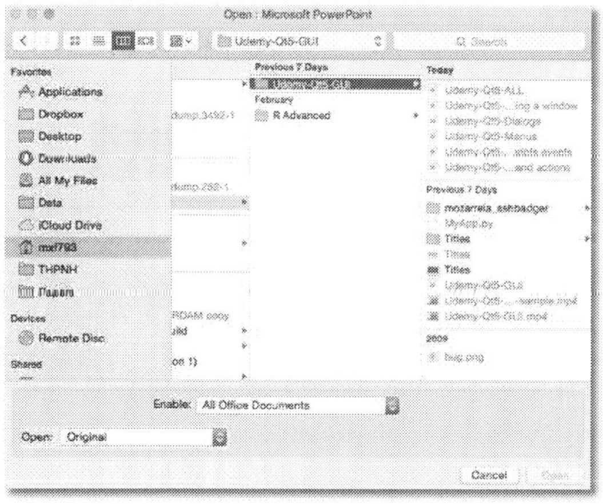

Figure 50. Standard GUI features — A file Open dialog

In Qt dialog boxes are handled by the `QDialog` class. To create a new dialog box simply create a new object of `QDialog` type passing in a parent widget, e.g. `QMainWindow`, as its parent.

Let's create our own `QDialog`. We'll start with a simple skeleton app with a button to press hooked up to a slot method.

Listing 44. basic/dialogs_start.py

```
import sys

from PyQt5.QtWidgets import QApplication, QMainWindow, QPushButton


class MainWindow(QMainWindow):
    def __init__(self):
        super().__init__()

        self.setWindowTitle("My App")

        button = QPushButton("Press me for a dialog!")
        button.clicked.connect(self.button_clicked)
        self.setCentralWidget(button)

    def button_clicked(self, s):
        print("click", s)


app = QApplication(sys.argv)

window = MainWindow()
window.show()

app.exec_()
```

In the slot `button_clicked` (which receives the signal from the button press) we create the dialog instance, passing our `QMainWindow` instance as a parent. This will make the dialog a *modal window* of `QMainWindow`. This means the dialog will completely block interaction with the parent window.

Listing 45. basic/dialogs_1.py

```
import sys

from PyQt5.QtWidgets import QApplication, QDialog, QMainWindow,
QPushButton


class MainWindow(QMainWindow):
    def __init__(self):
        super().__init__()

        self.setWindowTitle("My App")

        button = QPushButton("Press me for a dialog!")
        button.clicked.connect(self.button_clicked)
        self.setCentralWidget(button)

    def button_clicked(self, s):
        print("click", s)

        dlg = QDialog(self)
        dlg.setWindowTitle("HELLO!")
        dlg.exec_()


app = QApplication(sys.argv)

window = MainWindow()
window.show()

app.exec_()
```

Run it! Click the button and you'll see an empty dialog appear.

Once we have created the dialog, we start it using `.exec_()` - just like we did for `QApplication` to create the main event loop of our application. That's not a coincidence: when you exec the `QDialog` an entirely new event loop - specific for the dialog - is created.

One event loop to rule them all

Remember I said there can only be one Qt event loop running at any time? I meant it! The `QDialog` completely blocks your application execution. Don't start a dialog and expect anything else to happen anywhere else in your app.

We'll see later how you can use multithreading to get you out of this pickle.

Figure 51. Our empty dialog overlaying the window.

Like our very first window, this isn't very interesting. Let's fix that by adding a dialog title and a set of OK and Cancel buttons to allow the user to *accept* or *reject* the modal.

To customize the `QDialog` we can subclass it.

Listing 46. basic/dialogs_2a.py

```python
class CustomDialog(QDialog):
    def __init__(self):
        super().__init__()

        self.setWindowTitle("HELLO!")

        QBtn = QDialogButtonBox.Ok | QDialogButtonBox.Cancel

        self.buttonBox = QDialogButtonBox(QBtn)
        self.buttonBox.accepted.connect(self.accept)
        self.buttonBox.rejected.connect(self.reject)

        self.layout = QVBoxLayout()
        message = QLabel("Something happened, is that OK?")
        self.layout.addWidget(message)
        self.layout.addWidget(self.buttonBox)
        self.setLayout(self.layout)
```

In the above code, we first create our subclass of `QDialog` which we've called `CustomDialog`. As for the `QMainWindow` we apply our customizations in the class `__init__` block so our customizations are applied as the object is created. First we set a title for the `QDialog` using `.setWindowTitle()`, exactly the same as we did for our main window.

The next block of code is concerned with creating and displaying the dialog buttons. This is probably a bit more involved than you were expecting. However, this is due to Qt's flexibility in handling dialog button positioning on different platforms.

> *Easy way out?*
>
> You could of course choose to ignore this and use a standard `QButton` in a layout, but the approach outlined here ensures that your dialog respects the host desktop standards (OK on left vs. right for example). Messing around with these behaviors can be incredibly annoying to your users, so I wouldn't recommend it.

The first step in creating a dialog button box is to define the buttons want to show, using namespace attributes from `QDialogButtonBox`. The full list of buttons available is below:

Table 1. `QDialogButtonBox` available button types.

Button types
`QDialogButtonBox.Ok`
`QDialogButtonBox.Open`
`QDialogButtonBox.Save`
`QDialogButtonBox.Cancel`
`QDialogButtonBox.Close`
`QDialogButtonBox.Discard`
`QDialogButtonBox.Apply`
`QDialogButtonBox.Reset`
`QDialogButtonBox.RestoreDefaults`
`QDialogButtonBox.Help`
`QDialogButtonBox.SaveAll`
`QDialogButtonBox.Yes`
`QDialogButtonBox.YesToAll`
`QDialogButtonBox.No`
`QDialogButtonBox.NoToAll`
`QDialogButtonBox.Abort`
`QDialogButtonBox.Retry`
`QDialogButtonBox.Ignore`
`QDialogButtonBox.NoButton`

These should be sufficient to create any dialog box you can think of. You can construct a line of multiple buttons by OR-ing them together using a pipe (|). Qt will handle the order automatically, according to platform standards. For example, to show an OK and a Cancel button we used:

```
buttons = QDialogButtonBox.Ok | QDialogButtonBox.Cancel
```

The variable `buttons` now contains an integer value representing those two buttons. Next, we must create the `QDialogButtonBox` instance to hold the buttons. The flag for the buttons to display is passed in as the first parameter.

To make the buttons have any effect, you must connect the correct `QDialogButtonBox` signals to the slots on the dialog. In our case we've connected the `.accepted` and `.rejected` signals from the `QDialogButtonBox` to the handlers for `.accept()` and `.reject()` on our subclass of `QDialog`.

Lastly, to make the `QDialogButtonBox` appear in our dialog box we must add it to the dialog layout. So, as for the main window we create a layout, and add our `QDialogButtonBox` to it (`QDialogButtonBox` is a widget), and then set that layout on our dialog.

Finally, we launch the `CustomDialog` in our `MainWindow.button_clicked` slot.

Listing 47. basic/dialogs_2a.py

```
    def button_clicked(self, s):
        print("click", s)

        dlg = CustomDialog()
        if dlg.exec_():
            print("Success!")
        else:
            print("Cancel!")
```

🚀 **Run it!** Click to launch the dialog and you will see a dialog box with buttons in it.

Figure 52. Our dialog with a label and buttons.

When you click the button to launch the dialog, you may notice that it appears away from the parent window—probably in the center of the screen. Normally you want dialogs to appear over their launching window to make them easier for users to find. To do this we need to give Qt a **parent** for the dialog. If we pass our main window as the parent, Qt will position the new dialog so that the center of the dialog aligns with the center of the window.

We can modify our `CustomDialog` class to accept a `parent` parameter.

Listing 48. basic/dialogs_2b.py

```
class CustomDialog(QDialog):
    def __init__(self, parent=None):  ①
        super().__init__(parent)

        self.setWindowTitle("HELLO!")

        QBtn = QDialogButtonBox.Ok | QDialogButtonBox.Cancel

        self.buttonBox = QDialogButtonBox(QBtn)
        self.buttonBox.accepted.connect(self.accept)
        self.buttonBox.rejected.connect(self.reject)

        self.layout = QVBoxLayout()
        message = QLabel("Something happened, is that OK?")
        self.layout.addWidget(message)
        self.layout.addWidget(self.buttonBox)
        self.setLayout(self.layout)
```

① We set a default value of `None` so we can omit the parent if we wish.

Then, when we create our instance of `CustomDialog` we can pass the main window in as a parameter. In our `button_clicked` method, `self` is our main window object.

Listing 49. basic/dialogs_2b.py

```
    def button_clicked(self, s):
        print("click", s)

        dlg = CustomDialog(self)
        if dlg.exec_():
            print("Success!")
        else:
            print("Cancel!")
```

Run it! Click to launch the dialog and you should see the dialog pop up right in the middle of the parent window.

Figure 53. Our dialog, centered over the parent window.

Congratulations! You've created your first dialog box. Of course, you can continue to add any other content to the dialog box that you like. Simply insert it into the layout as normal.

Simple message dialogs with `QMessageBox`

There are many dialogs which follow the simple pattern we just saw—a message with buttons with which you can accept or cancel the dialog. While you can construct these dialogs yourself, Qt also provides a built-in message dialog class called `QMessageBox`. This can be used to create information, warning, about or question dialogs.

The example below creates a simple `QMessageBox` and shows it.

Listing 50. basic/dialogs_3.py

```
    def button_clicked(self, s):
        dlg = QMessageBox(self)
        dlg.setWindowTitle("I have a question!")
        dlg.setText("This is a simple dialog")
        button = dlg.exec_()

        if button == QMessageBox.Ok:
            print("OK!")
```

Run it! You'll see a simple dialog with an *OK* button.

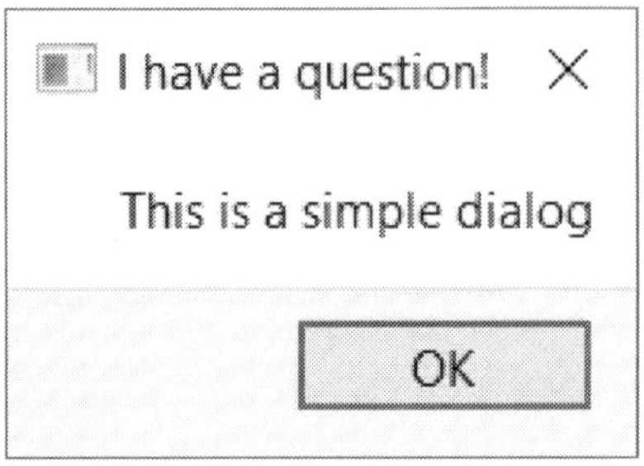

Figure 54. A `QMessageBox` *dialog.*

As with the dialog button box we looked at already, the buttons shown on a `QMessageBox` are also configured with a set of constants which can be combined with | to show multiple buttons. The full list of available button types is shown below.

Table 2. `QMessageBox` *available button types.*

Button types
`QMessageBox.Ok`
`QMessageBox.Open`
`QMessageBox.Save`
`QMessageBox.Cancel`
`QMessageBox.Close`
`QMessageBox.Discard`
`QMessageBox.Apply`
`QMessageBox.Reset`
`QMessageBox.RestoreDefaults`
`QMessageBox.Help`
`QMessageBox.SaveAll`
`QMessageBox.Yes`
`QMessageBox.YesToAll`
`QMessageBox.No`
`QMessageBox.NoToAll`
`QMessageBox.Abort`

Button types
`QMessageBox.Retry`
`QMessageBox.Ignore`
`QMessageBox.NoButton`

You can also tweak the icon shown on the dialog by setting the icon with one of the following.

Table 3. `QMessageBox` *icon constants.*

Icon state	Description
QMessageBox.NoIcon	The message box does not have an icon.
QMessageBox.Question	The message is asking a question.
QMessageBox.Information	The message is informational only.
QMessageBox.Warning	The message is warning.
QMessageBox.Critical	The message indicates a critical problem.

For example, the following creates a question dialog with *Yes* and *No* buttons.

Listing 51. basic/dialogs_4.py

```
from PyQt5.QtWidgets import QApplication, QDialog, QMainWindow,
QMessageBox, QPushButton

class MainWindow(QMainWindow):

    # __init__ skipped for clarity
    def button_clicked(self, s):
        dlg = QMessageBox(self)
        dlg.setWindowTitle("I have a question!")
        dlg.setText("This is a question dialog")
        dlg.setStandardButtons(QMessageBox.Yes | QMessageBox.No)
        dlg.setIcon(QMessageBox.Question)
        button = dlg.exec_()

        if button == QMessageBox.Yes:
            print("Yes!")
        else:
            print("No!")
```

Run it! You'll see a question dialog with *Yes* and *No* buttons.

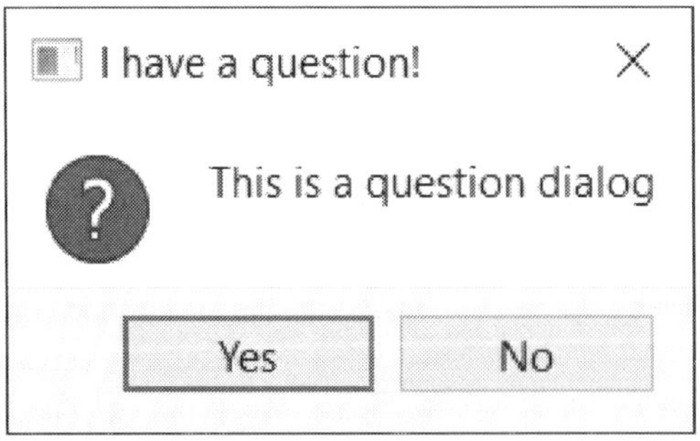

Figure 55. Question dialog created using `QMessageBox`.

Built in `QMessageBox` dialogs

To make things even simpler the `QMessageBox` has a number of methods which can be used to construct these types of message dialog. These methods are shown below—

```
QMessageBox.about(parent, title, message)
QMessageBox.critical(parent, title, message)
QMessageBox.information(parent, title, message)
QMessageBox.question(parent, title, message)
QMessageBox.warning(parent, title, message)
```

The `parent` parameter is the window which the dialog will be a child of. If you're launching your dialog from your main window, you can just pass in `self`. The following example creates a question dialog, as before, with *Yes* and *No* buttons.

Listing 52. basic/dialogs_5.py

```
    def button_clicked(self, s):

        button = QMessageBox.question(self, "Question dialog", "The
longer message")

        if button == QMessageBox.Yes:
            print("Yes!")
        else:
            print("No!")
```

🚀 **Run it!** You'll see the same result, this time using the built in `.question()` method.

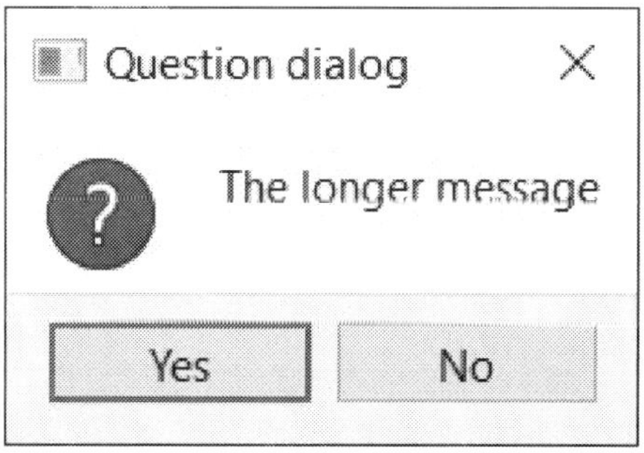

Figure 56. The built-in question dialog.

Notice that rather than call `exec()` we now simply call the dialog method and the dialog is created. The return value of each of the methods is the button which was pressed. We can detect what has been pressed by comparing the return value to the button constants.

The four `information`, `question`, `warning` and `critical` methods also accept optional `buttons` and `defaultButton` arguments which can be used to tweak the buttons shown on the dialog and select one by default. Generally though you don't want to change this from the default.

Listing 53. basic/dialogs_6.py

```
    def button_clicked(self, s):

        button = QMessageBox.critical(
            self,
            "Oh dear!",
            "Something went very wrong.",
            buttons=QMessageBox.Discard | QMessageBox.NoToAll |
QMessageBox.Ignore,
            defaultButton=QMessageBox.Discard,
        )

        if button == QMessageBox.Yes:
            print("Yes!")
        else:
            print("No!")
```

Run it! You'll see a critical dialog with customized buttons.

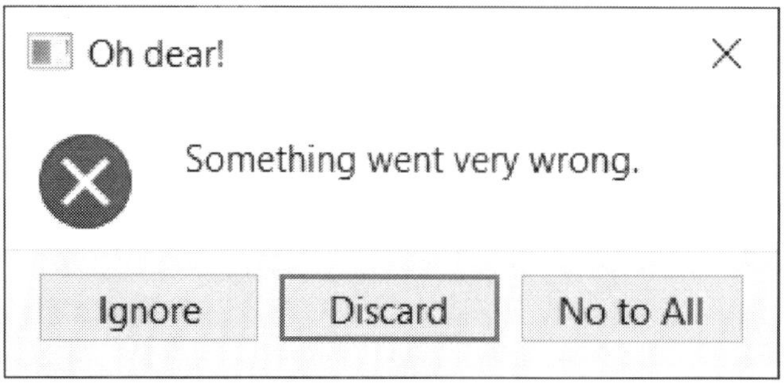

Figure 57. Critical error! This is a terrible dialog.

For most situations these simple dialogs are all you need.

Dialogs

It's particularly easy to create bad dialogs. From dialogs that trap users with confusing options to nested never-ending popups. There are plenty of ways to hurt your users.

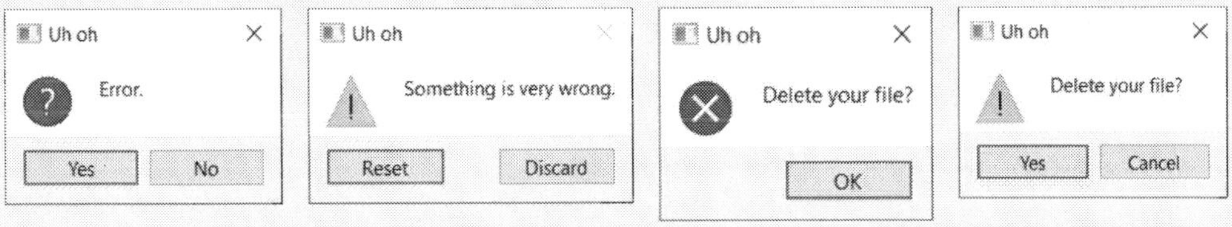

Figure 58. Some examples of bad dialogs.[2]

Dialog buttons are defined by system standards. You may never have noticed that the OK & Cancel buttons are in different locations on macOS & Linux vs. Windows, but your brain did. If you do not follow system standards, you'll confuse your users, and make them make mistakes.

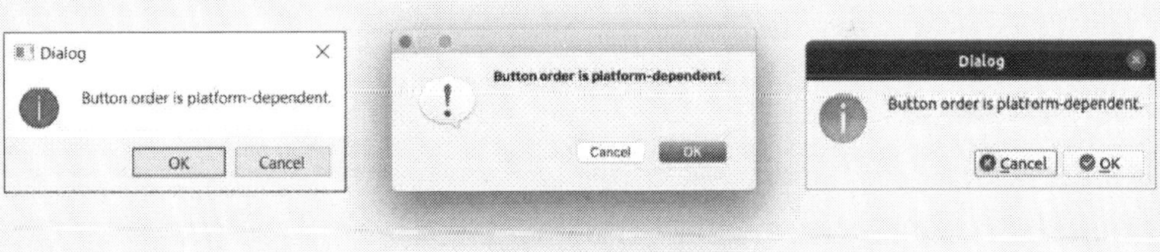

Figure 59. Dialog button order is platform dependent.

With Qt you get this consistency for *free* when using the built-in `QDialogButtonBox` controls. But you *must use them*!

Error dialogs annoy users. When you show an error dialog you're giving your users *bad news*. When you give someone bad news, you need to consider the impact it will have on them.

Take for example this (thankfully imaginary) dialog produced when we encounter an error in a document. The dialog tells you there is a error, but neither what the consequences are or what to do about it. Reading this your users will ask (possibly scream) "...and now what?"

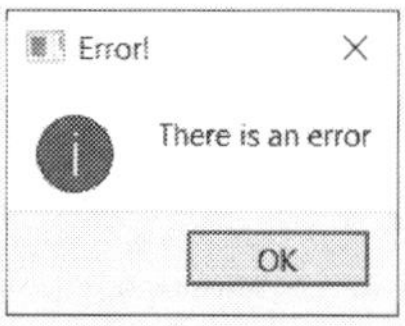

Figure 60. An example of a bad error dialog.

This real dialog from Acrobat Reader DC is better. This explains that there is an error, what the consequences may be, and potentially how to resolve it.

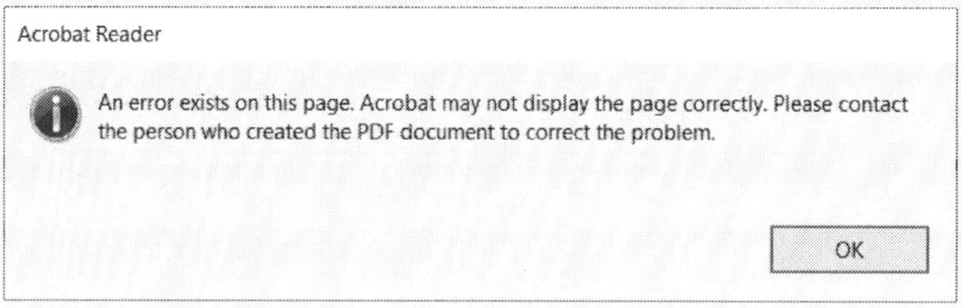

Figure 61. Adobe Acrobat Reader DC dialog

But this still isn't *perfect*. The error is shown as an *information* dialog, which doesn't suggest anything is wrong. The error is fired on every page, and can appear multiple times in a document—a warning dialog should be fired only *once*. The error could also be improved by making it clear that the error is permanent.

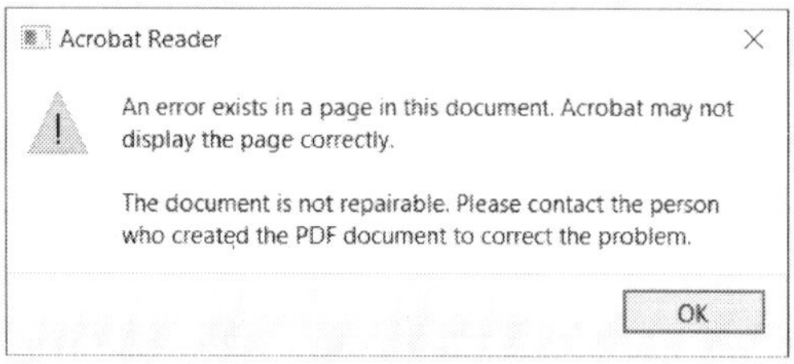

Figure 62. An improved version of the Adobe Acrobat Reader DC dialog

Good error messages should explain.

- ☐ What happened
- ☐ What was affected
- ☐ What are the consequences of it
- ☐ What can be done about it

11. Windows

In the previous chapter we looked at how to open *dialog* windows. These are special windows which (by default) grab the focus of the user, and run their own event loop, effectively blocking the execution of the rest of your app.

However, quite often you will want to open a second window in an application, without blocking the main window – for example, to show the output of some long-running process, or to display graphs or other visualizations. Alternatively, you may want to create an application that allows you to work on multiple documents at once, all in their own windows.

It's relatively straightforward to open new windows in PyQt5, but there are a few things to keep in mind to make sure they work well. In this tutorial we'll step through how to create a new window and how to show and hide external windows on demand.

Creating a new window

To create a new window in PyQt5 you just need to create a new instance of a widget object without a parent. This can be any widget (technically any subclass of `QWidget`) including another `QMainWindow` if you prefer.

> There is no restriction on the number of `QMainWindow` instances you can have, and if you need toolbars or menus on your second window you will need to use `QMainWindow` for that too.

As with your main window, *creating* a window is not sufficient, you must also show it.

Listing 54. basic/windows_1.py

```
import sys

from PyQt5.QtWidgets import (QApplication, QLabel, QMainWindow,
QPushButton,
                             QVBoxLayout, QWidget)


class AnotherWindow(QWidget):
    """
    This "window" is a QWidget. If it has no parent, it
    will appear as a free-floating window.
    """

    def __init__(self):
        super().__init__()
        layout = QVBoxLayout()
        self.label = QLabel("Another Window")
        layout.addWidget(self.label)
        self.setLayout(layout)


class MainWindow(QMainWindow):
    def __init__(self):
        super().__init__()
        self.button = QPushButton("Push for Window")
        self.button.clicked.connect(self.show_new_window)
        self.setCentralWidget(self.button)

    def show_new_window(self, checked):
        w = AnotherWindow()
        w.show()


app = QApplication(sys.argv)
w = MainWindow()
w.show()
app.exec_()
```

If you run this, you'll see the main window. Clicking the button *may* show the second window, but if you see it it will only be visible for a fraction of a second. What's happening?

```
def show_new_window(self, checked):
    w = AnotherWindow()
    w.show()
```

We are creating our second window inside this method, storing it in the variable `w` and showing it. However, once we leave this method the `w` variable will be cleaned up by Python, and the window destroyed. To fix this we need to keep a reference to the window *somewhere*—on the main window `self` object, for example.

Listing 55. basic/windows_1b.py

```
def show_new_window(self, checked):
    self.w = AnotherWindow()
    self.w.show()
```

Now, when you click the button to show the new window, it will persist.

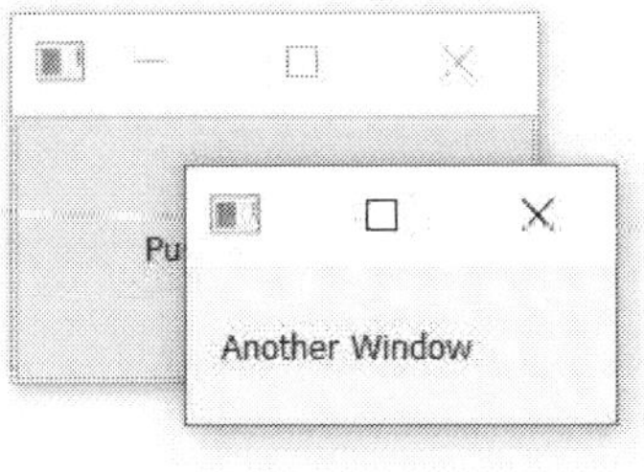

Figure 63. The second window persisting.

However, what happens if you click the button again? The window will be re-created! This new window will replace the old in the `self.w` variable, and the previous window will be destroyed. You can see this more clearly if you change the `AnotherWindow` definition to show a random number in the label each time it is created.

Listing 56. basic/windows_2.py

```
from random import randint

from PyQt5.QtWidgets import (
    QApplication,
    QLabel,
    QMainWindow,
    QPushButton,
    QVBoxLayout,
    QWidget,
)

class AnotherWindow(QWidget):
    """
    This "window" is a QWidget. If it has no parent, it
    will appear as a free-floating window.
    """

    def __init__(self):
        super().__init__()
        layout = QVBoxLayout()
        self.label = QLabel("Another Window % d" % randint(0, 100))
        layout.addWidget(self.label)
        self.setLayout(layout)
```

The `__init__` block is only run when *creating* the window. If you keep clicking the button the number will change, showing that the window is being re-created.

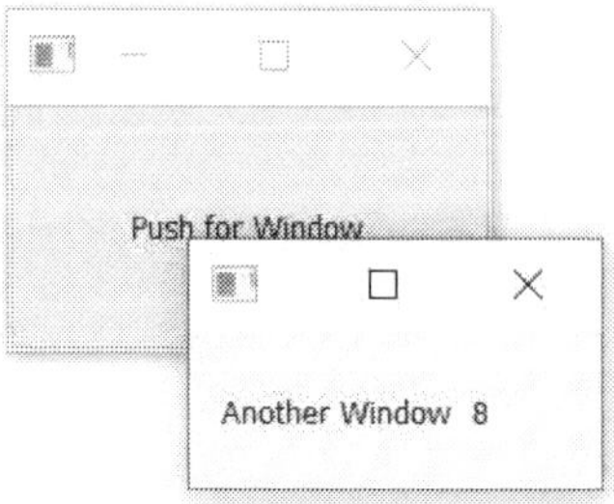

Figure 64. The number will change if the button is pressed again.

One solution is to simply check whether the window has already being created before creating it. The full example below shows this in action

Listing 57. basic/windows_3.py

```
class MainWindow(QMainWindow):
    def __init__(self):
        super().__init__()
        self.w = None  # No external window yet.
        self.button = QPushButton("Push for Window")
        self.button.clicked.connect(self.show_new_window)
        self.setCentralWidget(self.button)

    def show_new_window(self, checked):
        if self.w is None:
            self.w = AnotherWindow()
            self.w.show()
```

This approach is fine for windows that you create temporarily, or need to change dependent on the current state of the program – for example if you want to show a particular plot, or log output. However, for many applications you have a number of standard windows that you want to be able to show/hide on demand.

In the next part we'll look at how to work with these types of windows.

Closing a window

As we previously saw, if no reference to a window is kept, it will be discarded (and closed). We can use this behavior to close a window, replacing the `show_new_window` method from the previous example with –

Listing 58. basic/windows_4.py

```
    def show_new_window(self, checked):
        if self.w is None:
            self.w = AnotherWindow()
            self.w.show()

        else:
            self.w = None  # Discard reference, close window.
```

By setting `self.w` to `None` (or any other value) the reference to the window will be lost, and the window will close. However, if we set it to any other value than `None` the first test will not pass, and we will not be able to recreate a window.

This will only work if you have not kept a reference to this window somewhere else. To make sure the window closes regardless, you may want to explicitly call `.close()` on it.

Listing 59. basic/windows_4b.py

```
    def show_new_window(self, checked):
        if self.w is None:
            self.w = AnotherWindow()
            self.w.show()

        else:
            self.w.close()
            self.w = None  # Discard reference, close window.
```

Persistent windows

So far we've looked at how to create new windows on demand. However, sometimes you have a number of standard application windows. In this case it can often make more sense to create the additional windows first, then use `.show()` to display them when needed.

In the following example we create our external window in the `__init__` block for the main window, and then our show_new_window method simply calls self.w.show() to display it.

Listing 60. basic/windows_5.py

```
import sys
from random import randint

from PyQt5.QtWidgets import (
    QApplication,
    QLabel,
    QMainWindow,
    QPushButton,
    QVBoxLayout,
    QWidget,
)


class AnotherWindow(QWidget):
    """
    This "window" is a QWidget. If it has no parent, it
    will appear as a free-floating window.
    """

    def __init__(self):
        super().__init__()
        layout = QVBoxLayout()
        self.label = QLabel("Another Window % d" % randint(0, 100))
        layout.addWidget(self.label)
        self.setLayout(layout)


class MainWindow(QMainWindow):
    def __init__(self):
        super().__init__()
        self.w = AnotherWindow()
        self.button = QPushButton("Push for Window")
        self.button.clicked.connect(self.show_new_window)
        self.setCentralWidget(self.button)

    def show_new_window(self, checked):
        self.w.show()
```

```python
app = QApplication(sys.argv)
w = MainWindow()
w.show()
app.exec_()
```

If you run this, clicking on the button will show the window as before. Note that the window is only created once and calling `.show()` on an already visible window has no effect.

Showing & hiding windows

Once you have created a persistent window you can show and hide it without recreating it. Once hidden the window still exists, but will not be visible and accept mouse/other input. However you can continue to call methods on the window and update it's state – including changing it's appearance. Once re-shown any changes will be visible.

Below we update our main window to create a `toggle_window` method which checks, using `.isVisible()` to see if the window is currently visible. If it is not, it is shown using `.show()` , if it is already visible we hide it with `.hide()`.

```python
class MainWindow(QMainWindow):

    def __init__(self):
        super().__init__()
        self.w = AnotherWindow()
        self.button = QPushButton("Push for Window")
        self.button.clicked.connect(self.toggle_window)
        self.setCentralWidget(self.button)

    def toggle_window(self, checked):
        if self.w.isVisible():
            self.w.hide()

        else:
            self.w.show()
```

The complete working example of this persistent window and toggling the show/hide state is shown below.

Listing 61. basic/windows_6.py

```
import sys
from random import randint

from PyQt5.QtWidgets import (
    QApplication,
    QLabel,
    QMainWindow,
    QPushButton,
    QVBoxLayout,
    QWidget,
)


class AnotherWindow(QWidget):
    """
    This "window" is a QWidget. If it has no parent, it
    will appear as a free-floating window.
    """

    def __init__(self):
        super().__init__()
        layout = QVBoxLayout()
        self.label = QLabel("Another Window % d" % randint(0, 100))
        layout.addWidget(self.label)
        self.setLayout(layout)


class MainWindow(QMainWindow):
    def __init__(self):
        super().__init__()
        self.w = AnotherWindow()
        self.button = QPushButton("Push for Window")
        self.button.clicked.connect(self.toggle_window)
        self.setCentralWidget(self.button)

    def toggle_window(self, checked):
        if self.w.isVisible():
            self.w.hide()
```

```
        else:
            self.w.show()


app = QApplication(sys.argv)
w = MainWindow()
w.show()
app.exec_()
```

Again, the window is only created once – the window's `__init__` block is not re-run (so the number in the label does not change) each time the window is re-shown.

Connecting signals between windows

In the signals chapter we saw how it was possible to connect widgets together directly using signals and slots. All we needed was for the destination widget to have been created and to have a reference to via a variable. The same principle applies when connecting signals across windows—you can hook up signals in one window to slots in another, you just need to be able to access the slot.

In the example below, we connect a text input on our main window to a `QLabel` on a sub-window.

Listing 62. basic/windows_7.py

```
import sys
from random import randint

from PyQt5.QtWidgets import (
    QApplication,
    QLabel,
    QMainWindow,
    QPushButton,
    QVBoxLayout,
    QWidget,
    QLineEdit
```

```
)


class AnotherWindow(QWidget):
    """
    This "window" is a QWidget. If it has no parent, it
    will appear as a free-floating window.
    """

    def __init__(self):
        super().__init__()
        layout = QVBoxLayout()
        self.label = QLabel("Another Window")  ②
        layout.addWidget(self.label)
        self.setLayout(layout)


class MainWindow(QMainWindow):
    def __init__(self):
        super().__init__()
        self.w = AnotherWindow()
        self.button = QPushButton("Push for Window")
        self.button.clicked.connect(self.toggle_window)

        self.input = QLineEdit()
        self.input.textChanged.connect(self.w.label.setText)  ①

        layout = QVBoxLayout()
        layout.addWidget(self.button)
        layout.addWidget(self.input)
        container = QWidget()
        container.setLayout(layout)

        self.setCentralWidget(container)

    def toggle_window(self, checked):
        if self.w.isVisible():
            self.w.hide()

        else:
            self.w.show()
```

```python
app = QApplication(sys.argv)
w = MainWindow()
w.show()
app.exec_()
```

① The `AnotherWindow` window object is available via the variable `self.w`. The `QLabel` via `self.w.label` and the `.setText` slot by `self.w.label.setText`.

② When we create the `QLabel` we store a reference to it on `self` as `self.label`, so it is accessible externally on the object.

Run it! Type some text in the upper box, and you'll see it appear immediately on the label. Look what happens if you type text in the box while the window is hidden—it is still updated in the background! Updating the state of widgets is not dependent on them being visible.

Of course, you're also free to connect signals on one window to custom methods on another. Anything goes, as long as it is accessible (and for Qt slots the types match) you can connect it with signals.

Making sure components are importable and so accessible to one another is a good motivation for building a logical project structure. It often makes sense to hook up components centrally, in your main window/module to avoid cross-importing everything.

12. Events

Every interaction the user has with a Qt application is an *event*. There are many types of event, each representing a different type of interaction. Qt represents these events using *event objects* which package up information about what happened. These events are passed to specific *event handlers* on the widget where the interaction occurred.

By defining custom, or extended *event handlers* you can alter the way your widgets respond to these events. Event handlers are defined just like any other method, but the name is specific for the type of event they handle.

One of the main events which widgets receive is the `QMouseEvent`. QMouseEvent events are created for each and every mouse movement and button click on a widget. The following event handlers are available for handling mouse events—

Event handler	Event type moved
`mouseMoveEvent`	Mouse moved
`mousePressEvent`	Mouse button pressed
`mouseReleaseEvent`	Mouse button released
`mouseDoubleClickEvent`	Double click detected

For example, clicking on a widget will cause a `QMouseEvent` to be sent to the `.mousePressEvent` event handler on that widget. This handler can use the event object to find out information about what happened, such as what triggered the event and where specifically it occurred.

You can intercept events by sub-classing and overriding the handler method on the class. You can choose to filter, modify, or ignore events, passing them up to the normal handler for the event by calling the parent class function with `super()`. These could be added to your main window class as follows. In each case `e` will receive the incoming event.

Listing 63. basic/events_1.py

```python
import sys

from PyQt5.QtCore import Qt
from PyQt5.QtWidgets import QApplication, QLabel, QMainWindow,
QTextEdit


class MainWindow(QMainWindow):
    def __init__(self):
        super().__init__()
        self.label = QLabel("Click in this window")
        self.setCentralWidget(self.label)

    def mouseMoveEvent(self, e):
        self.label.setText("mouseMoveEvent")

    def mousePressEvent(self, e):
        self.label.setText("mousePressEvent")

    def mouseReleaseEvent(self, e):
        self.label.setText("mouseReleaseEvent")

    def mouseDoubleClickEvent(self, e):
        self.label.setText("mouseDoubleClickEvent")


app = QApplication(sys.argv)

window = MainWindow()
window.show()

app.exec_()
```

Run it! Try moving and clicking (and double-clicking) in the window and watch the events appear.

You'll notice that mouse move events are only registered when you have the button pressed down. You can change this by calling `self.setMouseTracking(True)` on the window. You may also notice that the press (click) and double-click events both fire when the button is pressed down. Only the release event fires when the button is released. Typically to register a click from a user you should watch for both the mouse down *and* the release.

Inside the event handlers you have access to an event object. This object contains information about the event and can be used to respond differently depending on what exactly has occurred. We'll look at the mouse event objects next.

Mouse events

All mouse events in Qt are tracked with the `QMouseEvent` object, with information about the event being readable from the following event methods.

Method	Returns
`.button()`	Specific button that trigger this event
`.buttons()`	State of all mouse buttons (OR'ed flags)
`.globalPos()`	Application-global position as a `QPoint`
`.globalX()`	Application-global *horizontal* X position
`.globalY()`	Application-global *vertical* Y position
`.pos()`	Widget-relative position as a `QPoint` *integer*
`.posF()`	Widget-relative position as a `QPointF` *float*

You can use these methods within an event handler to respond to different events differently, or ignore them completely. The positional methods provide both *global* and *local* (widget-relative) position information as `QPoint` objects, while buttons are reported using the mouse button types from the `Qt` namespace.

For example, the following allows us to respond differently to a left, right or middle click on the window.

Listing 64. basic/events_2.py

```python
    def mousePressEvent(self, e):
        if e.button() == Qt.LeftButton:
            # handle the left-button press in here
            self.label.setText("mousePressEvent LEFT")

        elif e.button() == Qt.MiddleButton:
            # handle the middle-button press in here.
            self.label.setText("mousePressEvent MIDDLE")

        elif e.button() == Qt.RightButton:
            # handle the right-button press in here.
            self.label.setText("mousePressEvent RIGHT")

    def mouseReleaseEvent(self, e):
        if e.button() == Qt.LeftButton:
            self.label.setText("mouseReleaseEvent LEFT")

        elif e.button() == Qt.MiddleButton:
            self.label.setText("mouseReleaseEvent MIDDLE")

        elif e.button() == Qt.RightButton:
            self.label.setText("mouseReleaseEvent RIGHT")

    def mouseDoubleClickEvent(self, e):
        if e.button() == Qt.LeftButton:
            self.label.setText("mouseDoubleClickEvent LEFT")

        elif e.button() == Qt.MiddleButton:
            self.label.setText("mouseDoubleClickEvent MIDDLE")

        elif e.button() == Qt.RightButton:
            self.label.setText("mouseDoubleClickEvent RIGHT")
```

On right-handed mice the left and right button positions are reversed, i.e. pressing the right-most button will return `Qt.LeftButton`. This means you don't need to account for the mouse orientation in your code.

The button identifiers are defined in the Qt namespace, as follows—

Identifier	Value (binary)	Represents
`Qt.NoButton`	0 (`000`)	No button pressed, or the event is not related to button press.
`Qt.LeftButton`	1 (`001`)	The left button is pressed
`Qt.RightButton`	2 (`010`)	The right button is pressed.
`Qt.MiddleButton`	4 (`100`)	The middle button is pressed.

For a more in-depth look at how this all works check out Enums & the Qt Namespace later.

Context menus

Context menus are small context-sensitive menus which typically appear when right clicking on a window. Qt has support for generating these menus, and widgets have a specific event used to trigger them. In the following example we're going to intercept the `.contextMenuEvent` a `QMainWindow`. This event is fired whenever a context menu is *about to be* shown, and is passed a single value `event` of type `QContextMenuEvent`.

To intercept the event, we simply override the object method with our new method of the same name. So in this case we can create a method on our `MainWindow` subclass with the name `contextMenuEvent` and it will receive all events of this type.

Listing 65. basic/events_3.py

```
import sys

from PyQt5.QtCore import Qt
from PyQt5.QtWidgets import QAction, QApplication, QLabel,
QMainWindow, QMenu


class MainWindow(QMainWindow):
    def __init__(self):
        super().__init__()

    def contextMenuEvent(self, e):
        context = QMenu(self)
        context.addAction(QAction("test 1", self))
        context.addAction(QAction("test 2", self))
        context.addAction(QAction("test 3", self))
        context.exec_(e.globalPos())


app = QApplication(sys.argv)

window = MainWindow()
window.show()

app.exec_()
```

If you run the above code and right-click within the window, you'll see a context menu appear. You can set up `.triggered` slots on your menu actions as normal (and re-use actions defined for menus and toolbars).

> When passing the initial position to the `exec_` function, this must be relative to the parent passed in while defining. In this case we pass `self` as the parent, so we can use the global position.

Just for completeness, there is actually a signal-based approach to creating context menus.

Listing 66. basic/events_4.py

```
class MainWindow(QMainWindow):
    def __init__(self):
        super().__init__()
        self.show()

        self.setContextMenuPolicy(Qt.CustomContextMenu)
        self.customContextMenuRequested.connect(self.on_context_menu)

    def on_context_menu(self, pos):
        context = QMenu(self)
        context.addAction(QAction("test 1", self))
        context.addAction(QAction("test 2", self))
        context.addAction(QAction("test 3", self))
        context.exec_(self.mapToGlobal(pos))
```

It's entirely up to you which you choose.

Event hierarchy

In pyqt5 every widget is part of two distinct hierarchies: the Python object hierarchy, and the Qt layout hierarchy. How you respond or ignore events can affect how your UI behaves.

Python inheritance forwarding

Often you may want to intercept an event, do something with it, yet still trigger the default event handling behavior. If your object is inherited from a standard widget, it will likely have sensible behavior implemented by default. You can trigger this by calling up to the parent implementation using `super()`.

> This is the Python parent class, not the pyqt5 `.parent()`.

```python
def mousePressEvent(self, event):
    print("Mouse pressed!")
    super(self, MainWindow).contextMenuEvent(event)
```

The event will continue to behave as normal, yet you've added some non-interfering behavior.

Layout forwarding

When you add a widget to your application, it also gets another *parent* from the layout. The parent of a widget can be found by calling `.parent()`. Sometimes you specify these parents manually, such as for `QMenu` or `QDialog`, often it is automatic. When you add a widget to your main window for example, the main window will become the widget's parent.

When events are created for user interaction with the UI, these events are passed to the *uppermost* widget in the UI. So, if you have a button on a window, and click the button, the button will receive the event first.

If the first widget cannot handle the event, or chooses not to, the event will *bubble up* to the parent widget, which will be given a turn. This *bubbling* continues all the way up nested widgets, until the event is handled or it reaches the main window.

In your own event handlers you can choose to mark an event as *handled* calling `.accept()`—

```python
    class CustomButton(Qbutton)
        def mousePressEvent(self, e):
            e.accept()
```

Alternatively, you can mark it as *unhandled* by calling `.ignore()` on the event object. In this case the event will continue to bubble up the hierarchy.

```python
class CustomButton(Qbutton)
    def event(self, e):
        e.ignore()
```

If you want your widget to appear transparent to events, you can safely ignore events which you've actually responded to in some way. Similarly, you can choose to accept events you are not responding to in order to silence them.

Qt Designer

So far we have been creating apps using Python code. This works great in many cases, but as your applications get larger or interfaces more complicated, it can get a bit cumbersome to define all widgets programmatically. The good news is that Qt comes with a graphical editor — *Qt Designer* — which contains a drag-and-drop UI editor. Using *Qt Designer* you can define your UIs visually and then simply hook up the application logic later.

In this chapter we'll cover the basics of creating UIs with *Qt Designer*. The principles, layouts and widgets are identical, so you can apply everything you've already learnt. You'll also need your knowledge of the Python API to hook up your application logic later.

13. Installing Qt Designer

Qt Designer is available in the installation packages for Qt available from the Qt downloads page [https://www.qt.io/download-qt-installer]. Download and run the appropriate installer for your system, the following the platform-specific instructions below. Installing *Qt Designer* will not affect your PyQt5 installation.

> *Qt Creator vs. Qt Designer*
>
> You may also see mentions of *Qt Creator*. *Qt Creator* a fully-fledged IDE for Qt projects, while *Qt Designer* is the UI design component. *Qt Designer* is available within *Qt Creator* so you can install that instead if you wish, although it doesn't provide any added value for Python projects.

Windows

Qt Designer is not mentioned in the Windows Qt installer, but is automatically installed when you install any version of the Qt core libraries. For example, in the following screenshot we've opted to install the *MSVC 2017 64-bit* version of Qt—what you choose will have no effect on your *Designer* install.

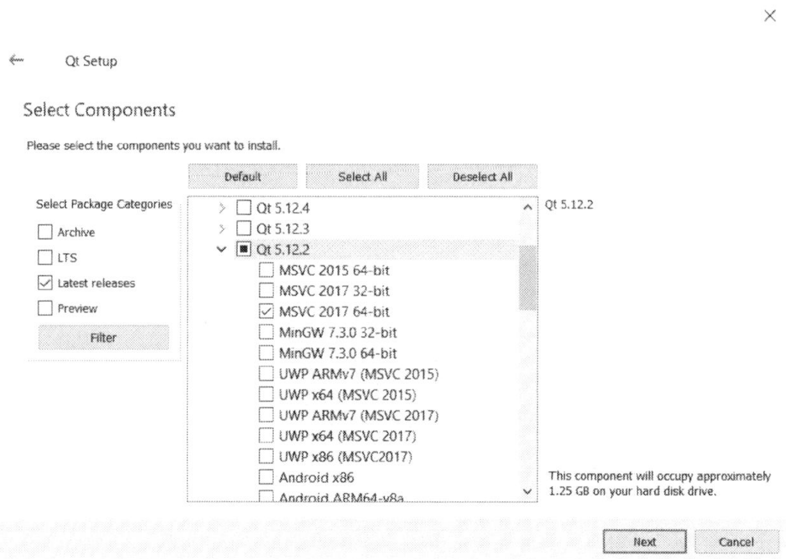

Figure 65. Installing Qt, will also install Qt Designer.

If you want to install *Qt Creator* it is listed under "Developer and Designer Tools". Rather confusingly, *Qt Designer* isn't in here.

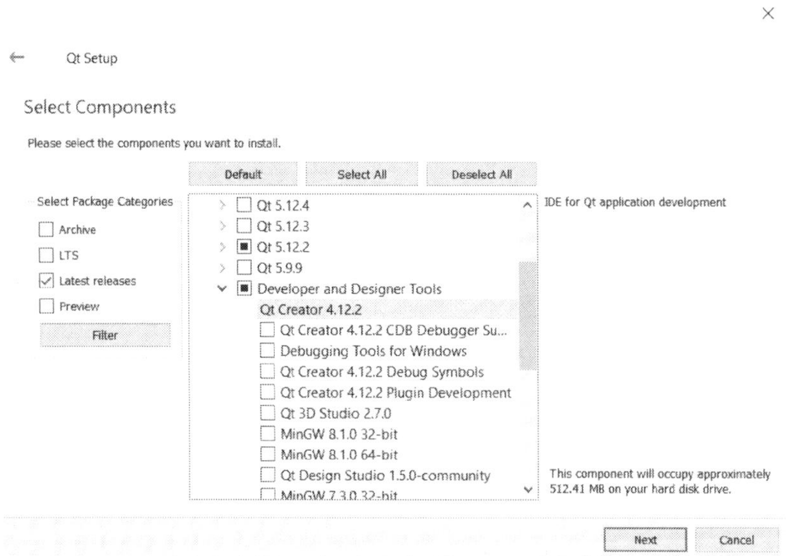

Figure 66. Installing the Qt Creator component.

macOS

Qt Designer is not mentioned in the macOS Qt installer, but is automatically installed when you install any version of the Qt core libraries. Download the installer from the Qt website—you can opt for the open source version.

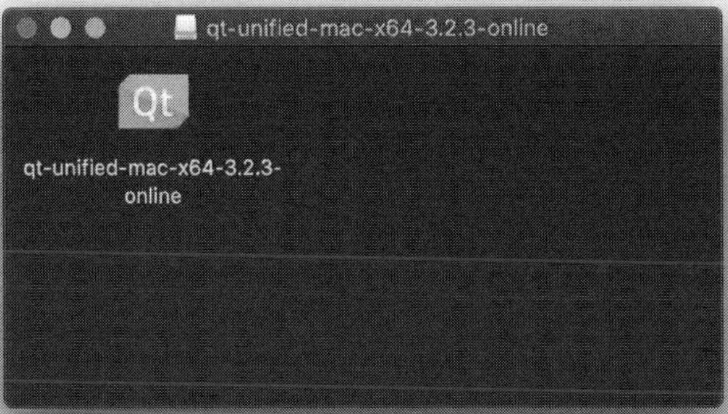

Figure 67. Inside the downloaded `.dmg` *file you'll find the installer.*

Open the installer to start the installation. Go through to where it asks you to choose which components to install. Select the *macOS* package under the latest version of Qt.

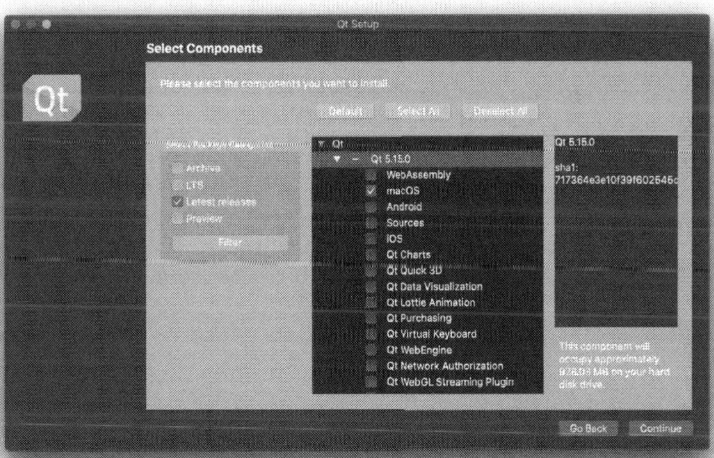

Figure 68. You only need the macOS package under the latest version.

Once the installation is complete, open the folder where you installed Qt. The launcher for *Designer* is under `<version>/clang_64/bin`. You'll notice that *Qt Creator* is also installed in the root of the Qt installation folder.

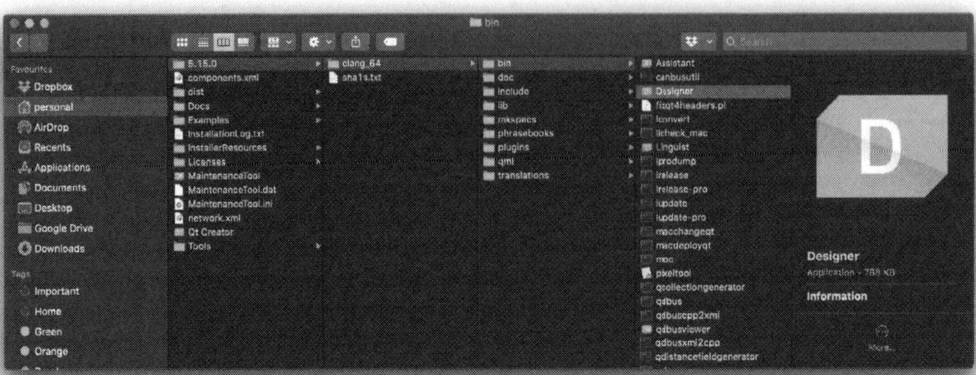

Figure 69. You can find the Designer launcher under the <version>/clang_64/bin folder.

You can run *Designer* from where it is located, or move it into your Applications folder so it is available to launch from the macOS Launchpad.

Linux (Ubuntu & Debian)

You can install *Qt Designer* from the command line with the following. *Qt Designer* is in the `qttools5-dev-tools` package.

```
sudo apt-get install qttools5-dev-tools
```

Once installed, *Qt Designer* will be available in the launcher.

Figure 70. Qt Designer in Ubuntu launcher.

14. Getting started with Qt Designer

In this chapter we'll take a quick tour through using *Qt Designer* to design a UI and exporting that UI for use in your PyQt5 application. We'll only scratch the surface of what you can do with *Qt Designer* here, but once you've got the basics down, feel free to experiment in more detail.

Open up *Qt Designer* and you will be presented with the main window. The designer is available via the tab on the left hand side. However, to activate this you first need to start creating a `.ui` file.

Qt Designer

Qt Designer starts up with the *New Form* dialog. Here you can choose the type of interface you're building—this decides the base widget you will build your interface on. If you are starting an application then *Main Window* is usually the right choice. However, you can also create `.ui` files for dialog boxes and custom compound widgets.

> Form is the technical name given to a UI layout, since many UIs resemble a paper form with various input boxes.

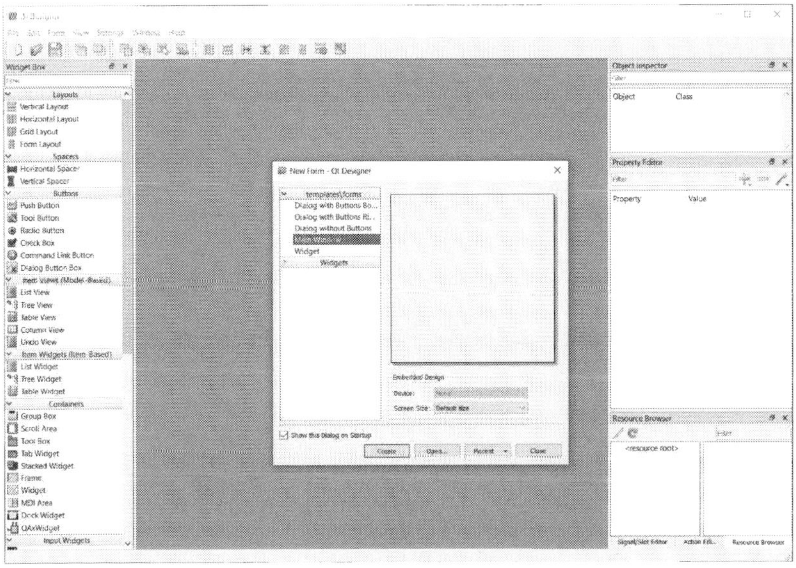

Figure 71. The Qt Designer interface

If you click *Create* then a new UI will be created, with a single empty widget in it. You're now ready to start designing your app.

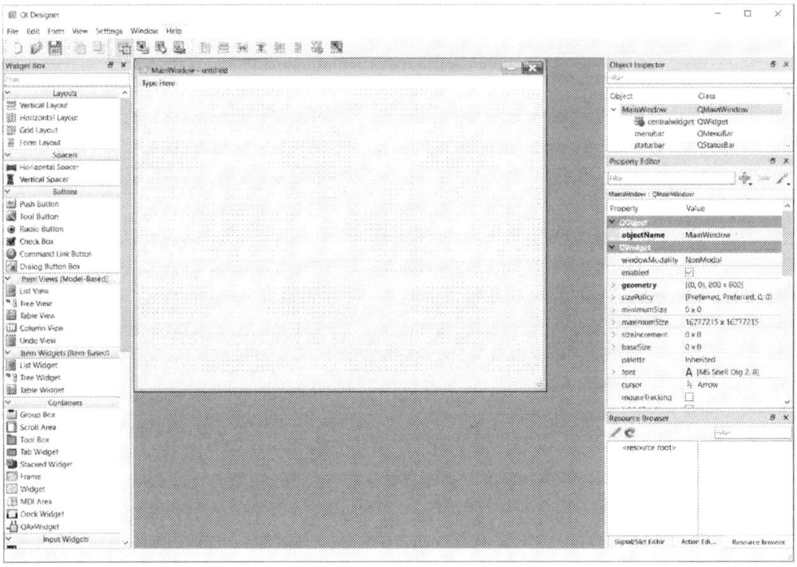

Figure 72. The Qt Designer editor interface, with an empty `QMainWindow` *widget.*

Qt Creator

If you've installed *Qt Creator* the interface and process is slightly different. The left-hand side has a tab-like interface where you can select from the various components of the application. One of these is *Design* which shows *Qt Designer* in the main panel.

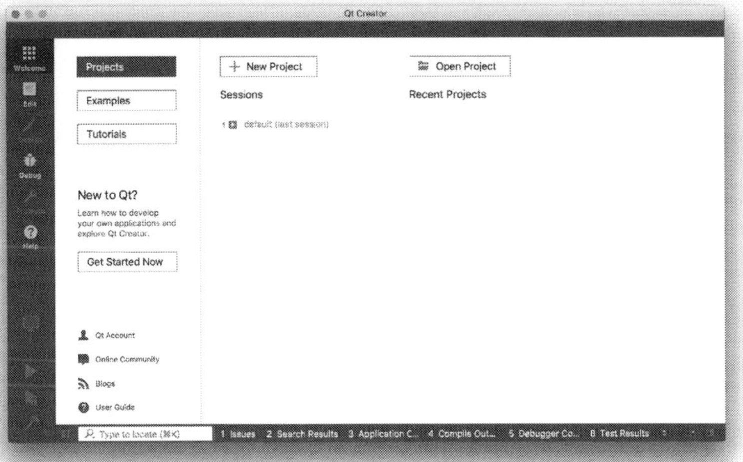

Figure 73. The Qt Creator interface, with the Design section selected on the left. The Qt Designer interface is identical to the nested Designer.

> All the features of *Qt Designer* are available in *Qt Creator* but some aspects of the user interface are different.

To create a `.ui` file go to File → New File or Project… In the window that appears select *Qt* under *Files and Classes* on the left, then select *Qt Designer Form* on the right. You'll notice the icon has "ui" on it, showing the type of file you're creating.

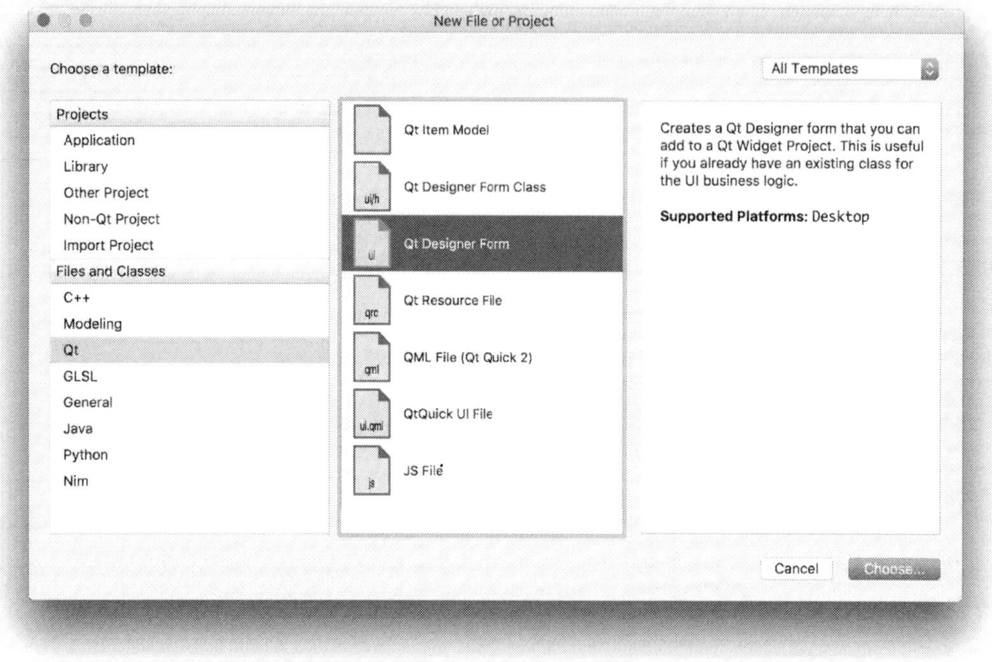

Figure 74. Create a new Qt .ui file.

In the next step you'll be asked what type of UI you want to create. For most applications *Main Window* is the right choice. However, you can also create `.ui` files for other dialog boxes or build custom widgets using `QWidget` (listed as "Widget").

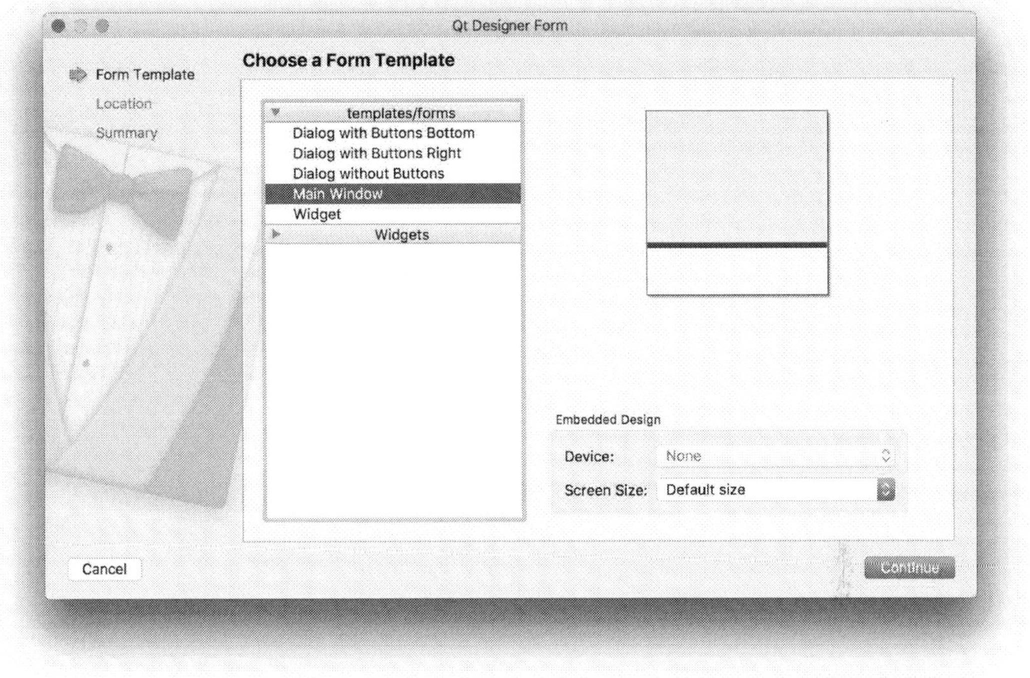

Figure 75. Select the type of widget to create, for most applications this will be Main Window.

Next choose a filename and save folder for your file. Save your `.ui` file with the same name as the class you'll be creating, just to make make subsequent commands simpler.

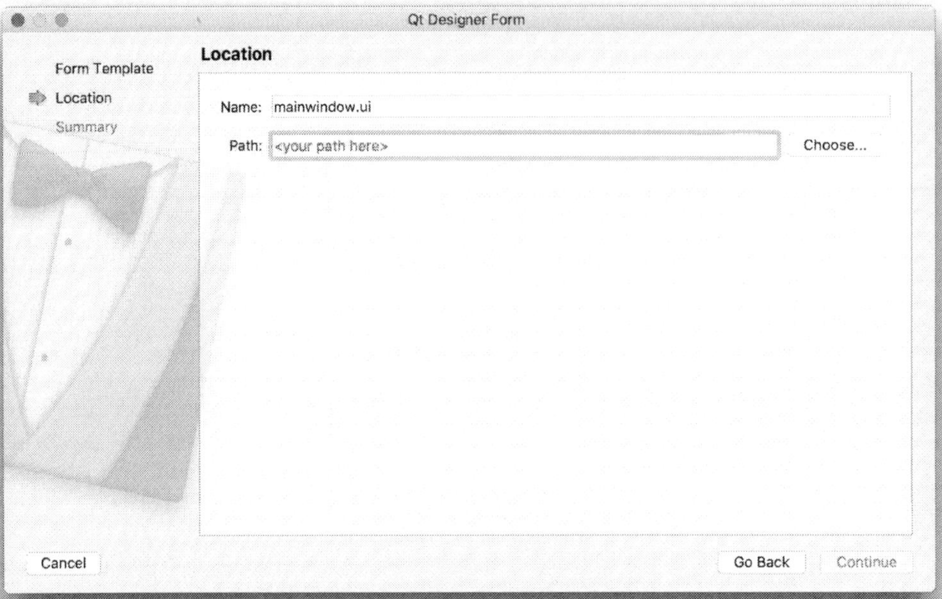

Figure 76. Choose save name and folder your your file.

Finally, you can choose to add the file to your version control system if you're using one. Feel free to skip this step — it doesn't affect your UI.

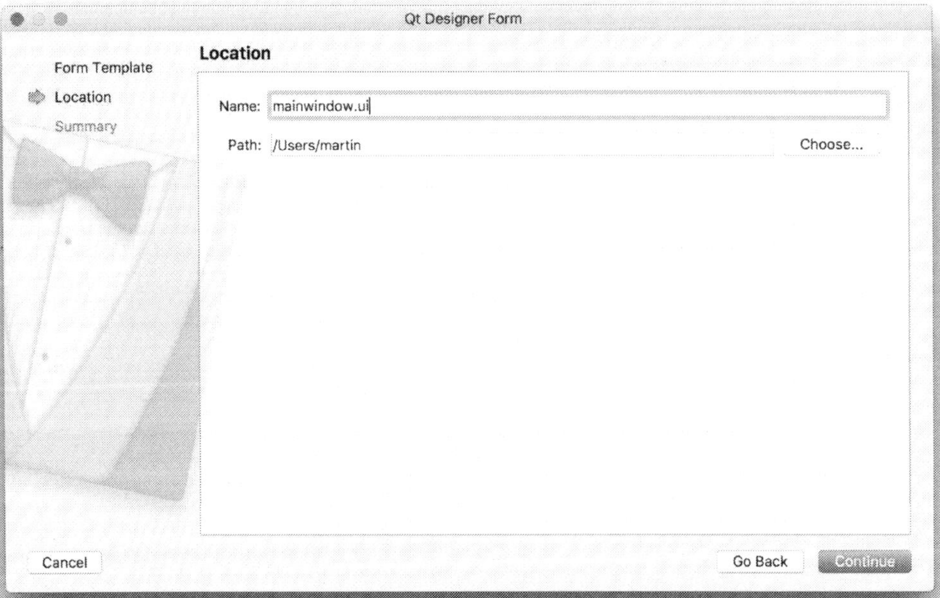

Figure 77. Optionally add the file to your version control, e.g. Git.

Laying out your Main Window

You'll be presented with your newly created main window in the UI designer. There isn't much to see to begin with, just a grey working area representing the window, together with the beginnings of a window menu bar.

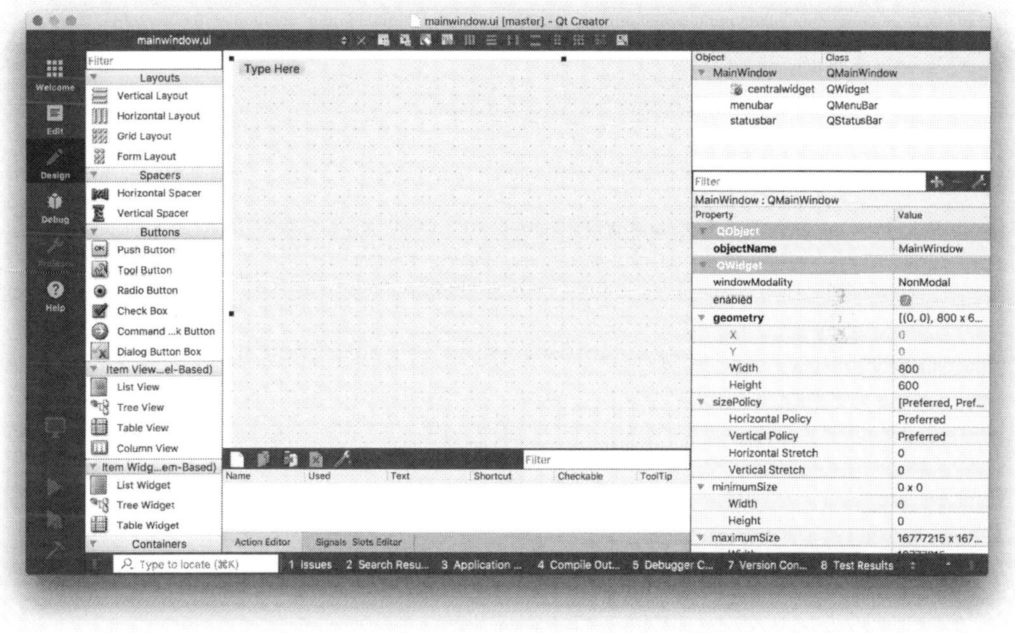

Figure 78. The initial view of the created main window.

You can resize the window by clicking the window and dragging the blue handles on each corner.

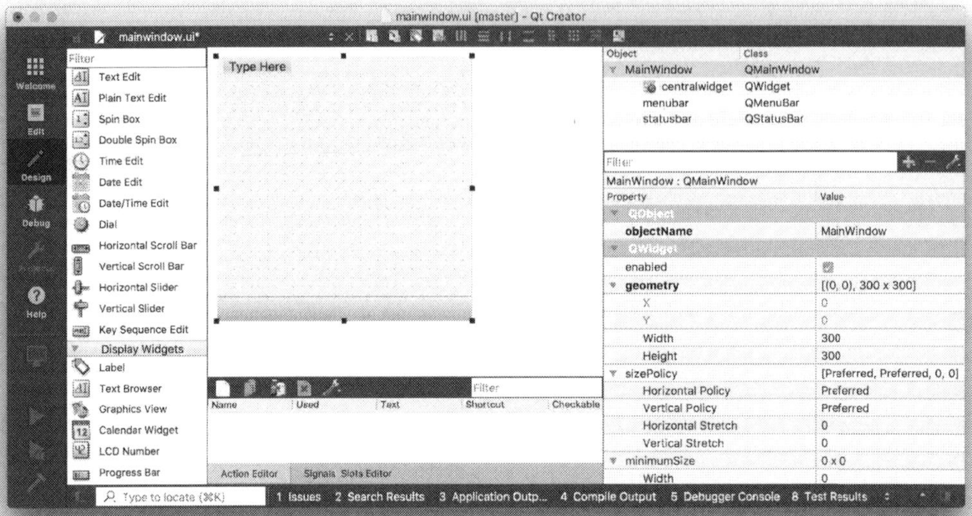

Figure 79. The main window resized to 300 x 300 pixels.

The first step in building an application is to add some widgets to your window. In our first applications we learnt that to set the central widget for a `QMainWindow` we need to use `.setCentralWidget()`. We also saw that to add multiple widgets with a layout, we need an intermediary `QWidget` to apply the layout to, rather than adding the layout to the window directly.

Qt Designer takes care of this for you automatically, although it's not particularly obvious about it.

To add multiple widgets to the main window with a layout, first drag your widgets onto the `QMainWindow`. Here we've dragged a `QLabel` and a `QPushButton`, it doesn't matter where you drop them.

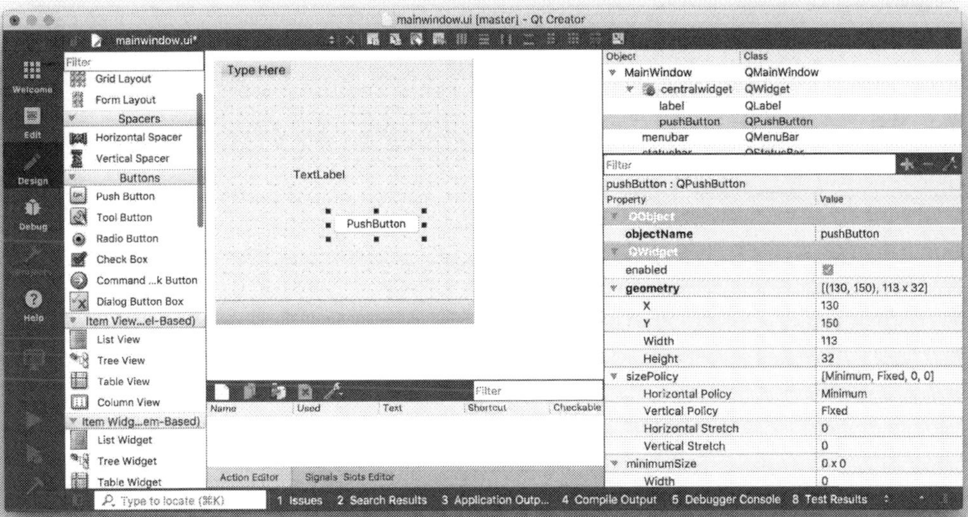

Figure 80. Main window with 1 labels and 1 button added.

We've created 2 widgets by dragging them onto the window, made them children of that window. We can now apply a layout.

Find the `QMainWindow` in the right hand panel (it should be right at the top). Underneath you see *centralwidget* representing the window's central widget. The icon for the central widget shows the current layout applied. Initially it has a red circle-cross through it, showing that there is no layout active. Right click on the `QMainWindow` object, and find 'Layout' in the resulting dropdown.

Figure 81. Right click on the main window, and choose layout.

Next you'll see a list of layouts which you can apply to the window. Select *Lay Out Horizontally* and the layout will be applied to the widget.

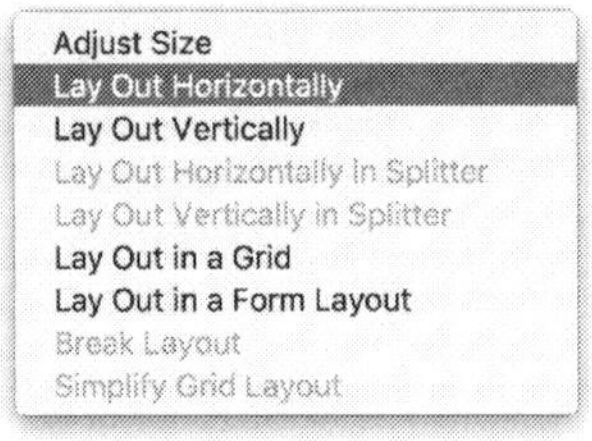

Figure 82. Select layout to apply to the main window.

The selected layout is applied to the *centralwidget* of the `QMainWindow` and the widgets are added the layout, being laid out depending on the selected layout. Note that in Qt Creator you can actually drag and re-order the widgets within the layout, or select a different layout, as you like. This makes it especially nice to prototyping and trying out things.

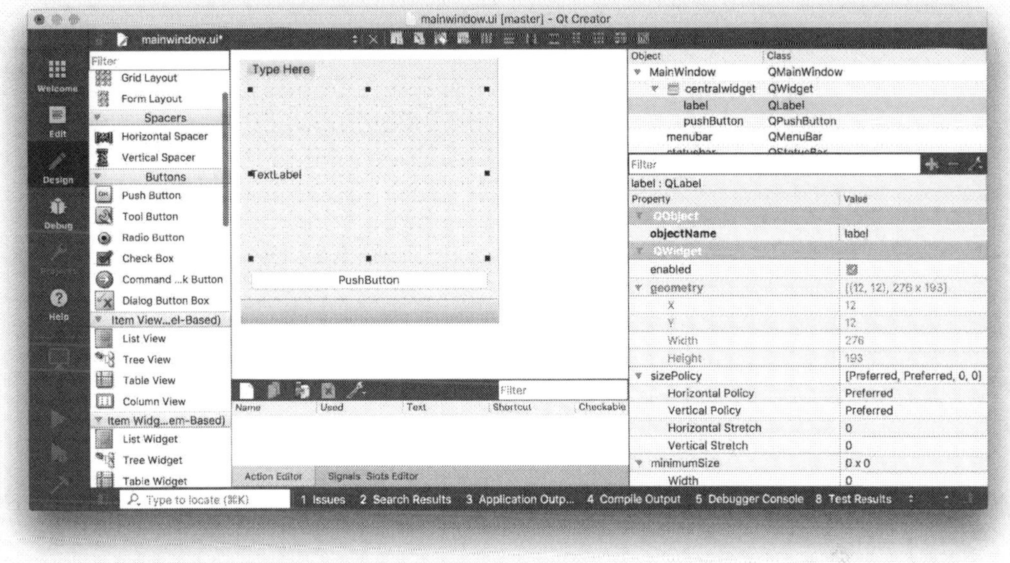

Figure 83. Horizontal layout applied to widgets on the main window.

We've created a very simple UI in *Qt Designer*. The next step is to get this UI into our Python code and use it to construct a working application.

First save your `.ui` file — by default it will save at the location you chosen while creating it, although you can choose another location if you like. The `.ui` file is in XML format. To use our UI in Python we can either load it directly from Python, *or* first convert it to a Python `.py` file using the `pyuic5` tool.

Loading your .ui file in Python

To load .ui files we can use the `uic` module included with PyQt5, specifically the `uic.loadUI()` method. This takes the filename of a UI file and loads it creating a fully-functional PyQt5 object.

Listing 67. designer/example_1.py

```
import sys

from PyQt5 import QtWidgets, uic

app = QtWidgets.QApplication(sys.argv)

window = uic.loadUi("mainwindow.ui")
window.show()
app.exec_()
```

To load a UI from the `__init__` block of an existing widget (e.g. a QMainWindow) you can use `uic.loadUI(filename, self)`.

Listing 68. designer/example_2.py

```
import sys

from PyQt5 import QtCore, QtGui, QtWidgets, uic


class MainWindow(QtWidgets.QMainWindow):
    def __init__(self, *args, **kwargs):
        super().__init__(*args, **kwargs)
        uic.loadUi("mainwindow.ui", self)


app = QtWidgets.QApplication(sys.argv)
window = MainWindow()
window.show()
app.exec_()
```

Converting your .ui file to Python

To generate a Python output file we can use the PyQt5 command line utility `pyuic5`. We run this, passing in the filename of the `.ui` file and the target file for output, with a `-o` parameter. The following will generate a Python file named `MainWindow.py` which contains our created UI. I use CamelCase on the filename to remind myself its a PyQt5 class file.

```
pyuic5 mainwindow.ui -o MainWindow.py
```

You can open the resulting `MainWindow.py` file in an editor to take a look, although you should *not* edit this file—if you do, any changes will be lost if you regenerate the UI from *Qt Designer*. The power of using *Qt Designer* is being able to edit and update your application as you go.

Building your application

Importing the resulting Python file works as for any other. You can import your class as follows. The `pyuic5` tool appends `Ui_` to the name of the object defined in *Qt Designer*, and it is this object you want to import.

```
from MainWindow import Ui_MainWindow
```

To create the main window in your application, create a class as normal but subclassing from both `QMainWindow` and your imported `Ui_MainWindow` class. Finally, call `self.setupUi(self)` from within the `__init__` to trigger the setup of the interface.

```
class MainWindow(QMainWindow, Ui_MainWindow):
    def __init__(self, *args, obj=None, **kwargs):
        super(MainWindow, self).__init__(*args, **kwargs)
        self.setupUi(self)
```

That's it. Your window is now fully set up.

Adding application logic

You can interact with widgets created through *Qt Designer* just as you would those created with code. To make things simpler, `pyuic5` adds all widgets to the window object.

The name used for objects can be found through *Qt Designer*. Simply click on it in the editor window, and then look for objectName in the properties panel.

In the follow example we use the generated main window class to build a working application.

```
import random
import sys

from PyQt5.QtCore import Qt
from PyQt5.QtWidgets import QApplication, QMainWindow

from MainWindow import Ui_MainWindow


class MainWindow(QMainWindow, Ui_MainWindow):
    def __init__(self):
        super().__init__()
        self.setupUi(self)
        self.show()

        # You can still override values from your UI file within your
code,
        # but if possible, set them in Qt Creator. See the properties
panel.
        f = self.label.font()
        f.setPointSize(25)
        self.label.setAlignment(Qt.AlignHCenter | Qt.AlignVCenter)
        self.label.setFont(f)

        # Signals from UI widgets can be connected as normal.
        self.pushButton.pressed.connect(self.update_label)

    def update_label(self):
        n = random.randint(1, 6)
        self.label.setText("%d" % n)


app = QApplication(sys.argv)
w = MainWindow()
app.exec_()
```

Notice that because we haven't set font size and alignment in the *Qt Designer* `.ui` definition, we must do so manually with code. You can change any widget parameters in this way, just as before. However, it is usually better to configure these things within *Qt Designer* itself.

You can set any widget properties through the properties panel on the bottom right of the window. Most widget properties are exposed here, for example, below we are updating the font size on the `QLabel` widget—

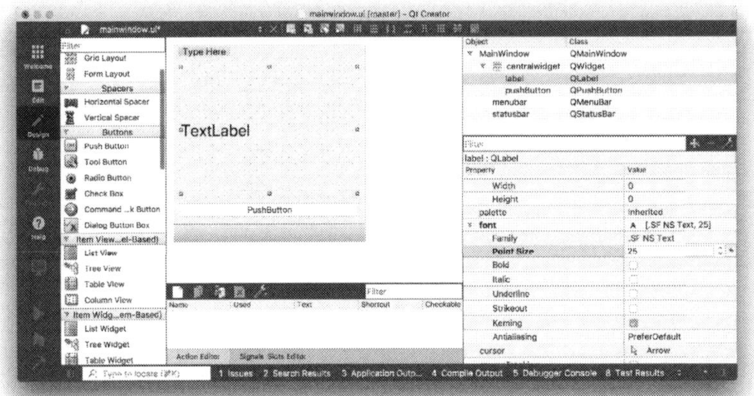

Figure 84. Setting the font size for the QLabel.

You can also configure alignment. For compound properties (where you can set multiple values, such as left + middle) they are nested.

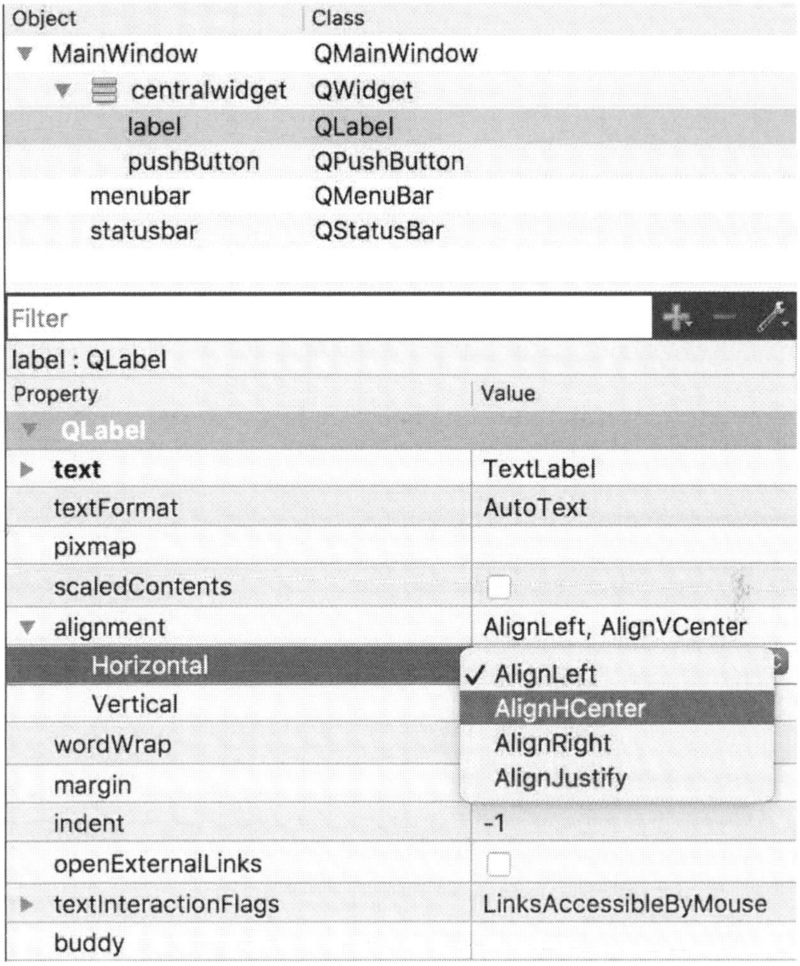

Figure 85. Detailed font properties.

All object properties are able to be edited from both places—it's up to you whether you make a particular modification in code or in *Qt Designer*. As a general rule, it makes sense to keep *dynamic* changes in your code and the base or default state in your designed UI.

This introduction has only scratched the surface of what *Qt Designer* is capable of. I highly recommend you dig a little deeper and experiment — remember you can still add or adjust widgets from code afterwards.

Aesthetics

If you're not a designer, it can be hard to create *beautiful* interfaces, or even know what they are. Thankfully there are simple rules you can follow to create interfaces that, if not *beautiful* at least won't be *ugly*. The key concepts are—alignment, groups and space.

Alignment is about reducing visual noise. Think of the corners of widgets as *alignment points* and aim to minimize the number of *unique* alignment points in the UI. In practice, this means making sure the edges of elements in the interface *line up* with one another.

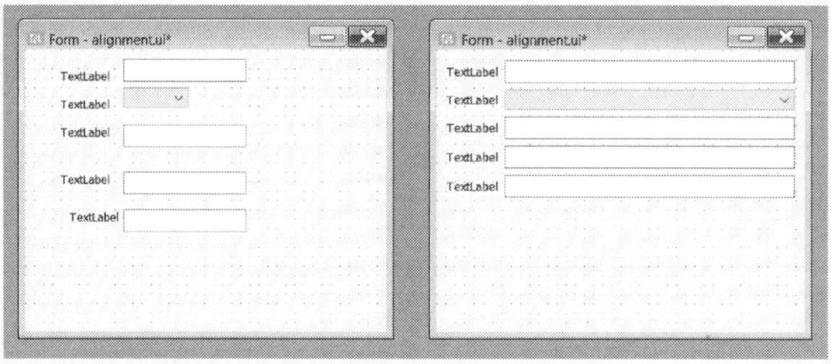

Figure 86. The effect of alignment of interface clarity.

> If you have differently sized inputs, align the edge you read *from*. English is a left-to-right language, so if your app is in English align the left.

Groups of related widgets gain context making them easier to *understand*. Structure your interface so related things are found together.

Space is key to creating visually distinct regions in your interface—without space between groups, there are no groups! Keep spacing consistent and meaningful.

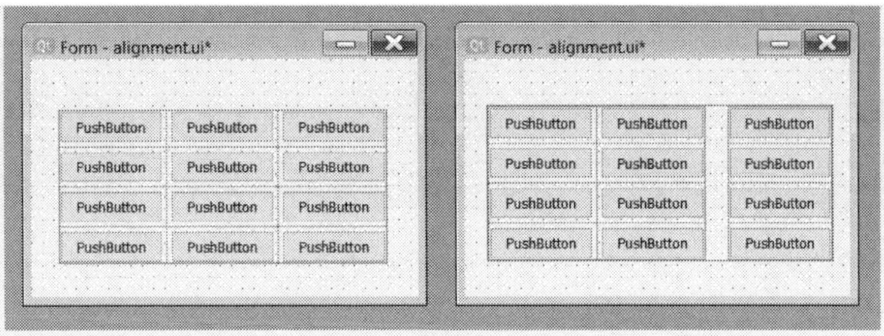

Figure 87. Group elements and add space between groups.

15. The Qt Resource system

Building applications takes more than just code. Usually your interface will need icons for actions, you may want to add illustrations or branding logos, or perhaps your application will need to load data files to pre-populate widgets. These *data files* are separate from the source code of your application but will ultimately need to be packaged and distributed with it in order for it to work.

Distributing data files with applications is a common cause of problems. If you reference data files with paths, your application won't work properly unless the exact same paths are available on the target computer. This can get even trickier when packaging applications for cross-platform (Windows, macOS and Linux) use. Thankfully, Qt comes to the rescue with it's *resource system*.

Since we're using Qt for our GUI we can make use of Qt Resource system to bundle, identify and load resources in our application. Resources are *bundled* into Python files which can be distributed along with your source code, guaranteeing they will continue to work on other platforms. You can manage Qt resources through Qt Designer (or Qt Creator) and use resource library to add icons (and other graphics) to your apps.

The QRC file

The core of the Qt Resources system is the *resource file* or QRC. The `.qrc` file is a simple XML file, which can be opened in any text editor.

> 💡 You can also create QRC files and add and remove resources using Qt Designer, which we'll cover later.

Simple QRC example

A very simple resource file is shown below, containing a single resource (a single icon `animal-penguin.png` we might add to a button).

```
<!DOCTYPE RCC>
<RCC version="1.0">
    <qresource prefix="icons">
        <file alias="animal-penguin.png">animal-penguin.png</file>
    </qresource>
</RCC>
```

The name between the `<file>` `</file>` tags is the path to the file, relative to the resource file. The `alias` is the name which this resource will be known by from within your application. You can use this *rename* icons to something more logical or simpler in your app, while keeping the original name externally.

For example, if we wanted to use the name `penguin.png` internally, we could change this line to.

```
<file alias="penguin.png">animal-penguin.png</file>
```

> This only changes the name used *inside* your application, the filename remains unchanged.

Outside this tag is the `qresource` tag which specifies a `prefix`. This is a *namespace* which can be used to group resources together. This is effectively a virtual folder, under which nested resources can all be found.

Using a QRC file

To use a `.qrc` file in your application you first need to compile it to Python. PyQt5 comes with a command line tool to do this, which takes a `.qrc` file as input and outputs a Python file containing the compiled data. This can then be imported into your app as for any other Python file or module.

To compile our `resources.qrc` file to a Python file named `resources.py` we can use—

```
pyrcc5 resources.qrc -o resources.py
```

To use the resource file in our application we need to make a few small changes. Firstly, we need to `import resources` at the top of our app, to load the resources into the Qt resource system, and then secondly we need to update the path to the icon file to use the resource path format as follows:

The prefix :/ indicates that this is a *resource path*. The first name "icons" is the *prefix* namespace and the filename is taken from the file *alias*, both as defined in our `resources.qrc` file.

The updated application is shown below.

```
import sys

from PyQt5 import QtGui, QtWidgets

import resources  # Import the compiled resource file.


class MainWindow(QtWidgets.QMainWindow):
    def __init__(self):
        super().__init__()

        self.setWindowTitle("Hello World")
        b = QtWidgets.QPushButton("My button")

        icon = QtGui.QIcon(":/icons/penguin.png")
        b.setIcon(icon)
        self.setCentralWidget(b)

        self.show()


app = QtWidgets.QApplication(sys.argv)
w = MainWindow()
app.exec_()
```

Resources in Qt Designer and Qt Creator

While it's fairly straightforward to manage your resources by editing the QRC file directly, **Qt Designer** can also be used to edit the resource library. This allows you to see all the icons (and other data) visually, rearrange them and edit them by drag-and-drop. If you are building your application UI in **Qt Designer** you can also select icons from the resource file directly, by browsing and selecting them. The UI file will keep a reference to the resource file and resources will be loaded automatically.

Adding Resources in Qt Designer

If you're using the standalone Qt Designer, the resource browser is available as a dockable widget, visible in the bottom right by default. If the Resource Browser is hidden you can show it through the "View" menu on the toolbar.

To add, edit and remove resource files click on the pencil icon in the Resource browser panel. This will open the resource editor.

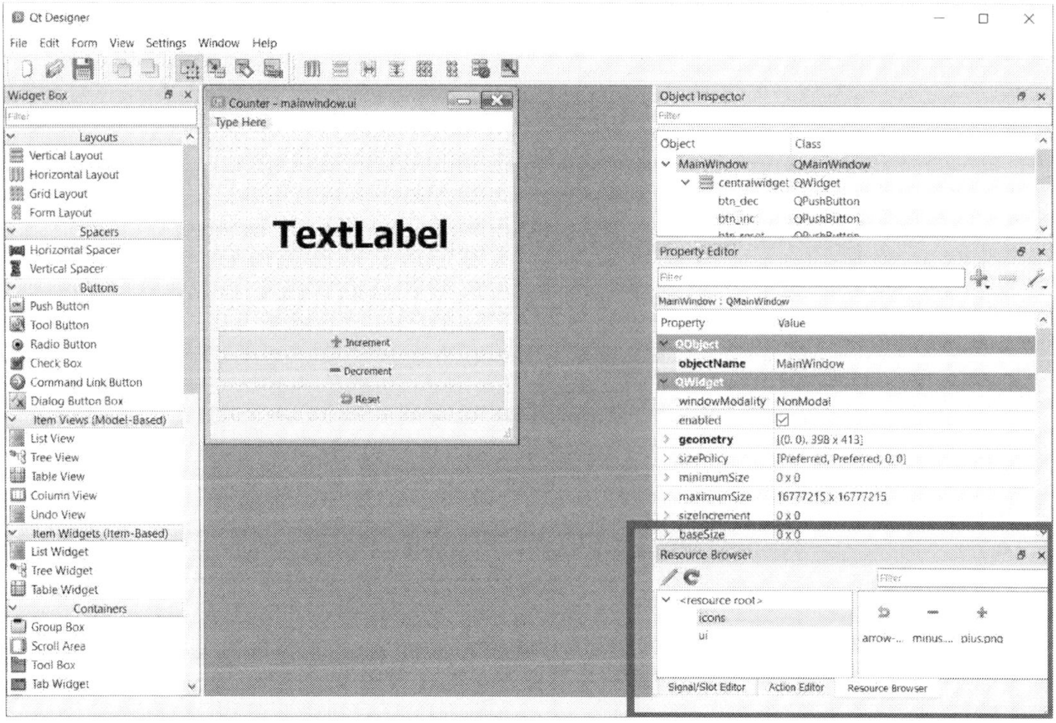

Figure 88. Standalone Qt Designer view

In the resource editor view you can open an existing resource file by clicking on the document folder icon (middle icon) on the bottom left.

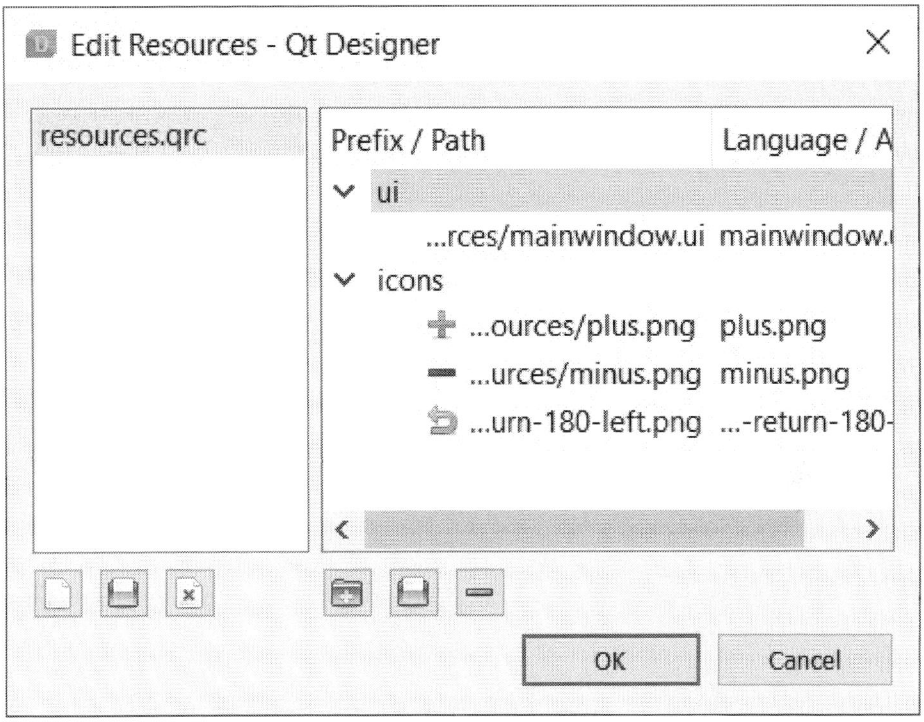

Figure 89. Edit Resources in Qt Designer

On the left hand panel you can also create and delete resource files from your UI. While on the right you can create new prefixes, add files to the prefix and delete items. Changes to the resource file are saved automatically.

Adding Resources in Qt Creator

In order to be able to add icons using the Qt Resource system from within Qt Creator you need to have an active Qt Project, and add both your UI and resource files to it.

If you don’t have a Qt Creator project set up you can create one in your existing source folder. Qt Creator will prompt before overwriting any of your files. Click on "+ New", choose "Qt for Python - Empty" for project type. Select the folder **above** your source folder for "Create in", and provide the name of your source folder as the project name. You can delete any files created, except the `.pyproject` which holds the project settings.

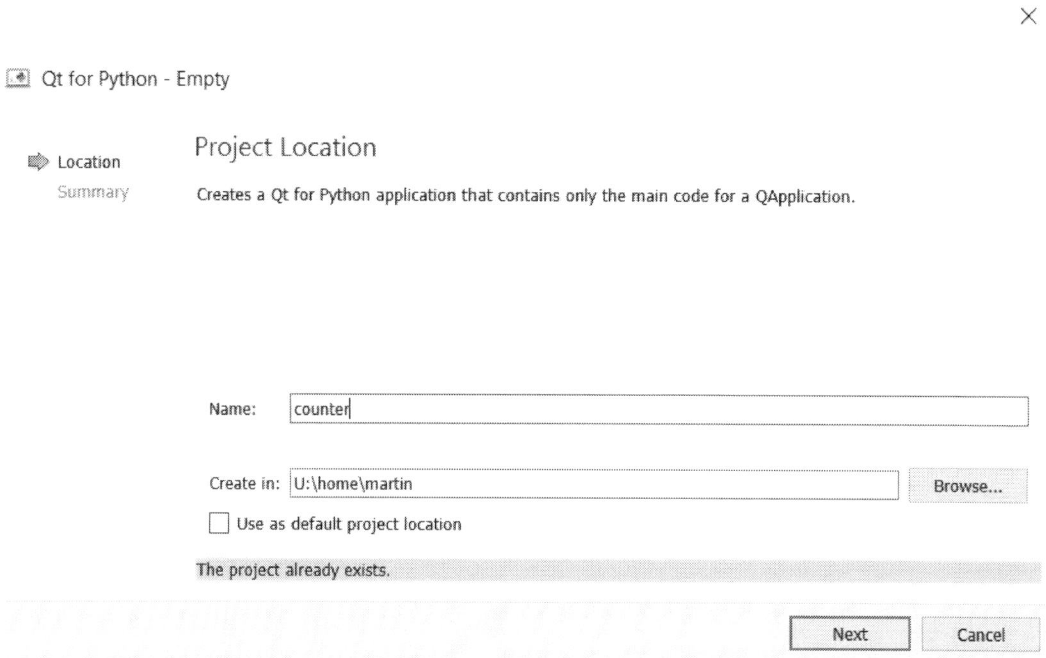

Figure 90. Select the location

To add resources to your existing project, select the "Edit" view on the left hand panel. You will see a file tree browser in the left hand panel. Right-click on the folder and choose "Add existing files..." and add your existing `.qrc` file to the project.

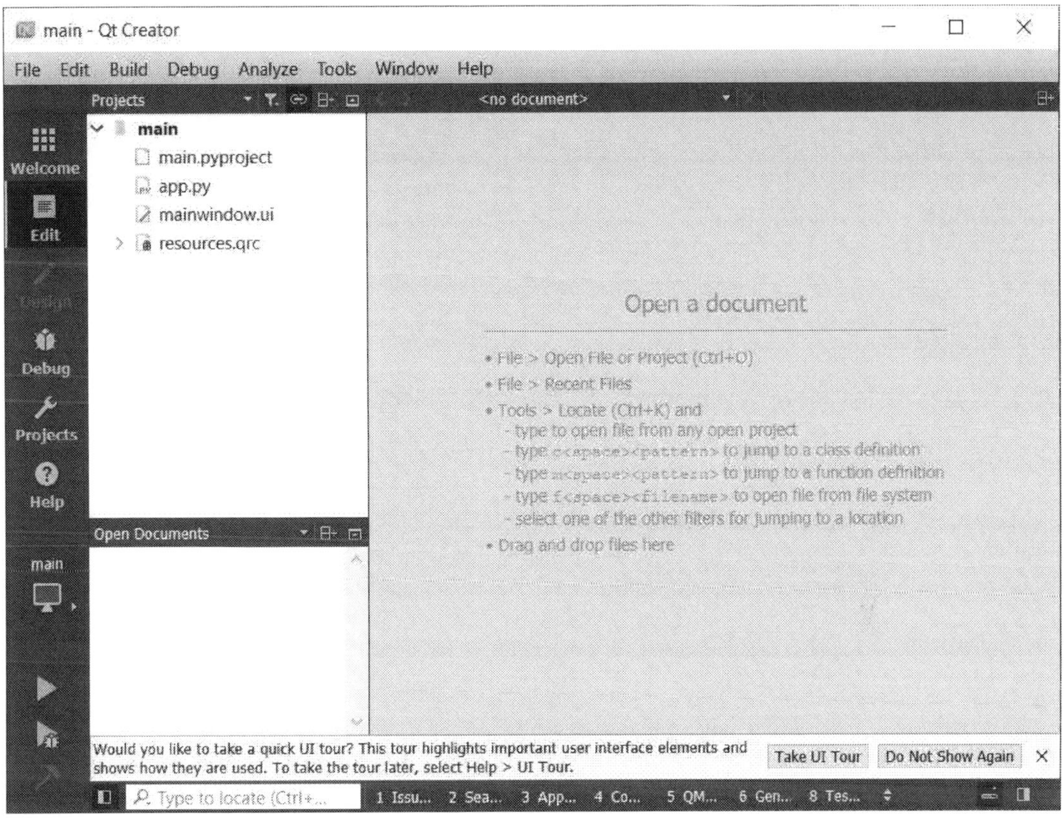

Figure 91. The Edit view, showing the added files

> The UI doesn't update when you add/remove things here, this seems to be a bug in Qt Creator. If you close and re-open Qt Creator the files will be there.

Once you have added the QRC file to the file listing you should be able to expand the file as if it were a folder, and browser the resources within. You can also add and remove resources using this interface.

Using resources in Qt Creator and Qt Designer

Once the Resource file is loaded you will be able to access it from the designer properties. The screenshot below shows the Designer with our counter app open, and the *increment* button selected. The icon for the button can be chosen by clicking the small black down arrow and selecting "Choose Resource..."

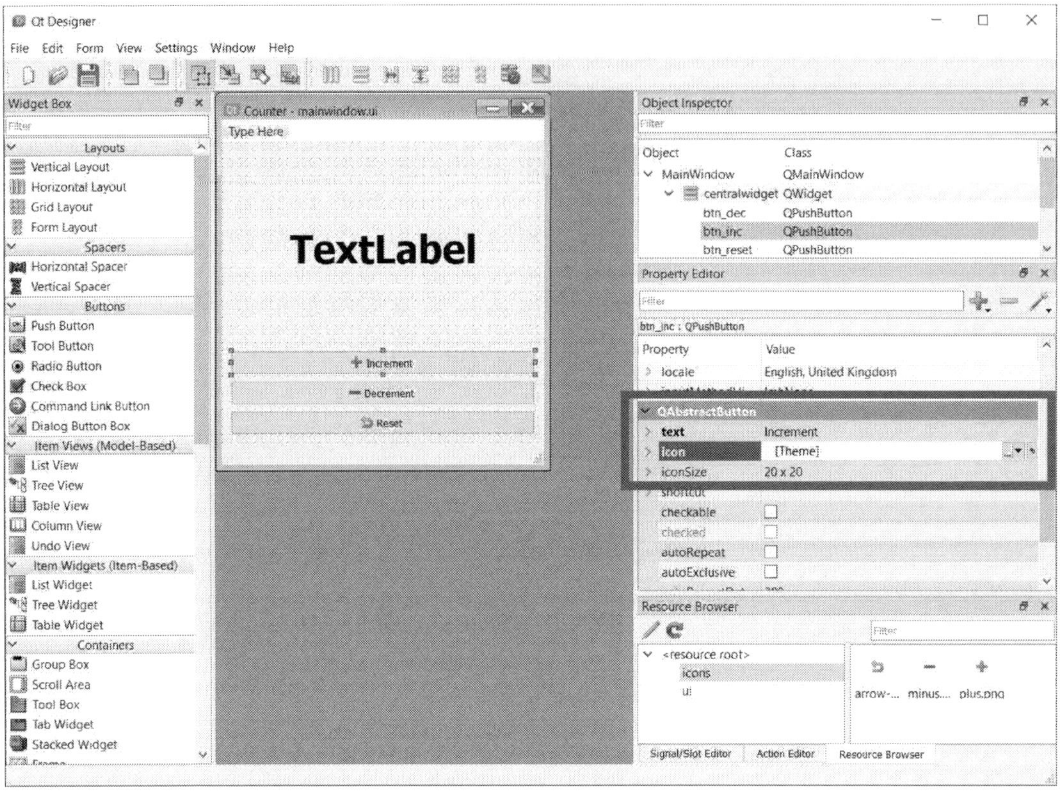

Figure 92. Select the location

The Resource chooser window that appears allows you to pick icons from the resource file(s) in the project to use in your UI.

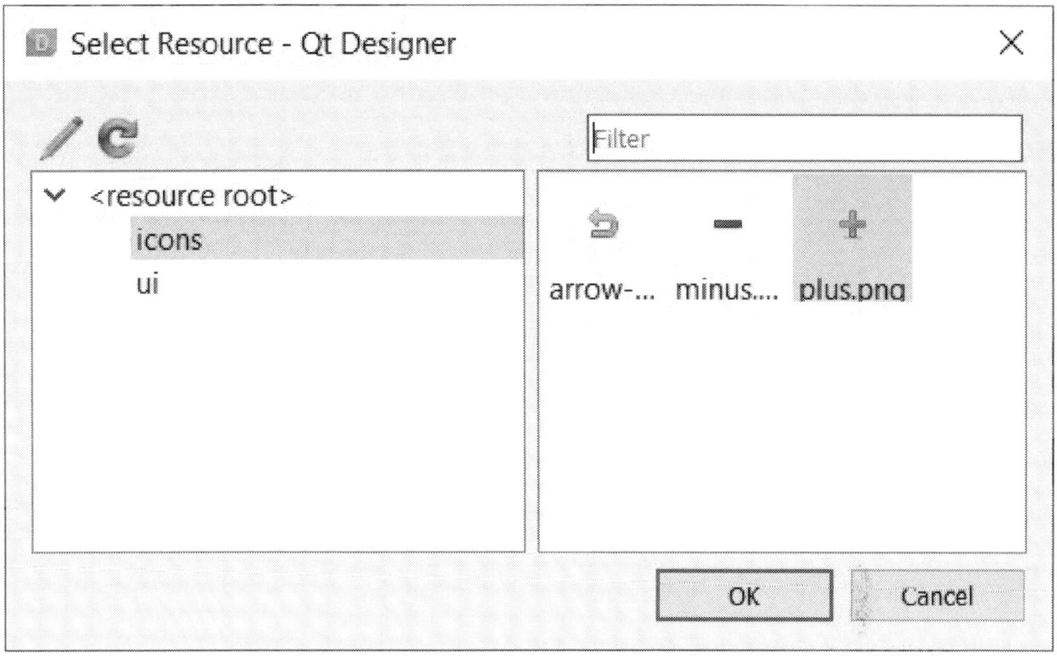

Figure 93. Select the location

Selecting the icons from the resource file in this way ensures that they will always work, as long as you compile and bundle the compiled resource file with your app.

Using a QRC file with compiled UI files

If you're designing your UIs in Qt Designer and compiling the resulting UI file to Python, then UI compiler automatically adds imports to a *compiled* version of your Qt Resource file for you. For example, if you run the following—

```
pyuic5 mainwindow.ui -o MainWindow.py
```

This build process also adds imports to `MainWindow.py` for the compiled version of the resources using in the UI, in our case `resources.qrc`. This means you do not need to import the resources separately into your app. However, we still need to build them, and use the specific name that is used for the import in `MainWindow.py`, here `resources_rc`.

```
pyrcc5 resources.qrc -o resources_rc.py
```

> `pyuic5` follows the pattern `<resource name>_rc.py` when adding imports for the resource file, so you will need to follow this when compiling resources yourself. You can check your compiled UI file (e.g. `MainWindow.py`) to double check the name of the import if you have problems.

When to use `QResource`?

You may be wondering when (or even *whether*) you should use the `QResource` system.

The main advantage of this method is that your data files are guaranteed to work cross-platform when distributed. The downside of course is you need to re-compile your resources any time you add/remove new resources. Whether this trade-off is worth it for your project is up to you, but if you plan to distribute your application to other people it almost always is.

Theming

Out of the box Qt applications look *platform native*. That is, they take on the *look and feel* of the operating system they are running on. This means they look at home on any system and feel natural to users. But it can also mean they look a bit *boring*. Helpfully, Qt gives you complete control over the appearance of widgets in your application.

Whether you want your application to stand out, or you are designing custom widgets and want them to fit in, this chapter will explain how to do that in PyQt5.

16. Styles

Styles are Qt's way of making broad look and feel changes to applications, modifying how widgets are displayed and behave. Qt automatically applies platform-specific styles when running your application on a given platform—this is why your application looks like an macOS application when run on macOS and a Windows application on Windows. These platform-specific styles make use of native widgets on the host platform, meaning they are not available to use on other platforms.

However, the platform styles are not the only options you have for styling your applications. Qt also ships with a cross-platform style called *Fusion*, which provides a consistent cross-platform, modern, style for your applications.

Fusion

Qt's Fusion style gives you the benefit of UI consistency across all systems, at the expense of some consistency with the operating system standards. Which is more important will depend on how much control you need over the UI you are creating, how much you are customizing it and which widgets you are using.

> The Fusion style is a platform-agnostic style that offers a desktop-oriented look'n'feel. It implements the same design language as the Fusion style for Qt Widgets.
>
> — Qt Documentation

To enable the style, call `.setStyle()` on the `QApplication` instance, passing in the name of the style (in this case *Fusion*) as a string.

```
app = QApplication(sys.argv)
app.setStyle('Fusion')
#...
app.exec_()
```

The widgets list example from earlier, but with the Fusion style applied, is shown below.

Figure 94. "Fusion" style widgets. They look identical on all platforms.

> There are more examples of widgets with Fusion style applied in the Qt documentation [https://doc.qt.io/archives/qt-5.8/gallery-fusion.html].

3rd Party Styles

In addition to the Fusion style provided with Qt there are 3rd party styles available too. These are all based on modifications to the base Fusion style. For example—

- Qt Modern [https://github.com/gmarull/qtmodern] provides a *frameless* window style, together with a dark mode palette and custom window decorations to give a modern macOS-like look.

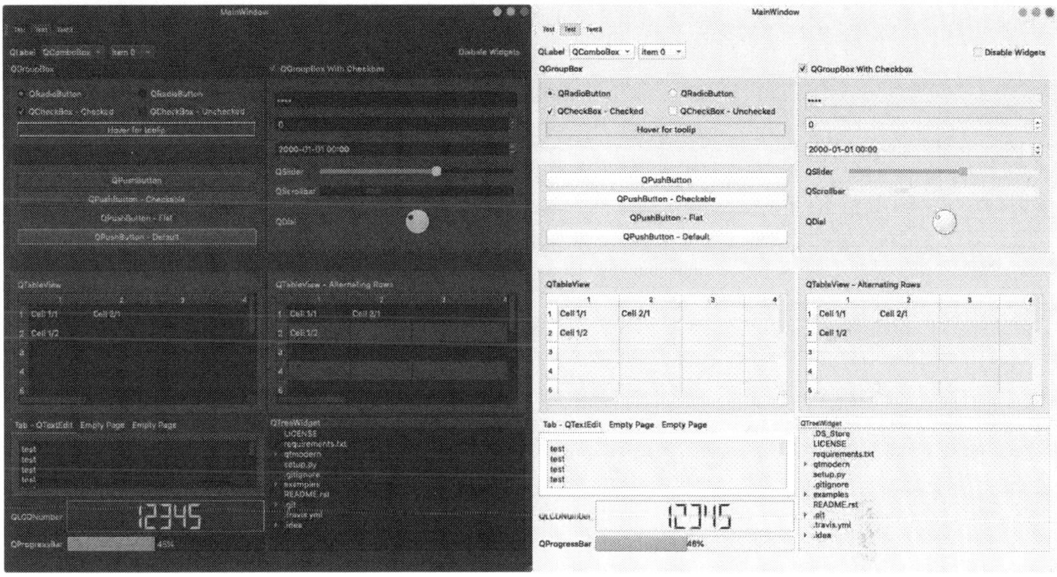

Figure 95. "Qt Modern" styles: Palette & window decorations.

17. Palettes

The selection of colors used to draw the user interface in Qt are termed *palettes*. Both application level and widget-specific palettes are managed through `QPalette` objects. Palettes can be set at both the application and widget level, allowing you to set a global standard palette and override this on a per-widget basis. The global palette is normally defined by the Qt theme (itself normally dependent on the OS) but you can override this to change the look of your entire app.

The active global palette can be accessed from `QApplication.palette()` or by creating a new *empty* `QPalette` instance. For example—

```
from PyQt5.QtGui import QPalette
palette = QPalette()
```

You can modify the palette by calling `palette.setColor(role, color)` where *role* determines what the color is used for, `QColor` the color to use. The color used can either by a custom `QColor` object, or one of the built-in basic colors from the `Qt` namespace.

```
palette.setColor(QPalette.Window, QColor(53,53,53))
palette.setColor(QPalette.WindowText, Qt.white)
```

> There are some limitations when using palettes on Windows 10 and macOS platform-specific themes.

There are rather a lot of different *roles*. The main roles are shown in the table below—

Table 4. Main roles

Constant	Value	Description
`QPalette.Window`	10	Background color for windows.

Constant	Value	Description
QPalette.WindowText	0	Default text color for windows.
QPalette.Base	9	Background of text entry widgets, combobox drop down lists and toolbar handles. *Usually white or light*
QPalette.AlternateBase	16	Second Base color used in striped (alternating) rows—e.g. QAbstractItemView.setAlternatingRowColors()
QPalette.ToolTipBase	18	Background color for QToolTip and QWhatsThis hover indicators. Both tips use the Inactive group (see later) because they are not active windows.
QPalette.ToolTipText	19	Foreground color for QToolTip and QWhatsThis. Both tips use the Inactive group (see later) because they are not active windows.
QPalette.PlaceholderText	20	Color for placeholder text in widgets.
QPalette.Text	6	Text color for widgets colored with Base background. Must provide a good contrast with both Window and Base.
QPalette.Button	1	Default button background color. This can differ from Window but must provide good contrast with ButtonText.
QPalette.ButtonText	8	Text color used on buttons, must contrast with Button color.
QPalette.BrightText	7	Text color which is very different from WindowText, contrasts well with black. Used were other Text and WindowText colors would give poor contrast. Note: Not just used for text.

You don't necessarily have to modify or set all of these in your custom palette, depending on widgets used in your application some can be omitted.

There are also smaller sets of roles used for 3D beveling on widgets and highlighting selected entries or links.

Table 5. 3D bevel roles

Constant	Value	Description
`QPalette.Light`	2	Lighter than `Button` color.
`QPalette.Midlight`	3	Between `Button` and `Light`.
`QPalette.Dark`	4	Darker than `Button`.
`QPalette.Mid`	5	Between `Button` and `Dark`.
`QPalette.Shadow`	11	A very dark color. By default, the shadow color is `Qt.black`.

Table 6. Highlighting & links

Constant	Value	Description
`QPalette.Highlight`	12	A color to indicate a selected item or the current item. By default, the highlight color is `Qt.darkBlue`.
`QPalette.HighlightedText`	13	A text color that contrasts with Highlight. By default, the highlighted text `Qt.white`.
`QPalette.Link`	14	A text color used for unvisited hyperlinks. By default, the link color is `Qt.blue`.
`QPalette.LinkVisited`	15	A text color used for already visited hyperlinks. By default, the link-visited color is `Qt.magenta`.

There is also technically a `QPalette.NoRole` value for widget drawing states where no role is assigned, this can be ignored when creating palettes.

For parts of the UI which change when a widget is active, inactive or disabled you must set a color for each of these states. To do this, you can call `palette.setColor(group, role, color)` passing additional *group* parameter. The available groups are shown below—

Constant	Value
`QPalette.Disabled`	1
`QPalette.Active`	0
`QPalette.Inactive`	2
`QPalette.Normal` *synonym for Active*	0

For example, the following will set the `WindowText` color for a disabled window to *white* in the palette.

```
palette.setColor(QPalette.Disabled, QPalette.WindowText, Qt.white)
```

Once the palette is defined, you can use `.setPalette()` to set it onto the `QApplication` object to apply it to your application, or to a a single widget. For example, the following example will change the color of the window text and background (here text is added using a `QLabel`).

Listing 69. themes/palette_test.py

```
from PyQt5.QtWidgets import QApplication, QLabel
from PyQt5.QtGui import QPalette, QColor
from PyQt5.QtCore import Qt

import sys


app = QApplication(sys.argv)
palette = QPalette()
palette.setColor(QPalette.Window, QColor(0, 128, 255))
palette.setColor(QPalette.WindowText, Qt.white)
app.setPalette(palette)

w = QLabel("Palette Test")
w.show()

app.exec_()
```

When run, this gives the following output. The background of the window is changed to a light blue, and the window text is white.

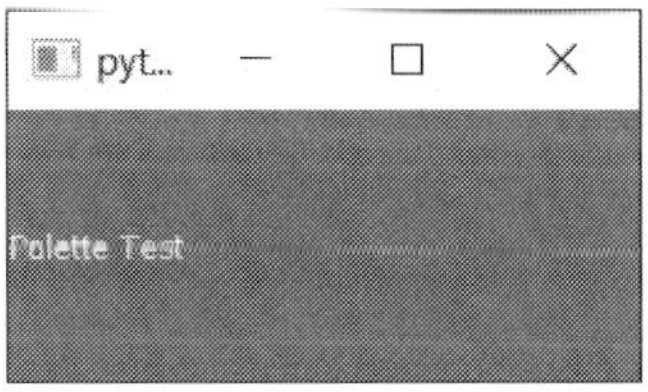

Figure 96. Changing the Window and WindowText colors.

To show palette use in practice and see some limitations of it, we'll now create an application using a custom dark palette.

> Using this palette all widgets will be drawn with a dark background, regardless of the dark mode state of your app. See later for using system dark modes.

While you should avoid overriding user settings in general, it can make sense in certain classes of applications such as photo viewers or video editors, where a bright UI will interfere with the users ability to judge color. The following app skeleton uses a custom palette by Jürgen Skrotzky [https://github.com/Jorgen-VikingGod/Qt-Frameless-Window-DarkStyle/blob/master/DarkStyle.cpp] to give the application a global dark theme.

```
from PyQt5.QtWidgets import QApplication, QMainWindow
from PyQt5.QtGui import QPalette, QColor
from PyQt5.QtCore import Qt

import sys

darkPalette = QPalette()
darkPalette.setColor(QPalette.Window, QColor(53, 53, 53))
darkPalette.setColor(QPalette.WindowText, Qt.white)
darkPalette.setColor(QPalette.Disabled, QPalette.WindowText, QColor
(127, 127, 127))
darkPalette.setColor(QPalette.Base, QColor(42, 42, 42))
darkPalette.setColor(QPalette.AlternateBase, QColor(66, 66, 66))
darkPalette.setColor(QPalette.ToolTipBase, Qt.white)
darkPalette.setColor(QPalette.ToolTipText, Qt.white)
darkPalette.setColor(QPalette.Text, Qt.white)
darkPalette.setColor(QPalette.Disabled, QPalette.Text, QColor(127,
127, 127))
darkPalette.setColor(QPalette.Dark, QColor(35, 35, 35))
darkPalette.setColor(QPalette.Shadow, QColor(20, 20, 20))
darkPalette.setColor(QPalette.Button, QColor(53, 53, 53))
darkPalette.setColor(QPalette.ButtonText, Qt.white)
darkPalette.setColor(QPalette.Disabled, QPalette.ButtonText, QColor
(127, 127, 127))
darkPalette.setColor(QPalette.BrightText, Qt.red)
darkPalette.setColor(QPalette.Link, QColor(42, 130, 218))
darkPalette.setColor(QPalette.Highlight, QColor(42, 130, 218))
darkPalette.setColor(QPalette.Disabled, QPalette.Highlight, QColor(
80, 80, 80))
darkPalette.setColor(QPalette.HighlightedText, Qt.white)
darkPalette.setColor(QPalette.Disabled, QPalette.HighlightedText,
QColor(127, 127, 127))

app = QApplication(sys.argv)
app.setPalette(darkPalette)

w = QMainWindow()  # Replace with your QMainWindow instance.
w.show()

app.exec_()
```

As before, once the palette is constructed it must be applied to take effect. Here we apply it to the application as a whole by calling `app.setPalette()`. All widgets will adopt the theme once applied. You can use this skeleton to construct your own applications using this theme.

In the code examples with this book you can also find `themes/palette_dark_widgets.py` which reproduces the widgets demo, using this palette. The result on each platform is shown below.

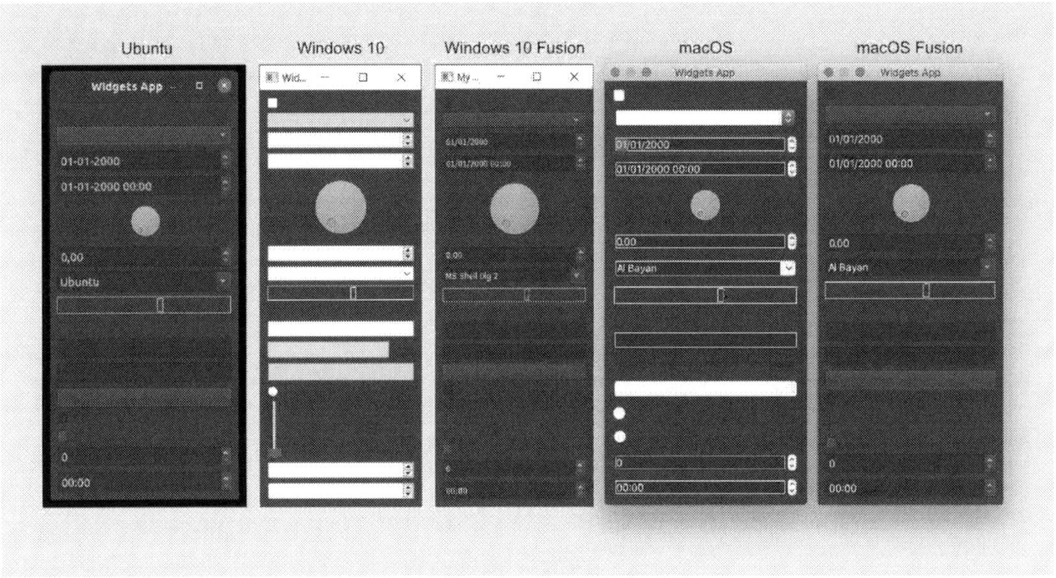

Figure 97. Custom dark palette on different platforms and themes

You'll notice that when using the default Windows and macOS themes some widgets do not have their colors applied correctly. This is because these themes make use of platform-native controls to give a true native feel. If you want to use a dark or heavily customized theme on Windows 10, it is recommended to use the *Fusion* style on these platforms.

Dark Mode

Dark mode is becoming popular as people spend more and more time on screens. Darker themed OS and applications help to minimize eye strain and reduce sleep distribution if working in the evening.

Windows, macOS and Linux all provide support for dark mode themes, and the good news is that if you build your application with PyQt5 you get dark mode support for free. However, the support is incomplete in earlier versions of PyQt5. Remember to test your application with dark mode enabled and disabled on all your target platforms.

> When building macOS packages for distribution you will need to set `NSRequiresAquaSystemAppearance` to `False` in your app for dark mode to be respected by the bundled `.app`—this is covered in the packaging chapter.

Color

Your operating system has a standard theme which is respected by most software. Qt picks up this color scheme automatically and will apply it to your PyQt5 applications to help them fit in. Using these colors has some advantages—

1. Your app will look at home on your users desktop
2. Your users are familiar with the meaning of contextual colors
3. Somebody else has spent time designing colors that work

If you want to replace the color scheme, make sure that the benefits outweigh the costs.

Sometimes your applications may require additional contextual colors or tweaks to highlights. For data visualization a good resource is Color Brewer [https://colorbrewer2.org] from *Cynthia Brewer* which has both qualitative and quantitative schemes. If you only need a few colors coolors.co [https://coolors.co] lets you generate custom well-matched 4-color themes.

Figure 98. Example color scheme from coolors.co

Use colors simply and effectively, restricting your palette as far as possible. If particular colors have meaning somewhere use the same meaning *everywhere*. Avoid using multiple shades unless those shades have meaning.

✔ DO

- Consider using GUI-standard colors in your app first.

- When using custom colors define a color scheme and stick to it.
- Keep color-blind users in mind when choosing colors and contrasts.

✕ DON'T

- Use standard colors for non-standard purposes, e.g. Red = OK.

18. Icons

Icons are small pictures which are used to aid navigation or understanding within a user interface. They are commonly found on buttons, either alongside or in place of text, or alongside actions in menus. By using easily recognizable indicators you can make your interface easier to use.

In PyQt5 you have a number of different options for how to source and integrate icons into your application. In this section we'll look at those options and the pros and cons of each.

Qt Standard Icons

The easiest way to add simple icons to your application is to use the built-in icons which ship with Qt itself. This small set of icons cover a number of standard use cases, from file operations, forward & backward arrows and message box indicators.

The full list of built-in icons is shown below.

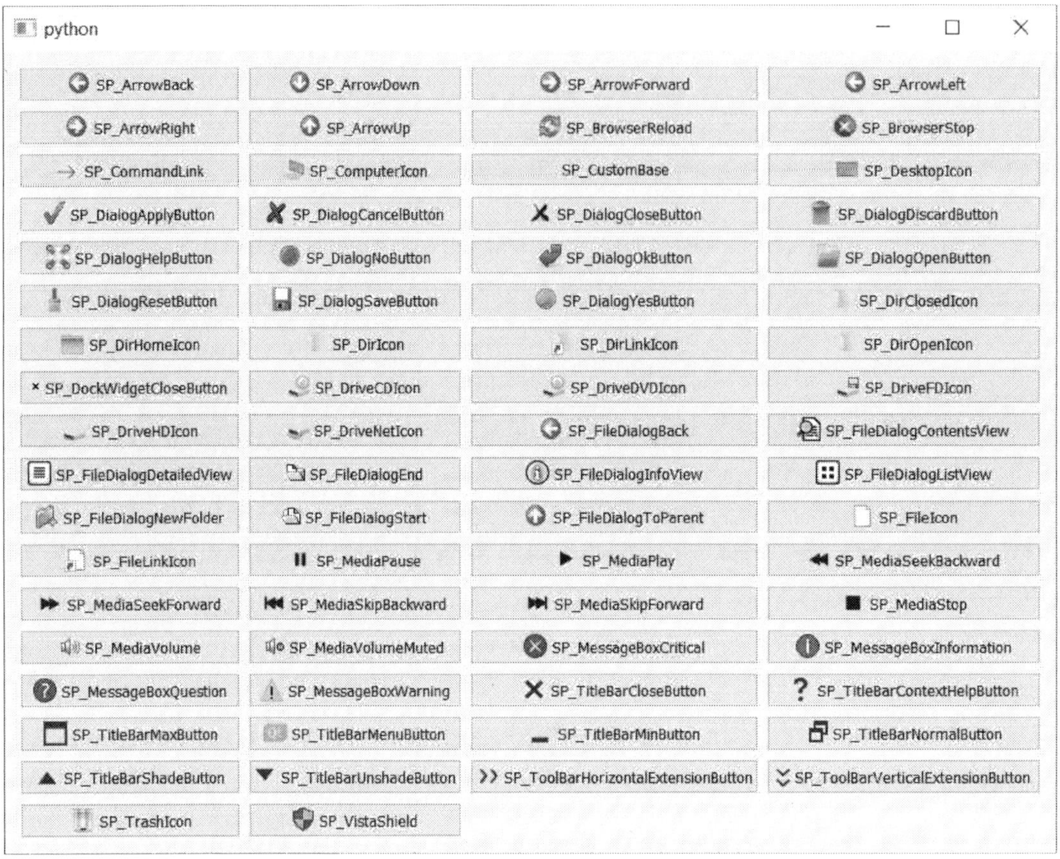

Figure 99. Qt Builtin icons

You'll notice that this set of icons is a bit *restrictive*. If that's not a problem for the app you're building, or if you only need a few icons for your app it might still be a viable option for you.

The icons are accessible through the current application style using `QStyle.standardIcon(name)` or `QStyle.<constant>`. The full table of built-in icon names is shown below—

`SP_ArrowBack`	`SP_DirIcon`	`SP_MediaSkipBackward`
`SP_ArrowDown`	`SP_DirLinkIcon`	`SP_MediaSkipForward`
`SP_ArrowForward`	`SP_DirOpenIcon`	`SP_MediaStop`
`SP_ArrowLeft`	`SP_DockWidgetCloseButton`	`SP_MediaVolume`
`SP_ArrowRight`	`SP_DriveCDIcon`	`SP_MediaVolumeMuted`
`SP_ArrowUp`	`SP_DriveDVDIcon`	`SP_MessageBoxCritical`

SP_BrowserReload	SP_DriveFDIcon	SP_MessageBoxInformation
SP_BrowserStop	SP_DriveHDIcon	SP_MessageBoxQuestion
SP_CommandLink	SP_DriveNetIcon	SP_MessageBoxWarning
SP_ComputerIcon	SP_FileDialogBack	SP_TitleBarCloseButton
SP_CustomBase	SP_FileDialogContentsView	SP_TitleBarContextHelpButton
SP_DesktopIcon	SP_FileDialogDetailedView	SP_TitleBarMaxButton
SP_DialogApplyButton	SP_FileDialogEnd	SP_TitleBarMenuButton
SP_DialogCancelButton	SP_FileDialogInfoView	SP_TitleBarMinButton
SP_DialogCloseButton	SP_FileDialogListView	SP_TitleBarNormalButton
SP_DialogDiscardButton	SP_FileDialogNewFolder	SP_TitleBarShadeButton
SP_DialogHelpButton	SP_FileDialogStart	SP_TitleBarUnshadeButton
SP_DialogNoButton	SP_FileDialogToParent	SP_ToolBarHorizontalExtensionButton
SP_DialogOkButton	SP_FileIcon	SP_ToolBarVerticalExtensionButton
SP_DialogResetButton	SP_FileLinkIcon	SP_TrashIcon
SP_DialogSaveButton	SP_MediaPause	SP_VistaShield
SP_DialogYesButton	SP_MediaPlay	SP_DirClosedIcon
SP_MediaSeekBackward	SP_DirHomeIcon	SP_MediaSeekForward

You can access these icons directly via the QStyle namespace, as follows.

```
style = button.style() # Get the QStyle object from the widget.
icon = style.standardIcon(QStyle.SP_MessageBoxCritical)
button.setIcon(icon)
```

You can also use the style object from a specific widget. It doesn't matter which you use, since we're only accessing the built-ins anyway.

```
style = button.style() # Get the QStyle object from the widget.
icon = style.standardIcon(style.SP_MessageBoxCritical)
button.setIcon(icon)
```

If you can't find an icon you need in this standard set, you will need to use one of the other approaches outlined below.

> While you *can* mix and match icons from different icon sets together, it's better to use a single style throughout to keep your app feeling coherent.

Icon files

If the standard icons aren't what your looking for, or you need icons not available, you can use any custom icons you like. Icons can be any of the Qt supported image types on your platform, although for most use cases PNG or SVG images are preferable.

> To get list of supported image formats on your own platform you can call `QtGui.QImageReader.supportedImageFormats()`.

Icon sets

If you're not a graphic designer you will save yourself a lot of time (and trouble) by using one of the many available icon sets. There are thousands of these available online, with varying licenses depending on their use in open source or commercial software.

In this book and example apps I've used the Fugue [http://p.yusukekamiyamane.com/] icon set, which is also free to use in your software with acknowledgement of the author. The Tango icon set is a large icon set developed for use on Linux, however there are no licensing requirements and it can be used on any platform.

Resource	Description	License
Fugue by p.yusukekamiyamane [http://p.yusukekamiyamane.com/]	3,570 16x16 icons in PNG format	CC BY 3.0
Diagona by p.yusukekamiyamane [http://p.yusukekamiyamane.com/]	400 16x16 and 10x10 icons in PNG format	CC BY 3.0
Tango Icons by The Tango Desktop Project [http://tango.freedesktop.org/Tango_Icon_Library]	Icons using the Tango project color theme.	Public domain

While you do have control over the size of icons using in menus and toolbars, in most cases you should leave these as-is. A good standard icon size for menus is 20x20 pixels.

Sizes smaller than this are fine too, the icon will be centered rather than scaled up.

Create your own

If you don't like any of the available icon sets, or want a unique look to your application, you can of course design your own icons. Icons can be created using any standard graphics software and saved as PNG images with transparent background. The icons should be square and of a resolution that they do not need to be scaled up or down when used in your application.

Using icon files

Once you have your icon files—whether from icon sets or self-drawn—they can be used in your Qt applications by creating instances of `QtGui.QIcon`, passing in the filename of the icon directly.

```
QtGui.QIcon("<filename>")
```

While you can use both absolute (complete) and relative (partial) to point to your file, absolute paths are prone to break when distributing your applications. Relative paths will work as long as the icon files are stored in the same location relative to your script, although even this can be difficult to manage when packaging. If you are using many icons in your application, or will be distributing your application, you may want to use the The Qt Resource system.

> In order to create icon instances you must have already created a `QApplication` instance. To ensure this is the case, you can create your app instance at the top of your source file, or create your `QIcon` instances in the `__init__` for the widget or window that uses them.

Free Desktop Specification Icons (Linux)

On Linux desktops there is a thing called the *Free Desktop Specification* which defines standard names for icons for specific actions.

If your application uses these specific icon names (and loads the icon from a "theme") then on Linux your application will use the current icon set which is enabled on the desktop. The idea is making all application have the same look & feel while remaining configurable.

To use these within Qt Designer you would select the drop-down and choose "Set Icon From Theme..."

Figure 100. Selecting an icon theme

You then enter the **name** of the icon you want to use, e.g. `document-new` (the full list of valid names [https://specifications.freedesktop.org/icon-naming-spec/latest/ar01s04.html]).

Figure 101. Selecting an icon theme

In code, you can get icons from the active Linux desktop theme using `icon = QtGui.QIcon.fromTheme("document-new")`. The following snippet produces a small window (button) with the "new document" icon showing, from the active theme.

Listing 70. icons/linux.py

```python
from PyQt5.QtWidgets import QApplication, QPushButton
from PyQt5.QtGui import QIcon

import sys

app = QApplication(sys.argv)
button = QPushButton("Hello")
icon = QIcon.fromTheme("document-new")
button.setIcon(icon)
button.show()

app.exec_()
```

The resulting window will look like the following on Ubuntu, with the default icon theme.

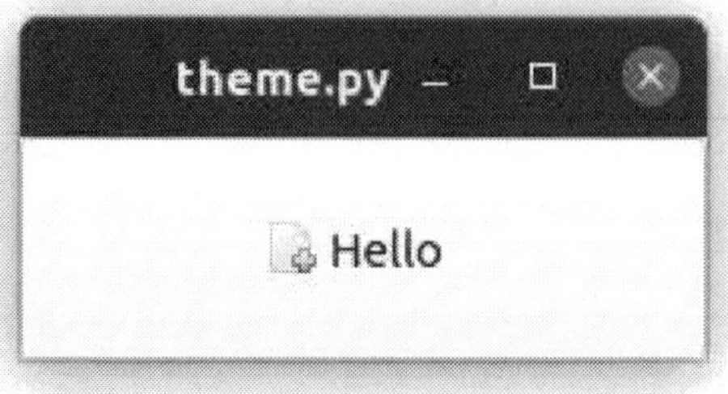

Figure 102. Linux Free Desktop Specification "document-new" icon

If you’re developing a cross-platform application you can still make use of these standard icons on Linux. To do this, use your own icons for Windows and macOS and create a custom theme in Qt Designer, using the Free Desktop Specification names for the icons.

19. Qt Style Sheets (QSS)

So far we've looked at how you can apply custom colors to your PyQt5 apps using `QPalette`. However, there are many other customizations you can make to the appearance of widgets in Qt5. The system provided to allow this customization is called Qt Style Sheets (QSS).

QSS is conceptually very similar to Cascading Style Sheets (CSS) used to style the web, sharing a similar syntax and approach. In this section we'll look at some examples of QSS and how you can use it to modify widget appearance.

> Using QSS on widgets has a small performance impact, due to the need to look up the appropriate rules when redrawing widgets. However, unless you are doing very widget-heavy work this is unlikely to be of consequence.

Style editor

To make experimenting with QSS rules a little bit easier, we can create a simple demo app which allows rules to be input and applied to some example widgets. We'll use this to test out the various style properties and rules.

> The source code for the style viewer is shown below, but it's also available in the source code with this book.

Listing 71. themes/qss_tester.py

```
import sys

from PyQt5.QtCore import Qt
from PyQt5.QtGui import QColor, QPalette
from PyQt5.QtWidgets import (
    QApplication,
    QCheckBox,
    QComboBox,
    QLabel,
```

```
    QLineEdit,
    QMainWindow,
    QPlainTextEdit,
    QPushButton,
    QSpinBox,
    QVBoxLayout,
    QWidget,
)


class MainWindow(QMainWindow):
    def __init__(self):
        super().__init__()

        self.setWindowTitle("QSS Tester")

        self.editor = QPlainTextEdit()
        self.editor.textChanged.connect(self.update_styles)

        layout = QVBoxLayout()
        layout.addWidget(self.editor)

        # Define a set of simple widgets.
        cb = QCheckBox("Checkbox")
        layout.addWidget(cb)

        combo = QComboBox()
        combo.setObjectName("thecombo")
        combo.addItems(["First", "Second", "Third", "Fourth"])
        layout.addWidget(combo)

        sb = QSpinBox()
        sb.setRange(0, 99999)
        layout.addWidget(sb)

        l = QLabel("This is a label")
        layout.addWidget(l)

        le = QLineEdit()
        le.setObjectName("mylineedit")
        layout.addWidget(le)

        pb = QPushButton("Push me!")
```

```
        layout.addWidget(pb)

        self.container = QWidget()
        self.container.setLayout(layout)

        self.setCentralWidget(self.container)

    def update_styles(self):
        qss = self.editor.toPlainText()
        self.setStyleSheet(qss)


app = QApplication(sys.argv)
app.setStyle("Fusion")

w = MainWindow()
w.show()

app.exec_()
```

Running this app you'll see the following window, with a text editor at the top (where you can enter QSS rules) and a set of widgets to which these rules will be applied—we'll look at how applying rules and inheritance works in a bit.

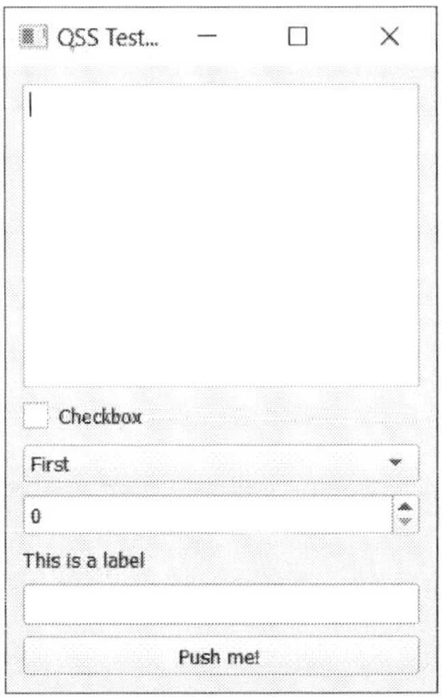

Figure 103. QSS tester application, no rules applied.

Try entering the following style rules in the box at the top, and comparing the result with the screenshots to make sure it's working.

```
QLabel { background-color: yellow }
```

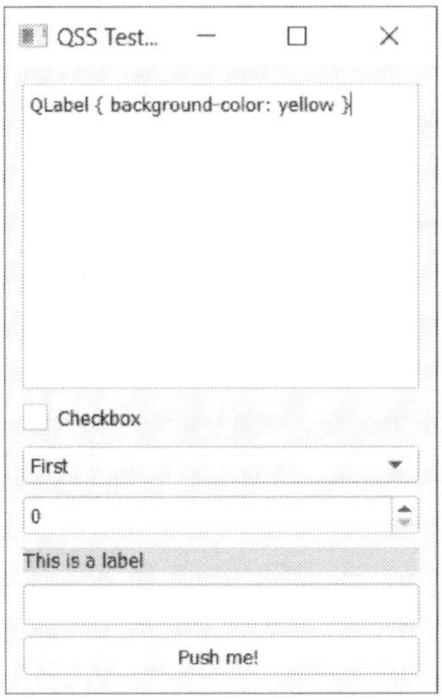

Figure 104. Applying background-color: yellow to QLabel

```
QLineEdit { background-color: rgb(255, 0, 0) }
```

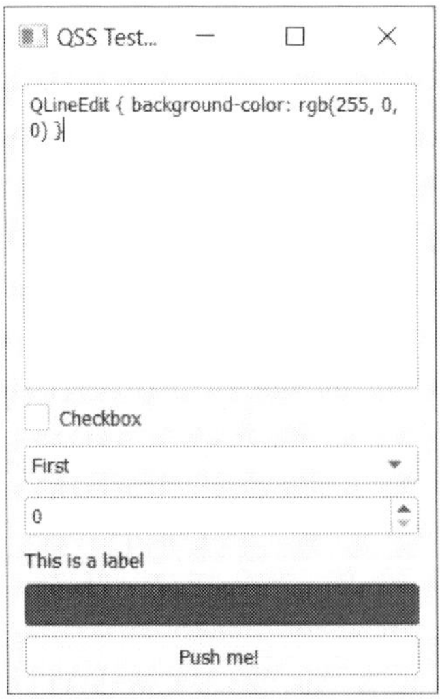

Figure 105. Applying background-color: rgb(255, 0, 0) (red) to QLineEdit

```
QLineEdit {
    border-width: 7px;
    border-style: dashed;
    border-color: red;
}
```

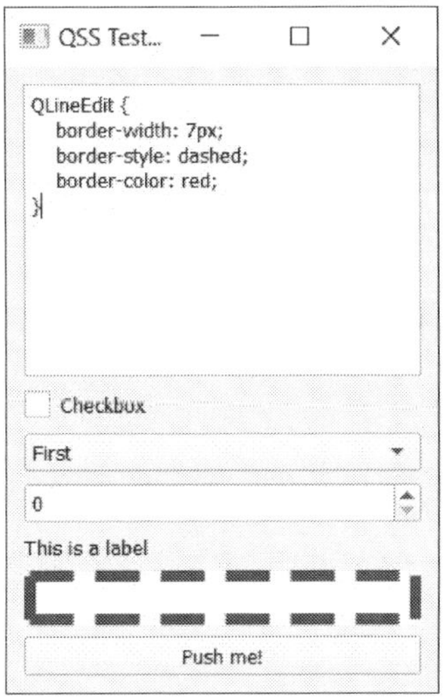

Figure 106. Applying dashed red border to QLineEdit

Next we'll look in some detail at how these QSS rules are styling the widgets, gradually building up to some more complex rule sets.

> A full list of styleable widgets is available in the Qt documentation [https://doc.qt.io/qt-5/stylesheet-reference.html].

Styling properties

Next we'll got through the properties available to style widgets with QSS. These have been broken down into logical sections, containing properties that are related to one another to make it easier to digest. You can use the QSS rule tester app we just created to test these styles out on the various widgets.

The types used in the following tables are listed below. Some of these are compound types, made up of other entries.

You can skip over this table for now, but will need it as a reference for interpreting the valid values for each property.

Property	Type	Description
`Alignment`	top | bottom | left | right | center	Horizontal and/or vertical alignment.
`Attachment`	scroll | fixed	Scroll or fixed attachment.
`Background`	Brush | Url | Repeat | Alignment	Compound type of Brush, Url,Repeat, andAlignment.
`Boolean`	0 | 1	True (1) or False (0).
`Border`	Border Style | Length | Brush	Shorthand border property.
`Border Image`	none | Url Number (stretch | repeat)	An image composed of nine parts (top left, top center, top right, center left, center, center right, bottom left, bottom center, and bottom right).
`Border Style`	dashed | dot-dash | dot-dot-dash | dotted | double | groove | inset | outset | ridge | solid | none	The pattern used to draw a border.

Property	Type	Description
Box Colors	Brush	Up to four values ofBrush, specifying the top, right, bottom, and left edges of a box, respectively. If the left color omitted will copy right, if bottom omitted will copy top.
Box Lengths	Length	Up to four values of Length, specifying the top, right, bottom, and left edges of a box, respectively. If the left color omitted will copy right, if bottom omitted will copy top.
Brush	Color | Gradient | PaletteRole	A Color, Gradient or an entry in the Palette.
Color	rgb(r,g,b) | rgba(r,g,b,a) | hsv(h,s,v) | hsva(h,s,v,a) | hsl(h,s,l) | hsla(h,s,l,a) | #rrggbb | Color Name	Specifies a color as RGB (red, green, blue), RGBA (red, green, blue, alpha), HSV (hue, saturation, value), HSVA (hue, saturation, value, alpha), HSL (hue, saturation, lightness), HSLA (hue, saturation, lightness, alpha) or a named color. Thergb()orrgba()syntax can be used with integer values between 0 and 255, or with percentages.
Font	(Font Style | Font Weight)Font Size	Shorthand font property.
Font Size	Length	The size of a font.
Font Style	normal | italic | oblique	The style of a font.
Font Weight	normal | bold | 100 | 200... | 900	The weight of a font.

Property	Type	Description
`Gradient`	qlineargradient | qradialgradient | qconicalgradient	Lineargradients between start and end points. Radialgradients between a focal point and end points on a circle surrounding it. Conical gradients around a center point. See the QLinearGradient documentation [https://doc.qt.io/qt-5/stylesheet-reference.html#gradient] for syntax.
`Icon`	Url(disabled | active | normal | selected) (on | off)	A list of url,QIcon.ModeandQIcon.State. e.g. `file-icon: url(file.png), url(file_selected.png) selected;`
`Length`	Number(px | pt | em | ex)	A number followed by a measurement unit. If no unit is given, uses pixels in most contexts. One of px: pixels pt: the size of one point (i.e., 1/72 of an inch), em: the em ` width of the font (i.e., the width of 'M'), ex: the ex width of the font (i.e., the height of 'x')
`Number`	A decimal integer or a real number	e.g. 123, or 12.2312
`Origin`	margin | border | padding | content	See box model for more details.

Property	Type	Description
PaletteRole	alternate-base | base | bright-text | button | button-text | dark | highlight | highlighted-text | light | link | link-visited | mid | midlight | shadow | text | window | window-text	These values correspond theColor roles in the widget'sQPalette, e.g. `color: palette(dark);`
Radius	Length	One or two occurrences of Length.
Repeat	repeat-x | repeat-y | repeat | no-repeat	repeat-x: Repeat horizontally. repeat-y: Repeat vertically. repeat: Repeat horizontally and vertically. no-repeat: Don't repeat.
Url	url(filename)	filenameis the name of a file on the local disk or stored usingThe Qt Resource System.

The full details of these properties and types are also available in the QSS reference documentation [https://doc.qt.io/Qt-5/stylesheet-reference.html#list-of-properties].

Text styles

We'll start with text properties which can be used to modify fonts, colors and styles (bold, italic, underline) of text. These can be applied to any widget or control.

Property	Type (Default)	Description
color	Brush (QPalette Foreground)	The color used to render text.

Property	Type (Default)	Description
`font`	Font	Shorthand notation for setting the text's font. Equivalent to specifying font-family, font-size, font-style, and/or font-weight
`font-family`	String	The font family.
`font-size`	Font Size	The font size. In this version of Qt, only pt and px metrics are supported.
`font-style`	normal | italic | oblique	The font style.
`font-weight`	Font Weight	The weight of the font.
`selection-background-color`	Brush (`QPalette Highlight`)	The background of selected text or items.
`selection-color`	Brush (`Palette HighlightedText`)	The foreground of selected text or items.
`text-align`	Alignment	The alignment of text and icon within the contents of the widget.
`text-decoration`	none | underline | overline | line-through	Additional text effects

The example snippet below, sets the color on the `QLineEdit` to *red*, the background color for selected text to *yellow* and the color of selected text to *blue*.

```
QLineEdit {
    color: red;
    selection-color: blue;
    selection-background-color: yellow;
}
```

Try this in the QSS tester to see the effect on the `QLineEdit` and it will give the following result. Notice that only the targeted widget (`QLineEdit`) is affected by the styles.

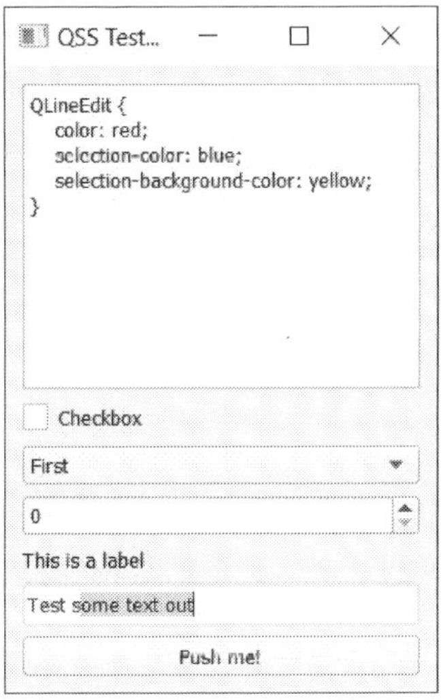

Figure 107. Applying text styles to a QLineEdit

We can apply this rule to two distinct types of widgets by giving them both as the target, separated by a comma.

```
QSpinBox, QLineEdit {
    color: red;
    selection-color: blue;
    selection-background-color: yellow;
}
```

Figure 108. Applying text styles to a QLineEdit & QSpinBox

In this final example, we make apply the styles to the `QSpinBox`, `QLineEdit` and `QPushButton`, setting the font bold & italic and the text-align to **right**.

```
QSpinBox, QLineEdit, QPushButton {
    color: red;
    selection-color: blue;
    selection-background-color: yellow;
    font-style: italic;
    font-weight: bold;
    text-align: right;
}
```

This produces the result shown below. Notice that the `text-align` property has not affected the alignment of the `QSpinBox` or `QLineEdit`. For both these widgets alignment must be set using the `.setAlignment()` method, rather than styles.

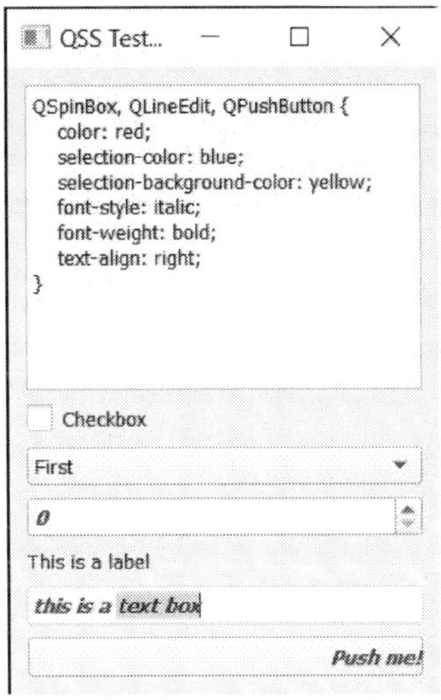

Figure 109. Applying text styles to a QPushButton, QLineEdit & QSpinBox

Backgrounds

In addition to styling text you can also style the widget background, with both solid colors and images. For images there are a number of additional properties which define how the image is repeated and positioned within the widget area.

Property	Type (Default)	Description
`background`	Background	Shorthand notation for setting the background. Equivalent to specifying background-color, background-image, background-repeat, and/or background-position. See also background-origin, selection-background-color, background-clip, background-attachment and alternate-background-color.
`background-color`	Brush	The background color used for the widget.
`background-image`	Url	The background image used for the widget. Semi-transparent parts of the image let the background-color shine through.
`background-repeat`	Repeat (both)	Whether and how the background image is repeated to fill the background-origin rectangle.

Property	Type (Default)	Description
`background-position`	Alignment (top-left)	The alignment of the background image within the background-origin rectangle.
`background-clip`	Origin (border)	The widget's rectangle, in which the background is drawn.
`background-origin`	Origin (padding)	The widget's background rectangle, to use in conjunction with background-position and background-image.

The following example will apply the specified image over the background of our `QPlainTextEdit` which we are using to enter the rules.

```
QPlainTextEdit {
    color: white;
    background-image: url(../otje.jpg);
}
```

Images are referenced using the `url()` syntax, passing in the path to the file. Here we're using `../otje.jpg` to point to a file in the parent directory. You can also use resource path syntax, e.g. `url(:/images/<imagename>.png)` to select images from the currently loaded resources.

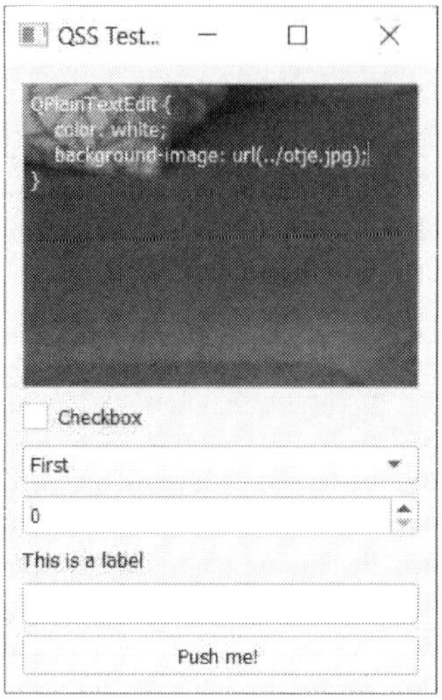

Figure 110. A background image.

> ℹ While this syntax is identical to that used in CSS, remote files cannot be loaded with URLs.

To position the background in the widget you can use the `background-position` property. This defines the point of the image which will be aligned with the *same* point on the widget's *origin rectangle*. By default the *origin rectangle* is the padded area of the widget.

Figure 111. Examples of background position

A position of `center, center` therefore means the center of the image will be aligned with the center of the widget, along both axes.

```
QPlainTextEdit {
    color: white;
    background-image: url(../otje.jpg);
    background-position: center center;
}
```

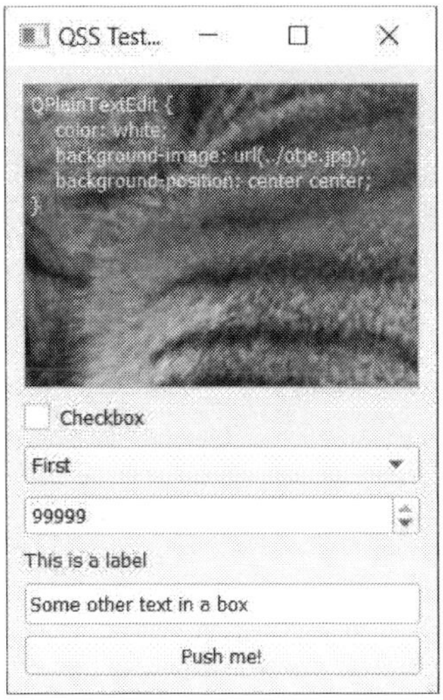

Figure 112. Centered background image.

To align the bottom-right of the image to the bottom-right of the *origin rectangle* of the widget, you would use.

```
QPlainTextEdit {
    color: white;
    background-image: url(../otje.jpg);
    background-position: bottom right;
}
```

The *origin rectangle* can be modified using the `background-origin` property. This accepts one of the values `margin`, `border`, `padding` or `content` which defines that specific box as the reference of background position alignment.

To understand what this means we'll need to take a look at the widget box model.

The widget Box Model

The term *box model* describes the relationships between the *boxes* (rectangles) which surround each widget and the effect these boxes have on the size or layout of widgets in relationship to one another. Each Qt widget is surrounded by four concentric boxes—from inside out, these are content, padding, border and margin.

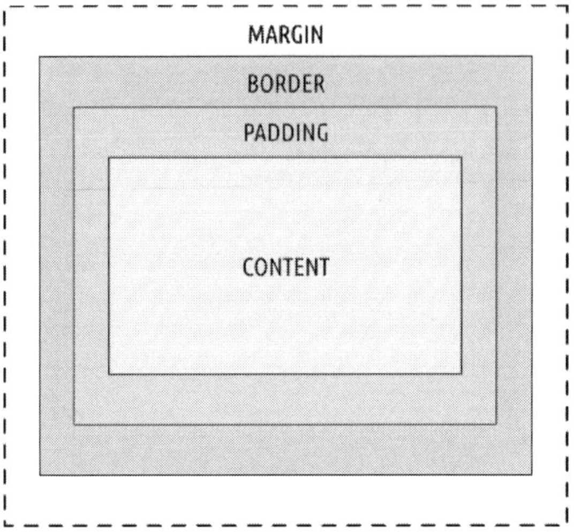

Figure 113. The box model.

Increasing the size of the inner boxes, increases the size of the outer boxes. This arrangement means, for example, that increasing the *padding* of a widget will add space between the content the border, while increasing the dimensions of the border itself.

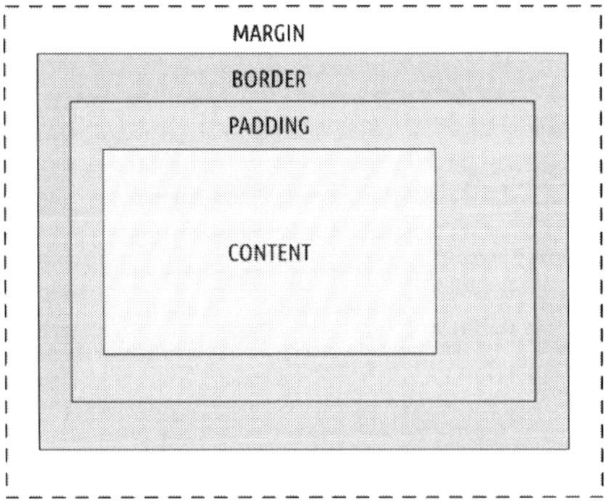

Figure 114. The effect on other boxes of adding padding to the right.

The properties available to modify the various boxes are given below.

Property	Type (Default)	Description
`border`	Border	Shorthand notation for setting the widget's border. Equivalent to specifying border-color, border-style, and/or border-width. Also `border-top`, `border-right`, `border-bottom` and `border-left`.
`border-color`	Box Colors (`QPalette Foreground`)	The color of all the border's edges. Also `border-top-color`, `border-right-color`, `border-bottom-color`, `border-left-color` for specific edges.
`border-image`	Border Image	The image used to fill the border. The image is cut into nine parts and stretched appropriately if necessary.
`border-radius`	Radius	The radius (curve) of the border's corners. Also `border-top-left-radius`, `border-top-right-radius`, `border-bottom-right-radius` and `border-bottom-left-radius` for specific corners.
`border-style`	Border Style (none)	The style of all the border's edges. Also `border-top-style`, `border-right-style`, `border-bottom-style` and `border-left-style` for specific edges.
`border-width`	Box Lengths	The width of the border. Also `border-top-width`, `border-right-width`, `border-bottom-width` and `border-left-width`.
`margin`	Box Lengths	The widget's margins. Also `margin-top`, `margin-right`, `margin-bottom` and `margin-left`.

Property	Type (Default)	Description
`outline`		The outline drawn around the object's border.
`outline-color`	Color	The color of the outline. See also border-color
`outline-offset`	Length	The outline's offset from the border of the widget.
`outline-style`		Specifies the pattern used to draw the outline. See also border-style
`outline-radius`		Adds rounded corners to the outline. Also `outline-bottom-left-radius`, `outline-bottom-right-radius`, `outline-top-left-radius` and `outline-top-right-radius`
`padding`	Box Lengths	The widget's padding. Also `padding-top`, `padding-right`, `padding-bottom` and `padding-left`.

The following example modifies the margin, border and padding of the `QPlainTextEdit` widget.

```
QPlainTextEdit {
    margin: 10;
    padding: 10px;
    border: 5px solid red;
}
```

A note on units

In this example we're using `px` or *pixel* units for the *padding* and *border* The value for *margin* is also in pixels, as this is the default unit when none is specified. You can also use one of the following units—

- `px` pixels
- `pt` the size of one point (i.e. 1/72 of an inch)
- `em` the *em* width of the font (i.e. the width of 'M')
- `ex` the *ex* width of the font (i.e. the height of 'x')

Looking at the result in the QSS tester, you can see the padding *inside* the red border and the margin *outside* the red border.

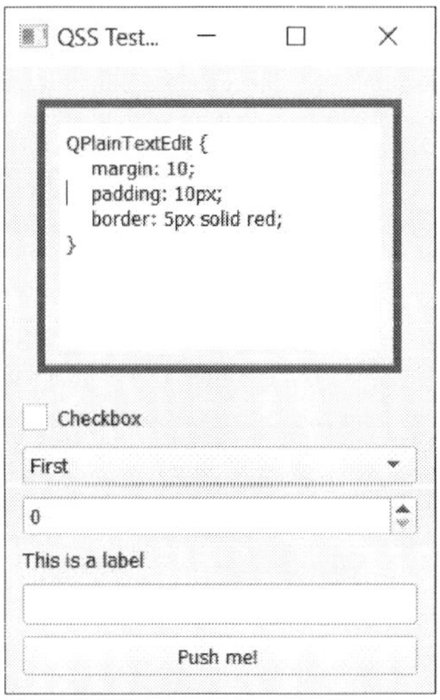

Figure 115. The box model

You can also add a *radius* to the outline to add curved edges.

```
QPlainTextEdit {
    margin: 10;
    padding: 10px;
    border: 5px solid red;
    border-radius: 15px;
}
```

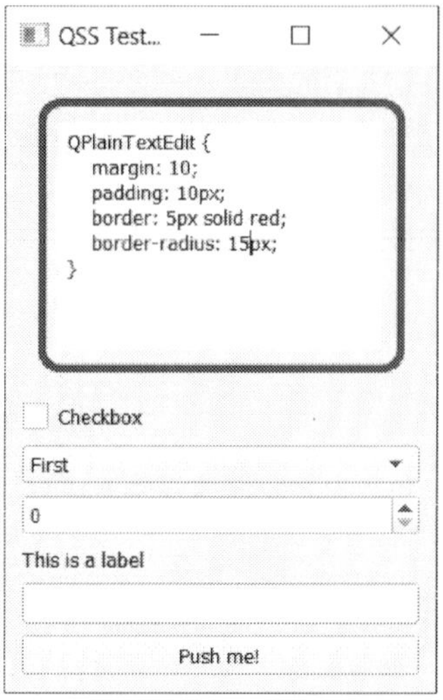

Figure 116. Borders with 15px radius (curve)

Sizing widgets

It is possible to control the size of widgets with QSS. However, while there are specific `width` and `height` properties (see later) these are only used to specify the sizes of sub-controls. To control widgets you must instead use the `max-` and `min-` properties.

Property	Type (Default)	Description
`max-height`	Length	The widget's or a subcontrol's maximum height.
`max-width`	Length	The widget's or a subcontrol's maximum width.
`min-height`	Length	The widget's or a subcontrol's minimum height.
`min-width`	Length	The widget's or a subcontrol's minimum width.

If you provide a `min-height` property larger than the widget *usually* is, then the widget will be enlarged.

```
QLineEdit {
    min-height: 50;
}
```

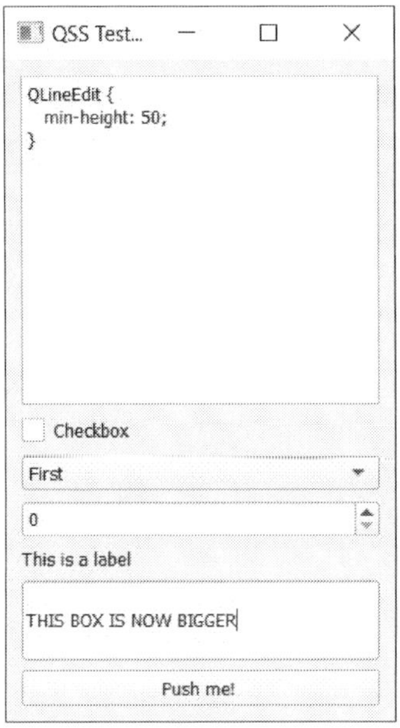

Figure 117. Setting a min-height on a QLineEdit, to enlarge it.

However, when setting `min-height` the widget can of course be larger than this. To specify an exact size for a widget, you can specify both a `min-` and `max-` value for the dimension.

```
QLineEdit {
    min-height: 50;
    max-height: 50;
}
```

This will lock the widget to this height, preventing it from resizing in response to changes in content.

> Be careful about using this, as you can render widgets unreadable!

Widget specific styles

The styles we've looked at so far are generic and can be used with most widgets. However, there are also a number of widget-specific properties which can be set.

Property	Type (Default)	Description
alternate-background-color	Brush (QPalette AlternateBase)	The alternate background color used in QAbstractItemView subclasses.
background-attachment	Attachment (scroll)	Determines whether the background-image in a QAbstractScrollArea is scrolled or fixed with respect to the viewport.
button-layout	Number (SH_DialogButtonLayout)	The layout of buttons in a QDialogButtonBox or a QMessageBox. The possible values are 0 (Win), 1 (Mac), 2 (KDE), 3 (Gnome) and 5 (Android).
dialogbuttonbox-buttons-have-icons	Boolean	Whether the buttons in a QDialogButtonBox show icons. If this property is set to 1, the buttons of a QDialogButtonBox show icons; if it is set to 0, the icons are not shown.
gridline-color	Color (SH_Table_GridLineColor)	The color of the grid line in a QTableView.

Property	Type (Default)	Description
icon	Url+	The widget icon. The only widget currently supporting this property is QPushButton.
icon-size	Length	The width and height of the icon in a widget.
lineedit-password-character	Number (SH_LineEdit_PasswordCharacter)	The QLineEdit password character as a Unicode number.
lineedit-password-mask-delay	Number (SH_LineEdit_PasswordMaskDelay)	The QLineEdit password mask delay in milliseconds before lineedit-password-character is applied.
messagebox-text-interaction-flags	Number (SH_MessageBox_TextInteractionFlags)	The interaction behavior for text in a message box.(from Qt.TextInteractionFlags)
opacity	Number (SH_ToolTipLabel_Opacity)	The opacity for a widget (tooltips only) 0-255.
paint-alternating-row-colors-for-empty-area	bool	Whether a QTreeView paints alternating rows past the end of the data.
show-decoration-selected	Boolean (SH_ItemView_ShowDecorationSelected)	Controls whether selections in a QListView cover the entire row or just the extent of the text.

Property	Type (Default)	Description
`titlebar-show-tooltips-on-buttons`	bool	Whether tool tips are shown on window title bar buttons.
`widget-animation-duration`	Number	How long an animation should last (milliseconds).

These only apply to the widgets specified in the description (or their subclasses).

Targeting

We've seen a range of different QSS properties and applied them to widgets based on their type. But how can you target individual widgets and how does Qt decide which rules to apply to which widgets and when? Next, we'll look at other options for targeting QSS rules and the effect of inheritance.

Type	Example	Description
Universal	`*`	Matches all widgets.
Type	`QPushButton`	Instances of QPushButton or its subclasses.
Property	`QPushButton[flat="false"]`	Instances of `QPushButton` that are not flat. Can compare with *any* property that supports `.toString()`. Can also use `class="classname"`
Property contains	`QPushButton[property~="something"]`	Instances of `QPushButton` where property (a list of `QString`) does not contain the given value.

Type	Example	Description
Class	`` `.QPushButton ``	Instances of QPushButton but not subclasses.
ID	`QPushButton#okButton`	A QPushButton instance whose object name is okButton.
Descendant	`QDialog QPushButton`	Instances of QPushButton that are descendants (children, grandchildren, etc.) of a QDialog.
Child	`QDialog > QPushButton`	Instances of QPushButton that are *immediate* children of a QDialog.

We'll look at each of these targeting rules in turn now, trying them out with our QSS tester.

Type

We've already seen *type targeting* in action in our QSS tester. Here we targeted rules against the type name of the individual widgets, for example `QComboBox` or `QLineEdit`.

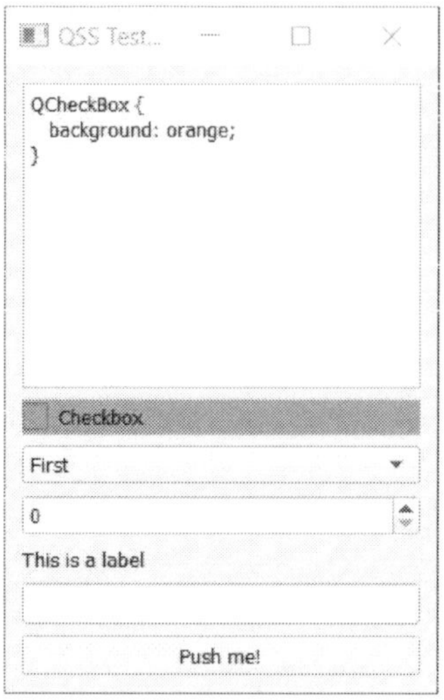

Figure 118. Targeting a QComboBox does not affect other unrelated types.

However, targeting types in this way *also* targets any subclasses of that type. So for example, we can target `QAbstractButton` to target any types that derive from it.

```
QAbstractButton {
    background: orange;
}
```

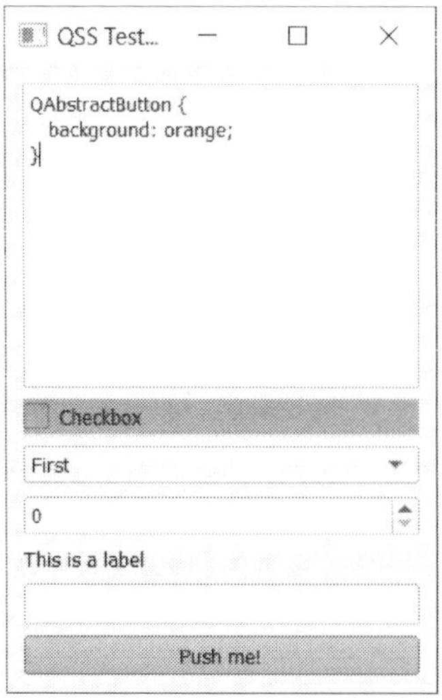

Figure 119. Targeting a QAbstractButton affects all child classes

This behavior means that *all* widgets can be targeted using `QWidget`. For example, the following will set the background of all widgets to *red*.

```
QWidget {
    background: red;
}
```

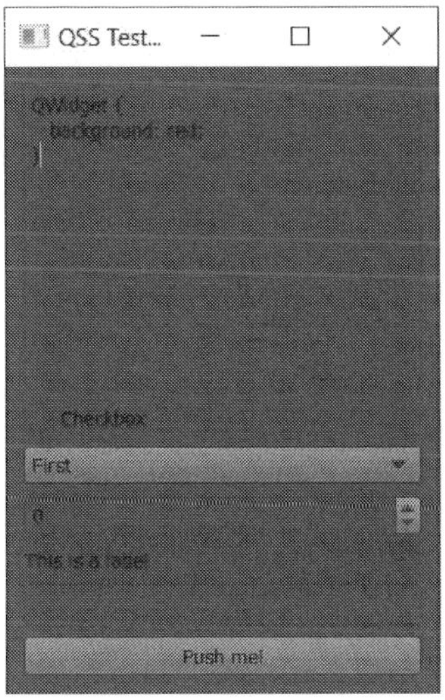

Figure 120. QSS selection via parent classes.

Class .

Sometimes however you *want* to only target a specific class of widget, and not any subclasses. To do this you can use *class targeting*—by prepending a `.` to the name of the type.

The following targets instances of `QWidget` but *not* any classes derived from `QWidget`. In our QSS tester the only `QWidget` we have is the central widget used for holding the layout. So the following will change the background of *that* container widget orange.

```
.QWidget {
    background: orange;
}
```

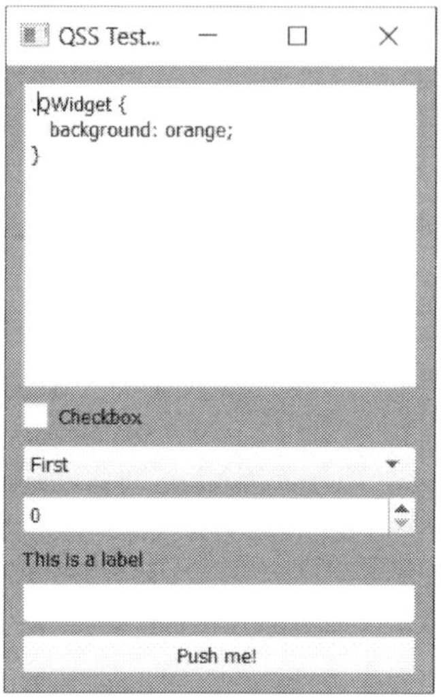

Figure 121. Targeting a class specifically will not target subclasses

ID targeting

All Qt widgets have an *object name* which uniquely identifies them. When creating widgets in Qt Designer you use the object name to specify the name that the object is available under on the parent window. However, this relationship is just for convenience—you can set any *object name* you want for a widget in your own code. These names can then be used to target QSS rules directly to specific widgets.

In our QSS tester app we've set IDs on our `QComboBox` and `QLineEdit` for testing.

```
combo.setObjectName('thecombo')
le.setObjectName('mylineedit')
```

Property `[property="<value>"]`

You can target widgets by any widget property which is available as a string (or who's value has a `.toString()` method). This can be used to define some quite complex states on widgets.

The following is a simple example targeting a `QPushButton` by the text label.

```
QPushButton[text="Push me!"] {
    background: red;
}
```

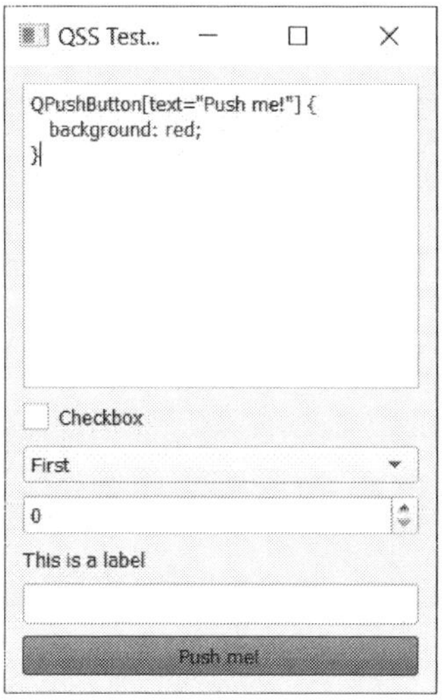

Figure 122. Targeting a QPushButton by the label text

> Targeting widgets by their visible text is a *very bad idea* in general as it will introduce bugs as you try and translate your application or change labels.

Rules are applied to widgets when the stylesheet is first set and will not respond to changes in properties. If a property targeted by a QSS rule is modified, you must trigger a stylesheet recalculation for it to take effect—for example by re-setting the stylesheet again.

Descendant

To target descendants of a given type of widget, you can chain widgets together. The following example targets any `QComboBox` which is a child of a `QMainWindow`—whether it is an immediate child, or nested within other widgets or layouts.

```
QMainWindow QComboBox {
   background: yellow;
}
```

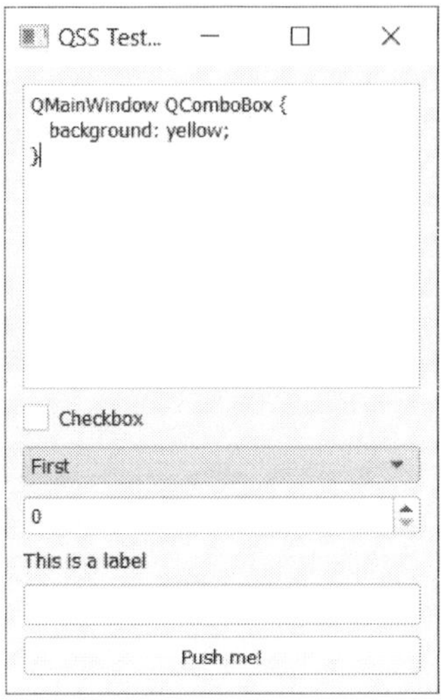

Figure 123. Targeting a QComboBox which is a child of a QMainWindow

To target *all* descendants you can use the global selector as the final element in the targeting. You can also chain many types together to target only those places in your app where that hierarchy exists.

```
QMainWindow QWidget * {
   background: yellow;
}
```

In our QSS tester application we have an outer `QMainWindow`, with a `QWidget` central widget holding the layout, and then our widgets in that layout. The rule above therefore matches only the individual widgets (which all have `QMainWindow QWidget` as parents, in that order).)

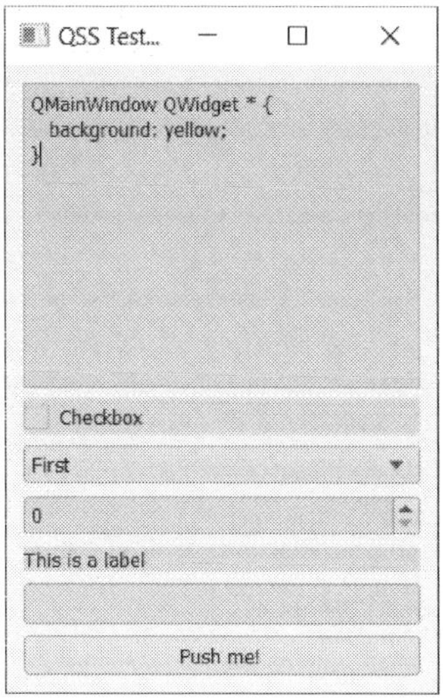

Figure 124. Targeting a QComboBox which is a child of a QMainWindow

Child >

You can also target a widget which is a *direct* child of another widget using the > selector. This will only match where that exact hierarchy is in place.

For example, the following will *only* target the `QWidget` container which is a direct child of the `QMainWindow`.

```
QMainWindow > QWidget {
   background: green;
}
```

But the following will not match anything, since in our QSS app the `QComboBox` widget is *not* a direct child of the `QMainWindow`.

```
QMainWindow > QComboBox {   /* matches nothing */
   background: yellow;
}
```

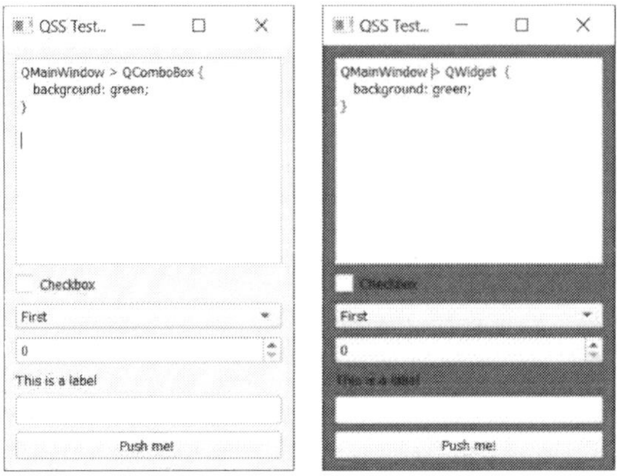

Figure 125. Targeting a QComboBox which is a direct child of a QWidget

Inheritance

Style sheets can be applied to `QApplication` and widgets and will apply to the styled widget and all of it's children. A widget's effective style sheet is determined by combining the style sheets of all it's ancestors (parent, grandparent, ...all the way up to the window) plus style sheets on `QApplication` itself.

Rules are applied in order of *specificity*. That means, a rule which targets a specific widget by ID, will override a rule which targets *all* widgets of that type. For example, the following will set the background of the `QLineEdit` in our QSS tester app to blue—the specific ID overrides the generic widget rule.

```
QLineEdit#mylineedit {
    background: blue;
}

QLineEdit {
    background: red;
}
```

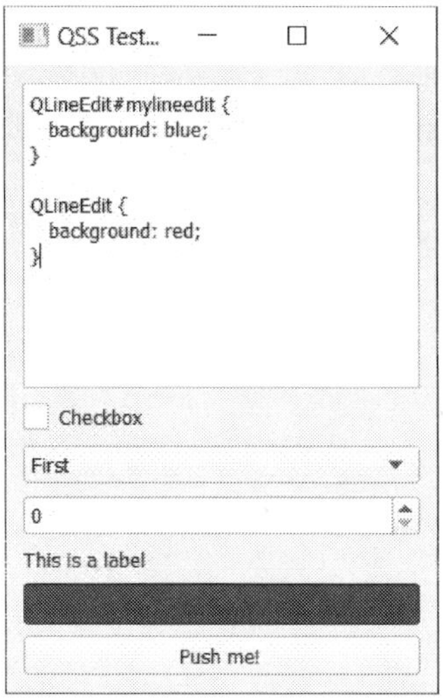

Figure 126. Specific ID targeting overrules generic widget targeting.

In cases where there are two conflicting rules the widgets' own style sheet will be preferred over inherited styles, and nearer ancestors will be preferred over more distance — parents will be preferred to grandparents for example.

No inherited properties

Widgets are only affected by rules which target them specifically. While rules can be *set* on a parent, they must still reference the target widget to affect it. Take the following rule —

```
QLineEdit {
    background: red;
}
```

If set on a `QMainWindow` all `QLineEdit` objects in that window will have a red background (assuming no other rules). However, if the following is set…

```
QMainWindow {
    background: red;
}
```

…only the `QMainWindow` itself will be set with a red background. The background color *itself* does not propogate to child widgets.

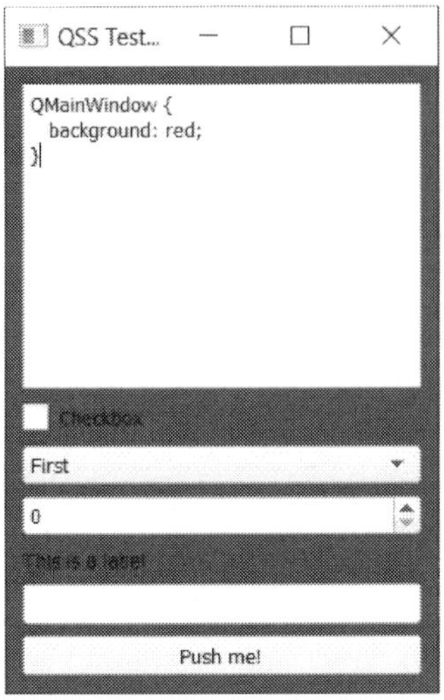

Figure 127. QSS properties do not propagate to children.

> If the child widgets have transparent backgrounds, the red *will* show through however.

Unless targeted by a matching rule, a widget will use it's default system style values for each property. Widgets do not inherit style properties from parent widgets, even inside compound widgets, and widgets must be targeted by rules directly to be affected by them.

> This is in contrast with CSS, where elements can inherit values from their parents.

Pseudo-selectors

So far we've looked at static styling, using properties to change the default appearance of a widget. However, QSS also allows you to style in response to dynamic widget states. An example of this is the highlight you see when buttons are hovered with the mouse—the highlight helps to indicate that the widget has focus and will respond if you click it.

There are many other uses for active styling, from usability (highlighting lines of data, or specific tabs) to visualizing data hierarchies. These can all be achieved using *pseudo-selectors* in QSS. Pseudo-selectors make QSS rules apply only in particular circumstances.

There are a lot of different pseudo selectors which you can apply to widgets. Some such as `:hover` are generic and can be used with all widgets, others are widget-specific. The full list is given below—

Pseudo-State	Description
`:active`	Widget is part of an active window.
`:adjoins-item`	The `::branch` of a `QTreeView` is adjacent to an item.
`:alternate`	Set for every alternate row when painting the row of a `QabstractItemView` (`QabstractItemView.alternatingRowColors()` is `True`)
`:bottom`	Positioned at the bottom, e.g. a `QTabBar` that has its tabs at the bottom.
`:checked`	Item is checked, e.g. the checked state of QAbstractButton.
`:closable`	Items can be closed, e.g. a `QDockWidget` has `QdockWidget.DockWidgetClosable` enabled.
`:closed`	Item is in the closed state, e.g. an non-expanded item in a `QtreeView`
`:default`	Item is the default action, e.g. a default `QPushButton` or a default action in a `QMenu`.
`:disabled`	Item is disabled.
`:editable`	`QcomboBox` is editable.
`:enabled`	Item is enabled.
`:exclusive`	Item is part of an exclusive item group, e.g. a menu item in a exclusive `QActionGroup`.
`:first`	Item is the first in a list, e.g. the first tab in a `QtabBar`.
`:flat`	Item is flat, e.g. a flat `QpushButton`.
`:floatable`	Items can be floated, e.g. the `QDockWidget` has `QDockWidget.DockWidgetFloatable` enabled.

Pseudo-State	Description
`:focus`	Item has input focus.
`:has-children`	Item has children, e.g. an item in a `QTreeView` with child items.
`:has-siblings`	Item has siblings, e.g. an item in a `QTreeView` with siblings.
`:horizontal`	Item has horizontal orientation
`:hover`	Mouse is hovering over the item.
`:indeterminate`	Item has indeterminate state, e.g. a `QCheckBox` or `QRadioButton` is partially checked.
`:last`	Item is the last (in a list), e.g. the last tab in a `QTabBar`.
`:left`	Item is positioned at the left, e.g. a `QTabBar` that has its tabs positioned at the left.
`:maximized`	Item is maximized, e.g. a maximized `QMdiSubWindow`.
`:middle`	Item is in the middle (in a list), e.g. a tab that is not in the beginning or the end in a `QTabBar`.
`:minimized`	Item is minimized, e.g. a minimized `QMdiSubWindow`.
`:movable`	Item can be moved around, e.g. the QDockWidget has `QDockWidget.DockWidgetMovable` enabled.
`:no-frame`	Item has no frame, e.g. a frameless `QSpinBox` or `QLineEdit`.
`:non-exclusive`	Item is part of a non-exclusive item group, e.g. a menu item in a non-exclusive `QActionGroup`.
`:off`	Items that can be toggled, this applies to items in the "off" state.
`:on`	Items that can be toggled, this applies to widgets in the "on" state.

Pseudo-State	Description
`:only-one`	Item is the only one (in a list), e.g. a lone tab in a `QTabBar`.
`:open`	Item is in the open state, e.g. an expanded item in a `QTreeView`, or a `QComboBox` or` QPushButton` with an open menu.
`:next-selected`	Next item is selected, e.g. the selected tab of a `QTabBar` is next to this item.
`:pressed`	Item is being pressed using the mouse.
`:previous-selected`	Previous item is selected, e.g. a tab in a `QTabBar` that is next to the selected tab.
`:read-only`	Item is marked read only or non-editable, e.g. a read only QLineEdit or a non-editable `QComboBox`.
`:right`	Item is positioned at the right, e.g. a `QTabBar` that has its tabs positioned at the right.
`:selected`	Item is selected, e.g. the selected tab in a `QTabBar` or the selected item in a `QMenu`.
`:top`	Item is positioned at the top, e.g. a `QTabBar` that has its tabs positioned at the top.
`:unchecked`	Item is unchecked.
`:vertical`	Item has vertical orientation.
`:window`	Widget is a window (i.e a top level widget)

We can use the QSS tester to see pseudo-selectors in action. For example, the following will change the background of the `QPushButton` *red* when the mouse hovers over the widget.

```
QPushButton:hover {
   background: red;
}
```

The following will change the background of all widgets when they are hovered.

```
*:hover {
    background: red;
}
```

Hovering a widget means all it's parents are also hovered (the mouse is within their bounding box) as the image below shows.

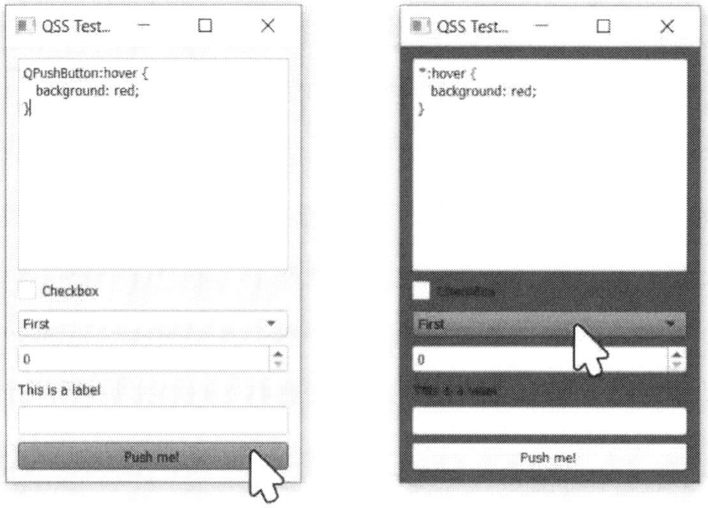

Figure 128. Left, QPushButton highlighted when hovered. Right, when a widget is hovered all parent widgets are also hovered.

You can also *negate* pseudo-selectors using !. This means that the rule will become active when that selector is inactive. For example the following...

```
QPushButton:!hover {
    background: yellow;
}
```

...will make the QPushButton yellow when it is *not hovered*.

You can also chain multiple pseudo-selectors together. For example, the following will set the background of a `QCheckBox` green when it is *checked* and *not hovered*, and yellow when it is *checked* and *hovered*.

```
QCheckBox:checked:!hover {
    background: green;
}

QCheckBox:checked:hover {
    background: yellow;
}
```

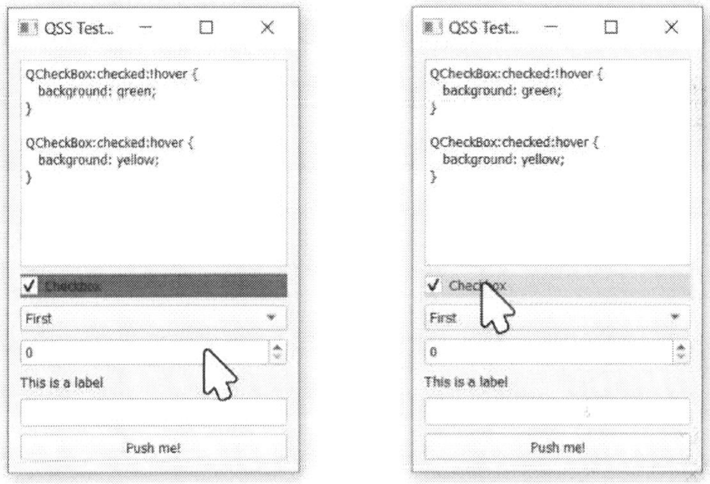

Figure 129. Chained pseudo selectors for hover state.

As for all other rules, you can also chain them using `,` separators to make the defined rule apply to both (or many) cases. For example, the following will set a checkbox background green when it is *checked* OR *hovered*.

```
QCheckBox:checked, QCheckBox:hover {
    background: yellow;
}
```

Styling Widget Sub controls

Many widgets are constructed from a combination of other sub-widgets or *controls*. QSS provides syntax for addressing these sub-controls directly, so you can make style changes to sub-controls individually. These sub-controls can be addressed by using the :: (double-colon) selector, followed by an identifier for the given sub control.

A good example of such a widget is the QComboBox. The following style snipped applies a custom style directly to the down-arrow on the right hand of the combo box.

```
QComboBox::drop-down {
    background: yellow;
    image: url('puzzle.png')
}
```

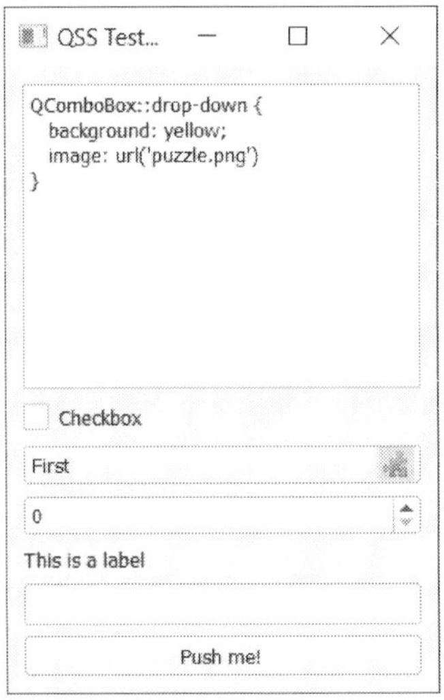

Figure 130. Setting background and icon for a QComboBox dropdown with QSS.

There are quite a few sub-control selectors available in QSS, which are listed below. You'll notice that many of them apply only to specific widgets (or types of widgets).

Sub-Control	Description
::add-line	Button to move to next line on a QScrollBar.
::add-page	Space between the handle and the add-line of a QScrollBar.
::branch	Branch indicator of a QTreeView.

Sub-Control	Description
::chunk	Progress chunk of a QProgressBar.
::close-button	Close button of a QDockWidget or tabs of QTabBar
::corner	Corner between two scrollbars in a QAbstractScrollArea
::down-arrow	Down arrow of a QComboBox, QHeaderView, QScrollBar or QSpinBox.
::down-button	Down button of a QScrollBar or a QSpinBox.
::drop-down	Drop-down button of a QComboBox.
::float-button	Float button of a QDockWidget.
::groove	Groove of a QSlider.
::indicator	Indicator of a QAbstractItemView, a QCheckBox, a QRadioButton, a checkable QMenu item or a checkable QGroupBox.
::handle	Handle of a QScrollBar, a QSplitter, or a QSlider.
::icon	Icon of a QAbstractItemView or a QMenu.
::item	Item of a QAbstractItemView, a QMenuBar, a QMenu, or a QStatusBar.
::left-arrow	Left arrow of a QScrollBar.
::left-corner	Left corner of a QTabWidget, e.g. control the left corner widget in a QTabWidget.
::menu-arrow	Arrow of a QToolButton with a menu.
::menu-button	Menu button of a QToolButton.
::menu-indicator	Menu indicator of a QPushButton.
::right-arrow	Right arrow of a QMenu or a QScrollBar.
::pane	The pane (frame) of a QTabWidget.

Sub-Control	Description
`::right-corner`	The right corner of a QTabWidget. For example, this control can be used to control the position the right corner widget in a QTabWidget.
`::scroller`	The scroller of a QMenu or QTabBar.
`::section`	The section of a QHeaderView.
`::separator`	The separator of a QMenu or in a QMainWindow.
`::sub-line`	The button to subtract a line of a QScrollBar.
`::sub-page`	The region between the handle (slider) and the sub-line of a QScrollBar.
`::tab`	The tab of a QTabBar or QToolBox.
`::tab-bar`	The tab bar of a QTabWidget. This subcontrol exists only to control the position of the QTabBar inside the QTabWidget. To style the tabs using the ::tab subcontrol.
`::tear`	The tear indicator of a QTabBar.
`::tearoff`	The tear-off indicator of a QMenu.
`::text`	The text of a QAbstractItemView.
`::title`	The title of a QGroupBox or a QDockWidget.
`::up-arrow`	The up arrow of a QHeaderView (sort indicator), QScrollBar or a QSpinBox.
`::up-button`	The up button of a QSpinBox.

The following targets the up and down buttons of a `QSpinBox` turning the background red and green respectively.

```
QSpinBox::up-button {
   background: green;
}

QSpinBox::down-button {
   background: red;
}
```

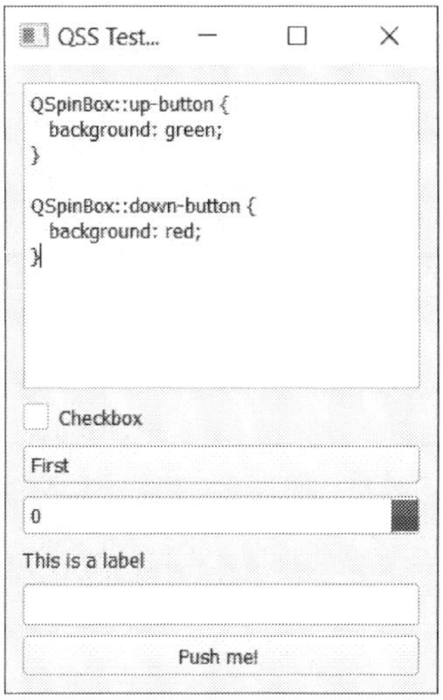

Figure 131. Setting background to the QSpinBox up and down buttons.

The arrows *inside* the up down buttons are also separately targetable. Below we're setting them with custom plus and minus icons — note we also need to resize the buttons to fit.

```
QSpinBox {
   min-height: 50;
}

QSpinBox::up-button {
    width: 50;
}

QSpinBox::up-arrow {
   image: url('plus.png');
}

QSpinBox::down-button {
    width: 50;
}

QSpinBox::down-arrow {
   image: url('minus.png')
}
```

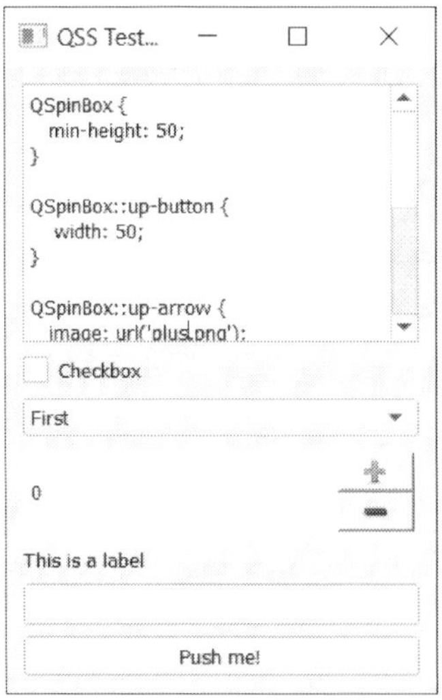

Figure 132. Setting background to the QSpinBox up and down buttons.

Subcontrol pseudostates

You can use pseudostates to target subcontrols, just as for other widgets. To do this, simply chain the pseudostate after the control. For example—

```
QSpinBox::up-button:hover {
   background: green;
}

QSpinBox::down-button:hover {
   background: red;
}
```

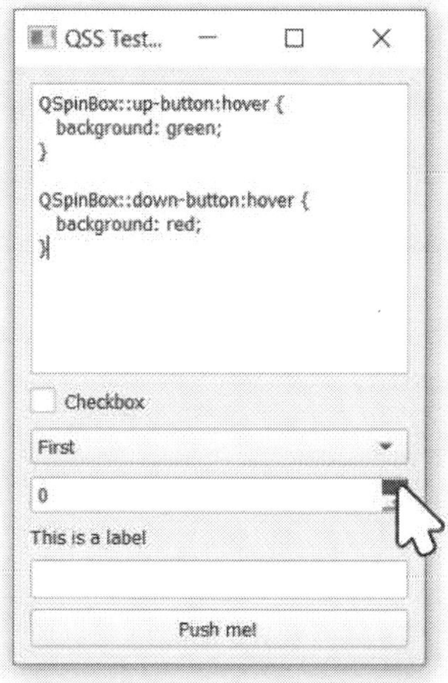

Figure 133. Combining subcontrol selectors with pseudo-selectors.

Positioning Sub-controls

Using QSS you also get precise control over the position of subcontrols inside widgets. These allow adjustment in position either *relative* to their normal position, or in *absolute* reference to their parent widget. We'll look at these positioning methods below.

Property	Type (Default)	Description
`position`	relative | absolute (relative)	Whether offsets specified using left, right, top, and bottom are relative or absolute coordinates.
`bottom`	Length	If position is relative (the default), moves a subcontrol by a certain offset up; specifying bottom: y is then equivalent to specifying top: -y. If position is absolute, the bottom property specifies the subcontrol's bottom edge in relation to the parent's bottom edge (see also subcontrol-origin).
`left`	Length	If position=relative move a subcontrol right by the given offset (i.e. specifies additional space on the left). If position is absolute, specifies the distance from the left edge of the parent.

Property	Type (Default)	Description
`right`	Length	If position=relative move a subcontrol left by the given offset (i.e. specifies additional space on the right). If position is absolute, specifies the distance from the right edge of the parent.
`top`	Length	If position=relative move a subcontrol down the given offset (i.e. specifies additional space on the top). If position is absolute, specifies the distance from the top edge of the parent.

By default, positioning is *relative*. In this mode, the *left*, *right*, *top* and *bottom* properties define additional spacing to be added on the respective side. This means, somewhat confusingly, that *left* moves widgets *right*.

To help you remember, think of these as "add space to the *left*" and so on.

```
QSpinBox {
    min-height: 100;
}

QSpinBox::up-button {
    width: 50;
}

QSpinBox::down-button {
    width: 50;
    left: 5;
}
```

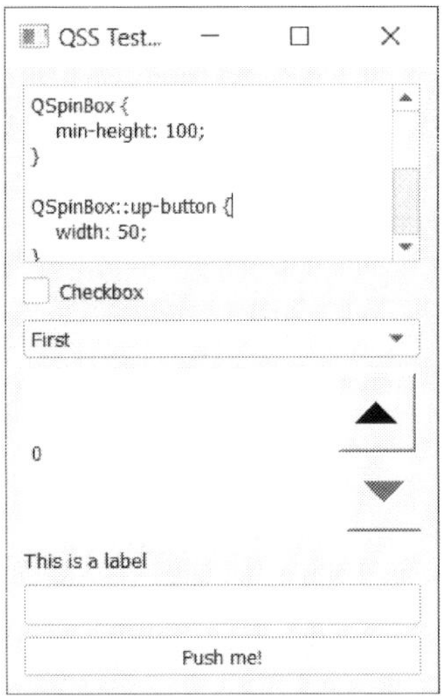

Figure 134. Adjusting the position of subcontrols with left.

When position is set to *absolute*, the *left*, *right*, *top* and *bottom* properties define the spacing between the widget and and it's parent's identical edges. So, for example, `top: 5, left: 5` will position a widget so it's top and left edges are 5 pixels from it's parent's top and left edge.

```
QSpinBox {
    min-height: 100;
}

QSpinBox::up-button {
    width: 50;
}

QSpinBox::down-button {
    position: absolute;
    width: 50;
    right: 25;
}
```

Below you can see the effect of positioning the down button using *absolute*, placing it 25 pixels from the right.

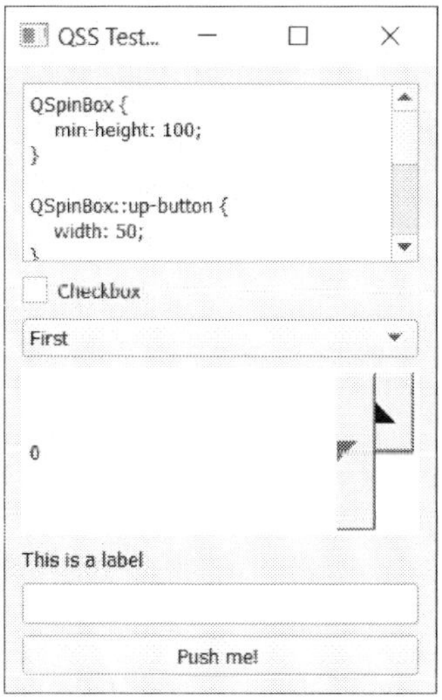

Figure 135. Adjusting the position of subcontrols absolute.

This is not the most practical example, but it demonstrates one constraint on positioning sub-controls in this way—you cannot position a subcontrol outside it's parent's bounding box.

Subcontrol styles

Finally, there are number of QSS properties which specifically target sub-controls for styling. These are shown below—see the description for the specific affected widgets and controls.

Property	Type (Default)	Description
`image`	Url+	The image that is drawn in the contents rectangle of a subcontrol. Setting the image property on sub controls implicitly sets the width and height of the sub-control (unless the image in a SVG).
`image-position`	alignment	The alignment of the image image's position can be specified using relative or absolute position. See relative and absolute for explanation.
`height`	Length	The height of a subcontrol. If you want a widget with a fixed height, set the min-height and max-height to the same value.
`spacing`	Length	Internal spacing in the widget.
`subcontrol-origin`	Origin (padding)	The origin rectangle of the subcontrol within the parent element.
`subcontrol-position`	Alignment	The alignment of the subcontrol within the origin rectangle specified by subcontrol-origin.

Property	Type (Default)	Description
`width`	Length	The width of a subcontrol. If you want a widget with a fixed width , set the min-width and max-width to the same value.

Editing Stylesheets in Qt Designer

So far the examples we've seen have applied QSS to widgets using code. However, you can also set stylesheets on widgets from within Qt Designer.

To set a QSS stylesheet on a widget in Qt Designer, right-click on the widget and select "Change stylesheet..." from the context menu.

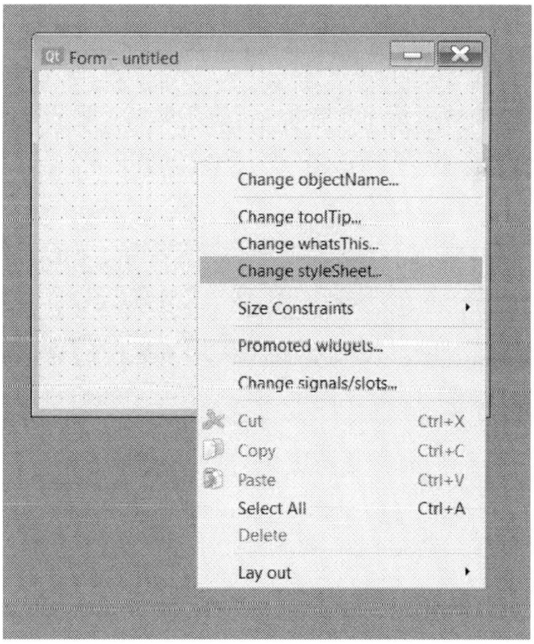

Figure 136. Accessing the QSS editor for a widget.

This will open up the following window, where you can enter QSS rules as text, which will be applied to this widget (and any children which match the rules).

Figure 137. The QSS editor in Qt Designer.

As well as entering rules as text, the QSS editor in Qt Designer gives you access to a resource lookup tool, color selection widget and a gradient designer. This tool (shown below) provides a number of built-in gradients you can add to your rules, but you can also define your own custom gradients if you prefer.

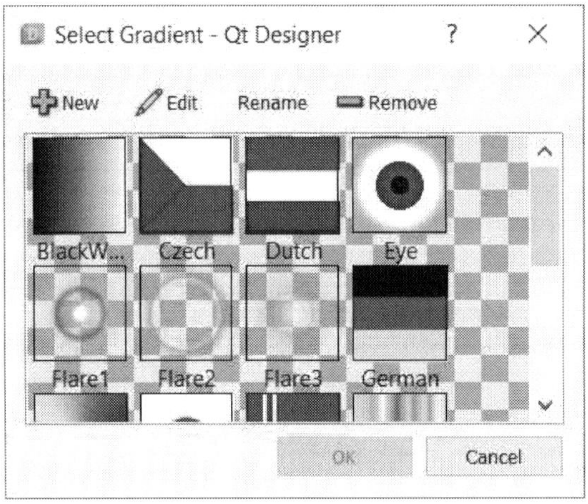

Figure 138. The QSS gradient designer in Qt Designer.

Gradients are defined using QSS rules so you can copy and paste them elsewhere (including into your code) to re-use them if you like.

Listing 72. The Dutch flag using a QSS qlineargradient rule.

```
QWidget {
background: qlineargradient(spread:pad, x1:0, y1:0, x2:0, y2:1, stop
:0 rgba(255, 0, 0, 255), stop:0.339795 rgba(255, 0, 0, 255), stop
:0.339799 rgba(255, 255, 255, 255), stop:0.662444 rgba(255, 255, 255,
255), stop:0.662469 rgba(0, 0, 255, 255), stop:1 rgba(0, 0, 255,
255))
}
```

Figure 139. The "Dutch flag" QSS gradient applied to a QWidget in Qt Designer

Model View Architecture

> ...with proper design, the features come cheaply.
>
> — Dennis Ritchie

As you start to build more complex applications with PyQt5 you'll likely come across issues keeping widgets in sync with your data.

Data stored in widgets (e.g. a simple `QListWidget`) is not easy to manipulate from Python — changes require you to get an item, get the data, and then set it back. The default solution to this is to keep an external data representation in Python, and then either duplicate updates to the both the data and the widget, or simply rewrite the whole widget from the data. As you start to work with larger data this approach can start to have performance impacts on your application.

Thankfully Qt has a solution for this — ModelViews. ModelViews are a powerful alternative to the standard display widgets, which use a standardized model interface to interact with data sources — from simple data structures to external databases. This isolates your data, meaning you can keep it in any structure you like, while the view takes care of presentation and updates.

This chapter introduces the key aspects of Qt's ModelView architecture and uses it to build simple desktop Todo application in PyQt5.

20. The Model View Architecture — Model View Controller

Model–View–Controller (MVC) is an architectural pattern used for developing user interfaces. It divides an application into three interconnected parts, separating the internal representation of data from how it is presented to and accepted from the user.

The MVC pattern splits the interface into the following components —

- **Model** holds the data structure which the app is working with.
- **View** is any representation of information as shown to the user, whether graphical or tables. Multiple views of the same data are allowed.
- **Controller** accepts input from the user, transforms it into commands and applies these to the model or view.

In Qt land the distinction between the View & Controller gets a little murky. Qt accepts input events from the user via the OS and delegates these to the widgets (Controller) to handle. However, widgets also handle presentation of their own state to the user, putting them squarely in the View. Rather than agonize over where to draw the line, in Qt-speak the View and Controller are instead merged together creating a Model/ViewController architecture — called "Model View" for simplicity.

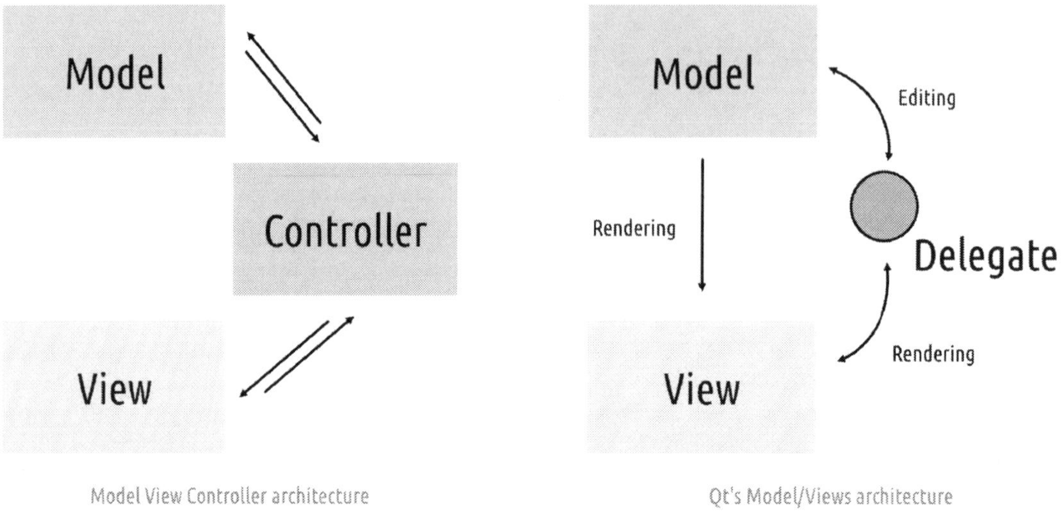

Figure 140. Comparing the MVC model and the Qt Model/View architecture.

Importantly, the distinction between the *data* and *how it is presented* is preserved.

The Model View

The Model acts as the interface between the data store and the ViewController. The Model holds the data (or a reference to it) and presents this data through a standardized API which Views then consume and present to the user. Multiple Views can share the same data, presenting it in completely different ways.

You can use any "data store" for your model, including for example a standard Python list or dictionary, or a database (via Qt itself, or SQLAlchemy) — it's entirely up to you.

The two parts are essentially responsible for —

1. The **model** stores the data, or a reference to it and returns individual or ranges of records, and associated metadata or *display* instructions.
2. The **view** requests data from the model and displays what is returned on the widget.

There is a good introduction to the Qt Model/View architecture in the Qt documentation [http://doc.qt.io/qt-5/model-view-programming.html].

21. A simple Model View — a Todo List

To demonstrate how to use the ModelViews in practice, we'll put together a very simple implementation of a desktop Todo List. This will consist of a `QListView` for the list of items, a `QLineEdit` to enter new items, and a set of buttons to add, delete, or mark items as done.

The files for this example are in the source code.

The UI

The simple UI was laid out using Qt Creator and saved as `mainwindow.ui`. The `.ui` file is included in the downloads for this book.

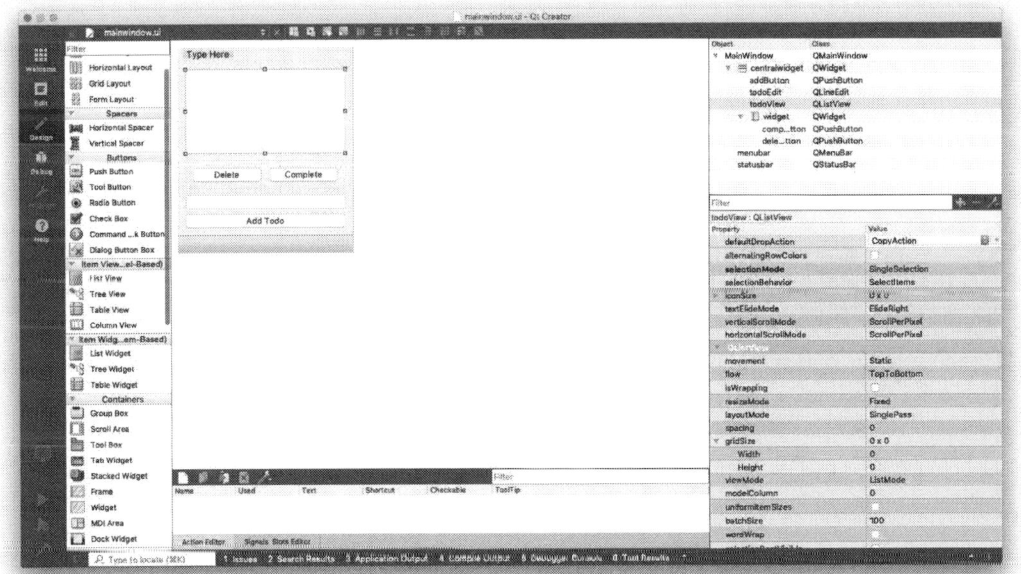

Figure 141. Designing the UI in Qt Creator

The `.ui` file was converted to a Python file as described previously using the command-line tool.

```
pyuic5 mainwindow.ui -o MainWindow.py
```

This generates a `MainWindow.py` file which contains our custom window class as designed in Qt Designer. This can be imported in our application code as normal—a basic skeleton app to display our UI is shown below.

Listing 73. model-views/todo_skeleton.py

```python
import sys

from PyQt5 import QtCore, QtGui, QtWidgets
from PyQt5.QtCore import Qt

from MainWindow import Ui_MainWindow


class MainWindow(QtWidgets.QMainWindow, Ui_MainWindow):
    def __init__(self):
        super().__init__()
        self.setupUi(self)


app = QtWidgets.QApplication(sys.argv)
window = MainWindow()
window.show()
app.exec_()
```

🚀 **Run it!** You'll see the window appear, although nothing is functional yet.

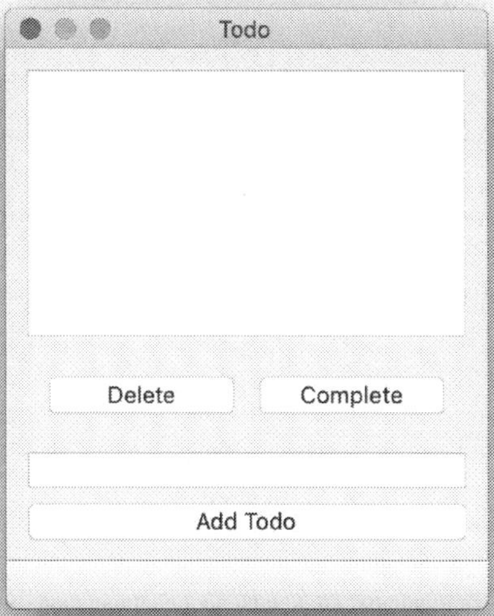

Figure 142. The MainWindow

The widgets added to in the interface were given the IDs shown in the table below.

objectName	Type	Description
`todoView`	`QListView`	The list of current todos
`todoEdit`	`QLineEdit`	The text input for creating a new todo item
`addButton`	`QPushButton`	Create the new todo, adding it to the todos list
`deleteButton`	`QPushButton`	Delete the current selected todo, removing it from the todos list
`completeButton`	`QPushButton`	Mark the current selected todo as done

We'll use these identifiers to hook up the application logic later.

The Model

We define our custom model by subclassing from a base implementation, allowing us to focus on the parts unique to our model. Qt provides a number of different model bases, including lists, trees and tables (ideal for spreadsheets).

For this example we are displaying the result to a `QListView`. The matching base model for this is `QAbstractListModel`. The outline definition for our model is shown below.

```
class TodoModel(QtCore.QAbstractListModel):
    def __init__(self, *args, todos=None, **kwargs):
        super(TodoModel, self).__init__(*args, **kwargs)
        self.todos = todos or []

    def data(self, index, role):
        if role == Qt.DisplayRole:
            # See below for the data structure.
            status, text = self.todos[index.row()]
            # Return the todo text only.
            return text

    def rowCount(self, index):
        return len(self.todos)
```

The`.todos` variable is our data store. The two methods `rowcount()` and `data()` are standard Model methods we must implement for a list model. We'll go through these in turn below.

.todos list

The data store for our model is `.todos`, a simple Python list in which we'll store a `tuple` of values in the format `[(bool, str), (bool, str), (bool, str)]` where `bool` is the **done** state of a given entry, and `str` is the text of the todo.

We initialize `self.todo` to an empty list on startup, unless a list is passed in via the `todos` keyword argument.

> `self.todos = todos or []` will set `self.todos` to the provided `todos` value if it is **truthy** (i.e. anything other than an empty list, the bool ` False` or `None` the default value), otherwise it will be set to the empty list [].

To create an instance of this model we can simply do —

```
model = TodoModel()   # create an empty todo list
```

Or to pass in an existing list —

```
todos = [(False, 'an item'), (False, 'another item')]
model = TodoModel(todos)
```

.rowcount()

The `.rowcount()` method is called by the view to get the number of rows in the current data. This is required for the view to know the maximum index it can request from the data store (`row count-1`). Since we're using a Python list as our data store, the return value for this is simply the `len()` of the list.

.data()

This is the core of your model, which handles requests for data from the view and returns the appropriate result. It receives two parameters `index` and `role`.

`index` is the position/coordinates of the data which the view is requesting, accessible by two methods `.row()` and `.column()` which give the position in each dimension. For a list view column can be ignored.

> For our `QListView` the column is always 0 and can be ignored, but you would need to use this for 2D data in a spreadsheet view.

`role` is a flag indicating the **type** of data the view is requesting. This is because the `.data()` method actually has more responsibility than just the core data. It also handles requests for style information, tooltips, status bars, etc. — basically anything that could be informed by the data itself.

The naming of `Qt.DisplayRole` is a bit weird, but this indicates that the **view** is asking us "please give me data for display". There are other **roles** which the `data` can receive for styling requests or requesting data in "edit-ready" format.

Role	Value	Description
`Qt.DisplayRole`	`0`	The key data to be rendered in the form of text. QString [https://doc.qt.io/qt-5/qstring.html]
`Qt.DecorationRole`	1	The data to be rendered as a decoration in the form of an icon. QColor [https://doc.qt.io/qt-5/qcolor.html], QIcon [https://doc.qt.io/qt-5/qicon.html] or QPixmap [https://doc.qt.io/qt-5/qpixmap.html]
`Qt.EditRole`	2	The data in a form suitable for editing in an editor. QString [https://doc.qt.io/qt-5/qstring.html]
`Qt.ToolTipRole`	3	The data displayed in the item's tooltip. QString [https://doc.qt.io/qt-5/qstring.html]
`Qt.StatusTipRole`	4	The data displayed in the status bar. QString [https://doc.qt.io/qt-5/qstring.html]
`Qt.WhatsThisRole`	5	The data displayed for the item in "What's This?" mode. QString [https://doc.qt.io/qt-5/qstring.html]
`Qt.SizeHintRole`	13	The size hint for the item that will be supplied to views. QSize [https://doc.qt.io/qt-5/qsize.html]

For a full list of available **roles** that you can receive see the Qt ItemDataRole documentation [https://doc.qt.io/qt-5/qt.html#ItemDataRole-enum]. Our todo list will only be using `Qt.DisplayRole` and `Qt.DecorationRole`.

Basic implementation

Below is the basic stub application needed to load the UI and display it. We'll add our model code and application logic to this base.

Listing 74. model-views/todo_1.py

```
import sys

from PyQt5 import QtCore, QtGui, QtWidgets
from PyQt5.QtCore import Qt

from MainWindow import Ui_MainWindow


class TodoModel(QtCore.QAbstractListModel):
    def __init__(self, todos=None):
        super().__init__()
        self.todos = todos or []

    def data(self, index, role):
        if role == Qt.DisplayRole:
            status, text = self.todos[index.row()]
            return text

    def rowCount(self, index):
        return len(self.todos)


class MainWindow(QtWidgets.QMainWindow, Ui_MainWindow):
    def __init__(self):
        super().__init__()
        self.setupUi(self)
        self.model = TodoModel()
        self.todoView.setModel(self.model)


app = QtWidgets.QApplication(sys.argv)
window = MainWindow()
window.show()
app.exec_()
```

We define our `TodoModel` as before, and initialize the `MainWindow` object. In the `__init__` for the MainWindow we create an instance of our todo model and set this model on the `todo_view`. Save this file as `todo.py` and run it with —

```
python3 todo.py
```

While there isn't much to see yet, the QListView and our model are actually working — if you add some default data you'll see it appear in the list.

```
self.model = TodoModel(todos=[(False, 'my first todo')])
```

Figure 143. QListView showing hard-coded todo item

You can keep adding items manually like this and they will show up in order in the QListView. Next we'll make it possible to add items from within the application.

First create a new method on the MainWindow named add. This is our callback which will take care of adding the current text from the input as a new todo. Connect this method to the addButton.pressed signal at the end of the __init__ block.

```
class MainWindow(QtWidgets.QMainWindow, Ui_MainWindow):
    def __init__(self):
        QtWidgets.QMainWindow.__init__(self)
        Ui_MainWindow.__init__(self)
        self.setupUi(self)
        self.model = TodoModel()
        self.todoView.setModel(self.model)
        # Connect the button.
        self.addButton.pressed.connect(self.add)

    def add(self):
        """
        Add an item to our todo list, getting the text from the
QLineEdit .todoEdit
        and then clearing it.
        """
        text = self.todoEdit.text()
        text = text.strip()  # Remove whitespace from the ends of the
string.
        if text: # Don't add empty strings.
            # Access the list via the model.
            self.model.todos.append((False, text))
            # Trigger refresh.
            self.model.layoutChanged.emit()  ①
            # Empty the input
            self.todoEdit.setText("")
```

① Here we're emitting a model signal `.layoutChanged` to let the view know that the **shape** of the data has been altered. This triggers a refresh of the entirety of the view. If you omit this line, the todo will still be added but the `QListView` won't update.

If just the data is altered, but the number of rows/columns are unaffected you can use the `.dataChanged()` signal instead. This also defines an altered region in the data using a top-left and bottom-right location to avoid redrawing the entire view.

Hooking up the other actions

We can now connect the rest of the button's signals and add helper functions for performing the **delete** and **complete** operations. We add the button signals to the `__init__` block as before.

```
        self.addButton.pressed.connect(self.add)
        self.deleteButton.pressed.connect(self.delete)
        self.completeButton.pressed.connect(self.complete)
```

Then define a new `delete` method as follows —

```
    def delete(self):
        indexes = self.todoView.selectedIndexes()
        if indexes:
            # Indexes is a list of a single item in single-select
mode.
            index = indexes[0]
            # Remove the item and refresh.
            del self.model.todos[index.row()]
            self.model.layoutChanged.emit()
            # Clear the selection (as it is no longer valid).
            self.todoView.clearSelection()
```

We use `self.todoView.selectedIndexes` to get the indexes (actually a list of a single item, as we're in single-selection mode) and then use the `.row()` as an index into our list of todos on our model. We delete the indexed item using Python's `del` operator, and then trigger a `layoutChanged` signal because the shape of the data has been modified.

Finally, we clear the active selection since the item you selected is now gone and the position itself could be out of bounds (if you had selected the last item).

> You could make this smarter and select the adjacent item in the list instead.

The `complete` method looks like this —

```
    def complete(self):
        indexes = self.todoView.selectedIndexes()
        if indexes:
            index = indexes[0]
            row = index.row()
            status, text = self.model.todos[row]
            self.model.todos[row] = (True, text)
            # .dataChanged takes top-left and bottom right, which are
equal
            # for a single selection.
            self.model.dataChanged.emit(index, index)
            # Clear the selection (as it is no longer valid).
            self.todoView.clearSelection()
```

This uses the same indexing as for delete, but this time we fetch the item from the model `.todos` list and then replace the status with `True`.

> We have to do this fetch-and-replace, as our data is stored as Python tuples which cannot be modified.

The key difference here vs. standard Qt widgets is that we make changes directly to our data, and simply need to notify Qt that some change has occurred — updating the widget state is handled automatically.

Using Qt.DecorationRole

If you run the application you should now find that adding and deleting both work, but while completing items is working, there is no indication of it in the view. We need to update our model to provide the view with an indicator to display when an item is complete. The updated model is shown below.

```python
tick = QtGui.QImage('tick.png')


class TodoModel(QtCore.QAbstractListModel):
    def __init__(self, *args, todos=None, **kwargs):
        super(TodoModel, self).__init__(*args, **kwargs)
        self.todos = todos or []

    def data(self, index, role):
        if role == Qt.DisplayRole:
            _, text = self.todos[index.row()]
            return text

        if role == Qt.DecorationRole:
            status, _ = self.todos[index.row()]
            if status:
                return tick

    def rowCount(self, index):
        return len(self.todos)
```

We're using a tick icon `tick.png` to indicate completed items, which we load into a `QImage` object named `tick`. In the model we've implemented a handler for the `Qt.DecorationRole` which returns the tick icon for rows who's `status` is `True` (for complete).

> The icon I'm using is taken from the Fugue set by p.yusukekamiyamane [http://p.yusukekamiyamane.com/]

> Instead of an icon you can also return a color, e.g. `QtGui.QColor('green')` which will be drawn as solid square.

Running the app you should now be able to mark items as complete.

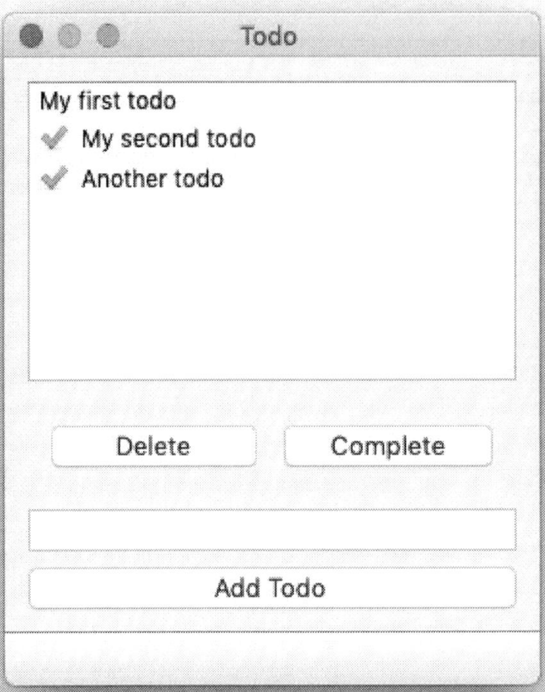

Figure 144. Todos complete

A persistent data store

Our todo app works nicely, but it has one fatal flaw — it forgets your todos as soon as you close the application While thinking you have nothing to do when you do may help to contribute to short-term feelings of Zen, long term it's probably a bad idea.

The solution is to implement some sort of persistent data store. The simplest approach is a simple file store, where we load items from a JSON or Pickle file at startup and write back any changes.

To do this we define two new methods on our `MainWindow` class — `load` and `save`. These load data from a JSON file name `data.json` (if it exists, ignoring the error if it doesn't) to `self.model.todos` and write the current `self.model.todos` out to the same file, respectively.

```
    def load(self):
        try:
            with open('data.json', 'r') as f:
                self.model.todos = json.load(f)
        except Exception:
            pass

    def save(self):
        with open('data.json', 'w') as f:
            data = json.dump(self.model.todos, f)
```

To persist the changes to the data we need to add the `.save()` handler to the end of any method that modifies the data, and the `.load()` handler to the `__init__` block after the model has been created.

The final code looks like this —

Listing 75. mode-views/todo_complete.py

```
import json
import sys

from PyQt5 import QtCore, QtGui, QtWidgets
from PyQt5.QtCore import Qt

from MainWindow import Ui_MainWindow

tick = QtGui.QImage("tick.png")


class TodoModel(QtCore.QAbstractListModel):
    def __init__(self, todos=None):
        super().__init__()
        self.todos = todos or []

    def data(self, index, role):
        if role == Qt.DisplayRole:
            _, text = self.todos[index.row()]
            return text

        if role == Qt.DecorationRole:
```

```
            status, _ = self.todos[index.row()]
            if status:
                return tick

    def rowCount(self, index):
        return len(self.todos)


class MainWindow(QtWidgets.QMainWindow, Ui_MainWindow):
    def __init__(self):
        super().__init__()

        self.setupUi(self)
        self.model = TodoModel()
        self.load()
        self.todoView.setModel(self.model)
        self.addButton.pressed.connect(self.add)
        self.deleteButton.pressed.connect(self.delete)
        self.completeButton.pressed.connect(self.complete)

    def add(self):
        """
        Add an item to our todo list, getting the text from the
QLineEdit .todoEdit
        and then clearing it.
        """
        text = self.todoEdit.text()
        if text:  # Don't add empty strings.
            # Access the list via the model.
            self.model.todos.append((False, text))
            # Trigger refresh.
            self.model.layoutChanged.emit()
            # Empty the input
            self.todoEdit.setText("")
            self.save()

    def delete(self):
        indexes = self.todoView.selectedIndexes()
        if indexes:
            # Indexes is a list of a single item in single-select
mode.
            index = indexes[0]
            # Remove the item and refresh.
```

```
            del self.model.todos[index.row()]
            self.model.layoutChanged.emit()
            # Clear the selection (as it is no longer valid).
            self.todoView.clearSelection()
            self.save()

    def complete(self):
        indexes = self.todoView.selectedIndexes()
        if indexes:
            index = indexes[0]
            row = index.row()
            status, text = self.model.todos[row]
            self.model.todos[row] = (True, text)
            # .dataChanged takes top-left and bottom right, which are
equal
            # for a single selection.
            self.model.dataChanged.emit(index, index)
            # Clear the selection (as it is no longer valid).
            self.todoView.clearSelection()
            self.save()

    def load(self):
        try:
            with open("data.json", "r") as f:
                self.model.todos = json.load(f)
        except Exception:
            pass

    def save(self):
        with open("data.json", "w") as f:
            data = json.dump(self.model.todos, f)


app = QtWidgets.QApplication(sys.argv)
window = MainWindow()
window.show()
app.exec_()
```

If the data in your application has the potential to get large or more complex, you may prefer to use an actual database to store it. Qt provides models for interacting with SQL databases which we'll cover shortly.

For another interesting example of a QListView see my example media player application [https://www.learnpyqt.com/apps/failamp-multimedia-player/]. This uses the Qt built-in QMediaPlaylist as the datastore, with the contents displayed to a QListView.

22. Tabular data in ModelViews, with numpy & pandas

In the previous section we covered an introduction to the Model View architecture. However, we only touched on one of the model views — `QListView`. There are two other Model Views available in Qt5 — `QTableView` and `QTreeView` which provide tabular (Excel-like) and tree (file directory browser-like) views using the same `QStandardItemModel`.

In this part we'll look at how to use `QTableView` from PyQt5, including how to model your data, format values for display and add conditional formatting.

You can use model views with *any* data source, as long as your model returns that data in a format that Qt can understand. Working with tabular data in Python opens up a number of possibilities for how we load and work with that data. Here we'll start with a simple nested `list` of `list` and then move onto integrating your Qt application with the popular *numpy* and *pandas* libraries. This will provide you with a great foundation for building data-focused applications.

Introduction to `QTableView`

`QTableView` is a Qt view widget which presents data in a spreadsheet-like table view. Like all widgets in the *Model View Architecture* this uses a separate *model* to provide data and presentation information to the view. Data in the model can be updated as required, and the view notified of these changes to redraw/display the changes. By customizing the model it is possible to have a huge amount of control over how the data is presented.

To use the model we'll need a basic application structure and some dummy data. A simple working example is shown below, which defines a custom model with a simple nested-list as a data store.

Listing 76. tableview_demo.py

```
import sys
from PyQt5 import QtCore, QtGui, QtWidgets
from PyQt5.QtCore import Qt


class TableModel(QtCore.QAbstractTableModel):
    def __init__(self, data):
        super().__init__()
        self._data = data

    def data(self, index, role):
        if role == Qt.DisplayRole:
            # See below for the nested-list data structure.
            # .row() indexes into the outer list,
            # .column() indexes into the sub-list
            return self._data[index.row()][index.column()]

    def rowCount(self, index):
        # The length of the outer list.
        return len(self._data)

    def columnCount(self, index):
        # The following takes the first sub-list, and returns
        # the length (only works if all rows are an equal length)
        return len(self._data[0])


class MainWindow(QtWidgets.QMainWindow):
    def __init__(self):
        super().__init__()

        self.table = QtWidgets.QTableView()

        data = [
            [4, 9, 2],
            [1, -1, -1],
            [3, 5, -5],
            [3, 3, 2],
            [7, 8, 9],
        ]
```

```
        self.model = TableModel(data)
        self.table.setModel(self.model)

        self.setCentralWidget(self.table)


app = QtWidgets.QApplication(sys.argv)
window = MainWindow()
window.show()
app.exec_()
```

As in our earlier model view examples, we create the `QTableView` widget, then create an instance of our custom model (which we've written to accept the data source as a parameter) and then we set the model on the view. That's all we need to do — the view widget now uses the model to get the data, and determine how to draw it.

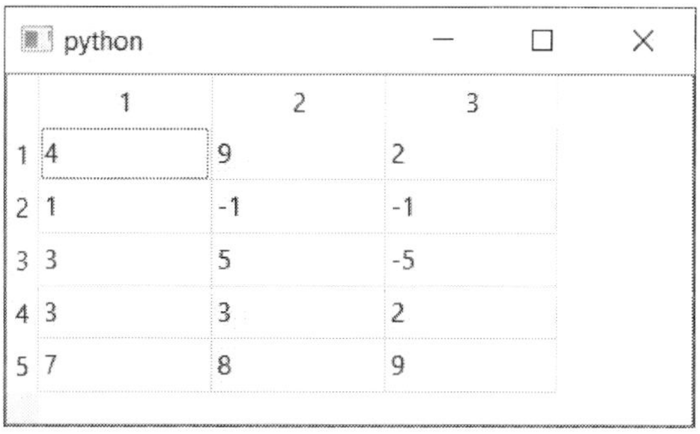

Figure 145. Basic table example

Nested `list` as a 2-dimensional data store

For a table you need a 2D data structure, with columns and rows. As shown in the example above you can model a simple 2D data structure using a nested Python `list`. We'll take a minute to look at this data structure, and it's limitations, below —

```
table = [
  [4, 1, 3, 3, 7],
  [9, 1, 5, 3, 8],
  [2, 1, 5, 3, 9],
]
```

The nested list is a "list of lists of values" — an outer list containing a number of sub-lists which themselves contain the values. With this structure, to index into individual values (or "cells") you must index twice, first to return one of the inner `list` objects and then again to index into that `list`.

The typical arrangement is for the outer list to hold the *rows* and each nested list to contain the values for the *columns*. With this arrangement when you index, you index first by *row*, then by *column* — making our example `table` a 3 row, 5 column table. Helpfully, this matches the visual layout in the source code.

The first index into the table will return a nested sub-list —

```
row = 2
col = 4

>>> table[row]
[2, 1, 5, 3, 9]
```

Which you then index again to return the value —

```
>>> table[row][col]
9
```

Note that using this type of structure you can't easily return an entire *column*, you would instead need to iterate all the rows. However, you are of course free to flip things on their head and use the first index as *column* depending on whether accessing by column or row is more useful to you.

```
table = [
  [4, 9, 2],
  [1, 1, 1],
  [3, 5, 5],
  [3, 3, 2],
  [7, 8, 9],
]

row = 4  # reversed
col = 2  # reversed

>>> table[col]
[3, 5, 5]

>>> table[col][row]
9
```

> Nothing about this data structure enforces equal row or column lengths — one row can be 5 elements long, another 200. Inconsistencies can lead to unexpected errors on the table view. See the alternative data stores later if you're working with large or complex data tables.

Next we'll look in a bit more detail at our custom `TableModel` and see how it works with this simple data structure to display the values.

Writing a custom `QAbstractTableModel`

In the *Model View Architecture* the model is responsible for providing both the data and presentation metadata for display by the view. In order to interface between our data object and the view we need to write our own custom model, which understands the structure of our data.

To write our custom model we can create a subclass of `QAbstractTableModel`. The only *required* methods for a custom table model are `data`, `rowCount` and `columnCount`. The first returns data (or presentation information) for given locations in the table, while the latter two must return a single integer value for the dimensions of the data source.

```
class TableModel(QtCore.QAbstractTableModel):

    def __init__(self, data):
        super(TableModel, self).__init__()
        self._data = data

    def data(self, index, role):
        if role == Qt.DisplayRole:
            # See below for the nested-list data structure.
            # .row() indexes into the outer list,
            # .column() indexes into the sub-list
            return self._data[index.row()][index.column()]

    def rowCount(self, index):
        # The length of the outer list.
        return len(self._data)

    def columnCount(self, index):
        # The following takes the first sub-list, and returns
        # the length (only works if all rows are an equal length)
        return len(self._data[0])
```

`QtCore.QAbstractTableModel` is an *abstract base class* meaning it does not have implementations for the methods. If you try and use it directly, it will not work. You must sub-class it.

In the `__init__` constructor we accept a single parameter `data` which we store as the instance attribute `self._data` so we can access it from our methods. The passed in data structure is stored by reference, so any external changes will be reflected here.

To notify the model of changes you need to trigger the model's `layoutChanged` signal, using `self.model.layoutChanged.emit()`.

The `data` method is called with two values `index` and `role`. The `index` parameter gives the location in the table for which information is currently being requested, and has two methods .row() and .column() which give the row and column number *in the view* respectively. In our example the data is stored as a nested list, and the row and column indices are used to index as follows data[row][column].

The view has no knowledge of the structure of the source data, and is the responsibility of the model to translate between the view's *row* and *column* and the relevant positions in your own data store.

The role parameter describes what *kind* of information the method should return on this call. To get the data to display the view calls this model method with the role of Qt.DisplayRole. However, role can have many other values including Qt.BackgroundRole, Qt.CheckStateRole, Qt.DecorationRole, Qt.FontRole, Qt.TextAlignmentRole and Qt.ForegroundRole, which each expect particular values in response (see later).

> Qt.DisplayRole actually expects a string to be returned, although other basic Python types including float, int and bool will also be displayed using their default string representations. However, formatting these types to your strings is usually preferable.

We'll cover how to use these other role types later, for now it is only necessary to know that you **must** check the role type is Qt.DisplayRole before returning your data for display.

The two custom methods columnCount and rowCount return the number of columns and rows in our data structure. In the case of a nested list of list in the arrangement we're using here, the number of rows is simply the number of elements in the outer list, and the number of columns is the number of elements in **one of** the inner lists — assuming they are all equal.

> If these methods return values that are too high you will see out of bounds errors, if they return values that are too low, you'll see the table cut off.

Formatting numbers and dates

The data returned by the model for display is expected to be a string. While `int` and `float` values will also be displayed, using their default string representation, complex Python types will not. To display these, or to override the default formatting of `float` , `int` or `bool` values, you must format these to strings yourself.

You might be tempted to do this by converting your data to a table of strings in advance. However, by doing this you make it very difficult to continue working with the data in your table, whether for calculations or for updates.

Instead, you should use the model's `data` method to perform the string conversion on demand. By doing this you can continue to work with the original data, yet have complete control over how it is presented to the user — including changing this on the fly while through configuration.

Below is a simple custom formatter which looks up the values in our data table, and displays them in a number of different ways depending on the Python `type` of the data.

Listing 77. tableview_format_1.py

```
import sys
from datetime import datetime  ①

from PyQt5 import QtCore, QtGui, QtWidgets
from PyQt5.QtCore import Qt


class TableModel(QtCore.QAbstractTableModel):
    def __init__(self, data):
        super().__init__()
        self._data = data

    def data(self, index, role):
        if role == Qt.DisplayRole:
            # Get the raw value
            value = self._data[index.row()][index.column()]

            # Perform per-type checks and render accordingly.
            if isinstance(value, datetime):
                # Render time to YYY-MM-DD.
                return value.strftime("%Y-%m-%d")

            if isinstance(value, float):
                # Render float to 2 dp
                return "%.2f" % value

            if isinstance(value, str):
                # Render strings with quotes
                return '"%s"' % value

            # Default (anything not captured above: e.g. int)
            return value

    def rowCount(self, index):
        return len(self._data)

    def columnCount(self, index):
        return len(self._data[0])
```

① Note the additional import for `from datetime import datetime` at the top of the file.

Use this together with the modified sample data below to see it in action.

```
data = [
    [4, 9, 2],
    [1, -1, 'hello'],
    [3.023, 5, -5],
    [3, 3, datetime(2017,10,1)],
    [7.555, 8, 9],
]
```

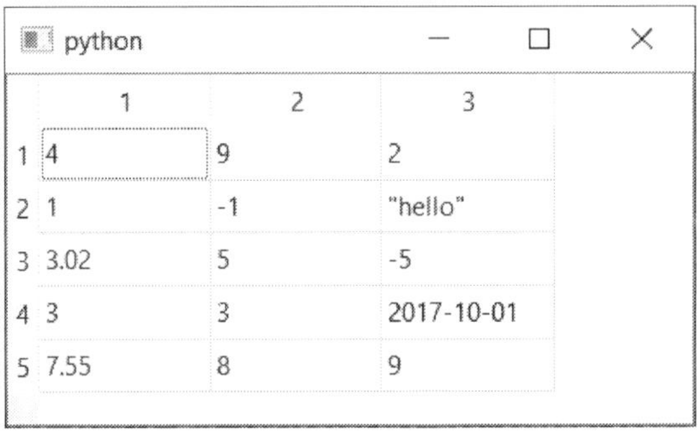

Figure 146. Custom data formatting

So far we've only looked at how we can customize how the data itself is formatted. However, the model interface gives you far more control over the display of table cells including colors and icons. In the next part we'll look at how to use the model to customize `QTableView` appearance.

Styles & Colors with Roles

Using colors and icons to highlight cells in data tables can help make data easier to find and understand, or help users to select or mark data of interest. Qt allows for complete control of all of these from the model, by responding to the relevant *role* on the `data` method.

The types expected to be returned in response to the various `role` types are shown below.

Role	Type

Qt.BackgroundRole	QBrush (also QColor)
Qt.CheckStateRole	Qt.CheckState
Qt.DecorationRole	QIcon, QPixmap, QColor
Qt.DisplayRole	QString (also int, float, bool)
Qt.FontRole	QFont
Qt.SizeHintRole	QSize
Qt.TextAlignmentRole	Qt.Alignment
Qt.ForegroundRole	QBrush (also QColor)

By responding to a particular combination of `role` and `index` we can modify the appearance of particular cells, columns or rows in the table — for example, setting a blue background for all cells in the 3rd column.

Listing 78. tableview_format_2.py

```
    def data(self, index, role):
        if role == Qt.BackgroundRole and index.column() == 2:
            # See below for the data structure.
            return QtGui.QColor(Qt.blue)

        # existing `if role == Qt.DisplayRole:` block hidden
        # hidden for clarity.
```

By using the `index` to lookup values from our own data, we can also customize appearance based on values in our data. We'll go through some of the more common use-cases below.

Text alignment

In our previous formatting examples we had used text formatting to display `float` down to 2 decimal places. However, it's also common when displaying numbers to right-align them, to make it easier to compare across lists of numbers. This can be accomplished by returning `Qt.AlignRight` in response to `Qt.TextAlignmentRole` for any numeric values.

The modified data method is shown below. We check for `role == Qt.TextAlignmentRole` and look up the value by index as before, then determine if the value is numeric. If it is we can return `Qt.AlignVCenter + Qt.AlignRight` to align in the middle vertically, and on the right horizontally.

Listing 79. tableview_format_3.py

```
    def data(self, index, role):
        if role == Qt.TextAlignmentRole:
            value = self._data[index.row()][index.column()]

            if isinstance(value, int) or isinstance(value, float):
                # Align right, vertical middle.
                return Qt.AlignVCenter | Qt.AlignRight

        # existing `if role == Qt.DisplayRole:` block hidden
        # hidden for clarity.
```

Other alignments are possible, including `Qt.AlignHCenter` to align center horizontally. You can combine them together by adding them together e.g. `Qt.AlignBottom + Qt.AlignRight`.

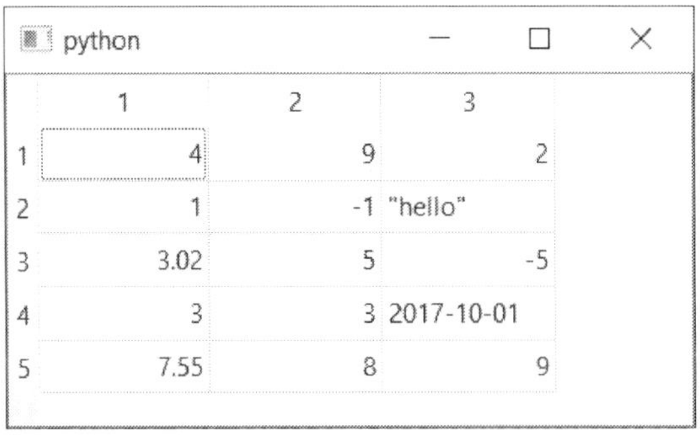

Figure 147. QTableView cell alignment

Text colors

If you've used spreadsheets like Excel you might be familiar with the concept of *conditional formatting*. These are rules you can apply to cells (or rows, or columns) which change text and background colors of cells depending on their value.

This can be useful to help visualize data, for example using red for negative numbers or highlighting ranges of numbers (e.g. low … high) with a gradient of blue to red.

First, the below example implements a `Qt.ForegroundRole` handler which checks if the value in the indexed cell is numeric, and below zero. If it is, then the handler returns the text (foreground) color red.

Listing 80. tableview_format_4.py

```
    def data(self, index, role):
        if role == Qt.ForegroundRole:
            value = self._data[index.row()][index.column()]

            if (isinstance(value, int) or isinstance(value, float))
and value < 0:
                return QtGui.QColor("red")

        # existing `if role == Qt.DisplayRole:` block hidden
        # hidden for clarity.
```

If you add this to your model's data handler, all negative numbers will now appear red.

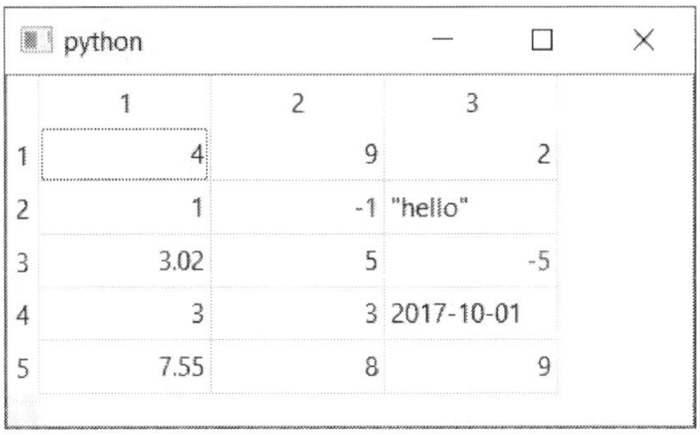

Figure 148. QTableView text formatting, with red negative numbers

Number range gradients

The same principle can be used to apply gradients to numeric values in a table to, for example, highlight low and high values. First we define our color scale, which is taken from colorbrewer2.org [http://colorbrewer2.org/#

type=diverging&scheme=RdBu&n=11].

```
COLORS = ['#053061', '#2166ac', '#4393c3', '#92c5de', '#d1e5f0',
'#f7f7f7', '#fddbc7', '#f4a582', '#d6604d', '#b2182b', '#67001f']
```

Next we define our custom handler, this time for `Qt.BackgroundRole`. This takes the value at the given index, checks that this is numeric then performs a series of operations to constrain it to the range 0…10 required to index into our list.

Listing 81. tableview_format_5.py

```
    def data(self, index, role):
        if role == Qt.BackgroundRole:
            value = self._data[index.row()][index.column()]
            if isinstance(value, int) or isinstance(value, float):
                value = int(value)  # Convert to integer for
indexing.

                # Limit to range -5 ... +5, then convert to 0..10
                value = max(-5, value)  # values < -5 become -5
                value = min(5, value)  # valaues > +5 become +5
                value = value + 5  # -5 becomes 0, +5 becomes + 10

                return QtGui.QColor(COLORS[value])

        # existing `if role == Qt.DisplayRole:` block hidden
        # hidden for clarity.
```

The logic used here for converting the value to the gradient is very basic, cutting off high/low values, and not adjusting to the range of the data. However, you can adapt this as needed, as long as the end result of your handler is to return a `QColor` or `QBrush`

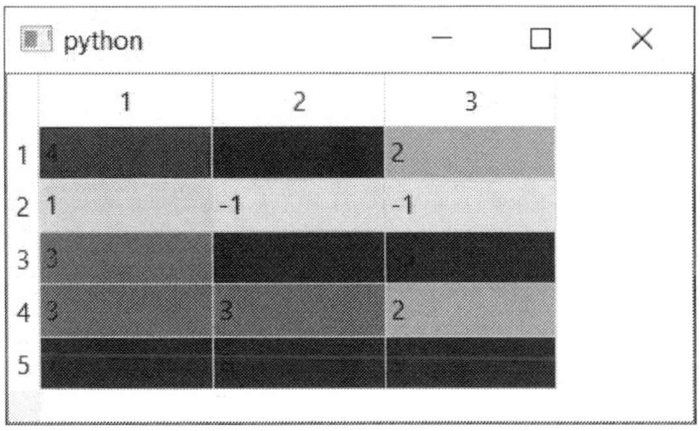

Figure 149. QTableView with number-range color gradients

Icon & Image decoration

Each table cell contains a small *decoration* area which can be used to display icons, images or a solid block of color, on the left hand side next to the data. This can be used to indicate data type, e.g. calendars for dates, ticks and crosses for `bool` values, or for a more subtle conditional-formatting for number ranges.

Below are some simple implementations of these ideas.

Indicating bool/date data types with icons

For dates we'll use Python's built-in `datetime` type. First, add the following import to the top of your file to import this type.

```
from datetime import datetime
```

Then, update the data (set in the `MainWindow.__init__`) to add `datetime` and `bool` (`True` or `False` values), for example.

```
data = [
    [True, 9, 2],
    [1, 0, -1],
    [3, 5, False],
    [3, 3, 2],
    [datetime(2019, 5, 4), 8, 9],
]
```

With these in place, you can update your model `data` method to show icons and formatted dates for date types, with the following.

Listing 82. tableview_format_6.py

```python
    def data(self, index, role):
        if role == Qt.DisplayRole:
            value = self._data[index.row()][index.column()]
            if isinstance(value, datetime):
                return value.strftime("%Y-%m-%d")

            return value

        if role == Qt.DecorationRole:
            value = self._data[index.row()][index.column()]
            if isinstance(value, datetime):
                return QtGui.QIcon("calendar.png")
```

Figure 150. QTableView formatted dates with indicator icon

The following shows how to use ticks and cross for boolean `True` and `False` values respectively.

Listing 83. tableview_format_7.py

```
    def data(self, index, role):
        if role == Qt.DecorationRole:
            value = self._data[index.row()][index.column()]
            if isinstance(value, bool):
                if value:
                    return QtGui.QIcon("tick.png")

                return QtGui.QIcon("cross.png")
```

You can of course combine the above together, or any other mix of `Qt.DecorationRole` and `Qt.DisplayRole` handlers. It's usually simpler to keep each type grouped under the same *if* branch, or as your model becomes more complex, to create sub-methods to handle each role.

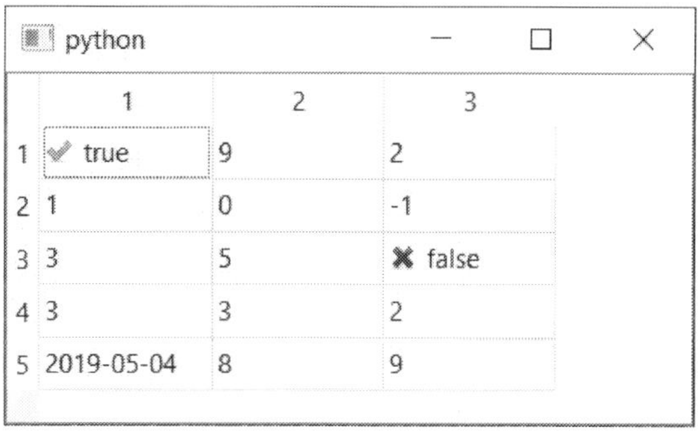

Figure 151. QTableView boolean indicators

Color blocks

If you return a `QColor` for `Qt.DecorationRole` a small square of color will be displayed on the left hand side of the cell, in the icon location. This is identical to the earlier `Qt.BackgroundRole` conditional formatting example, except now handling and responding to `Qt.DecorationRole`.

Listing 84. tableview_format_8.py

```python
    def data(self, index, role):
        if role == Qt.DecorationRole:
            value = self._data[index.row()][index.column()]

            if isinstance(value, datetime):
                return QtGui.QIcon("calendar.png")

            if isinstance(value, bool):
                if value:
                    return QtGui.QIcon("tick.png")

                return QtGui.QIcon("cross.png")

            if isinstance(value, int) or isinstance(value, float):
                value = int(value)

                # Limit to range -5 ... +5, then convert to 0..10
                value = max(-5, value)  # values < -5 become -5
                value = min(5, value)  # valaues > +5 become +5
                value = value + 5  # -5 becomes 0, +5 becomes + 10

                return QtGui.QColor(COLORS[value])
```

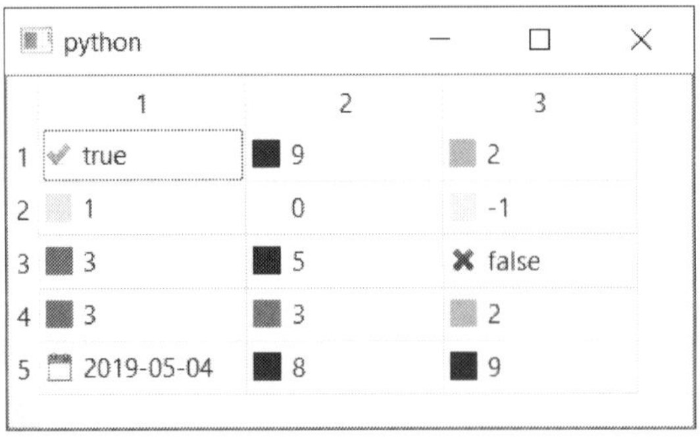

Figure 152. QTableView color block decorations

Alternative Python data structures

So far in our examples we've used simple nested Python lists to hold our data for display. This is fine for simple tables of data, however if you're working with large data tables there are some other better options in Python, which come with additional benefits. In the next parts we'll look at two Python data table libraries — *numpy* and *pandas* — and how to integrate these with Qt.

Numpy

Numpy is a library which provides support for large multi-dimensional arrays or matrix data structures in Python. The efficient and high-performance handling of large arrays makes *numpy* ideal for scientific and mathematical applications. This also makes *numpy* arrays an good data store for large, single-typed, data tables in PyQt5.

Using numpy as a data source

To support *numpy* arrays we need to make a number of changes to the model, first modifying the indexing in the `data` method, and then changing the row and column count calculations for `rowCount` and `columnCount`.

The standard *numpy* API provides element-level access to 2D arrays, by passing the row and column in the same slicing operation, e.g. `_data[index.row(), index.column()]`. This is more efficient than indexing in two steps, as for the `list` of `list` examples.

In *numpy* the dimensions of an array are available through `.shape` which returns a tuple of dimensions along each axis in turn. We get the length of each axis by selecting the correct item from this tuple, e.g. `_data.shape[0]` gets the size of the first axis.

The following complete example shows how to display a *numpy* array using Qt's `QTableView` via a custom model.

Listing 85. model-views/tableview_numpy.py

```
import sys

import numpy as np
from PyQt5 import QtCore, QtGui, QtWidgets
from PyQt5.QtCore import Qt
```

```
class TableModel(QtCore.QAbstractTableModel):
    def __init__(self, data):
        super().__init__()
        self._data = data

    def data(self, index, role):
        if role == Qt.DisplayRole:
            # Note: self._data[index.row()][index.column()] will also
work
            value = self._data[index.row(), index.column()]
            return str(value)

    def rowCount(self, index):
        return self._data.shape[0]

    def columnCount(self, index):
        return self._data.shape[1]


class MainWindow(QtWidgets.QMainWindow):
    def __init__(self):
        super().__init__()

        self.table = QtWidgets.QTableView()

        data = np.array([[1, 9, 2], [1, 0, -1], [3, 5, 2], [3, 3, 2],
[5, 8, 9],])

        self.model = TableModel(data)
        self.table.setModel(self.model)

        self.setCentralWidget(self.table)
        self.setGeometry(600, 100, 400, 200)


app = QtWidgets.QApplication(sys.argv)
window = MainWindow()
window.show()
app.exec_()
```

> ℹ While simple Python types such as `int` and `float` are displayed without converting to strings, *numpy* uses it's own types (e.g. `numpy.int32`) for array values. In order for these to be displayed we **must** first convert them to strings.

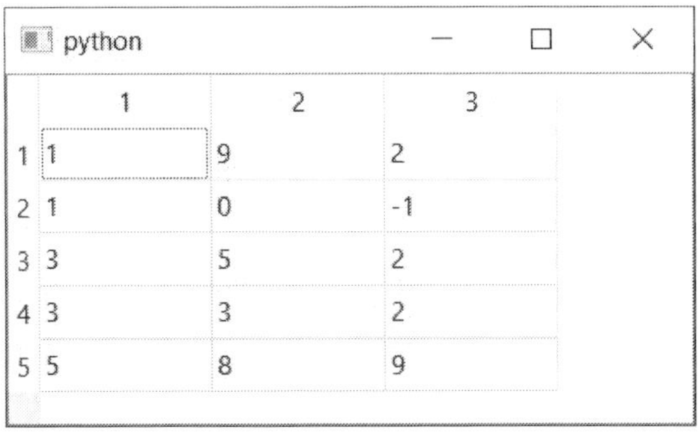

	1	2	3
1	1	9	2
2	1	0	-1
3	3	5	2
4	3	3	2
5	5	8	9

Figure 153. QTableView with numpy array

> 💡 With `QTableView` only 2D arrays can be displayed, however if you have a higher dimensional data structure you can combine the `QTableView` with a tabbed or scrollbar UI, to allow access to and display of these higher dimensions.

Pandas

Pandas is a Python library commonly used for data manipulation and analysis. It provides a nice API for loading 2D tabular data from various data sources and performing data analysis on it. By using the *numpy* `DataTable` as your `QTableView` model you can use these APIs to load and analyse your data from right within your application.

Using Pandas as a data source

The modifications of the model to work with *numpy* are fairly minor, requiring changes to the indexing in the `data` method and modifications to `rowCount` and `columnCount`. The changes for `rowCount` and `columnCount` are identical to *numpy* with *pandas* using a `_data.shape` tuple to represent the dimensions of the data.

For indexing we use the *pandas* `.iloc` method, for indexed locations — i.e.

lookup by column and/or row index. This is done by passing the row, and then column to the slice `_data.iloc[index.row(), index.column()]`.

The following complete example shows how to display a *pandas* data frame using Qt `QTableView` via a custom model.

Listing 86. model-views/tableview_pandas.py

```
import sys

import pandas as pd
from PyQt5 import QtCore, QtGui, QtWidgets
from PyQt5.QtCore import Qt


class TableModel(QtCore.QAbstractTableModel):
    def __init__(self, data):
        super().__init__()
        self._data = data

    def data(self, index, role):
        if role == Qt.DisplayRole:
            value = self._data.iloc[index.row(), index.column()]
            return str(value)

    def rowCount(self, index):
        return self._data.shape[0]

    def columnCount(self, index):
        return self._data.shape[1]

    def headerData(self, section, orientation, role):
        if role == Qt.DisplayRole:
            if orientation == Qt.Horizontal:
                return str(self._data.columns[section])

            if orientation == Qt.Vertical:
                return str(self._data.index[section])


class MainWindow(QtWidgets.QMainWindow):
    def __init__(self):
```

```python
        super().__init__()

        self.table = QtWidgets.QTableView()

        data = pd.DataFrame(
            [[1, 9, 2], [1, 0, -1], [3, 5, 2], [3, 3, 2], [5, 8,
9],],
            columns=["A", "B", "C"],
            index=["Row 1", "Row 2", "Row 3", "Row 4", "Row 5"],
        )

        self.model = TableModel(data)
        self.table.setModel(self.model)

        self.setCentralWidget(self.table)
        self.setGeometry(600, 100, 400, 200)


app = QtWidgets.QApplication(sys.argv)
window = MainWindow()
window.show()
app.exec_()
```

An interesting extension here is to use the table header of the `QTableView` to display row and *pandas* column header values, which can be taken from `DataFrame.index` and `DataFrame.columns` respectively.

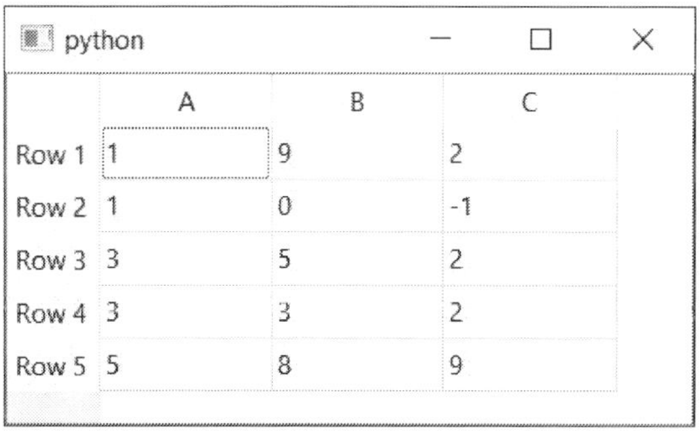

Figure 154. QTableView pandas DataTable, with column and row headers

For this we need to implement a `Qt.DisplayRole` handler in a custom `headerData` method. This receives `section`, the index of the row/column (0…n), `orientation` which can be either `Qt.Horizontal` for the column headers, or `Qt.Vertical` for the row headers, and `role` which works the same as for the `data` method.

> The `headerData` method also receives other roles, which can be used to customize the appearance of the headers further.

Conclusion

In this chapter we've covered the basics of using `QTableView` and a custom model to display tabular data in your applications. This was extended to demonstrate how to format data and decorate cells with icons and colors. Finally, we demonstrated using `QTableView` with tabular data from *numpy* and *pandas* structures including displaying custom column and row headers.

> If you want to run calculations on your table data, take a look at Using the thread pool.

23. Querying SQL databases with Qt models

So far we've used table models to access data loaded or stored in the application itself—from simple lists of lists to *numpy* and *pandas* tables. However, all of these approaches have in common that the data that you are viewing must be loaded entirely into memory.

To simplify interaction with SQL databases Qt provides a number of SQL models which can be connected to views to display the output of SQL queries, or database tables. In this chapter we'll look at two alternatives—displaying database data in a `QTableView` and with `QDataWidgetMapper` which allows you to map database fields to Qt widgets.

Which model you use depends on whether you want read-only access to a database, read-write access or read-only access with relationships (querying more than one table). In the next sections we'll look at each of those options in turn.

The following examples start from this simple skeleton, showing a table view in a window, but with no model set.

Listing 87. databases/tableview.py

```
import sys
from PyQt5.QtWidgets import QMainWindow, QApplication, QTableView
from PyQt5.QtCore import Qt


class MainWindow(QMainWindow):
    def __init__(self):
        super().__init__()

        self.table = QTableView()

        # self.model = ?
        # self.table.setModel(self.model)

        self.setCentralWidget(self.table)


app = QApplication(sys.argv)
window = MainWindow()
window.show()
app.exec_()
```

Before we connect a model, running this will just show an empty window.

> For these examples we're using a SQLite file database `demo.sqlite` which is included in the downloads for this book.

> You can use your own database if you prefer, including both SQLite databases or database servers (PostgreSQL, MySQL, etc.). See Authenticating with `QSqlDatabase` for instructions on how to connect to remote servers.

Connecting to a database

To be able to display data from a database in your app, you must first connect with it. Both server (IP, e.g. PostgreSQL or MySQL) and file-based (SQLite) databases are supported by Qt, the only difference being in how you set them up.

For all these examples we're using the Chinook sample database [https://github.com/lerocha/chinook-database]—a sample database designed for testing and demos. The database represents a digital media store, including tables for artists, albums, media tracks, invoices and customers.

> A copy of the SQLite version of this database is included in the code with this book, named `chinook.sqlite`. You can also download the latest version from here [https://github.com/lerocha/chinook-database/raw/master/ChinookDatabase/DataSources/Chinook_Sqlite.sqlite].

```
from PyQt5.QtSql import QSqlDatabase

db = QSqlDatabase("QSQLITE")
db.setDatabaseName("chinook.sqlite")
db.open()
```

> Where you place this code will depend on your application. Often you want to create a single database connection and use it throughout your app—in this case it's best to create a separate module, e.g. db.py to hold this (and other related functionality).

The process is the same for all databases—create the database object, set the name and the *open* the database to initialize the connection. However, if you want to connect to a remote database there are a few extra parameters. See Authenticating with `QSqlDatabase` for more information.

Displaying a table with `QSqlTableModel`

The simplest thing you can do once you've connected your app to a database store, is to display a single table in your application. To do this we can use `QSqlTableModel`. This model displays data directly from the table, allowing editing.

First we need to create the instance of the table mode, passing in the database we've created above. Then we need to set the table to query from—this is the name of the table in the database, here <table name>. Finally we need to call `.select()` on the model.

```
model = QSqlTableModel(db=db)
model.setTable('<table name>')
model.select()
```

By calling `.select()` we tell the model to query the database and keep the result, ready for display. To display this data in a `QTableView` we simply need to pass it to the views `.setModel()` method.

```
table = QTableView()
table.setModel(self.model)
```

The data will be displayed in the table model and can be browsed using the scrollbar. See below for the full code, which loads the database and displays the *track* table in the view.

Listing 88. tableview_tablemodel.py

```
import sys

from PyQt5.QtCore import QSize, Qt
from PyQt5.QtSql import QSqlDatabase, QSqlTableModel
from PyQt5.QtWidgets import QApplication, QMainWindow, QTableView

db = QSqlDatabase("QSQLITE")
db.setDatabaseName("chinook.sqlite")
db.open()


class MainWindow(QMainWindow):
    def __init__(self):
        super().__init__()

        self.table = QTableView()

        self.model = QSqlTableModel(db=db)

        self.table.setModel(self.model)

        self.model.setTable("Track")
        self.model.select()

        self.setMinimumSize(QSize(1024, 600))
        self.setCentralWidget(self.table)


app = QApplication(sys.argv)
window = MainWindow()
window.show()
app.exec_()
```

This will give you the following window when run.

	TrackId	Name	AlbumId	MediaTypeId	GenreId	Composer	Milliseconds	Bytes
1	1	To Rock (We ...	1	1	1	Malcolm Young,...	343719	11170334
2	2	Balls to the Wall	2	2	1		342562	5510424
3	3	Fast As a Shark	3	2	1	Kaufman, U. Dirkscneider & ...	230619	3990994
4	4	Restless and Wild	3	2	1	Kaufman, U. ...	252051	4331779
5	5	Princess of the Dawn	3	2	1	Deaffy & R.A. Smith-Diesel	375418	6290521
6	6	Put The Finger On You	1	1	1	Malcolm Young,...	205662	6713451
7	7	Let's Get It Up	1	1	1	Malcolm Young,...	233926	7636561
8	8	Inject The Venom	1	1	1	Malcolm Young,...	210834	6852860
9	9	Snowballed	1	1	1	Malcolm Young,...	203102	6599424
10	10	Evil Walks	1	1	1	Malcolm Young,...	263497	8611245
11	11	C.O.D.	1	1	1	Malcolm Young,...	199836	6566314
12	12	Breaking The Rules	1	1	1	Malcolm Young,...	263288	8596840
13	13	Night Of The Long Knives	1	1	1	Malcolm Young,...	205688	6706347
14	14	Spellbound	1	1	1	Malcolm Young,...	270863	8817038
15	15	Go Down	4	1	1	AC/DC	331180	10847611

Figure 155. The tracks table displayed in a `QTableView`*.*

> You can resize the columns by dragging the right hand edge. Resize to fit the contents by double-clicking on the right hand edge.

Editing the data

Database data displayed in a `QTableView` is editable by default—just double-click on any cell and you will be able to modify the contents. The changes are persisted back to the database immediately after you finish editing.

Qt provides some control over this editing behavior, which you may want to change depending on the type of app you are building. Qt terms these behaviors *editing strategy* and they can be one of the following -

Strategy	**Description**
`QSqlTableModel.OnFieldChange`	Changes are applied automatically, when the user deselects the edited cell.
`QSqlTableModel.OnRowChange`	Changes are applied automatically, when the user selects a different row.

Strategy	Description
`QSqlTableModel.OnManualSubmit`	Changes are cached in the model, and written to the database only when `.submitAll()` is called, or discarded when `revertAll()` is called.

You can set the current edit strategy for the model by calling `.setEditStrategy` on it. For example—

```
self.model.setEditStrategy(QSqlTableModel.OnRowChange)
```

Sorting columns

To sort the table by a given column, we can call `.setSort()` on the model, passing in the column index and `Qt.AscendingOrder` or `Qt.DescendingOrder`.

Listing 89. databases/tableview_tablemodel_sort.py

```
import sys

from PyQt5.QtCore import QSize, Qt
from PyQt5.QtSql import QSqlDatabase, QSqlTableModel
from PyQt5.QtWidgets import QApplication, QMainWindow, QTableView

db = QSqlDatabase("QSQLITE")
db.setDatabaseName("chinook.sqlite")
db.open()


class MainWindow(QMainWindow):
    def __init__(self):
        super().__init__()

        self.table = QTableView()

        self.model = QSqlTableModel(db=db)

        self.table.setModel(self.model)

        # tag::sortTable[]
        self.model.setTable("Track")
        self.model.setSort(2, Qt.DescendingOrder)
        self.model.select()
        # end::sortTable[]

        self.setMinimumSize(QSize(1024, 600))
        self.setCentralWidget(self.table)


app = QApplication(sys.argv)
window = MainWindow()
window.show()
app.exec_()
```

This must be done *before* the call to `.select()`. If you want to sort after you've got the data, you can perform another `.select()` call to refresh.

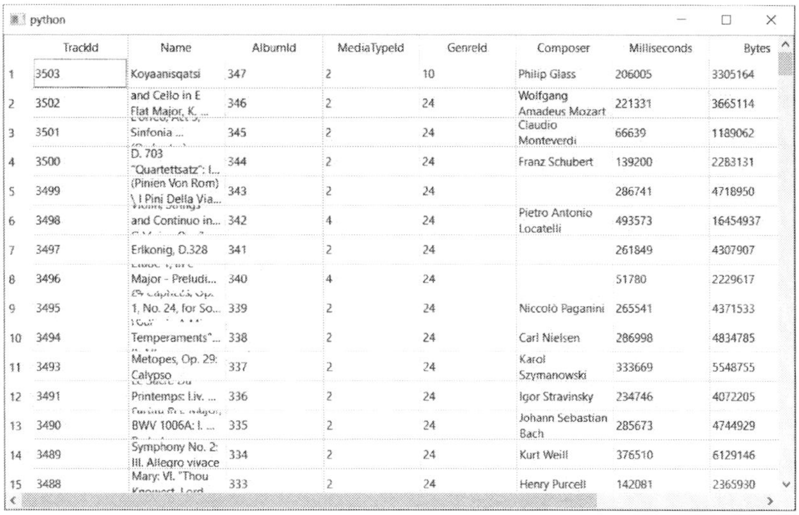

	TrackId	Name	AlbumId	MediaTypeId	GenreId	Composer	Milliseconds	Bytes
1	3503	Koyaanisqatsi	347	2	10	Philip Glass	206005	3305164
2	3502	and Cello in E Flat Major, K. ...	346	2	24	Wolfgang Amadeus Mozart	221331	3665114
3	3501	Sinfonia ...	345	2	24	Claudio Monteverdi	66639	1189062
4	3500	D. 703 "Quartettsatz": I...	344	2	24	Franz Schubert	139200	2283131
5	3499	(Pinien Von Rom) \ I Pini Della Via...	343	2	24		286741	4718950
6	3498	and Continuo in...	342	4	24	Pietro Antonio Locatelli	493573	16454937
7	3497	Erlkonig, D.328	341	2	24		261849	4307907
8	3496	Major - Preludi...	340	4	24		51780	2229617
9	3495	1, No. 24, for So...	339	2	24	Niccolò Paganini	265541	4371533
10	3494	Temperaments"...	338	2	24	Carl Nielsen	286998	4834785
11	3493	Metopes, Op. 29: Calypso	337	2	24	Karol Szymanowski	333669	5548755
12	3491	Printemps: I.iv. ...	336	2	24	Igor Stravinsky	234746	4072205
13	3490	BWV 1006A: I. ...	335	2	24	Johann Sebastian Bach	285673	4744929
14	3489	Symphony No. 2: III. Allegro vivace	334	2	24	Kurt Weill	376510	6129146
15	3488	Mary: VI. "Thou ...	333	2	24	Henry Purcell	142081	2365930

Figure 156. The tracks table sorted on column index 2, the `album_id`.

You may prefer to sort the table using the *column name* rather than the column index. To do this, you can look up the column index with the name.

Listing 90. databases/tableview_tablemodel_sortname.py

```
        self.model.setTable("Track")
        idx = self.model.fieldIndex("Milliseconds")
        self.model.setSort(idx, Qt.DescendingOrder)
        self.model.select()
```

The table is now sorted on the `milliseconds` column.

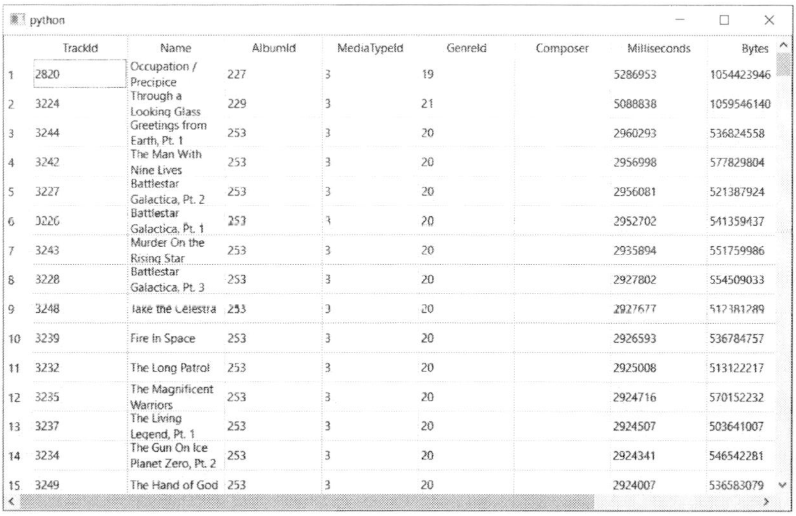

	TrackId	Name	AlbumId	MediaTypeId	GenreId	Composer	Milliseconds	Bytes
1	2820	Occupation / Precipice	227	3	19		5286953	1054423946
2	3224	Through a Looking Glass	229	3	21		5088838	1059546140
3	3244	Greetings from Earth, Pt. 1	253	3	20		2960293	536824558
4	3242	The Man With Nine Lives	253	3	20		2956998	577829804
5	3227	Battlestar Galactica, Pt. 2	253	3	20		2956081	521387924
6	3226	Battlestar Galactica, Pt. 1	253	3	20		2952702	541359437
7	3243	Murder On the Rising Star	253	3	20		2935894	551759986
8	3228	Battlestar Galactica, Pt. 3	253	3	20		2927802	554509033
9	3248	Take the Celestra	253	3	20		2927677	512381289
10	3239	Fire In Space	253	3	20		2926593	536784757
11	3232	The Long Patrol	253	3	20		2925008	513122217
12	3235	The Magnificent Warriors	253	3	20		2924716	570152232
13	3237	The Living Legend, Pt. 1	253	3	20		2924507	503641007
14	3234	The Gun On Ice Planet Zero, Pt. 2	253	3	20		2924341	546542281
15	3249	The Hand of God	253	3	20		2924007	536583079

Figure 157. The tracks table sorted on the `milliseconds` *column.*

Column titles

By default the column header titles on the table come from the column names in the database. Often this isn't very user-friendly, so you can replace them with proper titles using `.setHeaderData`, passing in the column index, the direction—horizontal (top) or vertical (left) header—and the label.

Listing 91. database/tableview_tablemodel_titles.py

```
        self.model.setTable("Track")
        self.model.setHeaderData(1, Qt.Horizontal, "Name")
        self.model.setHeaderData(2, Qt.Horizontal, "Album (ID)")
        self.model.setHeaderData(3, Qt.Horizontal, "Media Type (ID)")
        self.model.setHeaderData(4, Qt.Horizontal, "Genre (ID)")
        self.model.setHeaderData(5, Qt.Horizontal, "Composer")
        self.model.select()
```

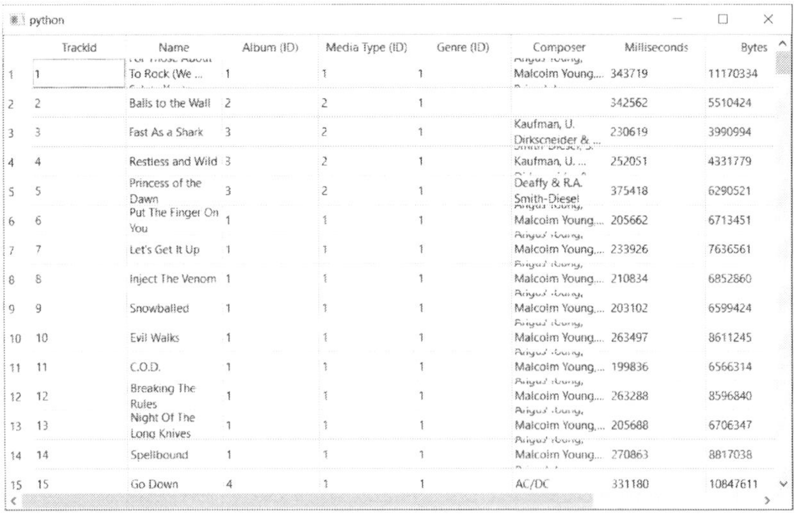

Figure 158. The tracks table with nicer column titles.

As when sorting, it is not always convenient to use the column indexes for this—if the column order changes on the database, the names set in your application will be out of sync.

As before, we can use `.fieldIndex()` to lookup the index for a given name. You can go a step further and define a Python `dict` of column name and title to apply in one go, when setting up the model.

Listing 92. database/tableview_tablemodel_titlesname.py

```
        self.model.setTable("Track")
        column_titles = {
            "Name": "Name",
            "AlbumId": "Album (ID)",
            "MediaTypeId": "Media Type (ID)",
            "GenreId": "Genre (ID)",
            "Composer": "Composer",
        }
        for n, t in column_titles.items():
            idx = self.model.fieldIndex(n)
            self.model.setHeaderData(idx, Qt.Horizontal, t)

        self.model.select()
```

Selecting columns

Often you will not want to display all the columns from a table. You can select which columns to display by removing columns from the model. To do this call `.removeColumns()` passing in the index of the first column to remove and the number of subsequent columns.

```
self.model.removeColumns(2, 5)
```

Once removed the columns will no longer be shown on the table. You can use the same name-lookup approach used for column labelling to remove columns by name.

```
columns_to_remove = ['name', 'something']

for cn in columns_to_remove:
    idx = self.model.fieldIndex(cn)
    self.model.removeColumns(idx, 1)
```

Removing columns in this way just removes them from the view. If you want to filter the columns out with SQL see the query models below.

Filtering a table

We can filter the table by calling `.setFilter()` on the model, passing in a parameter which describes the filter. The filter parameter can be any valid SQL `WHERE` clause without the `WHERE` prepended. For example `name="Martin"` to match exactly, or `name LIKE "Ma%"` to match fields beginning with "Ma".

In case you're not familiar with SQL, below are a few example search patterns you can use to perform different types of searches.

Pattern	Description
`field="{}"`	Field matches the string exactly.
`field LIKE "{}%"`	Field begins with the given string.
`field LIKE "%{}"`	Field ends with the given string.
`field LIKE "%{}%"`	Field contains the given string.

In each example {} is the search string, which you must interpolate using python `"{}".format(search_str)`. Unlike the sort, the filter will be applied automatically to the data, without the need to call `.select()` again.

If `.select()` hasn't been called yet, the filter will be applied the first time it is.

In the following example we add a `QLineEdit` field and hook this up to search the table on the track `name` field. We connect the line edit changed signal to construct and apply the filter to the model.

Listing 93. databases/tableview_tablemodel_filter.py

```
import sys
```

```python
from PyQt5.QtCore import QSize, Qt
from PyQt5.QtSql import QSqlDatabase, QSqlTableModel
from PyQt5.QtWidgets import (
    QApplication,
    QLineEdit,
    QMainWindow,
    QTableView,
    QVBoxLayout,
    QWidget,
)

db = QSqlDatabase("QSQLITE")
db.setDatabaseName("chinook.sqlite")
db.open()


class MainWindow(QMainWindow):
    def __init__(self):
        super().__init__()

        container = QWidget()
        layout = QVBoxLayout()

        self.search = QLineEdit()
        self.search.textChanged.connect(self.update_filter)
        self.table = QTableView()

        layout.addWidget(self.search)
        layout.addWidget(self.table)
        container.setLayout(layout)

        self.model = QSqlTableModel(db=db)

        self.table.setModel(self.model)

        self.model.setTable("Track")
        self.model.select()

        self.setMinimumSize(QSize(1024, 600))
        self.setCentralWidget(container)

    def update_filter(self, s):
        filter_str = 'Name LIKE "%{}%"'.format(s)
```

```
        self.model.setFilter(filter_str)


app = QApplication(sys.argv)
window = MainWindow()
window.show()
app.exec_()
```

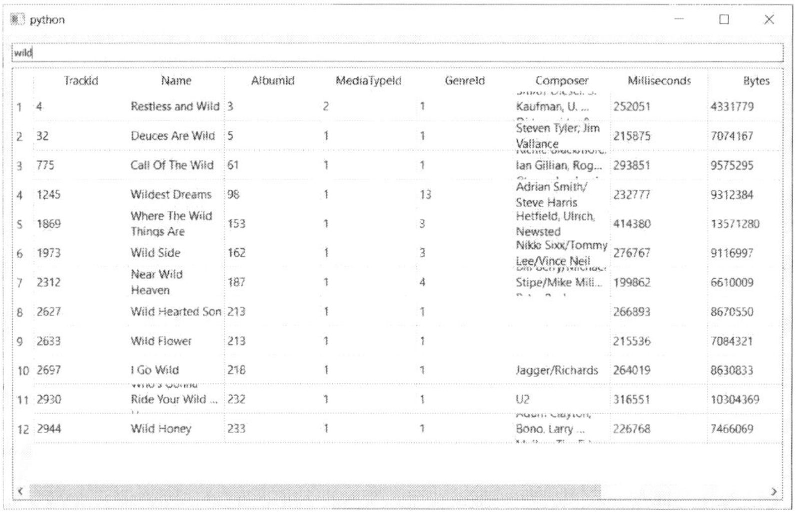

python

wild

	TrackId	Name	AlbumId	MediaTypeId	GenreId	Composer	Milliseconds	Bytes
1	4	Restless and Wild	3	2	1	Kaufman, U. ...	252051	4331779
2	32	Deuces Are Wild	5	1	1	Steven Tyler, Jim Vallance	215875	7074167
3	775	Call Of The Wild	61	1	1	Ian Gillian, Rog...	293851	9575295
4	1245	Wildest Dreams	98	1	13	Adrian Smith/ Steve Harris	232777	9312384
5	1869	Where The Wild Things Are	153	1	3	Hetfield, Ulrich, Newsted	414380	13571280
6	1973	Wild Side	162	1	3	Nikki Sixx/Tommy Lee/Vince Neil	276767	9116997
7	2312	Near Wild Heaven	187	1	4	Stipe/Mike Mil...	199862	6610009
8	2627	Wild Hearted Son	213	1	1		266893	8670550
9	2633	Wild Flower	213	1	1		215536	7084321
10	2697	I Go Wild	218	1	1	Jagger/Richards	264019	8630833
11	2930	Ride Your Wild ...	232	1	1	U2	316551	10304369
12	2944	Wild Honey	233	1	1	Bono, Larry ...	226768	7466069

Figure 159. Filtering the tracks table on the name.

> ⚠ This is prone to SQL injection attacks.

While this works, this is *really* bad way to enable searching on a table, since the user can construct invalid or malicious SQL statements. For example, try entering the single character " in the search box—the filtering will stop working, and won't work again until you restart the app.

This is because you've created an invalid SQL statement e.g.

```
'name LIKE "%"%"'
```

The ideal way to work around this problem is to use parameterized queries—leaving escaping of the input to the database, to ensure that nothing dangerous or malformed is passed. However, this isn't possible with the Qt filter interface, we can only pass a string.

For simple plain-text searching we can instead simply strip out any non-alphanumeric or space characters from the string. It will depend on your use case whether this is appropriate.

```
import re

s = re.sub('[\W_]+', '', s)
query = 'field="%s"' % s
```

Putting that into our filter method from our example, we get the following code.

Listing 94. databases/tableview_tablemodel_filter_clean.py

```
    def update_filter(self, s):
        s = re.sub("[\W_]+", "", s)
        filter_str = 'Name LIKE "%{}%"'.format(s)
        self.model.setFilter(filter_str)
```

Try running the example again, and entering "—and any other garbage you can think of. You should find that the search continues to work.

Displaying related data with `QSqlRelationalTableModel`

In the previous examples we've used `QSqlTableModel` to display data from a single table. However, in relational databases tables can have *relationships* with other tables and it is often useful to be able to view that related data inline.

Relationships in relational databases are handled through *foreign keys*. These are a (usually) numeric value, stored in a column of one table, which references the *primary key* for a row in another table.

An example of a *foreign key* in our example *tracks* table would be `album_id` or `genre_id`. Both are numeric values which point to records in the *album* and *genre* table respectively. Displaying these values to the user (1, 2, 3.. etc.) is not helpful because they have no meaning themselves.

What would be nicer, would be to pull through the name of the album, or the genre and display it in our table view. For that, we can use `QSqlRelationalTableModel`.

The setup for this model is identical for the previous. To define the relationships we call `.setRelation()` passing the column index, and a `QSqlRelation` object.

```
from PyQt5.QtSql import QSqlRelation, QSqlRelationalTableModel

self.model = QSqlRelationalTableModel(db=db)

relation = QSqlRelation('<related_table>',
'<related_table_foreign_key_column', '<column_to_display>')
self.model.setRelation(<column>, relation)
```

The `QSqlRelation` object accepts three arguments, first the related *table* we will be pulling data from, the *foreign key column* on that table, and finally the *column* to pull data from.

For our test database *tracks* table, the following will pull data from the related tables for album ID, media_type ID and genre ID (columns 3, 4, 5 respectively).

Listing 95. databases/tableview_relationalmodel.py

```
        self.model.setTable("Track")
        self.model.setRelation(2, QSqlRelation("Album", "AlbumId",
"Title"))
        self.model.setRelation(3, QSqlRelation("MediaType",
"MediaTypeId", "Name"))
        self.model.setRelation(4, QSqlRelation("Genre", "GenreId",
"Name"))
        self.model.select()
```

When run you will see the three _id columns have been replaced by the data pulled through from the related tables. The columns take the names of the related fields, if they don't clash, or have a name constructed for them.

Figure 160. Displaying data from related fields.

Using `QSqlRelationalDelegate` to edit related fields.

If you try and edit fields in a `QSqlRelationalTableModel` you'll notice a problem—while you can edit the fields on the base table (here *Tracks*) any edits you make to the related fields (e.g. *Album Title*) are not saved. These fields are currently only views to the data.

Valid values for related fields are limited by the values in the related table—to have more choices, we need to add another row to the related table. Since the options are restricted, it often makes sense to display the choices in a `QComboBox`. Qt comes with a model item delegate which can do this lookup and display for us—`QSqlRelationalTableModel`.

Listing 96. databases/tableview_relationalmodel_delegate.py

```
        self.model.setTable("Track")
        self.model.setRelation(2, QSqlRelation("Album", "AlbumId",
"Title"))
        self.model.setRelation(3, QSqlRelation("MediaType",
"MediaTypeId", "Name"))
        self.model.setRelation(4, QSqlRelation("Genre", "GenreId",
"Name"))

        delegate = QSqlRelationalDelegate(self.table)
        self.table.setItemDelegate(delegate)

        self.model.select()
```

This delegate automatically handles the mapping for *any* relational fields. We simply create the delegate passing in the `QTableView` instance, and then set the resulting delegate on the model, everything is taken care of automatically.

Running this you will see drop-downs when you edit the related fields.

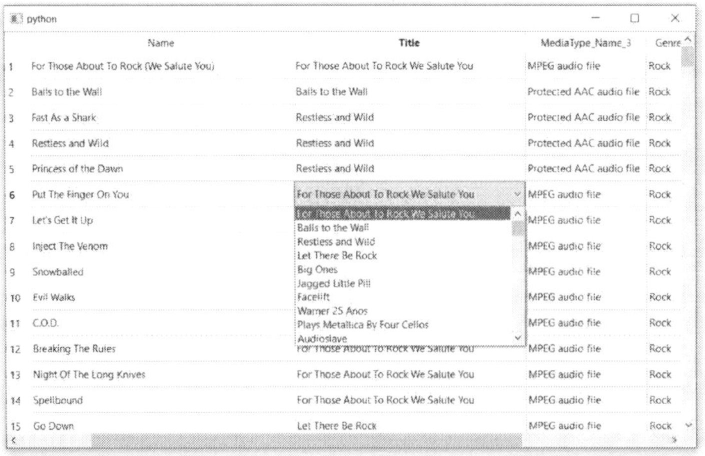

Figure 161. Making relatable fields editable through a drop-down with QSqlRelationalDelegate

Generic queries with QSqlQueryModel

So far we've been displaying an entire database table on our QTableView with some optional column filtering and sorting. However, Qt also allows for displaying more complex queries using QSqlQueryModel. In this part we'll look at how we can use QSqlQueryModel to display an SQL query, starting first with a simple single-table query and then relational and parameterized queries.

The process for querying with this model is slightly different. Rather than passing the database to the model constructor, here we instead create a QSqlQuery object which takes the database connection, and then pass *that* to the model.

```
query = QSqlQuery("SELECT name, composer FROM track ", db=db)
```

This means that you can use a single QSqlQueryModel and perform queries on different databases if you like. The complete working example of this query is shown below.

Listing 97. databases/tableview_querymodel.py

```
import sys

from PyQt5.QtCore import QSize, Qt
from PyQt5.QtSql import QSqlDatabase, QSqlQuery, QSqlQueryModel
from PyQt5.QtWidgets import QApplication, QMainWindow, QTableView

db = QSqlDatabase("QSQLITE")
db.setDatabaseName("chinook.sqlite")
db.open()


class MainWindow(QMainWindow):
    def __init__(self):
        super().__init__()

        self.table = QTableView()

        self.model = QSqlQueryModel()
        self.table.setModel(self.model)

        query = QSqlQuery("SELECT Name, Composer FROM track ", db=db)

        self.model.setQuery(query)

        self.setMinimumSize(QSize(1024, 600))
        self.setCentralWidget(self.table)


app = QApplication(sys.argv)
window = MainWindow()
window.show()
app.exec_()
```

Figure 162. Performing a simple query.

In this first example we've performed a very simple query against our *track* table, only returning two fields from that table. However, the `QSqlQuery` object can be used for more complex queries, including cross-table joins and parameterized queries—where we can pass values in to modify the query.

> Parameterized queries protect your app from SQL injection attacks.

In the following example we extend the simple query to add a related look up on the *album* table. In addition we bind a `album_title` parameter which is used for a *contains* search against the album table.

Listing 98. databases/tableview_querymodel_parameter.py

```
import sys

from PyQt5.QtCore import QSize, Qt
from PyQt5.QtSql import QSqlDatabase, QSqlQuery, QSqlQueryModel
from PyQt5.QtWidgets import QApplication, QMainWindow, QTableView

db = QSqlDatabase("QSQLITE")
db.setDatabaseName("chinook.sqlite")
db.open()


class MainWindow(QMainWindow):
    def __init__(self):
        super().__init__()

        self.table = QTableView()

        self.model = QSqlQueryModel()
        self.table.setModel(self.model)

        query = QSqlQuery(db=db)
        query.prepare(
            "SELECT Name, Composer, Album.Title FROM Track "
            "INNER JOIN Album ON Track.AlbumId = Album.AlbumId "
            "WHERE Album.Title LIKE '%' || :album_title || '%' "
        )
        query.bindValue(":album_title", "Sinatra")
        query.exec_()

        self.model.setQuery(query)
        self.setMinimumSize(QSize(1024, 600))
        self.setCentralWidget(self.table)


app = QApplication(sys.argv)
window = MainWindow()
window.show()
app.exec_()
```

Now that we want to add parameters to the query, we cannot pass it to

QSqlQuery as it is created. Doing this would execute it immediately, without the parameter-replacement. Instead we now need to pass the query into .prepare(), telling the driver to identify parameters in the query and wait for the values.

Next, we bind each of our parameters using .bindValue() and finally call query.exec_() to actually perform the query on the database.

This parameterized query is the equivalent of the following SQL—

```
SELECT Name, Composer, Album.Title FROM Track
INNER JOIN Album ON Track.AlbumId = Album.AlbumId
WHERE Album.Title LIKE '%Sinatra%'
```

This gives the following result—

Figure 163. The result of the parameterised query.

In this last example we add three search fields—one for the track title, one for the artist and one for the album title. We connect the .textChanged signals from each of these to a custom method that updates the parameters for the query.

Listing 99. databases/tableview_querymodel_search.py

```python
import sys
```

```python
from PyQt5.QtCore import QSize, Qt
from PyQt5.QtSql import QSqlDatabase, QSqlQuery, QSqlQueryModel
from PyQt5.QtWidgets import (
    QApplication,
    QHBoxLayout,
    QLineEdit,
    QMainWindow,
    QTableView,
    QVBoxLayout,
    QWidget,
)

db = QSqlDatabase("QSQLITE")
db.setDatabaseName("chinook.sqlite")
db.open()


class MainWindow(QMainWindow):
    def __init__(self):
        super().__init__()

        container = QWidget()
        layout_search = QHBoxLayout()

        self.track = QLineEdit()
        self.track.setPlaceholderText("Track name...")
        self.track.textChanged.connect(self.update_query)

        self.composer = QLineEdit()
        self.composer.setPlaceholderText("Artist name...")
        self.composer.textChanged.connect(self.update_query)

        self.album = QLineEdit()
        self.album.setPlaceholderText("Album name...")
        self.album.textChanged.connect(self.update_query)

        layout_search.addWidget(self.track)
        layout_search.addWidget(self.composer)
        layout_search.addWidget(self.album)

        layout_view = QVBoxLayout()
        layout_view.addLayout(layout_search)
```

```python
        self.table = QTableView()

        layout_view.addWidget(self.table)

        container.setLayout(layout_view)

        self.model = QSqlQueryModel()
        self.table.setModel(self.model)

        self.query = QSqlQuery(db=db)

        self.query.prepare(
            "SELECT Name, Composer, Album.Title FROM Track "
            "INNER JOIN Album ON Track.AlbumId=Album.AlbumId WHERE "
            "Track.Name LIKE '%' || :track_name || '%' AND "
            "Track.Composer LIKE '%' || :track_composer || '%' AND "
            "Album.Title LIKE '%' || :album_title || '%'"
        )

        self.update_query()

        self.setMinimumSize(QSize(1024, 600))
        self.setCentralWidget(container)

    def update_query(self, s=None):

        # Get the text values from the widgets.
        track_name = self.track.text()
        track_composer = self.composer.text()
        album_title = self.album.text()

        self.query.bindValue(":track_name", track_name)
        self.query.bindValue(":track_composer", track_composer)
        self.query.bindValue(":album_title", album_title)

        self.query.exec_()
        self.model.setQuery(self.query)


app = QApplication(sys.argv)
window = MainWindow()
window.show()
```

```
app.exec_()
```

If you run this you can search the database using each of the fields independently, with the results updating automatically each time the search query changes.

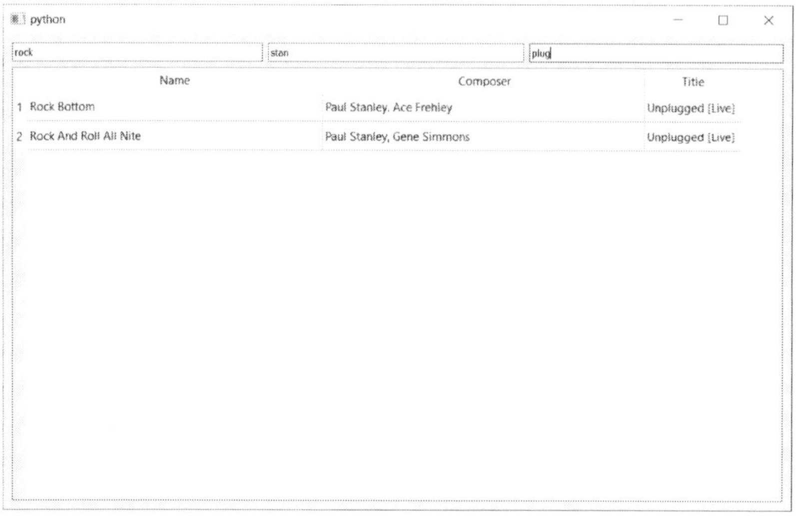

Figure 164. The result of the multi-parameter search query.

QDataWidgetMapper

In all the examples so far we've displayed the output data from the database in a table, using `QTableView`. While this often makes sense for *viewing* data, for data input or editing it is usually preferable to display the inputs as a form which can be typed into and tabbed between.

> These are called create, read, update and delete (CRUD) operations and interfaces.

The full working example is shown below.

Listing 100. databases/widget_mapper.py

```
import sys

from PyQt5.QtCore import QSize, Qt
from PyQt5.QtSql import QSqlDatabase, QSqlTableModel
from PyQt5.QtWidgets import (
```

```
    QApplication,
    QComboBox,
    QDataWidgetMapper,
    QDoubleSpinBox,
    QFormLayout,
    QLabel,
    QLineEdit,
    QMainWindow,
    QSpinBox,
    QTableView,
    QWidget,
)

db = QSqlDatabase("QSQLITE")
db.setDatabaseName("chinook.sqlite")
db.open()


class MainWindow(QMainWindow):
    def __init__(self):
        super().__init__()

        form = QFormLayout()

        self.track_id = QSpinBox()
        self.track_id.setDisabled(True)
        self.name = QLineEdit()
        self.album = QComboBox()
        self.media_type = QComboBox()
        self.genre = QComboBox()
        self.composer = QLineEdit()

        self.milliseconds = QSpinBox()
        self.milliseconds.setRange(0, 2147483647)  ①
        self.milliseconds.setSingleStep(1)

        self.bytes = QSpinBox()
        self.bytes.setRange(0, 2147483647)
        self.bytes.setSingleStep(1)

        self.unit_price = QDoubleSpinBox()
        self.unit_price.setRange(0, 999)
        self.unit_price.setSingleStep(0.01)
```

```python
        self.unit_price.setPrefix("$")

        form.addRow(QLabel("Track ID"), self.track_id)
        form.addRow(QLabel("Track name"), self.name)
        form.addRow(QLabel("Composer"), self.composer)
        form.addRow(QLabel("Milliseconds"), self.milliseconds)
        form.addRow(QLabel("Bytes"), self.bytes)
        form.addRow(QLabel("Unit Price"), self.unit_price)

        self.model = QSqlTableModel(db=db)

        self.mapper = QDataWidgetMapper()  ②
        self.mapper.setModel(self.model)

        self.mapper.addMapping(self.track_id, 0)  ③
        self.mapper.addMapping(self.name, 1)
        self.mapper.addMapping(self.composer, 5)
        self.mapper.addMapping(self.milliseconds, 6)
        self.mapper.addMapping(self.bytes, 7)
        self.mapper.addMapping(self.unit_price, 8)

        self.model.setTable("Track")
        self.model.select()  ④

        self.mapper.toFirst()  ⑤

        self.setMinimumSize(QSize(400, 400))

        widget = QWidget()
        widget.setLayout(form)
        self.setCentralWidget(widget)


app = QApplication(sys.argv)
window = MainWindow()
window.show()
app.exec_()
```

① Widgets must be configured to accept all valid values from the table.

② One `QDataWidgetMapper` for all widgets.

③ Widgets are mapped to _columns.

④ Perform the select to populate the model.

⑤ Step the mapper forward to the first record.

If you run this example, you'll see the following window. The `self.mapper.toFirst()` call selects the first record in the table and this is then displayed in the mapped widgets.

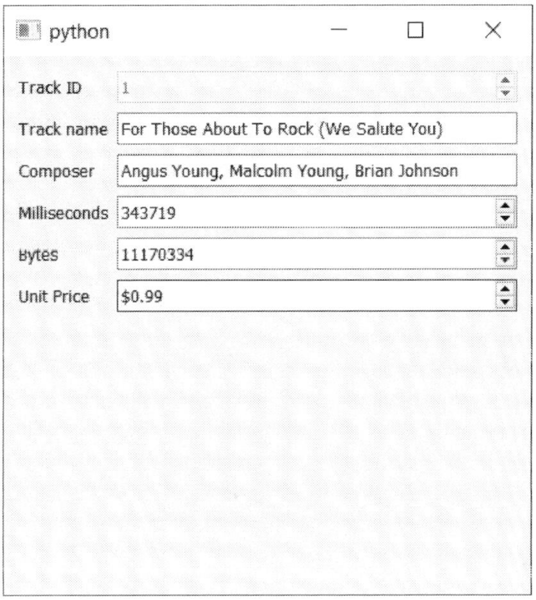

Figure 165. Viewing a record via mapped widgets.

We currently can't change which record we are viewing or save any changes we make to records. To make this possible we can add 3 buttons—one each for browse *previous* and *next* through the records, and *save* to commit changes to the database. To do this we can hook up some `QPushButton` widgets to the *mapper* slots `.toPrevious`, `.toNext` and `.submit`.

Update the end of the `__init__` method to add the following, adding the widgets into the existing layout.

Listing 101. databases/widget_mapper_controls.py

```
        self.setMinimumSize(QSize(400, 400))

        controls = QHBoxLayout()

        prev_rec = QPushButton("Previous")
        prev_rec.clicked.connect(self.mapper.toPrevious)

        next_rec = QPushButton("Next")
        next_rec.clicked.connect(self.mapper.toNext)

        save_rec = QPushButton("Save Changes")
        save_rec.clicked.connect(self.mapper.submit)

        controls.addWidget(prev_rec)
        controls.addWidget(next_rec)
        controls.addWidget(save_rec)

        layout.addLayout(form)
        layout.addLayout(controls)

        widget = QWidget()
        widget.setLayout(layout)
        self.setCentralWidget(widget)
```

You will also need to update the imports at the top of the file to import `QPushButton` and `QHBoxLayout`.

Listing 102. databases/widget_mapper_controls.py

```
from PyQt5.QtWidgets import (
    QApplication,
    QComboBox,
    QDataWidgetMapper,
    QDoubleSpinBox,
    QFormLayout,
    QHBoxLayout,
    QLabel,
    QLineEdit,
    QMainWindow,
    QPushButton,
    QSpinBox,
    QTableView,
    QVBoxLayout,
    QWidget,
)
```

Now you can browse between records in the *Tracks* table, make changes to the track data and submit these changes to the database. The full source code for this example is available at `databases/widget_mapper_controls.py` in the book source code.

Figure 166. Viewing records, with previous/next controls and save to submit.

Authenticating with QSqlDatabase

In the examples so far we've used SQLite database files. But often you'll want to connect to a remote SQL server instead. That requires a few additional parameters, including the hostname (where the database is located) and a username and password if appropriate.

```
# Create database connection.
db = QSqlDatabase('<driver>')
db.setHostName('<localhost>')
db.setDatabaseName('<databasename>')
db.setUserName('<username>')
db.setPassword('<password>')
db.open()
```

NOTE: The value of <driver> can be any one of the following `['QSQLITE', 'QMYSQL', 'QMYSQL3', 'QODBC', 'QODBC3', 'QPSQL', 'QPSQL7']`. To get this list on your system run `QSqlDatabase.drivers()`.

That's it! Once the connection is established, the models will behave exactly as before.

Further PyQt5 Features

The topics we've covered so far are enough to build perfectly functional desktop applications with PyQt5. In this chapter we'll take a look at some more technical and lesser-known aspects of the Qt framework to gain a deeper understanding of how things work.

For many applications the topics covered here are unnecessary, but they are good to have in your toolbox for when you need them!

24. Extending Signals

We've seen a basic introduction to signals already, but that only scratches the surface of what you can do with them. In this chapter we'll look at how you can create your own signals and customize the data sent with them.

Custom Signals

So far we've only looked at signals that Qt itself provides on the built-in widgets. However, you can also make use of signals in your own code for. This is a great way to *decouple* modular parts of your application—parts of your app can respond to things happening elsewhere, without needing to know anything about the structure of your app.

> A good indication that you need to *decouple* is use of `.parent()` to access data on other unrelated widgets.

By putting these updates in the event queue you also help to keep your app responsive—rather than having one big *update* method, you can split the work up into multiple slots and trigger them with a single signal.

You can define your own signals using the `pyqtSignal` method provided by PyQt5. Signals are defined as *class attributes* passing in the Python type (or types) that will emitted with the signal. You can choose any valid Python variable name for the name of the signal, and any Python type for the signal type.

Listing 103. further/signals_custom.py

```
import sys

from PyQt5.QtCore import Qt, pyqtSignal
from PyQt5.QtWidgets import QApplication, QMainWindow


class MainWindow(QMainWindow):

    message = pyqtSignal(str)  ①
    value = pyqtSignal(int, str, int)  ②
    another = pyqtSignal(list)  ③
    onemore = pyqtSignal(dict)  ④
    anything = pyqtSignal(object)  ⑤

    def __init__(self):
        super().__init__()

        self.message.connect(self.custom_slot)
        self.value.connect(self.custom_slot)
        self.another.connect(self.custom_slot)
        self.onemore.connect(self.custom_slot)
        self.anything.connect(self.custom_slot)

        self.message.emit("my message")
        self.value.emit(23, "abc", 1)
        self.another.emit([1, 2, 3, 4, 5])
        self.onemore.emit({"a": 2, "b": 7})
        self.anything.emit(1223)

    def custom_slot(self, a):
        print(a)


app = QApplication(sys.argv)
window = MainWindow()
window.show()

app.exec_()
```

① Signal emitting a string.

② Signal emitting 3 different types.

③ Signal emitting a list.

④ Signal emitting a dictionary.

⑤ Signal emitting *anything*.

As you can see the signals can be connected and emitted as normal. You can send any Python type, including multiple types, and compound types (e.g. dictionaries, lists).

If you define your signal as `pyqtSignal(object)` it will be able to transmit absolutely any Python type at all. But this isn't *usually* a good idea as receiving slots will then need to deal with all types.

> You can create signals on any class that is a subclass of `QObject`. That includes all widgets, including the main window and dialog boxes.

Forwarding Signals

Each signal object has an `.emit` method which triggers the sending of data. Like any other method this can be used as a *slot* target for a signal. This allows you to *chain* signals, so one being triggered can trigger another. Unless you modify the data (see the next section) the chained signal must carry the same data as the original signal.

Listing 104. further/signals_forward.py

```
import sys

from PyQt5.QtCore import Qt, pyqtSignal
from PyQt5.QtWidgets import QApplication, QLineEdit, QMainWindow


class MainWindow(QMainWindow):
    message = pyqtSignal(str)

    def __init__(self):
        super().__init__()

        self.message.connect(self.my_custom_fn)

        le = QLineEdit("Enter some text")
        le.textChanged.connect(self.message.emit)  ①

        self.setCentralWidget(le)

    def my_custom_fn(self, s):
        print(s)


app = QApplication(sys.argv)
window = MainWindow()
window.show()
app.exec_()
```

① By connecting the signal to the `.emit` of another, we can forward the signal to the receiving signals listeners.

If it's not immediately obvious why this would be useful, don't worry—it usually isn't! But it can help to maintain isolation between components, particularly where the receiving slot you are targeting is a private method. By hooking into the public signals you can have the intended effect while keeping your components properly decoupled.

Modifying Signal Data

Signals are connected to *slots* which are functions (or methods) which will be run every time the signal fires. Many signals also transmit data, providing information about the state change or widget that fired them. The receiving slot can use this data to perform different actions in response to the same signal.

However, there is a limitation—the signal can only emit the data it was designed to. Take for example, the `QPushButton.clicked` signal which fires when the button is clicked. The *clicked+ signal emits a single piece of data—the _checked* state of the button after being clicked.

> For non-checkable buttons, this will always be `False`.

The slot receives this data, but nothing more. It does not know *which* widget triggered it, or anything about it. This is usually fine. You can tie a particular widget to a unique function which does precisely what that widget requires. Sometimes however you want to add additional data so your slot methods can be a little smarter. There's a neat trick to do just that.

The additional data you send could be the triggered widget itself, or some associated metadata which your slot needs to perform the intended result of the signal.

Intercepting the signal

Instead of connecting the signal directly to the target slot function, you use an intermediate function to intercept the signal, modify the signal data and forward that on to your target slot. If you define the intermediate function in a context that has access to the widget that emitted the signal, you can pass that with the signal too.

This slot function must accept the value sent by the signal (here the `checked` state) and then call the *real* slot, passing any additional data with the arguments.

```
def fn(checked):
    self.button_clicked(checked, <additional args>)
```

Rather than define this intermediate function like this, you can also achieve the same thing inline using a `lambda` function. As above, this accepts a single parameter `checked` and then calls the real slot.

```
lambda checked: self.button_clicked(checked, <additional args>)
```

In both examples the `<additional args>` can be replaced with anything you want to forward to your slot. In the example below we're forwarding the `QPushButton` object `action` to the receiving slot.

```
btn = QPushButton()
btn.clicked.connect( lambda checked: self.button_clicked(checked,
btn) )
```

Our `button_clicked` slot method will receive both the original `checked` value and the `QPushButton` object. Our receiving slot could look something like this—

```
# a class method.
def button_clicked(self, checked, btn):
    # do something here.
```

> You can reorder arguments in your intermediate function if you like.

The following example shows it in practice, with our `button_clicked` slot receiving the check state and the widget object. In this example, we hide the button in the handler so you can't click it again!

Listing 105. further/signals_extra_1.py

```
import sys

from PyQt5.QtCore import Qt
from PyQt5.QtWidgets import QApplication, QMainWindow, QPushButton


class MainWindow(QMainWindow):
    def __init__(self):
        super().__init__()

        btn = QPushButton("Press me")
        btn.setCheckable(True)
        btn.clicked.connect(lambda checked: self.button_clicked
(checked, btn))

        self.setCentralWidget(btn)

    def button_clicked(self, checked, btn):
        print(btn, checked)
        btn.hide()


app = QApplication(sys.argv)

window = MainWindow()
window.show()
app.exec_()
```

Problems with loops

A common reason for wanting to connect signals in this way is when you're building a series of widgets and connecting signals programmatically in a loop. Unfortunately, then things aren't always so simple.

If you construct intercepted signals in a loop and want to pass the loop variable to the receiving slot, you'll hit a problem. For example, in the following example, we're creating a series of buttons, and trying to pass the sequence number with the signal. Clicking a button should update the label with the value of the button.

Listing 106. further/signals_extra_2.py

```
import sys

from PyQt5.QtCore import Qt
from PyQt5.QtWidgets import (
    QApplication,
    QHBoxLayout,
    QLabel,
    QMainWindow,
    QPushButton,
    QVBoxLayout,
    QWidget,
)


class MainWindow(QMainWindow):
    def __init__(self):
        super().__init__()

        v = QVBoxLayout()
        h = QHBoxLayout()

        for a in range(10):
            button = QPushButton(str(a))
            button.clicked.connect(lambda checked: self
.button_clicked(a))  ①
            h.addWidget(button)

        v.addLayout(h)
        self.label = QLabel("")
        v.addWidget(self.label)

        w = QWidget()
        w.setLayout(v)
        self.setCentralWidget(w)

    def button_clicked(self, n):
        self.label.setText(str(n))
```

```
app = QApplication(sys.argv)

window = MainWindow()
window.show()
app.exec_()
```

① We accept the `checked` variable on our `lambda` but discard it. This button is not checkable, so it will always be `False`.

If you run this you'll see the problem—no matter which button you click, you get the same number (9) shown on the label. Why 9? It's the last value of the loop.

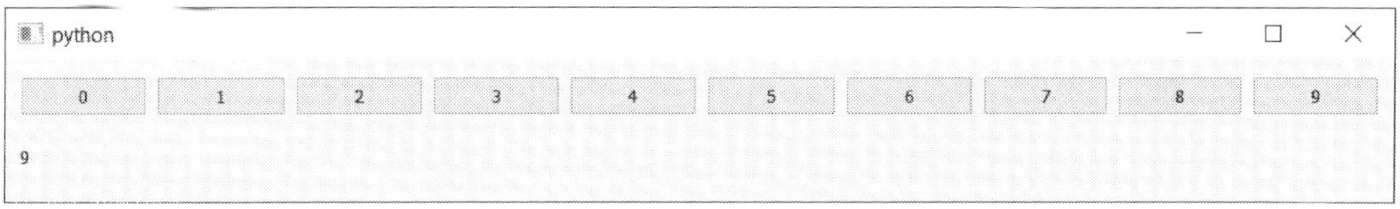

Figure 167. No matter which button you press, the label always shows 9.

The issue is here—

```
for a in range(10):
    button = QPushButton(str(a))
    button.clicked.connect(
        lambda checked: self.button_clicked(a)
    )
```

The problem is the line `lambda: self.button_clicked(a)` where we define the call to the final slot. Here we are passing `a`, but this remains bound to the loop variable. When the `lambda` is evaluated (when the signal fires) the value of `a` will be the value it had at *the end of the loop*, so clicking any of them will result in the same value being sent (here 9).

The solution is to pass the value in as a named parameter. By doing this the value is *bound* at the time the `lamdba` is created, and will hold value of `a` at *that iteration of the loop*. This ensures the correct value whenever it is called.

If this is gobbledygook, don't worry! Just remember to always used named parameters for your intermediate functions.

```
lambda checked, a=a: self.button_clicked(a) )
```

You don't *have* to use the same variable name, you could use `lambda val=a: self.button_clicked(val)` if you prefer. The important thing is to use *named parameters*.

Putting this into our loop, it would look like this:

Listing 107. further/signals_extra_3.py

```
        for a in range(10):
            button = QPushButton(str(a))
            button.clicked.connect(lambda checked, a=a: self
.button_clicked(a))  ①
            h.addWidget(button)
```

If you run this now, you'll see the expected behavior—clicking on a button will show the correct value in the label.

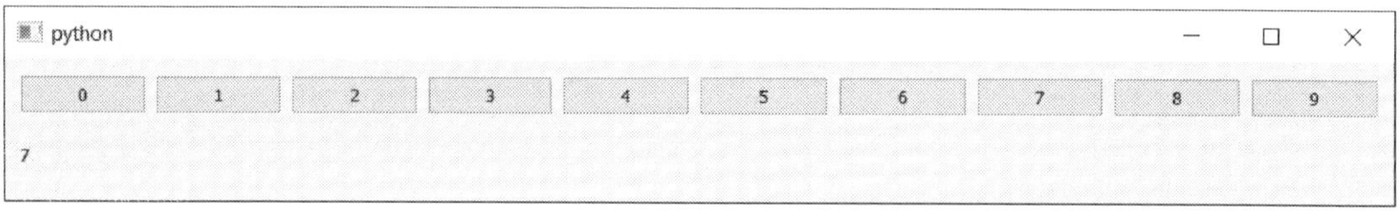

Figure 168. When you press a button, the number pressed is shown below.

Below are a few more examples using inline `lambda` functions to modify the data sent with the `MainWindow.windowTitleChanged` signal. They will all fire once the `.setWindowTitle` line is reached and the `my_custom_fn` slot will output what they receive.

Listing 108. further/signals_extra_4.py

```
import sys
```

```
from PyQt5.QtCore import Qt
from PyQt5.QtWidgets import QApplication, QLabel, QMainWindow


class MainWindow(QMainWindow):
    def __init__(self):
        super().__init__()

        # SIGNAL: The connected function will be called whenever the
window
        # title is changed. The new title will be passed to the
function.
        self.windowTitleChanged.connect(self.on_window_title_changed)

        # SIGNAL: The connected function will be called whenever the
window
        # title is changed. The new title is discarded in the lambda
and the
        # function is called without parameters.
        self.windowTitleChanged.connect(lambda x: self.
my_custom_fn())

        # SIGNAL: The connected function will be called whenever the
window
        # title is changed. The new title is passed to the function
        # and replaces the default parameter
        self.windowTitleChanged.connect(lambda x: self.my_custom_fn(
x))

        # SIGNAL: The connected function will be called whenever the
window
        # title is changed. The new title is passed to the function
        # and replaces the default parameter. Extra data is passed
from
        # within the lambda.
        self.windowTitleChanged.connect(lambda x: self.my_custom_fn(
x, 25))

        # This sets the window title which will trigger all the above
signals
        # sending the new title to the attached functions or lambdas
as the
        # first parameter.
```

```
        self.setWindowTitle("This will trigger all the signals.")

    # SLOT: This accepts a string, e.g. the window title, and prints
it
    def on_window_title_changed(self, s):
        print(s)

    # SLOT: This has default parameters and can be called without a
value
    def my_custom_fn(self, a="HELLLO!", b=5):
        print(a, b)


app = QApplication(sys.argv)

window = MainWindow()
window.show()
app.exec_()
```

25. Routing

In building maintainable software a good rule of thumb is that a function should do *one thing* and *only* one thing. This makes more readable and more maintainable code—it becomes easier to reason about what a function should be doing and spot bugs.

It can at times feel like Qt is actively working against you achieving this—there are many methods that receive multiple types of events, or states, and must handle them all. There is a good chance your PyQt5 application uses code like the following, with nested ifs and long function bodies.

Listing 109. further/routing_1.py

```
import sys

from PyQt5.QtCore import QSize, Qt
from PyQt5.QtWidgets import QApplication, QLabel, QMainWindow


class MainWindow(QMainWindow):
    def __init__(self):
        super().__init__()
        self.label = QLabel("Click in this window")
        self.status = self.statusBar()
        self.setFixedSize(QSize(200, 100))
        self.setCentralWidget(self.label)

    def mouseMoveEvent(self, e):
        self.label.setText("mouseMoveEvent")

    def mousePressEvent(self, e):
        button = e.button()
        if button == Qt.LeftButton:
            self.label.setText("mousePressEvent LEFT")
            if e.x() < 100:
                self.status.showMessage("Left click on left")
                self.move(self.x() - 10, self.y())
            else:
```

```
                self.status.showMessage("Left click on right")
                self.move(self.x() + 10, self.y())

        elif button == Qt.MiddleButton:
            self.label.setText("mousePressEvent MIDDLE")

        elif button == Qt.RightButton:
            self.label.setText("mousePressEvent RIGHT")
            if e.x() < 100:
                self.status.showMessage("Right click on left")
                print("Something else here.")
                self.move(10, 10)
            else:
                self.status.showMessage("Right click on right")
                self.move(400, 400)


app = QApplication(sys.argv)

window = MainWindow()
window.show()

app.exec_()
```

> This is a fun example that moves the window around the desktop depending where you click.

This code is a *mess*. Inside our `mousePressEvent` we're doing multiple things—one branch for each button. It's not immediately obvious if these buttons are self-contained or how differently we handle the middle button. Any time you want to change how *any* button behaves, you have to read through unrelated code to understand the context.

But, how can a method which handles multiple states *ever* have a *single purpose*? By redefining the purpose of the method! We modify our method not to *handle* the event, but to route it. *Routing* in this sense means taking *state information* and calling another method to handle that specific state.

The handling of your events than can then split out into separate methods, one for each event type, or state. This means better maintainability—no 100 line methods of `if` / `else` branches to wade through, but methods with single purpose routed through a single point.

Routing dictionaries

Some languages have *case* statements which allow you to branch off and handle different values of a variable. There is no direct equivalent in Python, but we can use dictionaries for the same result.

This makes use of the fact that in Python functions (and methods) are objects and can be stored as dictionary values. Using the input to our *routing* function we can look up which specific method to call, and pass through the data.

The following code shows how to do this for our example above.

Listing 110. further/routing_2.py

```
    def mousePressEvent(self, e):
        route = {  ①
            Qt.LeftButton: self.left_mousePressEvent,
            Qt.MiddleButton: self.middle_mousePressEvent,
            Qt.RightButton: self.right_mousePressEvent,
        }
        button = e.button()
        fn = route[button]  ②
        return fn(e)  ③

    def left_mousePressEvent(self, e):
        self.label.setText("mousePressEvent LEFT")
        if e.x() < 100:
            self.status.showMessage("Left click on left")
            self.move(self.x() - 10, self.y())
        else:
            self.status.showMessage("Left click on right")
            self.move(self.x() + 10, self.y())

    def middle_mousePressEvent(self, e):
        self.label.setText("mousePressEvent MIDDLE")

    def right_mousePressEvent(self, e):
        if e.x() < 100:
            self.status.showMessage("Right click on left")
            print("Something else here.")
            self.move(10, 10)
        else:
            self.status.showMessage("Right click on right")
            self.move(400, 400)
```

① Define the routing dictionary, keyed by the event type and with handler methods as the values.

② Get the route method from the dictionary.

③ Call the method, passing the event argument.

The value of `e.button()` is used to perform a lookup in our *routing* dictionary. This returns a single method, which we can call to handle that particular button state. We pass the e object as an argument, and return the return value (if any).

This will only work if the states handled are all in our routing dictionary—if there is a state which we haven't prepared for, the lookup will throw a KeyError and crash the application. To avoid needing to define routes for *all* states all the time, we need to handle this.

Listing 111. further/routing_3.py

```
    def mousePressEvent(self, e):
        route = {  ①
            Qt.LeftButton: self.left_mousePressEvent,
            Qt.MiddleButton: self.middle_mousePressEvent,
            # Qt.RightButton missing!
        }
        button = e.button()
        fn = route.get(button)  ②
        if fn:  ③
            return fn(e)
```

① Define the routing dictionary, we dropped the right-click state here.

② Using .get() will return None if there is no match.

③ Any method is *truthy*, None is *falsey*.

If you run this and right click, your app will handle it fine (and do nothing).

> An alternative is to define an empty function and set that as the default return value for the lookup. This will be returned and called for any states not in the routing dictionary.

Now we have a single routing method which calls a series of specific, well-defined methods, with descriptive names that say what they do. This is one of the most powerful methods for improving the *maintainability* of your event and model view code. You can use this same approach in model view .data handlers, and anywhere else that Qt passes state information into a method.

26. Working with command-line arguments

If you have created an application which works with specific file types—for example a video editor that opens videos, a document editor that opens document files—it can be useful to have your application open these files automatically. On all platforms, when you tell the OS to open a file with a specific application, the *filename* to open is passed to that application as a command-line *argument*.

When your application is run, the arguments passed to the application are always available in `sys.argv`. To open files automatically, you can check the value of `sys.argv` at startup and, if you find a filename in there, open it.

The following app when run will open a window with all the command line arguments received displayed.

Listing 112. further/arguments.py

```
from PyQt5.QtWidgets import QApplication, QWidget, QLabel,
QVBoxLayout

import sys


class Window(QWidget):
    def __init__(self):
        super().__init__()

        layout = QVBoxLayout()

        for arg in sys.argv:  ①
            l = QLabel(arg)
            layout.addWidget(l)

        self.setLayout(layout)
        self.setWindowTitle("Arguments")


app = QApplication(sys.argv)
w = Window()
w.show()

app.exec_()
```

① `sys.argv` is a list of strings. *All* arguments are strings.

Run this app from the command line, passing in a filename (you can make anything up, we don't load it). You can pass as many, or as few, arguments as you like.

Arguments are passed to your application as a `list` of `str`. *All* arguments are strings, even numeric ones. You can access any argument you like using normal list indexing—for example `sys.argv[1]` would return the 2nd argument.

Try running the script above with the following—

```
python arguments.py filename.mp4
```

This will produce the window below. Notice that when run with `python` the first argument is *actually* the Python file which is being executed.

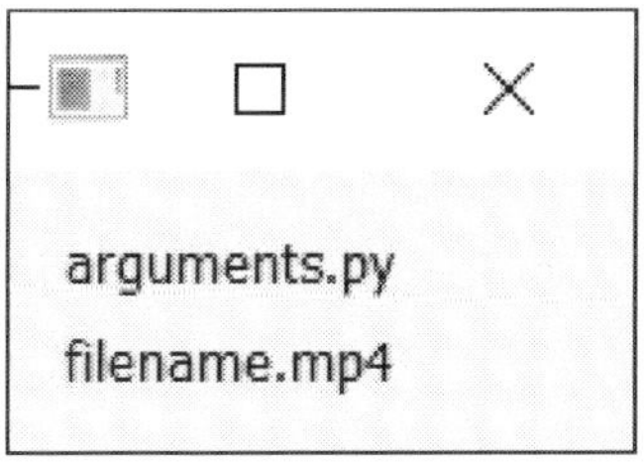

Figure 169. The window open showing the command line arguments.

If you package your application for distribution, this may no longer be the case—the first argument may now be the file you are opening, as there is no Python file passed as an argument. This can cause problems, but a simple way around this is to use the *last* argument passed to your application as the filename, e.g.

```
if len(sys.argv) > 0:
    filename_to_open = sys.argv[-1]
```

Alternatively, you can remove the currently executing script name if it is in the list. The currently executing Python script name is always available in `__file__`.

```
if __file__ in sys.argv:
    sys.argv.remove(__file__)
```

It will *always* be in the list, unless you have packaged your app.

Below is a further example, where we accept a filename on the command line, and then open that text file for display in a `QTextEdit`.

Listing 113. further/arguments_open.py

```
from PyQt5.QtWidgets import QApplication, QMainWindow, QTextEdit

import sys


class MainWindow(QMainWindow):
    def __init__(self):
        super().__init__()

        self.editor = QTextEdit()

        if __file__ in sys.argv:  ①
            sys.argv.remove(__file__)

        if sys.argv:  ②
            filename = sys.argv[0]  ③
            self.open_file(filename)

        self.setCentralWidget(self.editor)
        self.setWindowTitle("Text viewer")

    def open_file(self, fn):

        with open(fn, "r") as f:
            text = f.read()

        self.editor.setPlainText(text)


app = QApplication(sys.argv)
w = MainWindow()
w.show()

app.exec_()
```

① If the script name is in `sys.argv` remove it.

② If there is still something in `sys.argv` (not empty).

③ Take the first argument as the filename to open.

You can run this as follows, to view the passed in text file.

```
python arguments_open.py notes.txt
```

27. System tray & macOS menus

System tray applications (or menu bar applications) can be useful for making common functions available in a small number of clicks. For full desktop applications they're a useful shortcut to control apps without opening up the whole window.

Qt provides a simple interface for building cross-platform system tray (Windows) or menu bar (macOS) apps. Below is a minimal working example for showing an icon in the toolbar/system tray with a menu. The action in the menu isn't connected and so doesn't do anything yet.

Listing 114. further/systray.py

```
from PyQt5.QtWidgets import QApplication, QSystemTrayIcon,
QColorDialog, QMenu, QAction
from PyQt5.QtGui import QIcon

import sys


app = QApplication(sys.argv)
app.setQuitOnLastWindowClosed(False)

# Create the icon
icon = QIcon("icon.png")

# Create the tray
tray = QSystemTrayIcon()
tray.setIcon(icon)
tray.setVisible(True)

# Create the menu
menu = QMenu()
action = QAction("A menu item")
menu.addAction(action)

# Add a Quit option to the menu.
quit = QAction("Quit")
quit.triggered.connect(app.quit)
menu.addAction(quit)

# Add the menu to the tray
tray.setContextMenu(menu)

app.exec_()
```

You'll notice that there isn't a `QMainWindow`, simply because we don't have any window to show. You can create a window as normal without affecting the behavior of the system tray icon.

The default behavior in Qt is to close an application once all the active windows have closed. This won't affect this toy example, but will be an issue in application where you do create windows and then close them. Setting `app.setQuitOnLastWindowClosed(False)` stops this and will ensure your application keeps running.

The provided icon shows up in the toolbar (you can see it on the left hand side of the icons grouped on the right of the system tray or menubar).

Figure 170. The icon showing on the menubar.

Clicking (or right-clicking on Windows) on the icon shows the added menu.

Figure 171. The menubar app menu.

This application doesn't do anything yet, so in the next part we'll expand this example to create a mini color-picker.

Below is a more complete working example using the built in `QColorDialog` from Qt to give a toolbar accessible color picker. The menu lets you choose to get the picked color as HTML-format `#RRGGBB`, `rgb(R,G,B)` or `hsv(H,S,V)`.

Listing 115. further/systray_color.py

```
from PyQt5.QtWidgets import QApplication, QSystemTrayIcon,
QColorDialog, QMenu, QAction
from PyQt5.QtGui import QIcon

import sys


app = QApplication(sys.argv)
app.setQuitOnLastWindowClosed(False)

# Create the icon
icon = QIcon("color.png")

clipboard = QApplication.clipboard()
dialog = QColorDialog()


def copy_color_hex():
    if dialog.exec_():
        color = dialog.currentColor()
        clipboard.setText(color.name())


def copy_color_rgb():
    if dialog.exec_():
        color = dialog.currentColor()
        clipboard.setText(
            "rgb(%d, %d, %d)" % (color.red(), color.green(), color
.blue())
        )


def copy_color_hsv():
    if dialog.exec_():
        color = dialog.currentColor()
        clipboard.setText(
            "hsv(%d, %d, %d)" % (color.hue(), color.saturation(),
color.value())
        )


# Create the tray
tray = QSystemTrayIcon()
```

```
tray.setIcon(icon)
tray.setVisible(True)

# Create the menu
menu = QMenu()
action1 = QAction("Hex")
action1.triggered.connect(copy_color_hex)
menu.addAction(action1)

action2 = QAction("RGB")
action2.triggered.connect(copy_color_rgb)
menu.addAction(action2)

action3 = QAction("HSV")
action3.triggered.connect(copy_color_hsv)
menu.addAction(action3)

quit = QAction("Quit")
quit.triggered.connect(app.quit)
menu.addAction(quit)

# Add the menu to the tray
tray.setContextMenu(menu)

app.exec_()
```

As in the previous example there is no `QMainWindow` for this example. The menu is created as before, but adding 3 actions for the different output formats. Each action is connected to a specific handler function for the format it represents. Each handler shows a dialog and, if a color is selected, copies that color to the clipboard in the given format.

As before, the icon appears in the toolbar.

Figure 172. The Color picker on the toolbar.

Clicking the icon shows a menu, from which you can select the format of image you want to return.

Figure 173. The Color picker menu

Once you've chosen the format, you'll see the standard Qt color picker window.

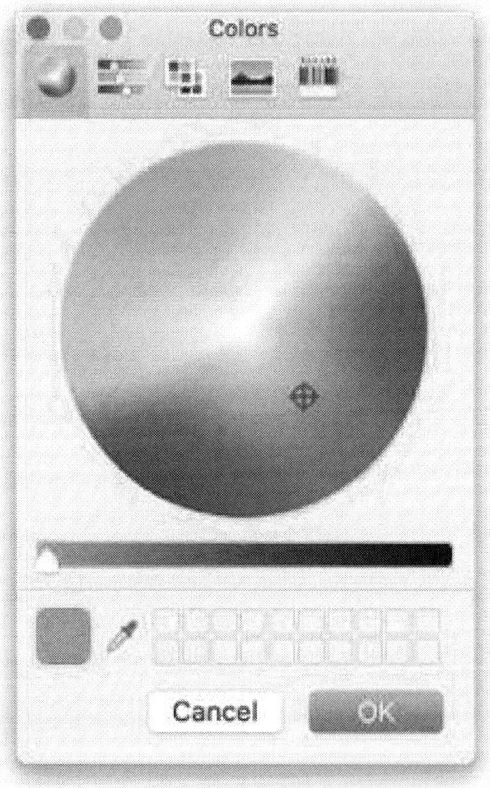

Figure 174. The system Color picker window

Select the color you want and click OK. The chosen color will be copied to the clipboard in the requested format. The formats available will product the following output:

Value	Ranges
#a2b3cc	00-FF
rgb(25, 28, 29)	0-255
hsv(14, 93, 199)	0-255

Adding a system tray icon for a full app

So far we've shown how to create a standalone system tray application with no main window. However, sometimes you may wish to have a system tray icon *as well* as a window. When this is done, typically the main window can be opened and closed (hidden) from the tray icon, without closing the application. In this section we'll look at how to build this kind of application with Qt5.

In principle it's quite straightforward—create our main window, and connect a signal from an action to the `.show()` method of the window.

Below is a small tray notes application called "PenguinNotes". When run, it puts a small penguin icon in your system track or macOS toolbar.

Clicking the small penguin icon in the tray will show the window. The window contains a `QTextEdit` editor into which you can write notes. You can close the window as normal, or by clicking again on the tray icon. The and app will remain running in the tray. To close the app you can use **File › Close**—closing will automatically save the notes.

Listing 116. further/systray_window.py

```
from PyQt5.QtWidgets import (
    QApplication,
    QSystemTrayIcon,
    QMainWindow,
    QTextEdit,
    QMenu,
    QAction,
)
from PyQt5.QtGui import QIcon
```

```
import sys


app = QApplication(sys.argv)
app.setQuitOnLastWindowClosed(False)

# Create the icon
icon = QIcon("animal-penguin.png")


# Create the tray
tray = QSystemTrayIcon()
tray.setIcon(icon)
tray.setVisible(True)


class MainWindow(QMainWindow):
    def __init__(self):
        super().__init__()

        self.editor = QTextEdit()
        self.load()  # Load up the text from file.

        menu = self.menuBar()
        file_menu = menu.addMenu("&File")

        self.reset = QAction("&Reset")
        self.reset.triggered.connect(self.editor.clear)
        file_menu.addAction(self.reset)

        self.quit = QAction("&Quit")
        self.quit.triggered.connect(app.quit)
        file_menu.addAction(self.quit)

        self.setCentralWidget(self.editor)

        self.setWindowTitle("PenguinNotes")

    def load(self):
        with open("notes.txt", "r") as f:
            text = f.read()
        self.editor.setPlainText(text)
```

```
    def save(self):
        text = self.editor.toPlainText()
        with open("notes.txt", "w") as f:
            f.write(text)

    def activate(self, reason):
        if reason == QSystemTrayIcon.Trigger:  # Icon clicked.
            self.show()


w = MainWindow()

tray.activated.connect(w.activate)
app.aboutToQuit.connect(w.save)

app.exec_()
```

On macOS the Quit action will appear in the application menu (on the far left, with the application name), not the File menu. If we didn't also add the **File › Reset** action, the File menu would be empty and hidden (try it!)

Below is a screenshot of the notes app with the window open.

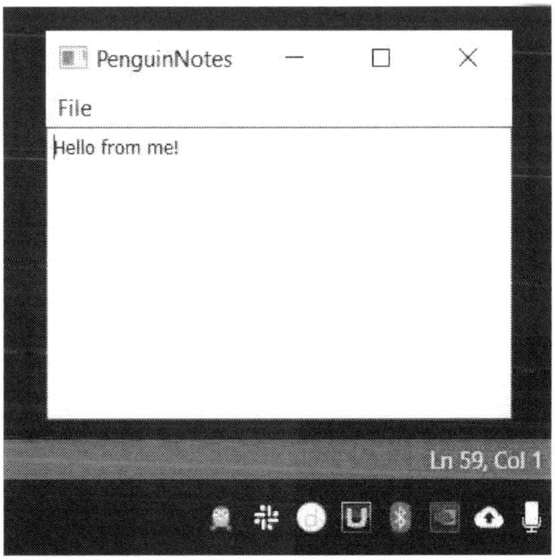

Figure 175. The notes editor window.

The control of showing and hiding the window is handled in the `activate` method on our `QMainWindow`. This is connected to the tray icon `.activated` signal at the bottom of the code, using `tray.activated.connect(w.activate)`.

```python
    def activate(self, reason):
        if reason == QSystemTrayIcon.Trigger:  # Icon clicked.
            if self.isVisible():
                self.hide()
            else:
                self.show()
```

This signal is triggered under a number of different circumstances, so we must first check to ensure we are only using `QSystemTrayIcon.Trigger`.

Reason	Value	Description
`QSystemTrayIcon.Unknown`	0	Unknown reason.
`QSystemTrayIcon.Context`	1	Context menu requested (single click macOS, right-click Windows).
`QSystemTrayIcon.DoubleClick`	2	Icon double clicked. On macOS double-click only fires if no context menu is set, as the menu opens with a single click.
`QSystemTrayIcon.Trigger`	3	Icon clicked once.
`QSystemTrayIcon.MiddleClick`	4	Icon clicked with the middle mouse button.

By listening to these events you should be able to construct any type of system tray behavior you wish. However, be sure to check the behavior on all your target platforms.

28. Enums & the Qt Namespace

When you see a line like the following in your application, you might have wondered what the `Qt.DisplayRole` or `Qt.CheckStateRole` objects actually *are*.

```
def data(self, role, index):

    if role == Qt.DisplayRole:
        # do something
```

Qt makes use of these types extensively for meaningful constants in code. Many of them are available in the Qt *namespace*, that is as `Qt.<something>`, although there are object-specific types such as `QDialogButtonBox.Ok` which work in exactly the same way.

But *how* do they work? In this chapter we'll take a close look at how these constants are formed and how to work with them effectively. To do that we'll need to touch on some fundamentals like binary numbers. But understanding these deeply isn't *necessary* to get something from this chapter—as always we'll focus on how we can apply things as we learn them.

All just numbers

If you check the `type()` of a flag you'll see the name of a class. These classes are the *group* that a given flag belongs to. For example, `Qt.DecorationRole` is of type `Qt.ItemDataRole`—you can see these groups in the Qt documentation [https://doc.qt.io/qt-5/qt.html#ItemDataRole-enum].

> You can run the following code in a Python shell, just import the `Qt` namespace first with `from PyQt5.QtCore import Qt`.

```
>>> type(Qt.DecorationRole)
<class 'PyQt5.QtCore.Qt.ItemDataRole'>
```

These types are *enums*—a type which restricts its values to a set of predefined values. In PyQt5 they are presented as a set of pre-defined class types.

Each of these values is *actually* a wrapper around a simple integer number. The value of `Qt.DisplayRole` is 0, while `Qt.EditRole` has a value of 2. The integer values themselves are *meaningless* but have a meaning in the particular context in which they are used.

```
>>> int(Qt.DecorationRole)
1
```

For example, would you expect the following to evaluate to `True`?

```
>>> Qt.DecorationRole == Qt.AlignLeft
True
```

Probably not. But both `Qt.DecorationRole` and `Qt.AlignLeft` have an integer value of 1 and so are numerically equal. These numeric values can usually be ignored. As long as you use the constants in their appropriate context they will always work as expected.

Table 7. Values given in the documentation can be in decimal or binary.

Identifier	Value (hex)	Value (decimal)	Description
`Qt.AlignLeft`	`0x0001`	1	Aligns with the left edge.
`Qt.AlignRight`	`0x0002`	2	Aligns with the right edge.
`Qt.AlignHCenter`	`0x0004`	4	Centers horizontally in the available space.

Identifier	Value (hex)	Value (decimal)	Description
`Qt.AlignJustify`	`0x0008`	8	Justifies the text in the available space.
`Qt.AlignTop`	`0x0020`	32	Aligns with the top.
`Qt.AlignBottom`	`0x0040`	64	Aligns with the bottom.
`Qt.AlignVCenter`	`0x0080`	128	Centers vertically in the available space.
`Qt.AlignBaseline`	`0x0100`	256	Aligns with the baseline.

If you look at the numbers in the table above you may notice something odd. Firstly, they don't increase by 1 for each constant, but double each time. Secondly, the horizontal alignment hex numbers are all in one column, while the vertical alignment numbers are in another.

This pattern of numbers is intentional and it allows us to do something very neat—combine flags together to create compound flags. To understand this we'll need to take a quick look at how integer numbers are represented by a computer.

Binary & Hexadecimal

When we count normally we use *decimal* a base-10 number system. It has 10 digits, from 0-9 and each digit in a decimal number is worth 10x that which preceded it. In the following example, our number 1251 is made up of 1x1000, 2x100, 5x10 and 1x1.

1000	100	10	1
1	2	5	1

Computers store data in binary, a series of on and off states represented in written form as 1s and 0s. Binary is a base-2 number system. It has 2 digits, from 0-1 and each digit in a binary number is worth 2x that which preceded it. In the following example, our number 5 is made up of 1x4 and 1x1.

8	4	2	1	Decimal
0	1	0	1	5

Writing binary numbers gets cumbersome quickly—5893 in binary is `1011100000101`—but converting back and forward to decimal is not much better. To make it easier to work with binary numbers *hexadecimal* is frequently used in computing. This is a numeric system with 16 digits (0-9A-F). Each hexadecimal digit has a value between 0-15 (0-A) equivalent to 4 binary digits. This makes it straightforward to convert between the two.

The table below shows the numbers 0-15, together with the same value in binary and hexadecimal. The value of a given binary number can be calculated by adding up the numbers at the top of each column with a 1 in them.

8	**4**	**2**	**1**	**Hex**	**Dec**
0	0	0	0	0	0
0	0	0	1	1	1
0	0	1	0	2	2
0	0	1	1	3	3
0	1	0	0	4	4
0	1	0	1	5	5
0	1	1	0	6	6
0	1	1	1	7	7
1	0	0	0	8	8

8	4	2	1	Hex	Dec
1	0	0	1	9	9
1	0	1	0	A	10
1	0	1	1	B	11
1	1	0	0	C	12
1	1	0	1	D	13
1	1	1	0	E	14
1	1	1	1	F	15

This pattern continues for higher numbers. For example, below is the number 25 in binary, constructed from 16 x 1, 8 x 1 and 1 x 1.

16	8	4	2	1
1	1	0	0	1

Because each digit in a binary value is either a 1 or a 0 (`True` or `False`) we can use individual binary digits as *boolean flags*. A single integer value can store multiple flags, using unique binary digits for each. Each of these flags would have their own *numerical value* based on the position of the binary digit they set to 1.

That is exactly how the Qt flags work. Looking at our alignment flags again, we can now see why the numbers were chosen—each flag is a unique non-overlapping bit. The *values* of the flags come from the binary digit the flag has set to 1.

`Qt.AlignLeft`	1	`00000001`
`Qt.AlignRight`	2	`00000010`
`Qt.AlignHCenter`	4	`00000100`
`Qt.AlignJustify`	8	`00001000`
`Qt.AlignTop`	32	`00100000`

`Qt.AlignBottom`	64	`01000000`
`Qt.AlignVCenter`	128	`10000000`

When testing these flags directly with == you don't need to worry about all this. But this arrangement of values unlocks the ability to *combine* the flags together to create compound flags which represent more than one state *at the same time*. This allows you to have a single flag variable representing, for example, left & bottom aligned.

Bitwise OR (|) combination

Any two numbers, with non-overlapping binary representations can be added together while leaving their original binary digits in place. For example, below we add 1 and 2 together, to get 3—

Table 8. Add

`001`	1
`010`	+ 2
`011`	= 3

The 1 digits in the original numbers are preserved in the output. In contrast, if we add together 1 and 3 to get 4, the 1 digits of the original numbers are not in the result—both are now zero.

`001`	1
`011`	+ 3
`100`	= 4

> You can see the same effect in decimal—compare adding 100 and 50 to give 150 vs. adding 161 and 50 to give 211.

Since we're using 1 values in specific binary positions to *mean* something, this poses a problem. For example, if we *added* the value of an alignment flag twice, we would get something else both entirely right (mathematically) and entirely wrong (in meaning).

Table 9. Add

00000001	1	Qt.AlignLeft
00000001	+ 1	+ Qt.AlignLeft
00000010	= 2	= Qt.AlignRight

```
>>> Qt.AlignLeft + Qt.AlignLeft == Qt.AlignRight
True
```

For this reason, when working with binary flags we combine them using a *bitwise OR*—which is performed in Python using the | (pipe) operator. In a *bitwise OR* you combine two numbers together by comparing them at the binary level. The result is a new number, where binary digits are set to 1 if they were 1 in *either* of the inputs. But importantly, *digits are not carried* and do not affect adjacent digits.

When you have non-overlapping digits bitwise OR is the same as add (+).

Qt.AlignLeft	00000001
Qt.AlignTop	00100000

Taking the two alignment constants above, we can combine their values together using a *bitwise OR* to produce the output to give align *top left*.

Table 10. Bitwise OR

00000001	1	Qt.AlignLeft
00100000	OR 32	| Qt.AlignTop

<table>
<tr><td>00100001</td><td>= 33</td><td>Qt.AlignLeft |
Qt.AlignTop</td></tr>
</table>

```
>>> int(Qt.AlignLeft | Qt.AlignTop)
33
```

So, if we combine 32 with 1 we get 33. This should hopefully not be too surprising. But what if we accidentally add `Qt.AlignLeft` multiple times?

```
>>> int(Qt.AlignLeft | Qt.AlignLeft | Qt.AlignTop)
33
```

The same result! The *bitwise OR* outputs a 1 in a binary position if there is a 1 in any of the inputs. It doesn't add them up, carry or overflow anything into other digits—meaning you can `|` the same value together multiple times and you just end up with what you started with.

```
>>> int(Qt.AlignLeft | Qt.AlignLeft | Qt.AlignLeft)
1
```

Or, in binary—

Table 11. Bitwise OR

<table>
<tr><td>00000001</td><td>1</td><td>Qt.AlignLeft</td></tr>
<tr><td>00000001</td><td>OR 1</td><td>| Qt.AlignLeft</td></tr>
<tr><td>00000001</td><td>= 1</td><td>= Qt.AlignLeft</td></tr>
</table>

And finally, comparing the values.

```
>>> Qt.AlignLeft | Qt.AlignLeft == Qt.AlignLeft
True

>>> Qt.AlignLeft | Qt.AlignLeft == Qt.AlignRight
False
```

Checking compound flags

We can check simple flags by comparing against the flag itself, as we've already seen —

```
>>> align = Qt.AlignLeft
>>> align == Qt.AlignLeft
True
```

For combined flags we can also check equality with the combination of flags —

```
>>> align = Qt.AlignLeft | Qt.AlignTop
>>> align == Qt.AlignLeft | Qt.AlignTop
True
```

But sometimes, you want to know if a given variable *contains* a specific flag. For example, perhaps we want to know if `align` has the *align left* flag set, regardless of any other alignment state.

How can we check that an element has `Qt.AlignLeft` applied, once it's been combined with another? In this case a `==` comparison will not work, since they are not numerically equal.

```
>> alignment = Qt.AlignLeft | Qt.AlignTop
>> alignment == Qt.AlignLeft  # 33 == 1
False
```

We need a way to compare the `Qt.AlignLeft` flag against the bits of our compound flag. For this we can use a *bitwise AND*.

Bitwise AND (&) checks

In Python, *bitwise AND* operations are performed using the & operator.

In the previous step we combined together `Qt.AlignLeft` (1) and `Qt.AlignTop` (32) to produce "Top Left" (33). Now we want to check if the resulting combined flag has the align left flag set. To test we need to use *bitwise AND* which checks bit by bit to see if both input values are 1, returning a 1 in that place if it is true.

Table 12. Bitwise AND

`00100001`	33	`Qt.AlignLeft | Qt.AlignTop`
`00000001`	AND 1	`& Qt.AlignLeft`
`00000001`	= 1	`= Qt.AlignLeft`

This has the effect of *filtering* the bits in our input variable to only those that are set in our target flag `Qt.AlignLeft`. If this one bit is set, the result is non-zero, if it is unset the result is 0.

```
>>> int(alignment & Qt.AlignLeft)
1  # result is the numerical value of the flag, here 1.
```

For example, if we tested our alignment variable against `Qt.AlignRight` the result is 0.

`00100001`	33	`Qt.AlignLeft | Qt.AlignTop`
`00000010`	2	`& Qt.AlignRight`
`00000000`	0	`= Qt.AlignLeft`

```
>>> int(alignment & Qt.AlignRight)
0
```

Because in Python 0 is equal to `False` and any other value is `True`. This means that when testing two numbers against one another with bitwise AND, if *any* bits are in common the result will be > 0, and be `True`.

With a combination of bitwise OR and AND you should be able to achieve everything you need with the Qt flags.

Custom Widgets

As we've seen, Qt comes with a wide range of widgets built-in, which you can use to build your applications. Even so, sometimes these simple widgets are not enough—maybe you need an input for some custom types, or want to visualize data in a unique way. In Qt you are free to create your own widgets, either from scratch or by combining existing widgets.

In this chapter we'll see how to use bitmap graphics and custom signals to create your very own widgets.

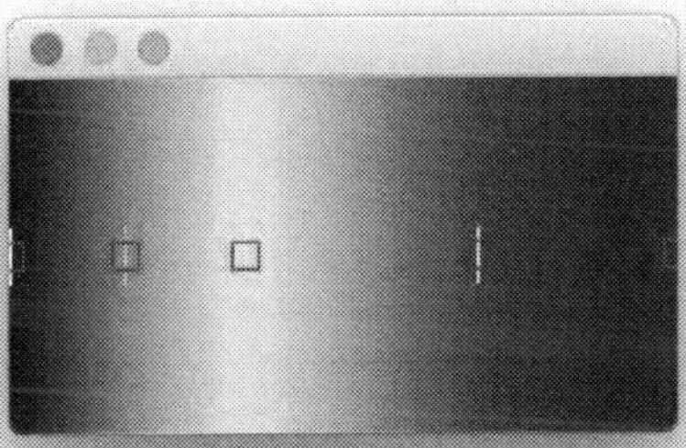

Figure 176. A custom color-gradient input, one of the widgets in our library.

> You may also want to check out our custom widget library [https://www.learnpyqt.com/widgets/].

29. Bitmap Graphics in Qt

The first step towards creating custom widgets in PyQt5 is understanding bitmap (pixel-based) graphic operations. All standard widgets draw themselves as bitmaps on a rectangular "canvas" that forms the shape of the widget. Once you understand how this works you can draw any custom widget you like!

INFO: Bitmaps are rectangular grids of *pixels*, where each pixel (and its color) is represented by a number of "bits". They are distinct from vector graphics, where the image is stored as a series of line (or *vector*) drawing shapes which are used to form the image. If you're viewing vector graphics on your screen they are being *rasterised*—converted into a bitmap image—to be displayed as pixels on the screen.

In this tutorial we'll take a look at `QPainter`, Qt's API for performing bitmap graphic operations and the basis for drawing your own widgets. We'll go through some basic drawing operations and finally put it all together to create our own little Paint app.

`QPainter`

Bitmap drawing operations in Qt are handled through the `QPainter` class. This is a generic interface which can be used to draw on various *surfaces* including, for example, `QPixmap`. In this chapter we'll look at the `QPainter` drawing methods, first using primitive operations on a `QPixmap` surface, and then building a simple Paint application using what we've learnt.

To make this easy to demonstrate we'll be using the following stub application which handles creating our container (a `QLabel`) creating a pixmap canvas, setting that into the container and adding the container to the main window.

Listing 117. bitmap/stub.py

```
import sys

from PyQt5 import QtCore, QtGui, QtWidgets
from PyQt5.QtCore import Qt


class MainWindow(QtWidgets.QMainWindow):
    def __init__(self):
        super().__init__()

        self.label = QtWidgets.QLabel()
        canvas = QtGui.QPixmap(400, 300)  ①
        canvas.fill(Qt.white)  ②

        self.setCentralWidget(self.label)
        self.draw_something()

    def draw_something(self):
        pass


app = QtWidgets.QApplication(sys.argv)
window = MainWindow()
window.show()
app.exec_()
```

① Create the `QPixmap` object we'll draw onto.

② Fill the entire canvas with white (so we can see our line).

> Why do we use `QLabel` to draw on? The `QLabel` widget can also be used to show images, and it's the simplest widget available for displaying a `QPixmap`.

We need to fill our canvas with white to begin with as depending on the platform and current dark mode, the background can be anything from light gray to black. We can start by drawing something really simple.

Listing 118. /bitmap/line.py

```
import sys

from PyQt5 import QtCore, QtGui, QtWidgets
from PyQt5.QtCore import Qt


class MainWindow(QtWidgets.QMainWindow):
    def __init__(self):
        super().__init__()

        self.label = QtWidgets.QLabel()
        canvas = QtGui.QPixmap(400, 300)  ①
        canvas.fill(Qt.white)  ②
        self.label.setPixmap(canvas)
        self.setCentralWidget(self.label)
        self.draw_something()

    def draw_something(self):
        painter = QtGui.QPainter(self.label.pixmap())
        painter.drawLine(10, 10, 300, 200)  ③
        painter.end()


app = QtWidgets.QApplication(sys.argv)
window = MainWindow()
window.show()
app.exec_()
```

① Create the `QPixmap` object we'll draw onto.

② Fill the entire canvas with white (so we can see our line).

③ Draw a line from (10, 10) to (300, 200). The coordinates are x, y with 0, 0 in the top left.

Save this to a file and run it and you should see the following — a single black line inside the window frame —

Figure 177. A single black line on the canvas.

All the drawing occurs within the `draw_something` method — we create a `QPainter` instance, passing in the canvas (`self.label.pixmap()`) and then issue a command to draw a line. Finally we call `.end()` to close the painter and apply the changes.

> You would usually also need to call `.update()` to trigger a refresh of the widget, but as we're drawing before the application window is shown a refresh is already going to occur automatically.

The coordinate system of `QPainter` puts 0, 0 in the top-left of the canvas, with x increasing towards the right and y increasing *down* the image. This may be surprising if you're used to graphing where 0, 0 is in the bottom-left.

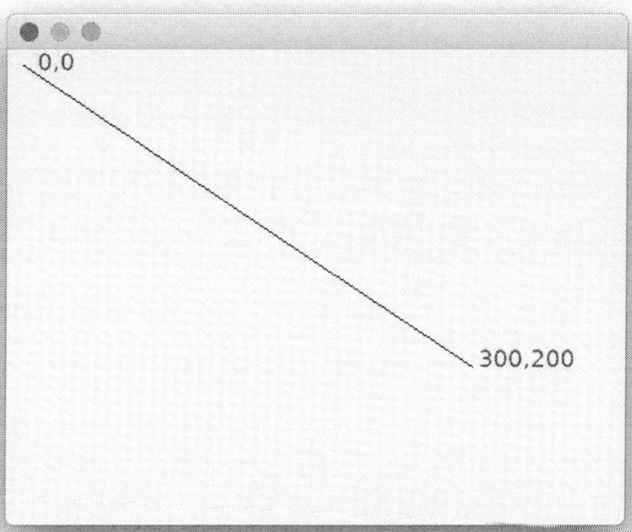

Figure 178. Black line annotated with the coordinates.

Drawing primitives

`QPainter` provides a huge number of methods for drawing shapes and lines on a bitmap surface (in 5.12 there are 192 `QPainter` specific non-event methods). The good news is that most of these are overloaded methods which are simply different ways of calling the same base methods.

For example, there are 5 different `drawLine` methods, all of which draw the same line, but differ in how the coordinates of what to draw are defined.

Method	Description
`drawLine(line)`	Draw a `QLine` instance
`drawLine(line)`	Draw a `QLineF` instance
`drawLine(x1, y1, x2, y2)`	Draw a line between x1, y2 and x2, y2 (both `int`).
`drawLine(p1, p2)`	Draw a line between point p1 and p2 (both `QPoint`)

Method	Description
`drawLine(p1, p2)`	Draw a line between point p1 and p2 (both `QPointF`)

If you're wondering what the difference is between a `QLine` and a `QLineF` , the latter has its coordinates specified as `float`. This is convenient if you have float positions as the result of other calculations, but otherwise not so much.

Ignoring the F-variants, we have 3 unique ways to draw a line — with a line object, with two sets of coordinates `(x1, y1), (x2, y2)` or with two `QPoint` objects. When you discover that a `QLine` itself is defined as `QLine(const QPoint & p1, const QPoint & p2)`or`QLine(int x1, int y1, int x2, int y2)`you see that they are all in fact, exactly the same thing. The different call signatures are simply there for convenience.

> Given the x1, y1, x2, y2 coordinates, the two `QPoint` objects would be defined as `QPoint(x1, y1)` and `QPoint(x2, y2)`.

So, leaving out the duplicates we have the following draw operations —`drawArc` , `drawChord`, `drawConvexPolygon`, `drawEllipse`,`drawLine`, `drawPath`, `drawPie`, `drawPoint`, `drawPolygon`, `drawPolyline`, `drawRect`, `drawRects` and `drawRoundedRect`. To avoid get overwhelmed we'll focus first on the primitive shapes and lines first and return to the more complicated operations once we have the basics down.

> For each example, replace the `draw_something` method in your stub application and re-run it to see the output.

`drawPoint`

This draws a point, or *pixel* at a given point on the canvas. Each call to `drawPoint` draws one pixel. Replace your `draw_something` code with the following.

Listing 119. bitmap/point.py

```
    def draw_something(self):
        painter = QtGui.QPainter(self.label.pixmap())
        painter.drawPoint(200, 150)
        painter.end()
```

If you re-run the file you will see a window, but this time there is a single dot, in black in the middle of it. You may need to move the window around to spot it.

Figure 179. Drawing a single point (pixel) with QPainter.

That really isn't much to look at. To make things more interesting we can change the color and size of the point we're drawing. In PyQt5 the color and thickness of lines is defined using the active *pen* on the QPainter. You can set this by creating a `QPen` instance and applying it.

Listing 120. bitmap/point_with_pen.py

```
    def draw_something(self):
        painter = QtGui.QPainter(self.label.pixmap())
        pen = QtGui.QPen()
        pen.setWidth(40)
        pen.setColor(QtGui.QColor('red'))
        painter.setPen(pen)
        painter.drawPoint(200, 150)
        painter.end()
```

This will give the following mildly more interesting result..

Figure 180. A big red dot.

You are free to perform multiple draw operations with your `QPainter` until the painter is *ended*. Drawing onto the canvas is very quick — here we're drawing 10k dots at random.

Listing 121. bitmap/points.py

```
from random import choice, randint  ①

    def draw_something(self):
        painter = QtGui.QPainter(self.label.pixmap())
        pen = QtGui.QPen()
        pen.setWidth(3)
        painter.setPen(pen)

        for n in range(10000):
            painter.drawPoint(
                200 + randint(-100, 100), 150 + randint(-100, 100)  #
x  # y
            )
        painter.end()
```

① Add this import at the top of the file.

The dots are 3 pixel-width and black (the default pen).

Figure 181. 10k 3-pixel dots on a canvas.

You will often want to update the current pen while drawing — e.g. to draw multiple points in different colors while keeping other characteristics (width) the same. To do this without recreating a new QPen instance each time you can get the current active pen from the QPainter using pen = painter.pen(). You can also re-apply an existing pen multiple times, changing it each time.

Listing 122. bitmap/points_color.py

```
    def draw_something(self):
        colors = ["#FFD141", "#376F9F", "#0D1F2D", "#E9EBEF",
"#EB5160"]

        painter = QtGui.QPainter(self.label.pixmap())
        pen = QtGui.QPen()
        pen.setWidth(3)
        painter.setPen(pen)

        for n in range(10000):
            # pen = painter.pen() you could get the active pen here
            pen.setColor(QtGui.QColor(choice(colors)))
            painter.setPen(pen)
            painter.drawPoint(
                200 + randint(-100, 100), 150 + randint(-100, 100)  #
x  # y
            )
        painter.end()
```

Will produce the following output —

Figure 182. Random pattern of 3 width dots.

> There can only ever be one `QPen` active on a `QPainter` — the current pen.

That's about as much excitement as you can have drawing dots onto a screen, so we'll move on to look at some other drawing operations.

`drawLine`

We already drew a line on the canvas at the beginning to test things are working. But what we didn't try was setting the pen to control the line appearance.

Listing 123. bitmap/line_with_pen.py

```
    def draw_something(self):
        painter = QtGui.QPainter(self.label.pixmap())
        pen = QtGui.QPen()
        pen.setWidth(15)
        pen.setColor(QtGui.QColor("blue"))
        painter.setPen(pen)
        painter.drawLine(QtCore.QPoint(100, 100), QtCore.QPoint(300,
200))
        painter.end()
```

In this example we're also using `QPoint` to define the two points to connect with a line, rather than passing individual `x1, y1, x2, y2` parameters — remember that both methods are functionally identical.

Figure 183. A thick blue line.

`drawRect`, `drawRects` and `drawRoundedRect`

These functions all draw rectangles, defined by a series of points, or by `QRect` or `QRectF` instances.

Listing 124. bitmap/rect.py

```
    def draw_something(self):
        painter = QtGui.QPainter(self.label.pixmap())
        pen = QtGui.QPen()
        pen.setWidth(3)
        pen.setColor(QtGui.QColor("#EB5160"))
        painter.setPen(pen)
        painter.drawRect(50, 50, 100, 100)
        painter.drawRect(60, 60, 150, 100)
        painter.drawRect(70, 70, 100, 150)
        painter.drawRect(80, 80, 150, 100)
        painter.drawRect(90, 90, 100, 150)
        painter.end()
```

A square is just a rectangle with the same width and height

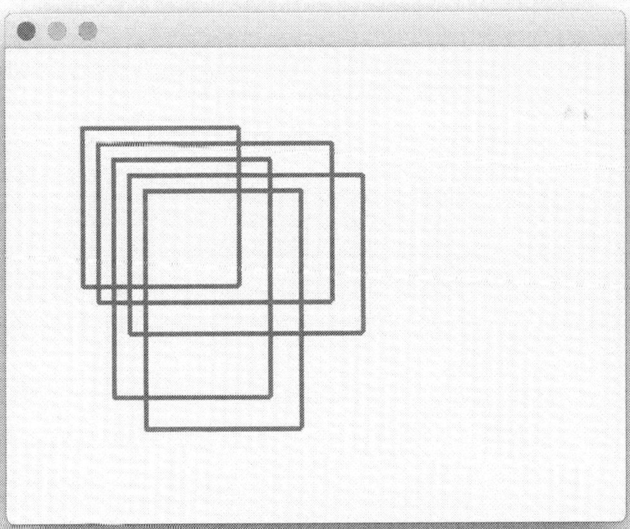

Figure 184. Drawing rectangles.

You can also replace the multiple calls to `drawRect` with a single call to `drawRects` passing in multiple `QRect` objects. This will product exactly the same result.

```python
painter.drawRects(
    QtCore.QRect(50, 50, 100, 100),
    QtCore.QRect(60, 60, 150, 100),
    QtCore.QRect(70, 70, 100, 150),
    QtCore.QRect(80, 80, 150, 100),
    QtCore.QRect(90, 90, 100, 150),
)
```

Drawn shapes can be filled in PyQt5 by setting the current active painter *brush*, passing in a `QBrush` instance to `painter.setBrush()`. The following example fills all rectangles with a patterned yellow color.

Listing 125. bitmap/rect_with_brush.py

```python
    def draw_something(self):
        painter = QtGui.QPainter(self.label.pixmap())
        pen = QtGui.QPen()
        pen.setWidth(3)
        pen.setColor(QtGui.QColor("#376F9F"))
        painter.setPen(pen)

        brush = QtGui.QBrush()
        brush.setColor(QtGui.QColor("#FFD141"))
        brush.setStyle(Qt.Dense1Pattern)
        painter.setBrush(brush)

        painter.drawRects(
            QtCore.QRect(50, 50, 100, 100),
            QtCore.QRect(60, 60, 150, 100),
            QtCore.QRect(70, 70, 100, 150),
            QtCore.QRect(80, 80, 150, 100),
            QtCore.QRect(90, 90, 100, 150),
        )
        painter.end()
```

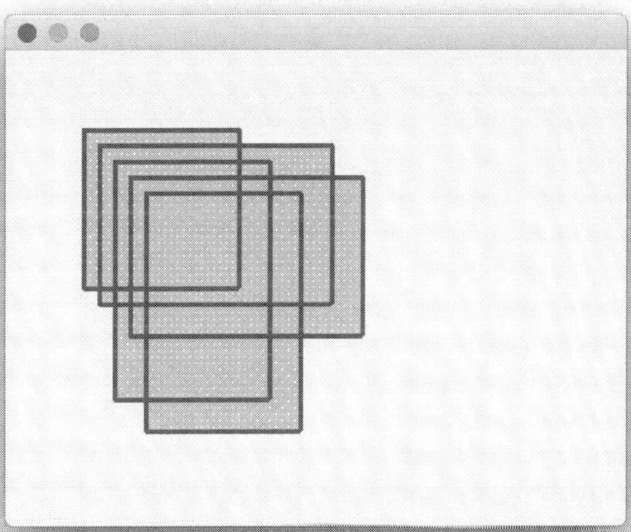

Figure 185. Filled rectangles.

As for the pen, there is only ever one brush active on a given painter, but you can switch between them or change them while drawing. There are a number of brush style patterns available [https://doc.qt.io/qt-5/qt.html#BrushStyle-enum]. You'll probably use `Qt.SolidPattern` more than any others though.

> You **must** set a style to see any fill at all as the default is `Qt.NoBrush`.

The `drawRoundedRect` methods draw a rectangle, but with rounded edges, and so take two extra parameters for the x & y *radius* of the corners.

Listing 126. bitmap/roundrect.py

```
    def draw_something(self):
        painter = QtGui.QPainter(self.label.pixmap())
        pen = QtGui.QPen()
        pen.setWidth(3)
        pen.setColor(QtGui.QColor("#376F9F"))
        painter.setPen(pen)
        painter.drawRoundedRect(40, 40, 100, 100, 10, 10)
        painter.drawRoundedRect(80, 80, 100, 100, 10, 50)
        painter.drawRoundedRect(120, 120, 100, 100, 50, 10)
        painter.drawRoundedRect(160, 160, 100, 100, 50, 50)
        painter.end()
```

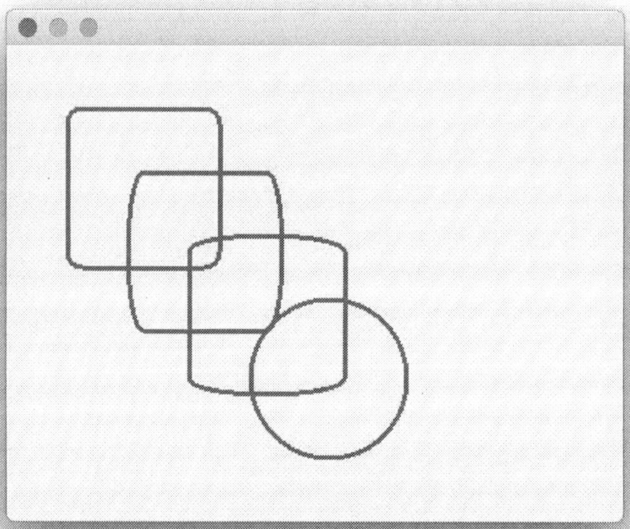

Figure 186. Rounded rectangles.

There is an optional final parameter to toggle between the x & y ellipse radii of the corners being defined in absolute pixel terms `Qt.RelativeSize` (the default) or relative to the size of the rectangle (passed as a value 0…100). Pass `Qt.RelativeSize` to enable this.

drawEllipse

The final primitive draw method we'll look at now is `drawEllipse` which can be used to draw an *ellipse* or a *circle*.

> A circle is just an ellipse with an equal width and height.

Listing 127. bitmap/ellipse.py

```python
    def draw_something(self):
        painter = QtGui.QPainter(self.label.pixmap())
        pen = QtGui.QPen()
        pen.setWidth(3)
        pen.setColor(QtGui.QColor(204, 0, 0))  # r, g, b
        painter.setPen(pen)

        painter.drawEllipse(10, 10, 100, 100)
        painter.drawEllipse(10, 10, 150, 200)
        painter.drawEllipse(10, 10, 200, 300)
        painter.end()
```

In this example `drawEllipse` is taking 4 parameters, with the first two being the x & y position of the *top left of the rectangle* in which the ellipse will be drawn, while the last two parameters are the width and height of that rectangle respectively.

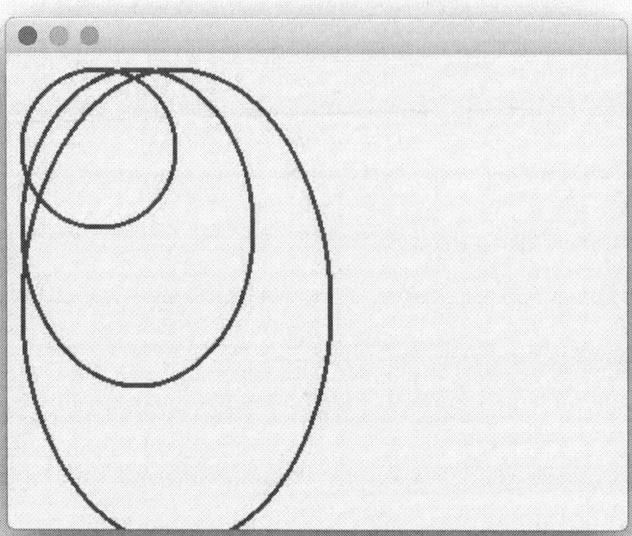

Figure 187. Drawing an ellipse with x, y, width, height or `QRect`.

> You can achieve the same by passing in a `QRect`

There is another call signature which takes the *center of the ellipse* as the first parameter, provided as `QPoint` or `QPointF` object, and then a x and y *radius*. The example below shows it in action.

```
painter.drawEllipse(QtCore.QPoint(100, 100), 10, 10)
painter.drawEllipse(QtCore.QPoint(100, 100), 15, 20)
painter.drawEllipse(QtCore.QPoint(100, 100), 20, 30)
painter.drawEllipse(QtCore.QPoint(100, 100), 25, 40)
painter.drawEllipse(QtCore.QPoint(100, 100), 30, 50)
painter.drawEllipse(QtCore.QPoint(100, 100), 35, 60)
```

Figure 188. Drawing an ellipse using Point & radius.

You can fill ellipses using the same `QBrush` approach described for rectangles.

Text

Finally, we'll take a brief tour through the `QPainter` text drawing methods. To control the current font on a `QPainter` you use `setFont` passing in a `QFont` instance. With this you can control the family, weight and size (among other things) of the text you write. The color of the text is still defined using the current pen, however the width of the pen has no effect.

Listing 128. bitmap/text.py

```
    def draw_something(self):
        painter = QtGui.QPainter(self.label.pixmap())

        pen = QtGui.QPen()
        pen.setWidth(1)
        pen.setColor(QtGui.QColor("green"))
        painter.setPen(pen)

        font = QtGui.QFont()
        font.setFamily("Times")
        font.setBold(True)
        font.setPointSize(40)
        painter.setFont(font)

        painter.drawText(100, 100, "Hello, world!")
        painter.end()
```

> You can also specify location with `QPoint` or `QPointF`.

Figure 189. Bitmap text hello world example.

There are also methods for drawing text within a specified area. Here the parameters define the x & y position and the width & height of the bounding box. Text outside this box is clipped (hidden). The 5th parameter *flags* can be used to control alignment of the text within the box among other things.

```
painter.drawText(100, 100, 100, 100, Qt.AlignHCenter, 'Hello,
world!')
```

Figure 190. Bounding box clipped on drawText.

You have complete control over the display of text by setting the active font on the painter via a `QFont` object. Check out the QFont documentation [https://doc.qt.io/archives/qt-4.8/qfont.html] for more information.

A bit of fun with QPainter

That got a bit heavy, so let's take a breather and make something fun. So far we've been programmatically defining the draw operations to perform on the `QPixmap` surface. But we can just as easily draw in response to user input — for example allowing a user to scribble all over the canvas. Let's take what we've learned so far and use it to build a rudimentary Paint app.

We can start with the same simple application outline, adding a `mouseMoveEvent` handler to the `MainWindow` class in place of our draw method. Here we take the current position of the user's mouse and draw it to the canvas.

Listing 129. bitmap/paint_start.py

```
import sys

from PyQt5 import QtCore, QtGui, QtWidgets
from PyQt5.QtCore import Qt


class MainWindow(QtWidgets.QMainWindow):
    def __init__(self):
        super().__init__()

        self.label = QtWidgets.QLabel()
        canvas = QtGui.QPixmap(400, 300)
        self.label.setPixmap(canvas)
        self.setCentralWidget(self.label)

    def mouseMoveEvent(self, e):
        painter = QtGui.QPainter(self.label.pixmap())
        painter.drawPoint(e.x(), e.y())
        painter.end()
        self.update()


app = QtWidgets.QApplication(sys.argv)
window = MainWindow()
window.show()
app.exec_()
```

Widgets by default only receive mouse move events when a mouse button is pressed, unless *mouse tracking* is enabled. This can be configured using the `.setMouseTracking` method — setting this to `True` (it is `False` by default) will track the mouse continuously.

If you save this and run it you should be able to move your mouse over the screen and click to draw individual points. It should look something like this —

Figure 191. Drawing individual mouseMoveEvent points.

The issue here is that when you move the mouse around quickly it actually jumps between locations on the screen, rather than moving smoothly from one place to the next. The `mouseMoveEvent` is fired for each location the mouse is in, but that's not enough to draw a continuous line, unless you move *very slowly*.

The solution to this is to draw *lines* instead of *points*. On each event we simply draw a line from where we were (previous `e.x()` and `e.y()`) to where we are now (current `e.x()` and `e.y()`). We can do this by tracking `last_x` and `last_y` ourselves.

We also need to *forget* the last position when releasing the mouse, or we'll start drawing from that location again after moving the mouse across the page — i.e. we won't be able to break the line.

Listing 130. bitmap/paint_line.py

```
import sys

from PyQt5 import QtCore, QtGui, QtWidgets
from PyQt5.QtCore import Qt


class MainWindow(QtWidgets.QMainWindow):

    def __init__(self):
        super().__init__()

        self.label = QtWidgets.QLabel()
        canvas = QtGui.QPixmap(400, 300)
        self.label.setPixmap(canvas)
        self.setCentralWidget(self.label)

        self.last_x, self.last_y = None, None

    def mouseMoveEvent(self, e):
        if self.last_x is None: # First event.
            self.last_x = e.x()
            self.last_y = e.y()
            return # Ignore the first time.

        painter = QtGui.QPainter(self.label.pixmap())
        painter.drawLine(self.last_x, self.last_y, e.x(), e.y())
        painter.end()
        self.update()

        # Update the origin for next time.
        self.last_x = e.x()
        self.last_y = e.y()

    def mouseReleaseEvent(self, e):
        self.last_x = None
        self.last_y = None
```

```
app = QtWidgets.QApplication(sys.argv)
window = MainWindow()
window.show()
app.exec_()
```

If you run this you should be able to scribble on the screen as you would expect.

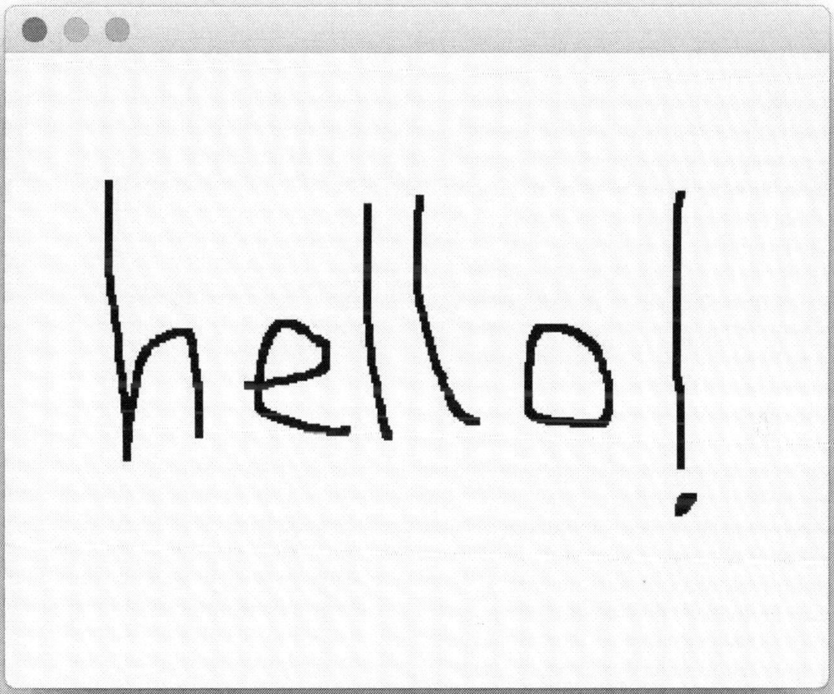

Figure 192. Drawing with the mouse, using a continuous line.

It's still a bit dull, so let's add a simple palette to allow us to change the pen color.

This requires a bit of re-architecting to ensure the mouse position is detected accurately. So far we've using the `mouseMoveEvent` on the `QMainWindow`. When we only have a single widget in the window this is fine — as long as you don't resize the window, the coordinates of the container and the single nested widget line up. However, if we add other widgets to the layout this won't hold — the coordinates of the `QLabel` will be offset from the window, and we'll be drawing in the wrong location.

This is easily fixed by moving the mouse handling onto the `QLabel` itself— it's event coordinates are always relative to itself. This we wrap up as an individual `Canvas` object, which handles the creation of the pixmap surface, sets up the x & y locations and the holds the current pen color (set to black by default).

> This self-contained `Canvas` is a drop-in drawable surface you could use in your own apps.

Listing 131. bitmap/paint.py

```
import sys

from PyQt5 import QtCore, QtGui, QtWidgets
from PyQt5.QtCore import Qt

class Canvas(QtWidgets.QLabel):
    def __init__(self):
        super().__init__()
        pixmap = QtGui.QPixmap(600, 300)
        pixmap.fill(Qt.white)
        self.setPixmap(pixmap)

        self.last_x, self.last_y = None, None
        self.pen_color = QtGui.QColor("#000000")

    def set_pen_color(self, c):
        self.pen_color = QtGui.QColor(c)

    def mouseMoveEvent(self, e):
        if self.last_x is None:  # First event.
            self.last_x = e.x()
            self.last_y = e.y()
            return  #  Ignore the first time.

        painter = QtGui.QPainter(self.pixmap())
        p = painter.pen()
        p.setWidth(4)
        p.setColor(self.pen_color)
        painter.setPen(p)
        painter.drawLine(self.last_x, self.last_y, e.x(), e.y())
        painter.end()
        self.update()

        # Update the origin for next time.
        self.last_x = e.x()
        self.last_y = e.y()

    def mouseReleaseEvent(self, e):
        self.last_x = None
        self.last_y = None
```

For the color selection we're going to build a custom widget, based off QPushButton. This widget accepts a color parameter which can be a QColor instance, or a color name ('red', 'black') or hex value. This color is set on the background of the widget to make it identifiable. We can use the standard QPushButton.pressed signal to hook it up to any actions.

Listing 132. bitmap/paint.py

```
COLORS = [
    # 17 undertones https://lospec.com/palette-list/17undertones
    "#000000",
    "#141923",
    "#414168",
    "#3a7fa7",
    "#35e3e3",
    "#8fd970",
    "#5ebb49",
    "#458352",
    "#dcd37b",
    "#fffee5",
    "#ffd035",
    "#cc9245",
    "#a15c3e",
    "#a42f3b",
    "#f45b7a",
    "#c24998",
    "#81588d",
    "#bcb0c2",
    "#ffffff",
]
class QPaletteButton(QtWidgets.QPushButton):
    def __init__(self, color):
        super().__init__()
        self.setFixedSize(QtCore.QSize(24, 24))
        self.color = color
        self.setStyleSheet("background-color: %s;" % color)
```

With those two new parts defined, we simply need to iterate over our list of colors, create a QPaletteButton for each, passing in the color. Then connect its pressed signal to the set_pen_color handler on the canvas (indirectly through a `lambda` to pass the additional color data) and add it to the palette layout.

Listing 133. bitmap/paint.py

```
class MainWindow(QtWidgets.QMainWindow):
    def __init__(self):
        super().__init__()

        self.canvas = Canvas()

        w = QtWidgets.QWidget()
        l = QtWidgets.QVBoxLayout()
        w.setLayout(l)
        l.addWidget(self.canvas)

        palette = QtWidgets.QHBoxLayout()
        self.add_palette_buttons(palette)
        l.addLayout(palette)

        self.setCentralWidget(w)

    def add_palette_buttons(self, layout):
        for c in COLORS:
            b = QPaletteButton(c)
            b.pressed.connect(lambda c=c: self.canvas.set_pen_color(
c))
            layout.addWidget(b)


app = QtWidgets.QApplication(sys.argv)
window = MainWindow()
window.show()
app.exec_()
```

This should give you a fully-functioning multicolor paint application, where you can draw lines on the canvas and select colors from the palette.

Figure 193. Unfortunately, it doesn't make you good.

Unfortunately, it doesn't make you a good artist.

Spray

For a final bit of fun you can switch out the `mouseMoveEvent` with the following to draw with a "spray can" effect instead of a line. This is simulated using `random.gauss` to generate a series of *normally distributed* dots around the current mouse position which we plot with `drawPoint`.

Listing 134. bitmap/spraypaint.py

```python
import random
import sys

from PyQt5 import QtCore, QtGui, QtWidgets
from PyQt5.QtCore import Qt

class Canvas(QtWidgets.QLabel):
    def __init__(self):
        super().__init__()
        pixmap = QtGui.QPixmap(600, 300)
        pixmap.fill(Qt.white)
        self.setPixmap(pixmap)

        self.pen_color = QtGui.QColor("#000000")

    def set_pen_color(self, c):
        self.pen_color = QtGui.QColor(c)

    def mouseMoveEvent(self, e):
        painter = QtGui.QPainter(self.pixmap())
        p = painter.pen()
        p.setWidth(1)
        p.setColor(self.pen_color)
        painter.setPen(p)

        for n in range(SPRAY_PARTICLES):
            xo = random.gauss(0, SPRAY_DIAMETER)
            yo = random.gauss(0, SPRAY_DIAMETER)
            painter.drawPoint(e.x() + xo, e.y() + yo)

        self.update()
```

For the spray can we don't need to track the previous position, as we always spray around the current point.

Define the `SPRAY_PARTICLES` and `SPRAY_DIAMETER` variables at the top of your file and import the `random` standard library module. The image below shows the spray behavior when using the following settings:

```python
import random

SPRAY_PARTICLES = 100
SPRAY_DIAMETER = 10
```

Figure 194. Just call me Picasso.

If you want a challenge, you could try adding an additional button to toggle between draw and spray mode, or an input widget to define the brush/spray diameter.

> For a fully-functional drawing app written with Python & Qt check out Piecasso [https://github.com/learnpyqt/15-minute-apps/tree/master/paint] in our "Minute apps" repository on Github.

This introduction should have given you a good idea of what you can do with `QPainter`. As described, this system is the basis of all widget drawing. If you want to look further, check out the widget `.paint()` method, which receives a `QPainter` instance, to allow the widget to draw on itself. The same methods you've learnt here can be used in `.paint()` to draw some basic custom widgets.

30. Creating Custom Widgets

In the previous chapter we introduced `QPainter` and looked at some basic bitmap drawing operations which you can used to draw dots, lines, rectangles and circles on a `QPainter` *surface* such as a `QPixmap`. This process of *drawing on a surface* with `QPainter` is in fact the basis by which all widgets in Qt are drawn. Now you know how to use `QPainter` you know how to draw your own custom widgets! In this chapter we'll take what we've learnt so far and use it to construct a completely new *custom* widget. For a working example we'll be building the following widget -- a customizable PowerBar meter with a dial control.

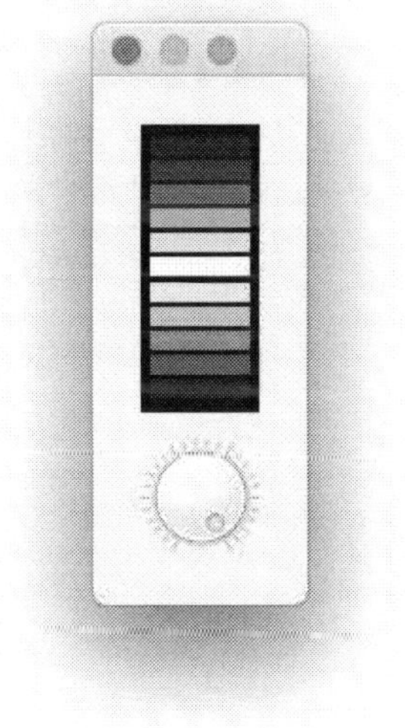

Figure 195. PowerBar meter.

This widget is actually a mix of a *compound widget* and *custom widget* in that we are using the built-in Qt `QDial` component for the dial, while drawing the power bar ourselves. We then assemble these two parts together into a parent widget which can be dropped into place seamlessly in any application, without needing to know how it's put together. The resulting widget provides the common `QAbstractSlider` interface with some additions for configuring the bar display.

After following this example you will be able to build your very own custom widgets—whether they are compounds of built-ins or completely novel self-drawn wonders.

Getting started

As we've previously seen compound widgets are simply widgets with a layout applied, which itself contains >1 other widget. The resulting "widget" can then be used as any other, with the internals hidden/exposed as you like.

The outline for our **PowerBar** widget is given below—we'll build our custom widget up gradually from this outline stub.

Listing 135. custom-widgets/stub.py

```python
import sys

from PyQt5 import QtCore, QtGui, QtWidgets
from PyQt5.QtCore import Qt


class _Bar(QtWidgets.QWidget):
    pass


class PowerBar(QtWidgets.QWidget):
    """
    Custom Qt Widget to show a power bar and dial.
    Demonstrating compound and custom-drawn widget.
    """

    def __init__(self, steps=5):
        super().__init__()

        layout = QtWidgets.QVBoxLayout()
        self._bar = _Bar()
        layout.addWidget(self._bar)

        self._dial = QtWidgets.QDial()
        layout.addWidget(self._dial)

        self.setLayout(layout)


app = QtWidgets.QApplication(sys.argv)
volume = PowerBar()
volume.show()
app.exec_()
```

This simply defines our custom power bar is defined in the `_Bar` object—here just unaltered subclass of `QWidget`. The `PowerBar` widget (which is the complete widget) combines this, using a `QVBoxLayout` with the built in `QDial` to display them together.

> We don't need to create a QMainWindow since any widget without a parent is a window in it's own right. Our custom PowerBar widget will appear as any normal window.

You can run this file at any time to see your widget in action. Run it now and you should see something like this:

Figure 196. PowerBar dial.

If you stretch the window down you'll see the dial has more space above it than below -- this is being taken up by our (currently invisible) _Bar widget.

paintEvent

The paintEvent handler is the core of all widget drawing in PyQt5. Every complete and partial re-draw of a widget is triggered through a paintEvent which the widget handles to draw itself. A paintEvent can be triggered by—

- repaint() [https://doc.qt.io/qt-5/qwidget.html#repaint] or update() [https://doc.qt.io/qt-5/qwidget.html#update] was called
- the widget was obscured and has now been uncovered
- the widget has been resized

—but it can also occur for many other reasons. What is important is that when a paintEvent is triggered your widget is able to redraw it.

If a widget is simple enough (like ours is) you can often get away with simply redrawing the entire thing any time *anything* happens. But for more complicated widgets this can get very inefficient. For these cases the paintEvent includes the specific region that needs to be updated. We'll make use of this in later, more complicated examples.

For now we'll do something very simple, and just fill the entire widget with a single color. This will allow us to see the area we're working with to start drawing the bar. Add the following code to the _Bar class.

Listing 136. custom-widgets/powerbar_1.py

```
    def paintEvent(self, e):
        painter = QtGui.QPainter(self)
        brush = QtGui.QBrush()
        brush.setColor(QtGui.QColor("black"))
        brush.setStyle(Qt.SolidPattern)
        rect = QtCore.QRect(0, 0, painter.device().width(), painter
.device().height())
        painter.fillRect(rect, brush)
```

Positioning

Now we can see the _Bar widget we can tweak its positioning and size. If you drag around the shape of the window you'll see the two widgets changing shape to fit the space available. This is what we want, but the QDial is also expanding vertically more than it should, and leaving empty space we could use for the bar.

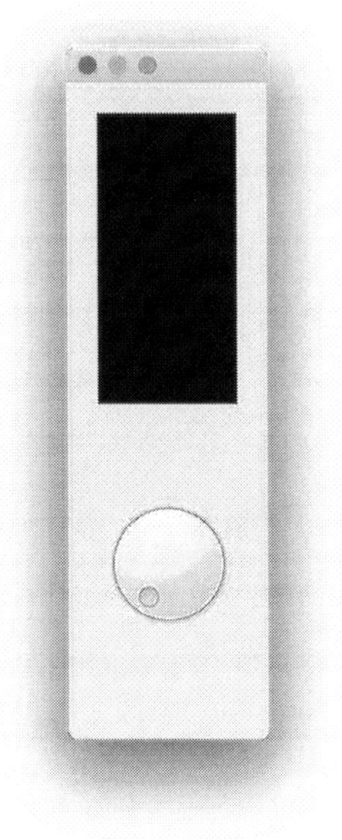

Figure 197. PowerBar stretched leaves empty space.

We can use `setSizePolicy` on our `_Bar` widget to make sure it expands as far as possible. By using the `QSizePolicy.MinimumExpanding` the provided `sizeHint` will be used as a minimum, and the widget will expand as much as possible.

Listing 137. custom-widgets/powerbar_2.py

```
class _Bar(QtWidgets.QWidget):
    def __init__(self, *args, **kwargs):
        super().__init__(*args, **kwargs)

        self.setSizePolicy(
            QtWidgets.QSizePolicy.MinimumExpanding,
            QtWidgets.QSizePolicy.MinimumExpanding,
        )

    def sizeHint(self):
        return QtCore.QSize(40, 120)

    def paintEvent(self, e):
        painter = QtGui.QPainter(self)
        brush = QtGui.QBrush()
        brush.setColor(QtGui.QColor("black"))
        brush.setStyle(Qt.SolidPattern)
        rect = QtCore.QRect(0, 0, painter.device().width(), painter
.device().height())
        painter.fillRect(rect, brush)
```

It's still not *perfect* as the `QDial` widget resizes itself a bit awkwardly, but our bar is now expanding to fill all the available space.

Figure 198. PowerBar with policy set to `QSizePolicy.MinimumExpanding`.

With the positioning sorted we can now move on to define our paint methods to draw our PowerBar meter in the top part (currently black) of the widget.

Updating the display

We now have our canvas completely filled in black, next we'll use `QPainter` draw commands to actually draw something on the widget.

Before we start on the bar, we've got a bit of testing to do to make sure we can update the display with the values of our dial. Update the `_Bar.paintEvent` with the following code.

Listing 138. custom-widgets/powerbar_3.py

```python
    def paintEvent(self, e):
        painter = QtGui.QPainter(self)

        brush = QtGui.QBrush()
        brush.setColor(QtGui.QColor("black"))
        brush.setStyle(Qt.SolidPattern)
        rect = QtCore.QRect(0, 0, painter.device().width(), painter
.device().height())
        painter.fillRect(rect, brush)

        # Get current state.
        dial = self.parent()._dial
        vmin, vmax = dial.minimum(), dial.maximum()
        value = dial.value()

        pen = painter.pen()
        pen.setColor(QtGui.QColor("red"))
        painter.setPen(pen)

        font = painter.font()
        font.setFamily("Times")
        font.setPointSize(18)
        painter.setFont(font)

        painter.drawText(25, 25, "{}-->{}<  {}".format(vmin, value,
vmax))
        painter.end()
```

This draws the black background as before, then uses `.parent()` to access our parent `PowerBar` widget and through that the `QDial` via `_dial`. From there we get the current value, as well as the allowed range minimum and maximum values. Finally we draw those using the painter, just like we did in the previous part.

> We're leaving handling of the current value, min and max values to the QDial here, but we could also store that value ourselves and use signals to/from the dial to keep things in sync.

Run this, wiggle the dial around and .....nothing happens. Although we've defined the paintEvent handler we're not triggering a repaint when the dial changes.

> You can force a refresh by resizing the window, as soon as you do this you should see the text appear. Neat, but terrible UX—"just resize your app to see your settings!"

To fix this we need to hook up our _Bar`widget to repaint itself in response to changing values on the dial. We can do this using the `QDial.valueChanged`signal, hooking it up to a custom slot method which calls `.refresh()—triggering a full-repaint.

Add the following method to the _Bar widget.

Listing 139. custom-widgets/powerbar_4.py

```
    def _trigger_refresh(self):
        self.update()
```

...and add the following to the __init__ block for the parent PowerBar widget.

Listing 140. custom-widgets/powerbar_4.py

```
        self._dial = QtWidgets.QDial()
        self._dial.valueChanged.connect(self._bar._trigger_refresh)
        layout.addWidget(self._dial)
```

If you re-run the code now, you will see the display updating automatically as you turn the dial (click and drag with your mouse). The current value is displayed as text.

Figure 199. PowerBar displaying current value as text.

Drawing the bar

Now we have the display updating and displaying the current value of the dial, we can move onto drawing the actual bar display. This is a little complicated, with a bit of maths to calculate bar positions, but we'll step through it to make it clear what's going on.

The sketch below shows what we are aiming for — a series of **N** boxes, inset from the edges of the widget, with spaces between them.

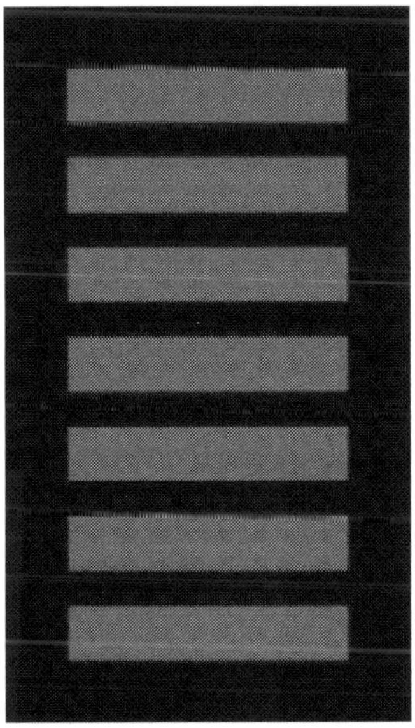

Figure 200. The bar segments and layout we're aiming for.

Calculating what to draw

The number of boxes to draw is determined by the current value—and how far along it is between the minimum and maximum value configured for the `QDial`. We already have that information in the example above.

```
dial = self.parent()._dial
vmin, vmax = dial.minimum(), dial.maximum()
value = dial.value()
```

If `value` is half way between `vmin` and `vmax` then we want to draw half of the boxes (if we have 4 boxes total, draw 2). If `value` is at `vmax` we want to draw them all.

To do this we first convert our `value` into a number between 0 and 1, where `0 = vmin` and `1 = vmax`. We first subtract `vmin` from `value` to adjust the range of possible values to start from zero—i.e. from `vmin…vmax` to `0…(vmax-vmin)`. Dividing this value by `vmax-vmin` (the new maximum) then gives us a number between 0 and 1.

The trick then is to multiply this value (called `pc` below) by the number of steps and that gives us a number between 0 and 5—the number of boxes to draw.

```
pc = (value - vmin) / (vmax - vmin)
n_steps_to_draw = int(pc * 5)
```

We're wrapping the result in `int` to convert it to a whole number (rounding down) to remove any partial boxes.

Update the `drawText` method in your paint event to write out this number instead.

Listing 141. custom-widgets/powerbar_5.py

```
    def paintEvent(self, e):
        painter = QtGui.QPainter(self)

        brush = QtGui.QBrush()
        brush.setColor(QtGui.QColor("black"))
        brush.setStyle(Qt.SolidPattern)
        rect = QtCore.QRect(0, 0, painter.device().width(), painter
.device().height())
        painter.fillRect(rect, brush)

        # Get current state.
        dial = self.parent()._dial
        vmin, vmax = dial.minimum(), dial.maximum()
        value = dial.value()

        pen = painter.pen()
        pen.setColor(QtGui.QColor("red"))
        painter.setPen(pen)

        font = painter.font()
        font.setFamily("Times")
        font.setPointSize(18)
        painter.setFont(font)

        pc = (value - vmin) / (vmax - vmin)
        n_steps_to_draw = int(pc * 5)
        painter.drawText(25, 25, "{}".format(n_steps_to_draw))
        painter.end()
```

As you turn the dial you will now see a number between 0 and 5.

Drawing boxes

Next we want to convert this number 0…5 to a number of bars drawn on the canvas. Start by removing the `drawText` and font and pen settings, as we no longer need those.

To draw accurately we need to know the size of our canvas—i.e the size of the widget. We will also add a bit of padding around the edges to give space around the edges of the blocks against the black background.

> All measurements in the QPainter are in pixels.

Listing 142. custom-widgets/powerbar_6.py

```
        padding = 5

        # Define our canvas.
        d_height = painter.device().height() - (padding * 2)
        d_width = painter.device().width() - (padding * 2)
```

We take the height and width and subtract `2 * padding` from each -- it's 2x because we're padding both the left and right (and top and bottom) edges. This gives us our resulting *active canvas* area in `d_height` and `d_width`.

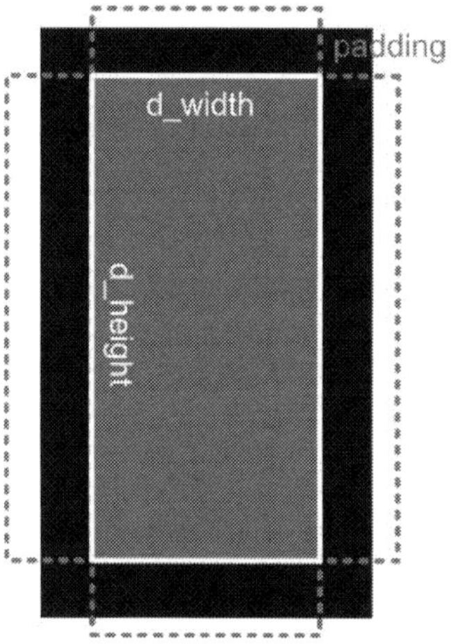

Figure 201. The padding on the outside of the layout.

We need to break up our `d_height` into 5 equal parts, one for each block -- we can calculate that height simply by `d_height / 5`. Additionally, since we want spaces between the blocks we need to calculate how much of this step size is taken up by space (top and bottom, so halved) and how much is actual block.

Listing 143. custom-widgets/powerbar_6.py

```
        step_size = d_height / 5
        bar_height = step_size * 0.6
        bar_spacer = step_size * 0.4 / 2
```

These values are all we need to draw our blocks on our canvas. To do this we count up to the number of steps-1 starting from 0 using `range` and then draw a `fillRect` over a region for each block.

Listing 144. custom-widgets/powerbar_6.py

```
        brush.setColor(QtGui.QColor("red"))

        for n in range(n_steps_to_draw):
            rect = QtCore.QRect(
                padding,
                padding + d_height - ((n + 1) * step_size) +
bar_spacer,
                d_width,
                bar_height,
            )
            painter.fillRect(rect, brush)
```

There is a lot going on in the placement calculations for the blocks, so let's step through those first.

The box to draw with `fillRect` is defined as a `QRect` object to which we pass, in turn, the left x, top y, width and height.

The *width* is the full canvas width minus the padding, which we previously calculated and stored in `d_width`. The *left x* is similarly just the `padding` value (5px) from the left hand side of the widget.

The *height* of the bar `bar_height`we calculated as 0.6 times the `step_size`.

This leaves parameter 2 `d_height - ((1 + n) * step_size) + bar_spacer` which gives the *top y* position of the rectangle to draw. This is the only calculation that changes as we draw the blocks.

Remember that *y* coordinates in `QPainter` start at the top and increase down the canvas. This means that plotting at `d_height` will be plotting at the very bottom of the canvas.

To draw a block at the very bottom we must start drawing at `d_height-step_size` i.e. one block up to leave space to draw downwards.

In our bar meter we're drawing blocks, in turn, starting at the bottom and working upwards. So our very first block must be placed at `d_height-step_size` and the second at `d_height-(step_size*2)`. Our loop iterates from 0 upwards, so we can achieve this with the following formula—

```
d_height - ((1 + n) * step_size)
```

The final adjustment is to account for our blocks only taking up part of each `step_size` (currently 0.6). We add a little padding to move the block away from the edge of the box and into the middle, and finally add the padding for the bottom edge. That gives us the final formula—

```
padding + d_height - ((n+1) * step_size) + bar_spacer,
```

This produces the following layout.

In the picture below the current value of `n` has been printed over the box, and a blue box has been drawn around the complete `step_size` so you can see the padding and spacers in effect.

Figure 202. Showing the whole area (in blue) taken up by each segment.

Putting this all together gives the following code, which when run will produce a working power-bar widget with blocks in red. You can drag the wheel back and forth and the bars will move up and down in response.

Listing 145. custom-widgets/powerbar_6.py

```
import sys

from PyQt5 import QtCore, QtGui, QtWidgets
from PyQt5.QtCore import Qt


class _Bar(QtWidgets.QWidget):
    def __init__(self, *args, **kwargs):
        super().__init__(*args, **kwargs)

        self.setSizePolicy(
            QtWidgets.QSizePolicy.MinimumExpanding,
            QtWidgets.QSizePolicy.MinimumExpanding,
        )

    def sizeHint(self):
        return QtCore.QSize(40, 120)

    def paintEvent(self, e):
        painter = QtGui.QPainter(self)

        brush = QtGui.QBrush()
        brush.setColor(QtGui.QColor("black"))
```

```
        brush.setStyle(Qt.SolidPattern)
        rect = QtCore.QRect(0, 0, painter.device().width(), painter
.device().height())
        painter.fillRect(rect, brush)

        # Get current state.
        dial = self.parent()._dial
        vmin, vmax = dial.minimum(), dial.maximum()
        value = dial.value()

        pc = (value - vmin) / (vmax - vmin)
        n_steps_to_draw = int(pc * 5)

        # tag::dimensions[]
        padding = 5

        # Define our canvas.
        d_height = painter.device().height() - (padding * 2)
        d_width = painter.device().width() - (padding * 2)
        # end::dimensions[]

        # tag::layout[]
        step_size = d_height / 5
        bar_height = step_size * 0.6
        bar_spacer = step_size * 0.4 / 2
        # end::layout[]

        # tag::draw[]
        brush.setColor(QtGui.QColor("red"))

        for n in range(n_steps_to_draw):
            rect = QtCore.QRect(
                padding,
                padding + d_height - ((n + 1) * step_size) +
bar_spacer,
                d_width,
                bar_height,
            )
            painter.fillRect(rect, brush)
        # end::draw[]
        painter.end()

    def _trigger_refresh(self):
```

```
        self.update()


class PowerBar(QtWidgets.QWidget):
    """
    Custom Qt Widget to show a power bar and dial.
    Demonstrating compound and custom-drawn widget.
    """

    def __init__(self, steps=5, *args, **kwargs):
        super().__init__(*args, **kwargs)

        layout = QtWidgets.QVBoxLayout()
        self._bar = _Bar()
        layout.addWidget(self._bar)

        self._dial = QtWidgets.QDial()
        self._dial.valueChanged.connect(self._bar._trigger_refresh)
        layout.addWidget(self._dial)

        self.setLayout(layout)


app = QtWidgets.QApplication(sys.argv)
volume = PowerBar()
volume.show()
app.exec_()
```

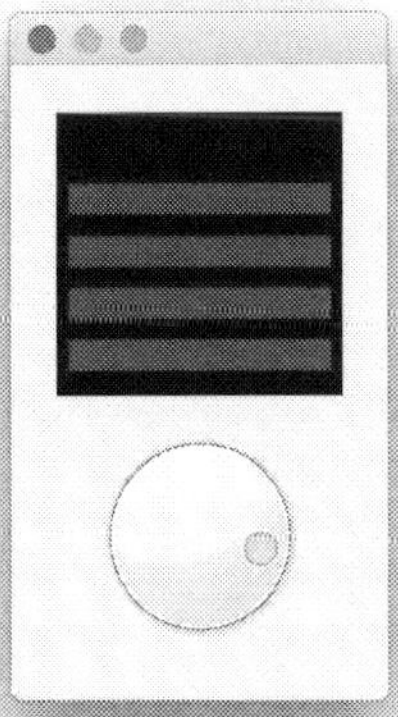

Figure 203. The basic complete PowerBar.

That already does the job, but we can go further to provide more customization, add some UX improvements and improve the API for working with our widget.

Customizing the Bar

We now have a working power bar, controllable with a dial. But it's nice when creating widgets to provide options to configure the behavior of your widget to make it more flexible. In this part we'll add methods to set customizable numbers of segments, colors, padding and spacing.

The elements we're going to provide customization for are—

Option	Description
number of bars	How many bars are displayed on the widget
colors	Individual colors for each of the bars
background color	The color of the draw canvas (default black)
padding	Space around the widget edge, between bars and edge of canvas
bar height / bar percent	Proportion (0…1) of the bar which is solid (the rest will be spacing between adjacent bars)

We can store each of these as attributes on the `_bar` object, and use them from the `paintEvent` method to change its behavior.

The `Bar.\__init_` is updated to accept an initial argument for either the number of bars (as an integer) or the colors of the bars (as a list of `QColor`, hex values or names). If a number is provided, all bars will be colored red. If the a list of colors is provided the number of bars will be determined from the length of the color list. Default values for`self._bar_solid_percent`, `self._background_color`, `self._padding` are also set.

Listing 146. custom-widgets/powerbar_7.py

```python
class _Bar(QtWidgets.QWidget):

    clickedValue = QtCore.pyqtSignal(int)

    def __init__(self, steps, *args, **kwargs):
        super().__init__(*args, **kwargs)

        self.setSizePolicy(
            QtWidgets.QSizePolicy.MinimumExpanding,
            QtWidgets.QSizePolicy.MinimumExpanding,
        )

        if isinstance(steps, list):
            # list of colors.
            self.n_steps = len(steps)
            self.steps = steps

        elif isinstance(steps, int):
            # int number of bars, defaults to red.
            self.n_steps = steps
            self.steps = ["red"] * steps

        else:
            raise TypeError("steps must be a list or int")

        self._bar_solid_percent = 0.8
        self._background_color = QtGui.QColor("black")
        self._padding = 4.0  # n-pixel gap around edge.
```

Likewise we update the `PowerBar.__init__` to accept the steps parameter, and pass it through.

Listing 147. custom-widgets/powerbar_7.py

```
class PowerBar(QtWidgets.QWidget):
    def __init__(self, steps=5, *args, **kwargs):
        super().__init__(*args, **kwargs)

        layout = QtWidgets.QVBoxLayout()
        self._bar = _Bar(steps)

        layout.addWidget(self._bar)

        self._dial = QtWidgets.QDial()
        self._dial.valueChanged.connect(self._bar._trigger_refresh)
        layout.addWidget(self._dial)

        self.setLayout(layout)
```

We now have the parameters in place to update the `paintEvent` method. The modified code is shown below.

Listing 148. custom-widgets/powerbar_7.py

```
    def paintEvent(self, e):
        painter = QtGui.QPainter(self)

        brush = QtGui.QBrush()
        brush.setColor(self._background_color)
        brush.setStyle(Qt.SolidPattern)
        rect = QtCore.QRect(0, 0, painter.device().width(), painter
.device().height())
        painter.fillRect(rect, brush)

        # Get current state.
        dial = self.parent()._dial
        vmin, vmax = dial.minimum(), dial.maximum()
        value = dial.value()

        # Define our canvas.
        d_height = painter.device().height() - (self._padding * 2)
        d_width = painter.device().width() - (self._padding * 2)

        # Draw the bars.
        step_size = d_height / self.n_steps
        bar_height = step_size * self._bar_solid_percent
        bar_spacer = step_size * (1 - self._bar_solid_percent) / 2

        # Calculate the y-stop position, from the value in range.
        pc = (value - vmin) / (vmax - vmin)
        n_steps_to_draw = int(pc * self.n_steps)

        for n in range(n_steps_to_draw):
            brush.setColor(QtGui.QColor(self.steps[n]))
            rect = QtCore.QRect(
                self._padding,
                self._padding + d_height - ((1 + n) * step_size) +
bar_spacer,
                d_width,
                bar_height,
            )
            painter.fillRect(rect, brush)

        painter.end()
```

You can now experiment with passing in different values for the `__init__` to `PowerBar`, e.g. increasing the number of bars, or providing a color list. Some examples are shown below.

> A good source of hex color palettes is the Bokeh source [https://github.com/bokeh/bokeh/blob/master/bokeh/palettes.py].

```
PowerBar(10)
PowerBar(3)
PowerBar(["#5e4fa2", "#3288bd", "#66c2a5", "#abdda4", "#e6f598",
"#ffffbf", "#fee08b", "#fdae61", "#f46d43", "#d53e4f", "#9e0142"])
PowerBar(["#a63603", "#e6550d", "#fd8d3c", "#fdae6b", "#fdd0a2",
"#feedde"])
```

Figure 204. Some PowerBar examples.

You could fiddle with the padding settings through the variables e.g. `self._bar_solid_percent` but it'd be nicer to provide proper methods to set these.

> We're following the Qt standard of camelCase method names for these external methods for consistency with the others inherited from `QDial`.

Listing 149. custom-widgets/powerbar_8.py

```
    def setColor(self, color):
        self._bar.steps = [color] * self._bar.n_steps
        self._bar.update()

    def setColors(self, colors):
        self._bar.n_steps = len(colors)
        self._bar.steps = colors
        self._bar.update()

    def setBarPadding(self, i):
        self._bar._padding = int(i)
        self._bar.update()

    def setBarSolidPercent(self, f):
        self._bar._bar_solid_percent = float(f)
        self._bar.update()

    def setBackgroundColor(self, color):
        self._bar._background_color = QtGui.QColor(color)
        self._bar.update()
```

In each case we set the private variable on the `_bar` object and then call `_bar.update()` to trigger a redraw of the widget. The method support changing the color to a single color, or updating a list of them—setting a list of colors can also be used to change the number of bars.

> There is no method to set the bar count, since expanding a list of colors would be faffy. But feel free to try adding this yourself!

Here's an example using 25px padding, a fully solid bar and a grey background.

```
bar = PowerBar(["#49006a", "#7a0177", "#ae017e", "#dd3497",
"#f768a1", "#fa9fb5", "#fcc5c0", "#fde0dd", "#fff7f3"])
bar.setBarPadding(2)
bar.setBarSolidPercent(0.9)
bar.setBackgroundColor('gray')
```

With these settings you get the following result.

Figure 205. Configuring the PowerBar.

Adding the QAbstractSlider Interface

We've added methods to configure the behavior of the power bar. But we currently provide no way to configure the standard `QDial` methods -- for example, setting the min, max or step size -- from our widget. We could work through and add wrapper methods for all of these, but it would get very tedious very quickly.

```
# Example of a single wrapper, we'd need 30+ of these.
def setNotchesVisible(self, b):
    return self._dial.setNotchesVisible(b)
```

Instead we can add a little handler onto our outer widget to automatically look for methods (or attributes) on the `QDial` instance, if they don't exist on our class directly. This way we can implement our own methods, yet still get all the `QAbstractSlider` goodness for free.

The wrapper is shown below, implemented as a custom `__getattr__` method.

Listing 150. custom-widgets/powerbar_8.py

```
    def __getattr__(self, name):
        if name in self.__dict__:
            return self[name]

        try:
            return getattr(self._dial, name)
        except AttributeError:
            raise AttributeError(
                "'{}' object has no attribute '{}'".format(
                    self.__class__.__name__, name
                )
            )
```

When accessing a property (or method) -- e.g. when we call `PowerBar.setNotchesVisible(true)` Python internally uses `__getattr__` to get the property from the current object. This handler does this through the object dictionary `self.__dict__`. We've overridden this method to provide our custom handling logic.

Now, when we call `PowerBar.setNotchesVisible(true)`, this handler first looks on our current object (a `PowerBar` instance) to see if `.setNotchesVisible` exists and if it does uses it. If **not** it then calls `getattr()` on `self._dial` instead returning what it finds there. This gives us access to all the methods of `QDial` from our custom `PowerBar` widget.

If `QDial` doesn't have the attribute either, and raises an `AttributeError` we catch it and raise it again from our custom widget, where it belongs.

This works for any properties or methods, including signals. So the standard `QDial` signals such as `.valueChanged` are available too.

Updating from the Meter display

Currently you can update the current value of the PowerBar meter by twiddling with the dial. But it would be nice if you could also update the value by clicking a position on the power bar, or by dragging you mouse up and down. To do this we can update our `_Bar` widget to handle mouse events.

Listing 151. custom-widgets/powerbar_9.py

```
class _Bar(QtWidgets.QWidget):

    clickedValue = QtCore.pyqtSignal(int)
```

In the `__init__` block for the `PowerBar` widget we can connect to the `_Bar.clickedValue` signal and send the values to `self._dial.setValue` to set the current value on the dial.

```
# Take feedback from click events on the meter.
self._bar.clickedValue.connect(self._dial.setValue)
```

If you run the widget now, you'll be able to click around in the bar area and the value will update, and the dial rotate in sync.

The final code

Below is the complete final code for our PowerBar meter widget, called `PowerBar`. You can save this as a separate file, e.g. `power_bar.py` and then import with `from power_bar import PowerBar` to use this widget in your own apps.

Listing 152. custom-widgets/powerbar_final.py

```
from PyQt5 import QtCore, QtGui, QtWidgets
from PyQt5.QtCore import Qt


class _Bar(QtWidgets.QWidget):
```

```
    clickedValue = QtCore.pyqtSignal(int)

    def __init__(self, steps, *args, **kwargs):
        super().__init__(*args, **kwargs)

        self.setSizePolicy(
            QtWidgets.QSizePolicy.MinimumExpanding,
            QtWidgets.QSizePolicy.MinimumExpanding,
        )

        if isinstance(steps, list):
            # list of colors.
            self.n_steps = len(steps)
            self.steps = steps

        elif isinstance(steps, int):
            # int number of bars, defaults to red.
            self.n_steps = steps
            self.steps = ["red"] * steps

        else:
            raise TypeError("steps must be a list or int")

        self._bar_solid_percent = 0.8
        self._background_color = QtGui.QColor("black")
        self._padding = 4.0  # n-pixel gap around edge.

    def paintEvent(self, e):
        painter = QtGui.QPainter(self)

        brush = QtGui.QBrush()
        brush.setColor(self._background_color)
        brush.setStyle(Qt.SolidPattern)
        rect = QtCore.QRect(0, 0, painter.device().width(), painter
.device().height())
        painter.fillRect(rect, brush)

        # Get current state.
        parent = self.parent()
        vmin, vmax = parent.minimum(), parent.maximum()
        value = parent.value()

        # Define our canvas.
```

```
        d_height = painter.device().height() - (self._padding * 2)
        d_width = painter.device().width() - (self._padding * 2)

        # Draw the bars.
        step_size = d_height / self.n_steps
        bar_height = step_size * self._bar_solid_percent
        bar_spacer = step_size * (1 - self._bar_solid_percent) / 2

        # Calculate the y-stop position, from the value in range.
        pc = (value - vmin) / (vmax - vmin)
        n_steps_to_draw = int(pc * self.n_steps)

        for n in range(n_steps_to_draw):
            brush.setColor(QtGui.QColor(self.steps[n]))
            rect = QtCore.QRect(
                self._padding,
                self._padding + d_height - ((1 + n) * step_size) +
bar_spacer,
                d_width,
                bar_height,
            )
            painter.fillRect(rect, brush)

        painter.end()

    def sizeHint(self):
        return QtCore.QSize(40, 120)

    def _trigger_refresh(self):
        self.update()

    def _calculate_clicked_value(self, e):
        parent = self.parent()
        vmin, vmax = parent.minimum(), parent.maximum()
        d_height = self.size().height() + (self._padding * 2)
        step_size = d_height / self.n_steps
        click_y = e.y() - self._padding - step_size / 2

        pc = (d_height - click_y) / d_height
        value = vmin + pc * (vmax - vmin)
        self.clickedValue.emit(value)

    def mouseMoveEvent(self, e):
```

```
        self._calculate_clicked_value(e)

    def mousePressEvent(self, e):
        self._calculate_clicked_value(e)


class PowerBar(QtWidgets.QWidget):
    """
    Custom Qt Widget to show a power bar and dial.
    Demonstrating compound and custom-drawn widget.

    Left-clicking the button shows the color-chooser, while
    right-clicking resets the color to None (no-color).
    """

    colorChanged = QtCore.pyqtSignal()

    def __init__(self, steps=5, *args, **kwargs):
        super().__init__(*args, **kwargs)

        layout = QtWidgets.QVBoxLayout()
        self._bar = _Bar(steps)
        layout.addWidget(self._bar)

        # Create the QDial widget and set up defaults.
        # - we provide accessors on this class to override.
        self._dial = QtWidgets.QDial()
        self._dial.setNotchesVisible(True)
        self._dial.setWrapping(False)
        self._dial.valueChanged.connect(self._bar._trigger_refresh)

        # Take feedback from click events on the meter.
        self._bar.clickedValue.connect(self._dial.setValue)

        layout.addWidget(self._dial)
        self.setLayout(layout)

    def __getattr__(self, name):
        if name in self.__dict__:
            return self[name]

        return getattr(self._dial, name)
```

```python
    def setColor(self, color):
        self._bar.steps = [color] * self._bar.n_steps
        self._bar.update()

    def setColors(self, colors):
        self._bar.n_steps = len(colors)
        self._bar.steps = colors
        self._bar.update()

    def setBarPadding(self, i):
        self._bar._padding = int(i)
        self._bar.update()

    def setBarSolidPercent(self, f):
        self._bar._bar_solid_percent = float(f)
        self._bar.update()

    def setBackgroundColor(self, color):
        self._bar._background_color = QtGui.QColor(color)
        self._bar.update()
```

You should be able to use many of these ideas in creating your own custom widgets. For some more examples, take a look at the Learn PyQt widget library [https://www.learnpyqt.com/widgets/] -- these widgets are all open source and free to use in your own projects.

✋ Familiarity & Skeuomorphism

One of the most powerful tools you can exploit when building user interfaces is *familiarity*. That is, giving your users the sense that your interface is something they have used before.

Good interfaces are often described as being *intuitive*. There is nothing naturally intuitive about moving a mouse pointer around a screen and clicking on square-ish bumps. But, after spending years of our lives doing exactly that, there is something very familiar about it. There is nothing more guaranteed to make an application incredibly user unfriendly than to ignore the value of this experience.

The search for *familiarity* in user interfaces led to the use of *skeuomorphism* in GUI design. Skeuomorphism is the application of non-functional design cues from other objects, where those design elements are functional. That can mean using common interface elements, or replicating some aspects of the manual process you're replacing. In the context of GUIs this often means user interfaces that look like real objects.

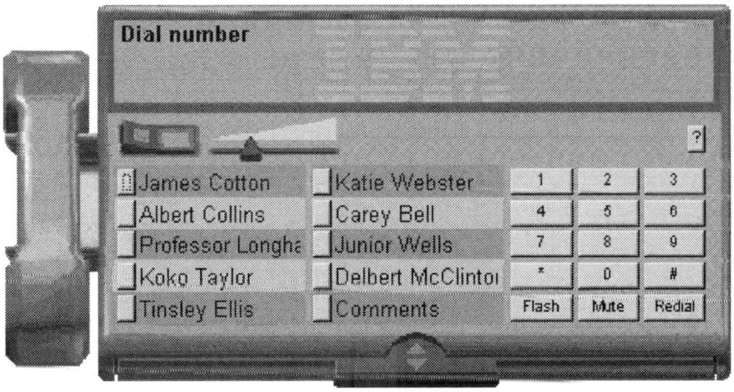

Figure 206. RealPhone — One of IBM's RealThings™

Apple was a big proponent of skeuomorphism during the Steve Jobs era. In recent years GUIs have, inspired by the web, moved increasingly to "flat" designs. Yet, modern user-interfaces all still have elements of skeuomorphism in them. Even though floppy disks are now defunct technology, they are still used to represent the **File › Save** and **File › Save As..** actions, and we put deleted documents in a trash can.

But there are more subtle ways to exploit *familiarity* in your interfaces. You can adapt the structure and layout of a manual process into your UI. The modern desktop calculator is a good example of this kind of abstract skeuomorphism.

Figure 207. Calculator & Upside down calculator—Windows 10

When we perform calculations we typically put the result at the *bottom*. So why is the screen at the top on a calculator? Because otherwise it would be obscured by your hand. The position of the screen is *functional*.

This position persists in calculators on computers, even though the screen position is no longer required—the mouse pointer will not obscure the screen and manual input is via the keyboard. But if you opened up a calculator and it had the screen at the bottom you would be confused. It looks *upside down*. It's *weird* or *unintuitive* despite being perfectly functional. That is the essence of skeuomorphism in GUI design—making user interfaces feel more intuitive by exploiting the familiarity of users with existing objects.

Where your own software sits on this scale is of course up to you. The important thing is to be aware of existing interfaces and to exploit them where you can to improve usability of your own apps. Your users will thank you for it!

✔ DO

- Take inspiration from existing interfaces when designing your own.
- Include skeuomorphic elements where they *help* your users.

Concurrent Execution

> A computer shall not waste your time or require you to do more work than is strictly necessary.
>
> — Jef Raskin, Second Law of User Interface Design

The event loop started by calling `.exec_()` on your `QApplication` object runs within the same thread as your Python code. The thread which runs this event loop — commonly referred to as the *GUI thread* — also handles all window communication with the host operating system.

By default, any execution triggered by the event loop will also run synchronously within this thread. In practise this means that any time your PyQt5 application spends *doing something* in your code, window communication and GUI interaction are frozen.

If what you're doing is simple, and returns control to the GUI loop quickly, this freeze will be imperceptible to the user. However, if you need to perform longer-running tasks, for example opening/writing a large file, downloading some data, or rendering some complex image, there are going to be problems. To your user the application will appear to be unresponsive. Because your app is no longer communicating with the OS the OS will think it has crashed—on macOS you see the spinning wheel of death, on Windows the window will dim. That's not a good look.

The solution is simple—get your work out of the *GUI thread*. PyQt5 provides straightforward interfaces to accomplish exactly that.

31. Introduction to Threads & Processes

Below is a minimal stub application for PyQt5 which will allow us to demonstrate the problem and later to fix it. You can copy and paste this into a new file, and save it with an appropriate filename like `concurrent.py`.

Listing 153. bad_example_1.py

```
import sys
import time

from PyQt5.QtCore import QTimer
from PyQt5.QtWidgets import (
    QApplication,
    QLabel,
    QMainWindow,
    QPushButton,
    QVBoxLayout,
    QWidget,
)


class MainWindow(QMainWindow):
    def __init__(self):
        super().__init__()

        self.counter = 0

        layout = QVBoxLayout()

        self.l = QLabel("Start")
        b = QPushButton("DANGER!")
        b.pressed.connect(self.oh_no)

        layout.addWidget(self.l)
        layout.addWidget(b)

        w = QWidget()
        w.setLayout(layout)
```

```
        self.setCentralWidget(w)

        self.show()

        self.timer = QTimer()
        self.timer.setInterval(1000)
        self.timer.timeout.connect(self.recurring_timer)
        self.timer.start()

    def oh_no(self):
        time.sleep(5)

    def recurring_timer(self):
        self.counter += 1
        self.l.setText("Counter: %d" % self.counter)


app = QApplication(sys.argv)
window = MainWindow()
app.exec_()
```

Run it! A window will appear, containing a button and a number counting upwards.

Figure 208. The number will increase by 1 every second, as long as the event loop is running.

This is generated by a simple recurring timer, firing once per second. Think of this as our *event loop indicator*—a simple way to let us known that out application is ticking over normally. There is also a button with the word **"DANGER!"**. Push it.

Figure 209. Push the button.

You'll notice that each time you push the button the counter stops ticking and your application freezes entirely. On Windows you may see the window turn pale, indicating it is not responding, while on macOS you may see the spinning wheel of death.

What appears as a *frozen interface* is in fact caused by the Qt event loop being blocked from processing (and responding to) window events. Your clicks on the window as still registered by the host OS and sent to your application, but because it's sat in your big ol' lump of code (`time.sleep`), it can't accept or react to them. Your app does not respond and the OS and it interprets this as a freeze or hang.

The wrong approach

The simplest way get around this is to accept events from within your code. This allows Qt to continue to respond to the host OS and your application will stay responsive. You can do this easily by using the static `.processEvents()` function on the `QApplication` class. Simply add a line like the following, somewhere in your long-running code block:

```
QApplication.processEvents()
```

If we take our long-running `time.sleep` code and break it down into multiple steps, we can insert `.processEvents` in between. The code for this would be:

```
def oh_no(self):
    for n in range(5):
        QApplication.processEvents()
        time.sleep(1)
```

Now when you push the button your code is entered as before. However, now `QApplication.processEvents()` intermittently passes control back to Qt, and allows it to respond to OS events as normal. Qt will now accept events *and handle them* before returning to run the remainder of your code.

This works, but it's horrible for a couple of reasons.

Firstly, when you pass control back to Qt, your code is no longer running. This means that whatever long-running thing you're trying to do will take *longer*. That is probably not what you want.

Secondly, processing events outside the main event loop (`app.exec_()`) causes your application to branch off into handling code (e.g. for triggered slots, or events) while in your loop. If your code depends on/responds to external state this can cause undefined behavior. The code below demonstrates this in action:

Listing 154. bad_example_2.py

```
import sys
import time

from PyQt5.QtCore import QTimer
from PyQt5.QtWidgets import (
    QApplication,
    QLabel,
    QMainWindow,
    QPushButton,
    QVBoxLayout,
    QWidget,
)
```

```python
class MainWindow(QMainWindow):
    def __init__(self):
        super().__init__()

        self.counter = 0

        layout = QVBoxLayout()

        self.l = QLabel("Start")
        b = QPushButton("DANGER!")
        b.pressed.connect(self.oh_no)

        c = QPushButton("?")
        c.pressed.connect(self.change_message)

        layout.addWidget(self.l)
        layout.addWidget(b)

        layout.addWidget(c)

        w = QWidget()
        w.setLayout(layout)

        self.setCentralWidget(w)

        self.show()

    def change_message(self):
        self.message = "OH NO"

    def oh_no(self):
        self.message = "Pressed"

        for _ in range(100):
            time.sleep(0.1)
            self.l.setText(self.message)
            QApplication.processEvents()


app = QApplication(sys.argv)
window = MainWindow()
app.exec_()
```

If you run this code you'll see the counter as before. Pressing "DANGER!" will change the displayed text to "Pressed", as defined at the entry point to the `oh_no` function. However, if you press the "?" button while `oh_no` is still running you'll see that the message changes. State is being changed from outside your loop.

This is a toy example. However, if you have multiple long-running processes within your application, with each calling `QApplication.processEvents()` to keep things ticking, your application behavior can quickly become unpredictable.

Threads and Processes

If you take a step back and think about what you want to happen in your application, it can probably be summed up with "stuff to happen at the same time as other stuff happens". There are two main approaches to running independent tasks on a computer: *threads* and *processes*.

Threads share the same memory space, so are quick to start up and consume minimal resources. The shared memory makes it trivial to pass data between threads, however reading/writing memory from different threads can lead to race conditions or segfaults. In Python there is the added issue that multiple threads are bound by the same Global Interpreter Lock GIL — meaning non-GIL-releasing Python code can only execute in one thread at a time. However, this is not a major issue with PyQt5 where most of the time is spent outside of Python.

Processes use separate memory space (and an entirely separate Python interpreter). This side-steps any potential problems with the GIL, but at the cost of slower start-up times, larger memory overhead and complexity in sending/receiving data.

For simplicity's sake it usually makes sense to use threads. Processes in Qt are better suited to running and communicating with external programs. In this chapter we'll look at the options available to you from within Qt to move work onto separate threads and processes.

32. Using the thread pool

Qt provides a very simple interface for running jobs in other threads, which is exposed nicely in PyQt5. This is built around two classes—`QRunnable` and `QThreadPool`. The former is the container for the work you want to perform, while the latter is the manager for your working threads.

The neat thing about using `QThreadPool` is that it handles queuing and execution of workers for you. Other than queuing up jobs and retrieving the results there is not very much to do at all.

To define a custom `QRunnable` you can subclass the base `QRunnable` class, then place the code you wish you execute within the `run()` method. The following is an implementation of our long running `time.sleep` job as a `QRunnable`. Add the following code to `multithread.py`, above the `MainWindow` class definition.

Listing 155. concurrent/qrunner_1.py

```
class Worker(QRunnable):
    """
    Worker thread
    """

    @pyqtSlot()
    def run(self):
        """
        Your code goes in this function
        """
        print("Thread start")
        time.sleep(5)
        print("Thread complete")
```

Executing our function in another thread is simply a matter of creating an instance of the `Worker` and then pass it to our `QThreadPool` instance and it will be executed automatically.

Next add the following within the `__init__` block, to set up our thread pool.

Listing 156. concurrent/qrunner_1.py

```
class MainWindow(QMainWindow):
    def __init__(self):
        super().__init__()

        self.threadpool = QThreadPool()
        print(
            "Multithreading with maximum %d threads" % self
.threadpool.maxThreadCount()
        )
```

Finally, replace the `oh_no` method with the following.

Listing 157. concurrent/qrunner_1.py

```
    def oh_no(self):
        worker = Worker()
        self.threadpool.start(worker)
```

Now, clicking on the button will create a worker to handle the (long-running) process and spin that off into another thread via `QThreadPool`` pool. If there are not enough threads available to process incoming workers, they'll be queued and executed in order at a later time.

Run it! You'll see that your application now handles you frantically bashing the button with no problems.

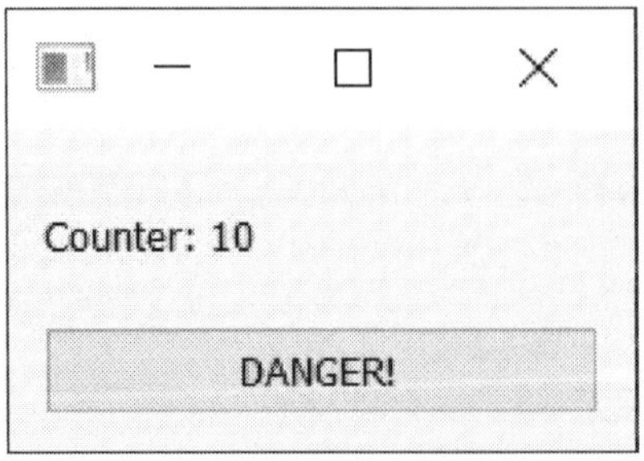

Figure 210. The simple `QRunner` example app. The counter will increase by one every second—as long as the GUI thread is running.

Look at the output in the console to see workers starting and finishing.

```
Multithreading with maximum 12 threads
Thread start
Thread start
Thread start
Thread complete
Thread complete
Thread complete
```

Check what happens if you hit the button multiple times. You should see your threads executed immediately *up to* the number reported by `.maxThreadCount`. If you hit the button again after there are already this number of active workers, the subsequent workers will be queued until a thread becomes available.

In this example we've let `QThreadPool` decide the *ideal* number of active threads to use. This number differs on different computers and is designed to get the optimum performance. However, sometimes you have a need for a *specific* number of threads—in that case, you can use `.setMaxThreadCount` to set this value explicitly. This value is *per thread pool*.

Extended Runners

If you want to pass custom data into the execution function you can set up your runner to take *arguments* or *keywords* and then store that data on the `QRunner` `self` object. The data will then be accessible from within the `run` method.

Listing 158. concurrent/qrunner_2.py

```
class Worker(QRunnable):
    """
    Worker thread

    :param args: Arguments to make available to the run code
    :param kwargs: Keywords arguments to make available to the run
    :code
    :
    """

    def __init__(self, *args, **kwargs):
        super().__init__()
        self.args = args
        self.kwargs = kwargs

    @pyqtSlot()
    def run(self):
        """
        Initialize the runner function with passed self.args,
self.kwargs.
        """
        print(self.args, self.kwargs)


    def oh_no(self):
        worker = Worker("some", "arguments", keywords=2)
        self.threadpool.start(worker)
```

As functions are also objects in Python, you can also pass a function to execute in to your runner. See The Generic for an example.

Thread IO

Sometimes it's helpful to be able to pass back *state* and *data* from running workers. This could include the outcome of calculations, raised exceptions or ongoing progress (think progress bars). Qt provides the *signals and slots* framework which allows you to do just that and is thread-safe, allowing safe communication directly from running threads to your GUI frontend. *Signals* allow you to `.emit` values, which are then picked up elsewhere in your code by *slot* functions which have been linked with `.connect`.

Below is a simple `WorkerSignals` class defined to contain a number of example signals.

> Custom signals can only be defined on objects derived from `QObject`. Since `QRunnable` is not derived from `QObject` we can't define the signals there directly. A custom `QObject` to hold the signals is the simplest solution.

Listing 159. concurrent/qrunner_3.py

```
class WorkerSignals(QObject):
    """
    Defines the signals available from a running worker thread.

    Supported signals are:

    finished
        No data

    error
        `str` Exception string

    result
        `dict` data returned from processing

    """

    finished = pyqtSignal()
    error = pyqtSignal(str)
    result = pyqtSignal(dict)
```

In this example we've defined 3 custom signals:

1. *finished* signal, with no data to indicate when the task is complete.

2. *error* signal which receives a `tuple` of `Exception` type, `Exception` value and formatted traceback.

3. *result* signal receiving any `object` type from the executed function.

You may not find a need for all of these signals, but they are included to give an indication of what is possible. In the following code we use these signals to notify about completion and errors in a simple calculation worker.

Listing 160. concurrent/qrunner_3.py

```
import random
import sys
import time

from PyQt5.QtCore import QObject, QRunnable, QThreadPool, QTimer,
pyqtSignal, pyqtSlot
from PyQt5.QtWidgets import (
    QApplication,
    QLabel,
    QMainWindow,
    QPushButton,
    QVBoxLayout,
    QWidget,
)

class WorkerSignals(QObject):
    """
    Defines the signals available from a running worker thread.

    Supported signals are:

    finished
        No data

    error
        `str` Exception string

    result
        `dict` data returned from processing

    """
```

```
    finished = pyqtSignal()
    error = pyqtSignal(str)
    result = pyqtSignal(dict)


class Worker(QRunnable):
    """
    Worker thread

    :param args: Arguments to make available to the run code
    :param kwargs: Keywords arguments to make available to the run
    :code
    :
    """

    def __init__(self, iterations=5):
        super().__init__()
        self.signals = WorkerSignals()  # Create an instance of our
signals class.
        self.iterations = iterations

    @pyqtSlot()
    def run(self):
        """
        Initialize the runner function with passed self.args,
self.kwargs.
        """
        try:
            for n in range(self.iterations):
                time.sleep(0.01)
                v = 5 / (40 - n)

        except Exception as e:
            self.signals.error.emit(str(e))

        else:
            self.signals.finished.emit()
            self.signals.result.emit({"n": n, "value": v})


class MainWindow(QMainWindow):
    def __init__(self):
```

```
        super().__init__()

        self.threadpool = QThreadPool()
        print(
            "Multithreading with maximum %d threads" % self
.threadpool.maxThreadCount()
        )

        self.counter = 0

        layout = QVBoxLayout()

        self.l = QLabel("Start")
        b = QPushButton("DANGER!")
        b.pressed.connect(self.oh_no)

        layout.addWidget(self.l)
        layout.addWidget(b)

        w = QWidget()
        w.setLayout(layout)

        self.setCentralWidget(w)

        self.show()

        self.timer = QTimer()
        self.timer.setInterval(1000)
        self.timer.timeout.connect(self.recurring_timer)
        self.timer.start()

    def oh_no(self):
        worker = Worker(iterations=random.randint(10, 50))
        worker.signals.result.connect(self.worker_output)
        worker.signals.finished.connect(self.worker_complete)
        worker.signals.error.connect(self.worker_error)
        self.threadpool.start(worker)

    def worker_output(self, s):
        print("RESULT", s)

    def worker_complete(self):
        print("THREAD COMPLETE!")
```

```
    def worker_error(self, t):
        print("ERROR: %s" % t)

    def recurring_timer(self):
        self.counter += 1
        self.l.setText("Counter: %d" % self.counter)


app = QApplication(sys.argv)
window = MainWindow()
app.exec_()
```

You can connect your own handler functions to these signals to receive notification of completion (or the result) of threads. The example is designed to occasionally throw a *division by zero* exception, which you'll see in the output.

```
Multithreading with maximum 12 threads
THREAD COMPLETE!
RESULT {'n': 16, 'value': 0.20833333333333334}
ERROR: division by zero
THREAD COMPLETE!
RESULT {'n': 11, 'value': 0.1724137931034483}
THREAD COMPLETE!
RESULT {'n': 22, 'value': 0.2777777777777778}
ERROR: division by zero
```

In the next section we'll look at a number of different variations on this approach which allow you to do some interesting things using `QThreadPool` in your own applications.

33. Threading examples

`QThreadPool` and `QRunnable` are an incredibly flexible way to run things in other threads. By tweaking the signals and parameters you can perform any tasks you can imagine. In this chapter we'll look some examples for how to construct runners for particular scenarios.

All the examples follow the same general pattern—a custom `QRunnable` class with custom `WorkerSignals`. The difference is in what we pass to the runner, what it does with those parameters, and how we hook up the signals.

Listing 161. concurrent/qrunner_base.py

```python
import sys
import time
import traceback

from PyQt5.QtCore import QObject, QRunnable, QThreadPool, pyqtSignal,
pyqtSlot
from PyQt5.QtWidgets import QApplication, QMainWindow


class WorkerSignals(QObject):
    pass


class Worker(QRunnable):
    def __init__(self, *args, **kwargs):
        super().__init__()
        # Store constructor arguments (re-used for processing)
        self.args = args
        self.kwargs = kwargs
        self.signals = WorkerSignals()

    @pyqtSlot()
    def run(self):
        pass


class MainWindow(QMainWindow):
    def __init__(self):
        super().__init__()


app = QApplication(sys.argv)
window = MainWindow()
app.exec_()
```

The progress watcher

If you're using threads to perform long-running actions you should keep your users informed about how the task is progressing. A common way to do this is by showing the user a *progress bar* which indicates, with a bar filling left to right, how much of the task is complete. In order to show a progress bar for your tasks, you need to emit the current progress state from your worker.

To do this we can define another signal called `progress` on the `WorkerSignals` object. This signal emits on each loop a number from 0..100 as the "task" progresses. The output of this progress signal is connected to a standard `QProgressBar` shown on the statusbar of our main window.

Listing 162. concurrent/qrunner_progress.py

```
import time

from PyQt5.QtCore import QObject, QRunnable, QThreadPool, QTimer,
pyqtSignal, pyqtSlot
from PyQt5.QtWidgets import (
    QApplication,
    QLabel,
    QMainWindow,
    QProgressBar,
    QPushButton,
    QVBoxLayout,
    QWidget,
)


class WorkerSignals(QObject):
    """
    Defines the signals available from a running worker thread.

    progress
        int progress complete,from 0-100
    """

    progress = pyqtSignal(int)


class Worker(QRunnable):
    """
    Worker thread

    Inherits from QRunnable to handle worker thread setup, signals
```

```
    and wrap-up.
    """

    def __init__(self):
        super().__init__()

        self.signals = WorkerSignals()

    @pyqtSlot()
    def run(self):
        total_n = 1000
        for n in range(total_n):
            progress_pc = int(100 * float(n + 1) / total_n)  #
Progress 0-100% as int
            self.signals.progress.emit(progress_pc)
            time.sleep(0.01)


class MainWindow(QMainWindow):
    def __init__(self, *args, **kwargs):
        super().__init__(*args, **kwargs)

        layout = QVBoxLayout()

        self.progress = QProgressBar()

        button = QPushButton("START IT UP")
        button.pressed.connect(self.execute)

        layout.addWidget(self.progress)
        layout.addWidget(button)

        w = QWidget()
        w.setLayout(layout)

        self.setCentralWidget(w)

        self.show()

        self.threadpool = QThreadPool()
        print(
            "Multithreading with maximum %d threads" % self
.threadpool.maxThreadCount()
```

```python
        )

    def execute(self):
        worker = Worker()
        worker.signals.progress.connect(self.update_progress)

        # Execute
        self.threadpool.start(worker)

    def update_progress(self, progress):
        self.progress.setValue(progress)


app = QApplication(sys.argv)
window = MainWindow()
app.exec_()
```

Figure 211. Progress bar showing current progress for a long-running worker.

If you press the button while another runner is already working, you'll notice a problem—the two runners emit their progress to the same progress bar, so the values will jump back and forward.

Tracking multiple workers with a single progress bar is possible—we just need two things: somewhere to *store* the progress values for each worker, and a unique identifier for each worker. On each progress update, we can then calculate the *average* progress across all workers, and display that.

Listing 163. concurrent/qrunner_progress_many.py

```python
import random
import sys
import time
import uuid
```

```
from PyQt5.QtCore import QObject, QRunnable, QThreadPool, QTimer,
pyqtSignal, pyqtSlot
from PyQt5.QtWidgets import (
    QApplication,
    QLabel,
    QMainWindow,
    QProgressBar,
    QPushButton,
    QVBoxLayout,
    QWidget,
)


class WorkerSignals(QObject):
    """
    Defines the signals available from a running worker thread.

    progress
        int progress complete,from 0-100
    """

    progress = pyqtSignal(str, int)
    finished = pyqtSignal(str)


class Worker(QRunnable):
    """
    Worker thread

    Inherits from QRunnable to handle worker thread setup, signals
    and wrap-up.
    """

    def __init__(self):
        super().__init__()
        self.job_id = uuid.uuid4().hex  ①
        self.signals = WorkerSignals()

    @pyqtSlot()
    def run(self):
        total_n = 1000
        delay = random.random() / 100  # Random delay value.
```

```
        for n in range(total_n):
            progress_pc = int(100 * float(n + 1) / total_n)  ②
            self.signals.progress.emit(self.job_id, progress_pc)
            time.sleep(delay)

        self.signals.finished.emit(self.job_id)


class MainWindow(QMainWindow):
    def __init__(self):
        super().__init__()

        layout = QVBoxLayout()

        self.progress = QProgressBar()

        button = QPushButton("START IT UP")
        button.pressed.connect(self.execute)

        self.status = QLabel("0 workers")

        layout.addWidget(self.progress)
        layout.addWidget(button)
        layout.addWidget(self.status)

        w = QWidget()
        w.setLayout(layout)

        # Dictionary holds the progress of current workers.
        self.worker_progress = {}

        self.setCentralWidget(w)

        self.show()

        self.threadpool = QThreadPool()
        print(
            "Multithreading with maximum %d threads" % self
.threadpool.maxThreadCount()
        )

        self.timer = QTimer()
        self.timer.setInterval(100)
```

```
        self.timer.timeout.connect(self.refresh_progress)
        self.timer.start()

    def execute(self):
        worker = Worker()
        worker.signals.progress.connect(self.update_progress)
        worker.signals.finished.connect(self.cleanup)  ③

        # Execute
        self.threadpool.start(worker)

    def cleanup(self, job_id):
        if job_id in self.worker_progress:
            del self.worker_progress[job_id]  ④

            # Update the progress bar if we've removed a value.
            self.refresh_progress()

    def update_progress(self, job_id, progress):
        self.worker_progress[job_id] = progress

    def calculate_progress(self):
        if not self.worker_progress:
            return 0

        return sum(v for v in self.worker_progress.values()) / len
(self.worker_progress)

    def refresh_progress(self):
        # Calculate total progress.
        progress = self.calculate_progress()
        print(self.worker_progress)
        self.progress.setValue(progress)
        self.status.setText("%d workers" % len(self.worker_progress))


app = QApplication(sys.argv)
window = MainWindow()
app.exec_()
```

① Use a unique UUID4 identifier for this runner.

② Progress 0-100% as an integer.

③ When the job finishes, we need to cleanup (delete) the workers progress.

④ Delete the progress for the finished worker.

If you run this, you'll see the global progress bar along with an indicator to show how many active workers there are running.

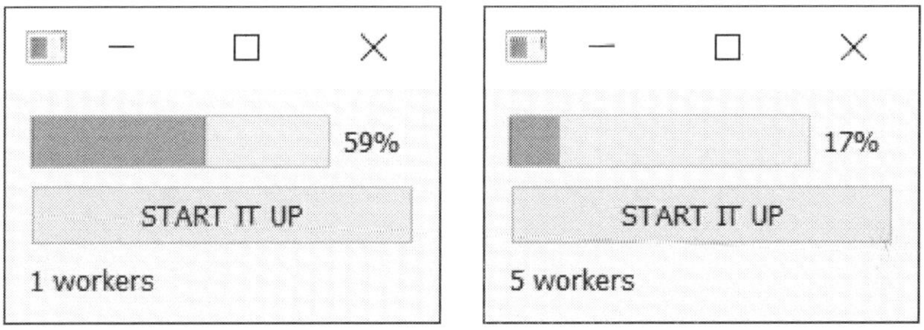

Figure 212. The window showing the global progress state, together with the number of active workers.

Checking the console output for the script you can see the actual status for each of the individual workers.

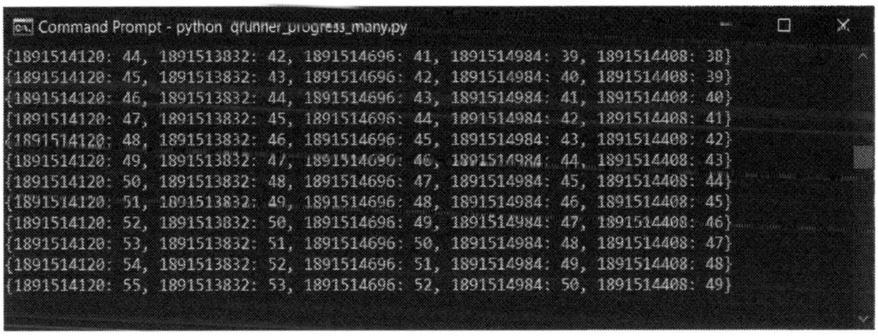

Figure 213. Check the shell output to see the individual worker progress.

Removing the worker immediately means that the progress will jump *backwards* when a job finishes—removing 100 from the average calculation will cause the average to fall. You can postpone the cleanup if you like, for example the following will only remove the entries when *all* progress bars reach 100.

Listing 164. concurrent/qrunner_progress_many_2.py

```
import random
```

```
import sys
import time
import uuid

from PyQt5.QtCore import QObject, QRunnable, QThreadPool, QTimer,
pyqtSignal, pyqtSlot
from PyQt5.QtWidgets import (
    QApplication,
    QLabel,
    QMainWindow,
    QProgressBar,
    QPushButton,
    QVBoxLayout,
    QWidget,
)


class WorkerSignals(QObject):
    """
    Defines the signals available from a running worker thread.

    progress
        int progress complete,from 0-100
    """

    progress = pyqtSignal(str, int)
    finished = pyqtSignal(str)


class Worker(QRunnable):
    """
    Worker thread

    Inherits from QRunnable to handle worker thread setup, signals
    and wrap-up.
    """

    def __init__(self):
        super().__init__()
        self.job_id = uuid.uuid4().hex  ①
        self.signals = WorkerSignals()

    @pyqtSlot()
```

```
    def run(self):
        total_n = 1000
        delay = random.random() / 100  # Random delay value.
        for n in range(total_n):
            progress_pc = int(100 * float(n + 1) / total_n)  ②
            self.signals.progress.emit(self.job_id, progress_pc)
            time.sleep(delay)

        self.signals.finished.emit(self.job_id)


class MainWindow(QMainWindow):
    def __init__(self):
        super().__init__()

        layout = QVBoxLayout()

        self.progress = QProgressBar()

        button = QPushButton("START IT UP")
        button.pressed.connect(self.execute)

        self.status = QLabel("0 workers")

        layout.addWidget(self.progress)
        layout.addWidget(button)
        layout.addWidget(self.status)

        w = QWidget()
        w.setLayout(layout)

        # Dictionary holds the progress of current workers.
        self.worker_progress = {}

        self.setCentralWidget(w)

        self.show()

        self.threadpool = QThreadPool()
        print(
            "Multithreading with maximum %d threads" % self
.threadpool.maxThreadCount()
        )
```

```
        self.timer = QTimer()
        self.timer.setInterval(100)
        self.timer.timeout.connect(self.refresh_progress)
        self.timer.start()

    def execute(self):
        worker = Worker()
        worker.signals.progress.connect(self.update_progress)
        worker.signals.finished.connect(self.cleanup)  ③

        # Execute
        self.threadpool.start(worker)

    def cleanup(self, job_id):
        if all(v == 100 for v in self.worker_progress.values()):
            self.worker_progress.clear()  # Empty the dict.

            # Update the progress bar if we've removed a value.
            self.refresh_progress()

    def update_progress(self, job_id, progress):
        self.worker_progress[job_id] = progress

    def calculate_progress(self):
        if not self.worker_progress:
            return 0

        return sum(v for v in self.worker_progress.values()) / len
(self.worker_progress)

    def refresh_progress(self):
        # Calculate total progress.
        progress = self.calculate_progress()
        print(self.worker_progress)
        self.progress.setValue(progress)
        self.status.setText("%d workers" % len(self.worker_progress))


app = QApplication(sys.argv)
window = MainWindow()
app.exec_()
```

While this works, and is fine for simple use-cases, it would be nicer if this worker state (and control) could be wrapped up into it's own *manager* component rather than being handled through the main window. Take a look at the later The Manager section to see how we can do that.

The calculator

Threading is a good option when you need to perform complex calculations. If you're using the Python *numpy*, *scipy* or *pandas* libraries then these calculations may also release the GIL meaning both your GUI and calculation thread can run at full speed.

In this example we'll create a number of workers which are all performing some simple calculations. The results of these calculations will be returned to the GUI thread and displayed in a plot.

> We cover PyQtGraph in detail in Plotting with PyQtGraph, for now just focus on the `QRunner`.

Listing 165. concurrent/qrunner_logger.py

```
import random
import sys
import time
import uuid

import pyqtgraph as pg
from PyQt5.QtCore import QObject, QRunnable, QThreadPool, QTimer,
pyqtSignal, pyqtSlot
from PyQt5.QtWidgets import QApplication, QMainWindow, QPushButton,
QVBoxLayout, QWidget
from pyqtgraph import PlotWidget, plot


class WorkerSignals(QObject):
    """
    Defines the signals available from a running worker thread.

    data
        tuple data point (worker_id, x, y)
    """

    data = pyqtSignal(tuple)  ①
```

```
class Worker(QRunnable):
    """
    Worker thread

    Inherits from QRunnable to handle worker thread setup, signals
    and wrap-up.
    """

    def __init__(self):
        super().__init__()
        self.worker_id = uuid.uuid4().hex  # Unique ID for this
worker.
        self.signals = WorkerSignals()

    @pyqtSlot()
    def run(self):

        total_n = 1000
        y2 = random.randint(0, 10)
        delay = random.random() / 100  # Random delay value.
        value = 0

        for n in range(total_n):
            # Dummy calculation, each worker will produce different
values,
            # because of the random y & y2 values.
            y = random.randint(0, 10)
            value += n * y2 - n * y

            self.signals.data.emit((self.worker_id, n, value))  ②
            time.sleep(delay)


class MainWindow(QMainWindow):
    def __init__(self):
        super().__init__()

        self.threadpool = QThreadPool()

        self.x = {}  # Keep timepoints.
        self.y = {}  # Keep data.
        self.lines = {}  # Keep references to plotted lines, to
update.
```

```
        layout = QVBoxLayout()
        self.graphWidget = pg.PlotWidget()
        self.graphWidget.setBackground("w")
        layout.addWidget(self.graphWidget)

        button = QPushButton("Create New Worker")
        button.pressed.connect(self.execute)

        # layout.addWidget(self.progress)
        layout.addWidget(button)

        w = QWidget()
        w.setLayout(layout)

        self.setCentralWidget(w)

        self.show()

    def execute(self):
        worker = Worker()
        worker.signals.data.connect(self.receive_data)

        # Execute
        self.threadpool.start(worker)

    def receive_data(self, data):
        worker_id, x, y = data  ③

        if worker_id not in self.lines:
            self.x[worker_id] = [x]
            self.y[worker_id] = [y]

            # Generate a random color.
            pen = pg.mkPen(
                width=2,
                color=(
                    random.randint(100, 255),
                    random.randint(100, 255),
                    random.randint(100, 255),
                ),
            )
            self.lines[worker_id] = self.graphWidget.plot(
```

```
                  self.x[worker_id], self.y[worker_id], pen=pen
              )
              return

          # Update existing plot/data
          self.x[worker_id].append(x)
          self.y[worker_id].append(y)

          self.lines[worker_id].setData(self.x[worker_id], self.y
[worker_id])


app = QApplication(sys.argv)
window = MainWindow()
app.exec_()
```

① Setup a custom signal to pass out the data. Using `tuple` allows you to send out any number of values wrapped in a `tuple`.

② Here we're emitting a *worker_id*, *x* and *y* value.

③ Receiver slot unpacks the data.

Once you've received the data from a worker, you can do what you like with it—perhaps add it to a table or model view. Here we're storing the *x* and *y* values in `dict` objects keyed by the *worker_id*. That keeps the data for each worker separate and allows us to plot them individually.

If you run this example press the button you'll see a line appear on the plot and gradually extend. If you press the button again, another worker will start, returning more data and adding another line to the plot. Each worker generates data at a different rate, each generating 100 values.

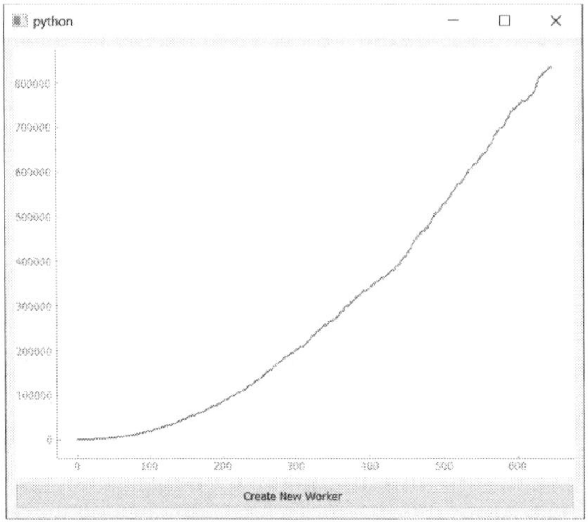

Figure 214. Plot output from a single runner after a few iterations.

You can start new workers up to the *max threads* available on your machine. After generating 100 values workers will shut-down and the next queued worker will start up—adding it's values as a new line.

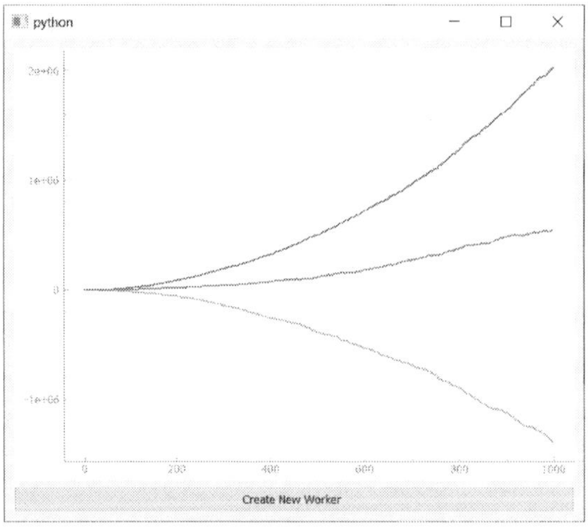

Figure 215. Plot from multiple runners.

The `tuple` is of course optional, you could send back bare strings if you have only one runner, or don't need to associated outputs with a source. It is also possible to send a `bytestring`, or any other type of data, by setting up the signals appropriately.

Stopping a running QRunner

Once you've started a QRunner there is, by default, no way to stop it. This isn't very nice from a usability point of view—if a user starts task by mistake, they then have to sit and wait for it to finish. Unfortunately, there is no way to *kill* a runner, however we can ask it nicely to stop. In this example we'll look at how we can use *flags* to indicate to the runner that it needs to stop.

> In computing *flags* are variables that are used to signal a current or change in state. Think of how ships use flags to communicate with one another.
>
> 
>
> *Figure 216. Lima, "You should stop your vessel instantly."*

The code below implements a simple runner with a progress bar which increases every 0.01 seconds from left to right, and a **[Stop]** button. If you click **[Stop]** the worker will exit, stopping the progress bar permanently.

Listing 166. concurrent/qrunner_stop.py

```python
import sys
import time

from PyQt5.QtCore import QObject, QRunnable, Qt, QThreadPool,
pyqtSignal, pyqtSlot
from PyQt5.QtWidgets import (
    QApplication,
    QHBoxLayout,
    QMainWindow,
    QProgressBar,
    QPushButton,
    QWidget,
)


class WorkerKilledException(Exception):
    pass
```

```
class WorkerSignals(QObject):
    progress = pyqtSignal(int)


class JobRunner(QRunnable):

    signals = WorkerSignals()

    def __init__(self):
        super().__init__()

        self.is_killed = False  ①

    @pyqtSlot()
    def run(self):
        try:
            for n in range(100):
                self.signals.progress.emit(n + 1)
                time.sleep(0.1)

                if self.is_killed:  ②
                    raise WorkerKilledException

        except WorkerKilledException:
            pass  ③

    def kill(self):  ④
        self.is_killed = True


class MainWindow(QMainWindow):
    def __init__(self):
        super().__init__()

        # Some buttons
        w = QWidget()
        l = QHBoxLayout()
        w.setLayout(l)

        btn_stop = QPushButton("Stop")
```

```
        l.addWidget(btn_stop)

        self.setCentralWidget(w)

        # Create a statusbar.
        self.status = self.statusBar()
        self.progress = QProgressBar()
        self.status.addPermanentWidget(self.progress)

        # Thread runner
        self.threadpool = QThreadPool()

        # Create a runner
        self.runner = JobRunner()
        self.runner.signals.progress.connect(self.update_progress)
        self.threadpool.start(self.runner)

        btn_stop.pressed.connect(self.runner.kill)

        self.show()

    def update_progress(self, n):
        self.progress.setValue(n)


app = QApplication(sys.argv)
w = MainWindow()
app.exec_()
```

① The flag to indicate whether the runner should be killed is called `.is_killed`.

② On each loop we test to see whether `.is_killed` is `True` in which case we throw an exception.

③ Catch the exception, we could emit a *finished* or *error* signal here.

④ `.kill()` convenience function so we can call `worker.kill()` to kill it.

If you want to stop the worker without throwing an error, you can simply `return` from the `run` method, e.g.

```
    def run(self):
        for n in range(100):
            self.signals.progress.emit(n + 1)
            time.sleep(0)

            if self.is_killed:
                return
```

In the above example we only have a single worker. However, in many applications you will have more. How do you handle stopping workers when you have multiple runners running?

If you want the stop to stop *all* workers, then nothing is changed. You can simply hook all the workers up to the same "Stop" signal, and when that signal is fired—e.g. by pressing a button—all the workers will stop simultaneously.

If you want to be able to stop individual workers you would either need to create a separate button somewhere in your UI for each runner, or implement a *manager* to keep track of workers and provide a nicer interface to kill them. Take a look at The Manager for a working example.

Pausing a runner

Pausing a runner is a rarer requirement—normally you want things to go *as fast as possible*. But sometimes you may want to put a worker to "sleep" so it temporarily stops reading from a data source. You can do this with a small modification to the approach used to stop the runner. The code to do this is shown below.

Listing 167. concurrent/qrunner_pause.py

```
import sys
import time

from PyQt5.QtCore import (QObject, QRunnable, Qt, QThreadPool,
pyqtSignal,
                          pyqtSlot)
```

```python
from PyQt5.QtWidgets import (QApplication, QHBoxLayout, QMainWindow,
                             QProgressBar, QPushButton, QWidget)


class WorkerKilledException(Exception):
    pass


class WorkerSignals(QObject):
    progress = pyqtSignal(int)


class JobRunner(QRunnable):

    signals = WorkerSignals()

    def __init__(self):
        super().__init__()

        self.is_paused = False
        self.is_killed = False

    @pyqtSlot()
    def run(self):
        for n in range(100):
            self.signals.progress.emit(n + 1)
            time.sleep(0.1)

            while self.is_paused:
                time.sleep(0)  ①

            if self.is_killed:
                raise WorkerKilledException

    def pause(self):
        self.is_paused = True

    def resume(self):
        self.is_paused = False

    def kill(self):
        self.is_killed = True
```

```python
class MainWindow(QMainWindow):
    def __init__(self):
        super().__init__()

        # Some buttons
        w = QWidget()
        l = QHBoxLayout()
        w.setLayout(l)

        btn_stop = QPushButton("Stop")
        btn_pause = QPushButton("Pause")
        btn_resume = QPushButton("Resume")

        l.addWidget(btn_stop)
        l.addWidget(btn_pause)
        l.addWidget(btn_resume)

        self.setCentralWidget(w)

        # Create a statusbar.
        self.status = self.statusBar()
        self.progress = QProgressBar()
        self.status.addPermanentWidget(self.progress)

        # Thread runner
        self.threadpool = QThreadPool()

        # Create a runner
        self.runner = JobRunner()
        self.runner.signals.progress.connect(self.update_progress)
        self.threadpool.start(self.runner)

        btn_stop.pressed.connect(self.runner.kill)
        btn_pause.pressed.connect(self.runner.pause)
        btn_resume.pressed.connect(self.runner.resume)

        self.show()

    def update_progress(self, n):
        self.progress.setValue(n)
```

```
app = QApplication(sys.argv)
w = MainWindow()
app.exec_()
```

① You can put a higher value that `0` in the `sleep` call if you don't want to check if it's time to wake up very often.

If you run this example you'll see a progress bar moving from left to right. If you click **[Pause]** the worker will pause. If you then click **[Resume]** the worker will continue from where it started. If you click **[Stop]** the worker will stop, permanently, as before.

Rather than throw an exception when receiving the `is_paused` signal, we enter a pause loop. This stops execution of the worker, but does not exit the `run` method or terminate the worker.

By using `while self.is_paused:` for this loop, we will exit the loop as soon as the worker is unpaused, and resume what we were doing before.

> You *must* include the `time.sleep()` call. This zero-second pause allows for Python to release the GIL, so this loop will not block other execution. Without that sleep you have a *busy loop* which will waste resources while doing nothing. Increase the sleep value if you want to check less often.

The Communicator

When running a thread you frequently want to be able get output from what is happening, while it's happening.

In this example we'll create a runner which performs requests to remote servers in a separate thread, and dumps the output to a logger. We'll also look at how we can pass a custom *parser* into the runner to extra data we're interested in from the requests.

> If you want to log data from external processes, rather than threads, take a look at Running External processes and Running external commands & processes.

Dumping data

In this first example we'll just dump the raw data (HTML) from each request to the output, using a custom signal.

Listing 168. concurrent/qrunner_io.py

```
import sys

import requests
from PyQt5.QtCore import QObject, QRunnable, QThreadPool, QTimer,
pyqtSignal, pyqtSlot
from PyQt5.QtWidgets import (
    QApplication,
    QLabel,
    QMainWindow,
    QPlainTextEdit,
    QPushButton,
    QVBoxLayout,
    QWidget,
)


class WorkerSignals(QObject):
    """
    Defines the signals available from a running worker thread.
```

```
    data
        tuple of (identifier, data)
    """

    data = pyqtSignal(tuple)


class Worker(QRunnable):
    """
    Worker thread

    Inherits from QRunnable to handle worker thread setup, signals
    and wrap-up.

    :param id: The id for this worker
    :param url: The url to retrieve
    """

    def __init__(self, id, url):
        super().__init__()
        self.id = id
        self.url = url

        self.signals = WorkerSignals()

    @pyqtSlot()
    def run(self):
        r = requests.get(self.url)

        for line in r.text.splitlines():
            self.signals.data.emit((self.id, line))


class MainWindow(QMainWindow):
    def __init__(self):
        super().__init__()

        self.urls = [
            "https://www.learnpyqt.com/",
            "https://www.mfitzp.com/",
            "https://www.google.com",
            "https://www.udemy.com/create-simple-gui-applications-
```

```
with-python-and-qt/",
        ]

        layout = QVBoxLayout()

        self.text = QPlainTextEdit()
        self.text.setReadOnly(True)

        button = QPushButton("GO GET EM!")
        button.pressed.connect(self.execute)

        layout.addWidget(self.text)
        layout.addWidget(button)

        w = QWidget()
        w.setLayout(layout)

        self.setCentralWidget(w)

        self.show()

        self.threadpool = QThreadPool()
        print(
            "Multithreading with maximum %d threads" % self
.threadpool.maxThreadCount()
        )

    def execute(self):
        for n, url in enumerate(self.urls):
            worker = Worker(n, url)
            worker.signals.data.connect(self.display_output)

            # Execute
            self.threadpool.start(worker)

    def display_output(self, data):
        id, s = data
        self.text.appendPlainText("WORKER %d: %s" % (id, s))


app = QApplication(sys.argv)
window = MainWindow()
app.exec_()
```

If you run this example and press the button you'll see the HTML output from a number of websites, prepended by the worker ID that retrieve them. Note that output from different workers is interleaved.

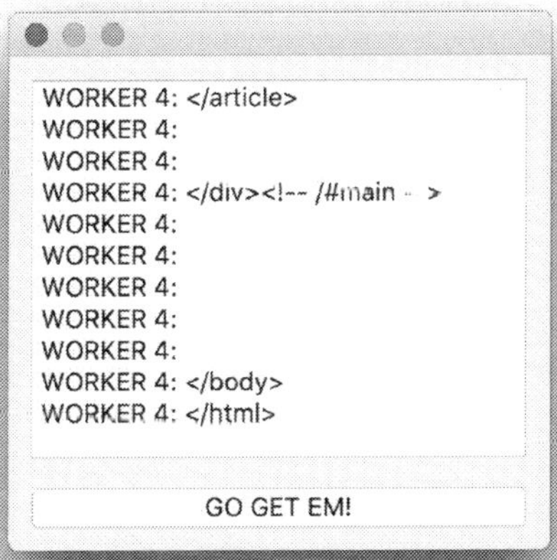

Figure 217. Logging output from multiple workers to the main window.

The `tuple` is of course optional, you could send back bare strings if you have only one runner, or don't need to associated outputs with a source. It is also possible to send a `bytestring`, or any other type of data, by setting up the signals appropriately.

Parsing data

Often you are not interested in the raw data from the thread (whether from a server or other external device) and instead want to process the data in some way first. In this example we create custom parsers, which can extract *specific* data from pages requested. We can create multiple workers, each receiving a different list of sites and parsers.

Listing 169. concurrent/qrunner_io_parser.py

```
        self.parsers = {  ①
            # Regular expression parsers, to extract data from the
HTML.
            "title": re.compile(r"<title.*?>(.*?)<\/title>", re.M |
re.S),
            "h1": re.compile(r"<h1.*?>(.*?)<\/h1>", re.M | re.S),
            "h2": re.compile(r"<h2.*?>(.*?)<\/h2>", re.M | re.S),
        }
```

① The parsers are defined as a series of compiled regular expressions. But you can define parsers however you like.

Listing 170. concurrent/qrunner_io_parser.py

```
    def execute(self):
        for n, url in enumerate(self.urls):
            worker = Worker(n, url, self.parsers)  ①
            worker.signals.data.connect(self.display_output)

            # Execute
            self.threadpool.start(worker)
```

① Pass the list of parsers to each worker.

Listing 171. concurrent/qrunner_io_parser.py

```
class Worker(QRunnable):
    """
    Worker thread

    Inherits from QRunnable to handle worker thread setup, signals
    and wrap-up.

    :param id: The id for this worker
    :param url: The url to retrieve
    """

    def __init__(self, id, url, parsers):
        super().__init__()
        self.id = id
        self.url = url
        self.parsers = parsers

        self.signals = WorkerSignals()

    @pyqtSlot()
    def run(self):
        r = requests.get(self.url)

        data = {}
        for name, parser in self.parsers.items():  ①
            m = parser.search(r.text)
            if m:  ②
                data[name] = m.group(1).strip()

        self.signals.data.emit((self.id, data))
```

① Iterate the parser list we passed to the worker. Run each parser on the data for this page.

② If the regular expression matched, add the data to our `data` dictionary.

Running this, you'll see the output from each worker, with the H1, H2 and TITLE tags extracted.

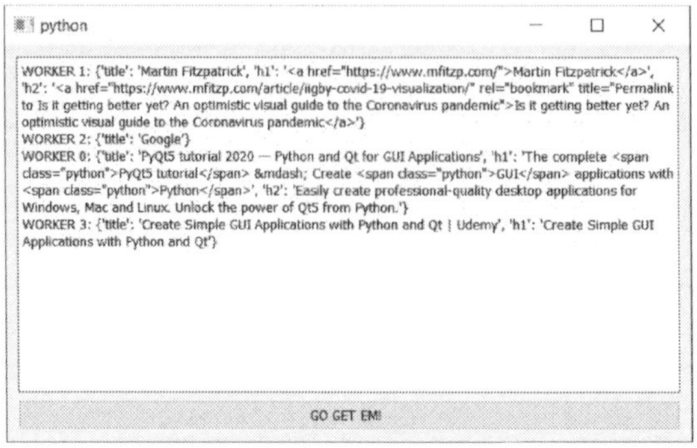

Figure 218. Displaying parsed output from multiple workers.

If you are building tools to extract data from websites, take a look at BeautifulSoup 4 [https://www.crummy.com/software/BeautifulSoup/bs4/doc/] which is far more robust than using regular expressions.

The Generic

You won't always know ahead of time what you want to use workers for. Or you may have a number of similar functions to perform and want a regular API for running them. In that case you can take advantage of the fact that in Python functions are objects to build a *generic* runner which accepts not just arguments, but also the function to run.

In the following example we create a single `Worker` class and then use it to run a number of different functions. With this setup you can pass in any Python function and have it executed in a separate thread.

The complete working example is given below, showcasing the custom `QRunnable` worker together with the worker & progress signals. You should be able to adapt this code to any application you develop.

Listing 172. concurrent/qrunner_generic.py

```
import sys
import time
import traceback

from PyQt5.QtCore import QObject, QRunnable, QThreadPool, QTimer,
pyqtSignal, pyqtSlot
from PyQt5.QtWidgets import (
    QApplication,
    QLabel,
    QMainWindow,
    QPushButton,
    QVBoxLayout,
    QWidget,
)


def execute_this_fn():
    for _ in range(0, 5):
        time.sleep(1)

    return "Done."
```

```python
class WorkerSignals(QObject):
    """
    Defines the signals available from a running worker thread.

    Supported signals are:

    finished
        No data

    error
        `tuple` (exctype, value, traceback.format_exc() )

    result
        `object` data returned from processing, anything

    """

    finished = pyqtSignal()
    error = pyqtSignal(tuple)
    result = pyqtSignal(object)


class Worker(QRunnable):
    """
    Worker thread

    Inherits from QRunnable to handle worker thread setup, signals
and wrap-up.

    :param callback: The function callback to run on this worker
    :thread. Supplied args and
                    kwargs will be passed through to the runner.
    :type callback: function
    :param args: Arguments to pass to the callback function
    :param kwargs: Keywords to pass to the callback function
    :
    """

    def __init__(self, fn, *args, **kwargs):
        super().__init__()
        # Store constructor arguments (re-used for processing)
        self.fn = fn
```

```
        self.args = args
        self.kwargs = kwargs
        self.signals = WorkerSignals()

    @pyqtSlot()
    def run(self):
        """
        Initialize the runner function with passed args, kwargs.
        """

        # Retrieve args/kwargs here; and fire processing using them
        try:
            result = self.fn(*self.args, **self.kwargs)
        except:
            traceback.print_exc()
            exctype, value = sys.exc_info()[:2]
            self.signals.error.emit((exctype, value, traceback
.format_exc()))
        else:
            self.signals.result.emit(result)  # Return the result of
the processing
        finally:
            self.signals.finished.emit()  # Done


class MainWindow(QMainWindow):
    def __init__(self):
        super().__init__()

        self.counter = 0

        layout = QVBoxLayout()

        self.l = QLabel("Start")
        b = QPushButton("DANGER!")
        b.pressed.connect(self.oh_no)

        layout.addWidget(self.l)
        layout.addWidget(b)

        w = QWidget()
        w.setLayout(layout)
```

```
        self.setCentralWidget(w)

        self.show()

        self.threadpool = QThreadPool()
        print(
            "Multithreading with maximum %d threads" % self
.threadpool.maxThreadCount()
        )

        self.timer = QTimer()
        self.timer.setInterval(1000)
        self.timer.timeout.connect(self.recurring_timer)
        self.timer.start()

    def print_output(self, s):
        print(s)

    def thread_complete(self):
        print("THREAD COMPLETE!")

    def oh_no(self):
        # Pass the function to execute
        worker = Worker(
            execute_this_fn
        )  # Any other args, kwargs are passed to the run function
        worker.signals.result.connect(self.print_output)
        worker.signals.finished.connect(self.thread_complete)

        # Execute
        self.threadpool.start(worker)

    def recurring_timer(self):
        self.counter += 1
        self.l.setText("Counter: %d" % self.counter)


app = QApplication(sys.argv)
window = MainWindow()
app.exec_()
```

The generic function approach adds a limitation that may not be immediately obvious—the run function does not have access to the self object of your runner, and therefore cannot access the signals to emit the data itself. We can only emit the return value of the function, once it has ended. While you can return a compound type, such as a tuple, to return multiple values, you can't get progress signals or in-progress data.

However, there is a way around this. Since you can pass anyting you want **into** the custom function, you can also pass self or the self.signals object to make them available to you.

Listing 173. concurrent/qrunner_generic_callback.py

```
import sys
import time
import traceback

from PyQt5.QtCore import QObject, QRunnable, QThreadPool, QTimer,
pyqtSignal, pyqtSlot
from PyQt5.QtWidgets import (
    QApplication,
    QLabel,
    QMainWindow,
    QPushButton,
    QVBoxLayout,
    QWidget,
)


def execute_this_fn(signals):
    for n in range(0, 5):
        time.sleep(1)
        signals.progress.emit(n * 100 / 4)

    return "Done."


class WorkerSignals(QObject):
    """
    Defines the signals available from a running worker thread.

    Supported signals are:
```

```
    finished
        No data

    error
        `tuple` (exctype, value, traceback.format_exc() )

    result
        `object` data returned from processing, anything

    progress
        `int` indicating % progress

    """

    finished = pyqtSignal()
    error = pyqtSignal(tuple)
    result = pyqtSignal(object)
    progress = pyqtSignal(int)


class Worker(QRunnable):
    """
    Worker thread

    Inherits from QRunnable to handle worker thread setup, signals
and wrap-up.

    :param callback: The function callback to run on this worker
    :thread. Supplied args and
                    kwargs will be passed through to the runner.
    :type callback: function
    :param args: Arguments to pass to the callback function
    :param kwargs: Keywords to pass to the callback function
    :
    """

    def __init__(self, fn, *args, **kwargs):
        super().__init__()
        # Store constructor arguments (re-used for processing)
        self.fn = fn
        self.args = args
        self.kwargs = kwargs
```

```
        self.signals = WorkerSignals()

        # Add the callback to our kwargs
        kwargs["signals"] = self.signals

    @pyqtSlot()
    def run(self):
        """
        Initialize the runner function with passed args, kwargs.
        """

        # Retrieve args/kwargs here; and fire processing using them
        try:
            result = self.fn(*self.args, **self.kwargs)
        except Exception:
            traceback.print_exc()
            exctype, value = sys.exc_info()[:2]
            self.signals.error.emit((exctype, value, traceback
.format_exc()))
        else:
            self.signals.result.emit(result)  # Return the result of
the processing
        finally:
            self.signals.finished.emit()  # Done


class MainWindow(QMainWindow):
    def __init__(self):
        super().__init__()

        self.counter = 0

        layout = QVBoxLayout()

        self.l = QLabel("Start")
        b = QPushButton("DANGER!")
        b.pressed.connect(self.oh_no)

        layout.addWidget(self.l)
        layout.addWidget(b)

        w = QWidget()
        w.setLayout(layout)
```

```
        self.setCentralWidget(w)

        self.show()

        self.threadpool = QThreadPool()
        print(
            "Multithreading with maximum %d threads" % self
.threadpool.maxThreadCount()
        )

        self.timer = QTimer()
        self.timer.setInterval(1000)
        self.timer.timeout.connect(self.recurring_timer)
        self.timer.start()

    def progress_fn(self, n):
        print("%d%% done" % n)

    def print_output(self, s):
        print(s)

    def thread_complete(self):
        print("THREAD COMPLETE!")

    def oh_no(self):
        # Pass the function to execute
        worker = Worker(
            execute_this_fn
        )  # Any other args, kwargs are passed to the run function
        worker.signals.result.connect(self.print_output)
        worker.signals.finished.connect(self.thread_complete)
        worker.signals.progress.connect(self.progress_fn)

        # Execute
        self.threadpool.start(worker)

    def recurring_timer(self):
        self.counter += 1
        self.l.setText("Counter: %d" % self.counter)


app = QApplication(sys.argv)
```

```
window = MainWindow()
app.exec_()
```

Note that for this to work, your custom function must be able to accept the additional argument. You can do this by defining the functions with `**kwargs` to silently swallow the extra arguments if they aren't used.

```
def execute_this_fn(**kwargs):  ①
    for _ in range(0, 5):
        time.sleep(1)

    return "Done."
```

① The `signals` keyword argument is swallowed up by `**kwargs`.

Running External processes

So far we've looked how we can run Python code in another *thread*. Sometimes however you need to run external programs—such as command line programs—in another *process*.

You actually have two options when starting external processes with PyQt5. You can either use Python's built-in `subprocess` module to start the processes, or you can use Qt's `QProcess`.

> For more information on running external processes using `QProcess` take a look at the Running external commands & processes chapter.

Starting a new process always comes with a small execution cost and will block your GUI momentarily. This is usually not perceptible but it can add up depending on your use case and may have performance impacts. You can get around this by starting your processes in another thread.

If you want to communicate with the process in real-time you will need a separate thread to avoid blocking the GUI. `QProcess` handles this separate thread for you internally, but with Python `subprocess` you will need to do this yourself.

In this `QRunner` example we use instances of workers to handle starting external processes through Python `subprocess`. This keeps the startup cost of the process out of the GUI thread and also allows us to interact with the processes directly through Python.

Listing 174. concurrent/qrunner_process.py

```
import subprocess
import sys
import time
import traceback
import uuid
from collections import namedtuple
```

```
from PyQt5.QtCore import (
    QObject,
    QRunnable,
    Qt,
    QThreadPool,
    QTimer,
    pyqtSignal,
    pyqtSlot,
)
from PyQt5.QtWidgets import (
    QApplication,
    QMainWindow,
    QPlainTextEdit,
    QPushButton,
    QVBoxLayout,
    QWidget,
)


class WorkerSignals(QObject):
    """
    Defines the signals available from a running worker thread.

    Supported signals are:

    finished: No data
    result: str
    """

    result = pyqtSignal(str)  # Send back the output from the process
as a string.
    finished = pyqtSignal()


class SubProcessWorker(QRunnable):
    """
    ProcessWorker worker thread

    Inherits from QRunnable to handle worker thread setup, signals
and wrap-up.

    :param command: command to execute with `subprocess`.
```

```python
    """

    def __init__(self, command):
        super().__init__()

        # Store constructor arguments (re-used for processing).
        self.signals = WorkerSignals()

        # The command to be executed.
        self.command = command

    @pyqtSlot()
    def run(self):
        """
        Execute the command, returning the result.
        """
        output = subprocess.getoutput(self.command)
        self.signals.result.emit(output)
        self.signals.finished.emit()


class MainWindow(QMainWindow):
    def __init__(self):
        super().__init__()

        # Some buttons
        layout = QVBoxLayout()

        self.text = QPlainTextEdit()
        layout.addWidget(self.text)

        btn_run = QPushButton("Execute")
        btn_run.clicked.connect(self.start)

        layout.addWidget(btn_run)

        w = QWidget()
        w.setLayout(layout)
        self.setCentralWidget(w)

        # Thread runner
        self.threadpool = QThreadPool()
```

```
        self.show()

    def start(self):
        # Create a runner
        self.runner = SubProcessWorker("python dummy_script.py")
        self.runner.signals.result.connect(self.result)
        self.threadpool.start(self.runner)

    def result(self, s):
        self.text.appendPlainText(s)


app = QApplication(sys.argv)
w = MainWindow()
app.exec_()
```

The "external program" in this example is a simple Python script `python dummy_script.py`. However can replace this with any other program you like.

Running processes have two streams of output—*standard out* and *standard error*. The standard output returns the actual result of the execution (if any) while standard error returns any error *or* logging information.

In this example we're running the external script using `subprocess.getoutput`. This runs the external program, waiting for it to complete before returning. Once it has completed, `getoutput` returns both the *standard output* and *standard error* together as a single string.

Parsing the result

You don't have to pass the output as-is. If you have post-processing to do on the output from the command, it can make sense to handle this in your worker thread as well, to keep it self-contained. The worker can then return the data to your GUI thread in a structured format, ready to be used.

In the following example, we pass in a function to post-process the result of the demo script to extract the values of interest into a dictionary. This data is used to update widgets on the GUI side.

Listing 175. concurrent/qrunner_process.py

```
import subprocess
import sys
import time
import traceback
import uuid
from collections import namedtuple

from PyQt5.QtCore import (QObject, QRunnable, Qt, QThreadPool,
QTimer,
                          pyqtSignal, pyqtSlot)
from PyQt5.QtWidgets import (
    QApplication, QLineEdit, QMainWindow, QPushButton, QSpinBox,
QVBoxLayout,
    QWidget)


def extract_vars(l):
    """
    Extracts variables from lines, looking for lines
    containing an equals, and splitting into key=value.
    """
    data = {}
    for s in l.splitlines():
        if '=' in s:
            name, value = s.split('=')
            data[name] = value

    data['number_of_lines'] = len(l)
    return data


class WorkerSignals(QObject):
    """
    Defines the signals available from a running worker thread.

    Supported signals are:

    finished: No data
```

```
    result: dict
    """

    result = pyqtSignal(dict)  # Send back the output as dictionary.
    finished = pyqtSignal()


class SubProcessWorker(QRunnable):
    """
    ProcessWorker worker thread

    Inherits from QRunnable to handle worker thread setup, signals
and wrap-up.

    :param command: command to execute with `subprocess`.

    """

    def __init__(self, command, process_result=None):
        super().__init__()

        # Store constructor arguments (re-used for processing).
        self.signals = WorkerSignals()

        # The command to be executed.
        self.command = command

        # The post-processing fn.
        self.process_result = process_result

    @pyqtSlot()
    def run(self):
        """
        Execute the command, returning the result.
        """
        output = subprocess.getoutput(self.command)

        if self.process_result:
            output = self.process_result(output)

        self.signals.result.emit(output)
        self.signals.finished.emit()
```

```python
class MainWindow(QMainWindow):
    def __init__(self):
        super().__init__()

        # Some buttons
        layout = QVBoxLayout()

        self.name = QLineEdit()
        layout.addWidget(self.name)

        self.country = QLineEdit()
        layout.addWidget(self.country)

        self.website = QLineEdit()
        layout.addWidget(self.website)

        self.number_of_lines = QSpinBox()
        layout.addWidget(self.number_of_lines)

        btn_run = QPushButton("Execute")
        btn_run.clicked.connect(self.start)

        layout.addWidget(btn_run)

        w = QWidget()
        w.setLayout(layout)
        self.setCentralWidget(w)

        # Thread runner
        self.threadpool = QThreadPool()

        self.show()

    def start(self):
        # Create a runner
        self.runner = SubProcessWorker(
            "python dummy_script.py", process_result=extract_vars
        )
        self.runner.signals.result.connect(self.result)
        self.threadpool.start(self.runner)

    def result(self, data):
```

```
        print(data)
        self.name.setText(data['name'])
        self.country.setText(data['country'])
        self.website.setText(data['website'])
        self.number_of_lines.setValue(data['number_of_lines'])


app = QApplication(sys.argv)
w = MainWindow()
app.exec_()
```

The simple parser in this case looks for any lines with a = in them, splits on this to produce a name and a value, which are then stored in a `dict`. However, you can use any tools you like to extract data from the string output.

Because `getoutput` *blocks* until the program is complete, we cannot see how the program is running—for example, to get progress information. In the next example we'll show how to get live output from a running process.

Tracking progress

Often external programs will output progress information to the console. You might want to capture this and either show it to your users, or use it to generate a progress bar.

For the result of the execution you usually want to capture standard out, for the progress to capture *standard error*. In this following example we capture both. As well as the command, we pass a custom parser function to the worker, to capture the current worker progress and emit it as a number 0-99.

This example is quite complex. The full source code is available in the source code with the book, but here we'll cover the key differences to the simpler one.

Listing 176. concurrent/qrunner_process_parser.py

```
    @pyqtSlot()
    def run(self):
        """
        Initialize the runner function with passed args, kwargs.
        """

        result = []

        with subprocess.Popen(  ①
            self.command,
            bufsize=1,
            stdout=subprocess.PIPE,
            stderr=subprocess.STDOUT,  ②
            universal_newlines=True,
        ) as proc:
            while proc.poll() is None:
                data = proc.stdout.readline()  ③
                result.append(data)
                if self.parser:  ④
                    value = self.parser(data)
                    if value:
                        self.signals.progress.emit(value)

        output = "".join(result)

        self.signals.result.emit(output)
```

① Run using Popen to give us access to output streams.

② We pipe *standard error* out together with *standard output*.

③ Read a line from the process (or wait for one).

④ Pass all collected data so far to the parser.

Parsing is handled by this simple parser function, which takes in a string and matches the regular expression `Total complete: (\d+)%`.

Listing 177. concurrent/qrunner_process_parser.py

```
progress_re = re.compile("Total complete: (\d+)%")


def simple_percent_parser(output):
    """
    Matches lines using the progress_re regex,
    returning a single integer for the % progress.
    """
    m = progress_re.search(output)
    if m:
        pc_complete = m.group(1)
        return int(pc_complete)
```

The parser is passed into the runner along with the command—this means we can use a generic runner for all subprocesses and handle the output differently for different commands.

Listing 178. concurrent/qrunner_process_parser.py

```
    def start(self):
        # Create a runner
        self.runner = SubProcessWorker(
            command="python dummy_script.py", parser
=simple_percent_parser
        )
        self.runner.signals.result.connect(self.result)
        self.runner.signals.progress.connect(self.progress.setValue)
        self.threadpool.start(self.runner)
```

In this simple example we only pass the *latest* line from the process, since our custom script outputs lines like `Total complete: 25%`. That means that we only need the *latest* line to be able to calculate the current progress.

Sometimes however, scripts can be a bit less helpful. For example `ffmpeg` the video encoder outputs the duration of the video file to be processed once at the beginning, then outputs the *duration* that has currently been processed. To calculate the % of progress you need *both* values.

To do that, you can pass the collected output to the parser instead. There is an example of this in the source code with the book, named `concurrent/qrunner_process_parser_elapsed.py`.

The Manager

In the previous examples we've created a number of different `QRunner` implementations that can be used for different purposes in your application. In all cases you can run as many of these runners as you like, on the same or multiple `QThreadPool` pools. However, sometimes you will want to keep track of the runners which you have running in order to do something with their output, or provide users with control over the runners directly.

`QThreadPool` itself does not give you access to the currently running runners, so we need to create our own *manager* ourselves, through which we start and control our workers.

The example below brings together some of the other worker features already introduced—progress, pause and stop control—together with the model views to present individual progress bars. This manager will likely work as a drop-in for most use-cases you have for running threads.

> This is quite a complex example, the full source code is available in the resources for the book. Here we'll go through the key parts of the `QRunner` manager in turn.

The worker manager

The worker manager class holds the threadpool, our workers and their progress and state information. It is derived from `QAbstractListModel` meaning it also provides a Qt model-like interface, allowing for it to be used as the model for a `QListView`—providing a per-worker progress bar and status indicator. The status tracking is handled through a number of internal signals, which attach automatically to every added worker.

Listing 179. concurrent/qrunner_manager.py

```
class WorkerManager(QAbstractListModel):
    """
    Manager to handle our worker queues and state.
    Also functions as a Qt data model for a view
```

```
    displaying progress for each worker.

    """

    _workers = {}
    _state = {}

    status = pyqtSignal(str)

    def __init__(self):
        super().__init__()

        # Create a threadpool for our workers.
        self.threadpool = QThreadPool()
        # self.threadpool.setMaxThreadCount(1)
        self.max_threads = self.threadpool.maxThreadCount()
        print("Multithreading with maximum %d threads" % self
.max_threads)

        self.status_timer = QTimer()
        self.status_timer.setInterval(100)
        self.status_timer.timeout.connect(self.notify_status)
        self.status_timer.start()

    def notify_status(self):
        n_workers = len(self._workers)
        running = min(n_workers, self.max_threads)
        waiting = max(0, n_workers - self.max_threads)
        self.status.emit(
            "{} running, {} waiting, {} threads".format(
                running, waiting, self.max_threads
            )
        )

    def enqueue(self, worker):
        """
        Enqueue a worker to run (at some point) by passing it to the
QThreadPool.
        """
        worker.signals.error.connect(self.receive_error)
        worker.signals.status.connect(self.receive_status)
        worker.signals.progress.connect(self.receive_progress)
        worker.signals.finished.connect(self.done)
```

```python
        self.threadpool.start(worker)
        self._workers[worker.job_id] = worker

        # Set default status to waiting, 0 progress.
        self._state[worker.job_id] = DEFAULT_STATE.copy()

        self.layoutChanged.emit()

    def receive_status(self, job_id, status):
        self._state[job_id]["status"] = status
        self.layoutChanged.emit()

    def receive_progress(self, job_id, progress):
        self._state[job_id]["progress"] = progress
        self.layoutChanged.emit()

    def receive_error(self, job_id, message):
        print(job_id, message)

    def done(self, job_id):
        """
        Task/worker complete. Remove it from the active workers
        dictionary. We leave it in worker_state, as this is used to
        to display past/complete workers too.
        """
        del self._workers[job_id]
        self.layoutChanged.emit()

    def cleanup(self):
        """
        Remove any complete/failed workers from worker_state.
        """
        for job_id, s in list(self._state.items()):
            if s["status"] in (STATUS_COMPLETE, STATUS_ERROR):
                del self._state[job_id]
        self.layoutChanged.emit()

    # Model interface
    def data(self, index, role):
        if role == Qt.DisplayRole:
            # See below for the data structure.
            job_ids = list(self._state.keys())
```

```
            job_id = job_ids[index.row()]
            return job_id, self._state[job_id]

    def rowCount(self, index):
        return len(self._state)
```

Workers are constructed outside the manager and passed in via `.enqueue()`. This connects all signals and adds the worker to the thread pool`. It will be executed, as normal once a thread is available.

The worker's are kept in an internal dictionary `_workers` keyed by the job id. There is a separate dictionary `_state` which stores the status and progress information about the workers. We keep them separate so we can delete jobs once complete, keeping an accurate count, yet continue to show information about completed jobs until cleared.

Signals from each submitted workers are connected to slots on the manager, which update the `_state` dictionary, print error messages or delete the completed job. Once any state is updated, we must call `.layoutChanged()` to trigger a refresh of the model view. The _clear_ method iterates through the `\_state` list and removes any that are complete or have failed.

Lastly, we set up a timer to regularly trigger a method to emit the current thread counts as a status message. The number of active threads is the *minimum* of the number of `_workers` and the `max_threads`. The waiting threads is the number of `\_workers` _minus_ the `max_threads` (as long as it is more than zero). The message is shown on the main window status bar.

The worker

The worker itself follows the same pattern as all our previous examples. The only *requirement* for our manager is the addition of a `.job_id` property which is set when the worker is created.

The signals from the workers must include this *job id* so the manager knows which worker sent the signal—updating the correct status, progress and finished states.

The worker itself is a simply dummy worker, which iterates 100 times (1 for each % progress) and performs a simple calculation. This worker calculation generates a series of numbers, but is constructed to occasionally throw *division by zero* errors.

Listing 180. concurrent/qrunner_manager.py

```python
class WorkerSignals(QObject):
    """
    Defines the signals available from a running worker thread.

    Supported signals are:

    finished
        No data

    error
        `tuple` (exctype, value, traceback.format_exc() )

    result
        `object` data returned from processing, anything

    progress
        `int` indicating % progress

    """

    error = pyqtSignal(str, str)
    result = pyqtSignal(str, object)  # We can send anything back.

    finished = pyqtSignal(str)
    progress = pyqtSignal(str, int)
    status = pyqtSignal(str, str)


class Worker(QRunnable):
    """
    Worker thread

    Inherits from QRunnable to handle worker thread setup, signals
and wrap-up.
```

```
    :param args: Arguments to pass for the worker
    :param kwargs: Keywords to pass for the worker

    """

    def __init__(self, *args, **kwargs):
        super().__init__()

        # Store constructor arguments (re-used for processing).
        self.signals = WorkerSignals()

        # Give this job a unique ID.
        self.job_id = str(uuid.uuid4())

        # The arguments for the worker
        self.args = args
        self.kwargs = kwargs

        self.signals.status.emit(self.job_id, STATUS_WAITING)

    @pyqtSlot()
    def run(self):
        """
        Initialize the runner function with passed args, kwargs.
        """

        self.signals.status.emit(self.job_id, STATUS_RUNNING)

        x, y = self.args

        try:

            value = random.randint(0, 100) * x
            delay = random.random() / 10
            result = []

            for n in range(100):
                #  Generate some numbers.
                value = value / y
                y -= 1

                # The following will sometimes throw a division by
zero error.
```

```
                result.append(value)

                # Pass out the current progress.
                self.signals.progress.emit(self.job_id, n + 1)
                time.sleep(delay)

        except Exception as e:
            print(e)
            # We swallow the error and continue.
            self.signals.error.emit(self.job_id, str(e))
            self.signals.status.emit(self.job_id, STATUS_ERROR)

        else:
            self.signals.result.emit(self.job_id, result)
            self.signals.status.emit(self.job_id, STATUS_COMPLETE)

        self.signals.finished.emit(self.job_id)
```

In addition to the progress signals we've seen before, we also have a *status* signal which emits one of the following statuses. Exceptions are caught and both the exception text and the error state are emitted using *error* and *status*.

Listing 181. concurrent/qrunner_manager.py

```
STATUS_WAITING = "waiting"
STATUS_RUNNING = "running"
STATUS_ERROR = "error"
STATUS_COMPLETE = "complete"


STATUS_COLORS = {
    STATUS_RUNNING: "#33a02c",
    STATUS_ERROR: "#e31a1c",
    STATUS_COMPLETE: "#b2df8a",
}

DEFAULT_STATE = {"progress": 0, "status": STATUS_WAITING}
```

Each of the active statuses have assigned colors which will be used in drawing on the progress bar.

Custom row display

We're using a `QListView` for the progress bar display. Normally a list view displays a simple text value for each row. To modify this we use a `QItemDelegate` which allows us to paint a custom widget for each row.

Listing 182. concurrent/qrunner_manager.py

```
class ProgressBarDelegate(QStyledItemDelegate):
    def paint(self, painter, option, index):
        # data is our status dict, containing progress, id, status
        job_id, data = index.model().data(index, Qt.DisplayRole)
        if data["progress"] > 0:
            color = QColor(STATUS_COLORS[data["status"]])

            brush = QBrush()
            brush.setColor(color)
            brush.setStyle(Qt.SolidPattern)

            width = option.rect.width() * data["progress"] / 100

            rect = QRect(option.rect)  #  Copy of the rect, so we can
modify.
            rect.setWidth(width)

            painter.fillRect(rect, brush)

        pen = QPen()
        pen.setColor(Qt.black)
        painter.drawText(option.rect, Qt.AlignLeft, job_id)
```

We get the data for the current row from the model using `index.model().data(index, Qt.DisplayRole)`. This is calling the `.data()` method on our custom model (manager) passing in the `index` and `role`. In our `.data()` method we are returning two bits of data — `job_id` and the `state` dictionary, containing *progress* and *status* keys.

For active jobs (`progress > 0`) *status* is used to select a color for the bar. This is drawn as a rectangle of the item row size `option.rect()`, with the width adjusted by the % completion. Finally, we write the `job_id` text over the top of this.

Starting a job

With everything in place, we can now enqueue jobs by calling `.self.worker.enqueue()` passing in arguments to the worker.

Listing 183. concurrent/qrunner_manager.py

```
    def start_worker(self):
        x = random.randint(0, 1000)
        y = random.randint(0, 1000)

        w = Worker(x, y)
        w.signals.result.connect(self.display_result)
        w.signals.error.connect(self.display_result)

        self.workers.enqueue(w)
```

The `.enqueue()` method accepts a constructed worker and attaches the internal signals to it to track progress. However, we can still attach any other external signals that we want.

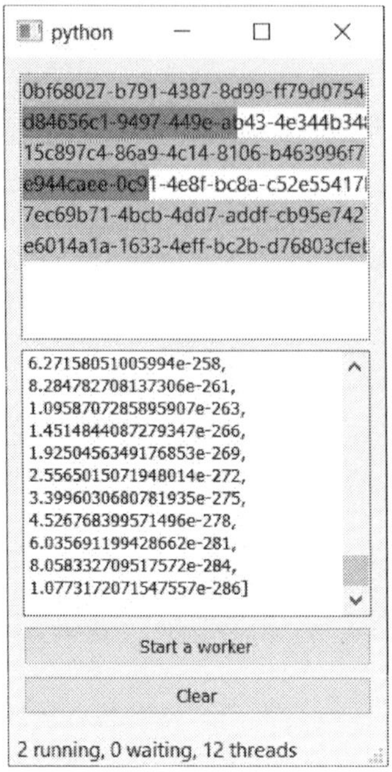

Figure 219. The manager interface, where you can start new jobs and see progress.

Also, while this example has only a single worker class, you can use this same manager with any other `QRunner`-derived classes, as long as they have the same signals available. This means you can use a single worker manager to manage all the workers in your app.

> Take a look at the full code in the source files with this book and experiment modifying the manager to your needs—for example, try adding kill & pause functionality, generic function runners.

Stopping jobs

We can start jobs, and some of them die due to errors. But what if we want to stop jobs that are taking too long? The `QListView` allows us to select rows and through the selected row we can kill a specific worker. The method below is linked to a button, and looks up the worker from the current selected item in the list.

Listing 184. concurrent/qrunner_manager_stop.py

```
    def stop_worker(self):
        selected = self.progress.selectedIndexes()
        for idx in selected:
            job_id, _ = self.workers.data(idx, Qt.DisplayRole)
            self.workers.kill(job_id)
```

In addition to this we need to modify the delegate to draw the currently selected item and update the worker and manager to pass through the *kill* signal. Take a look at the full source for this example to see how it all fits together.

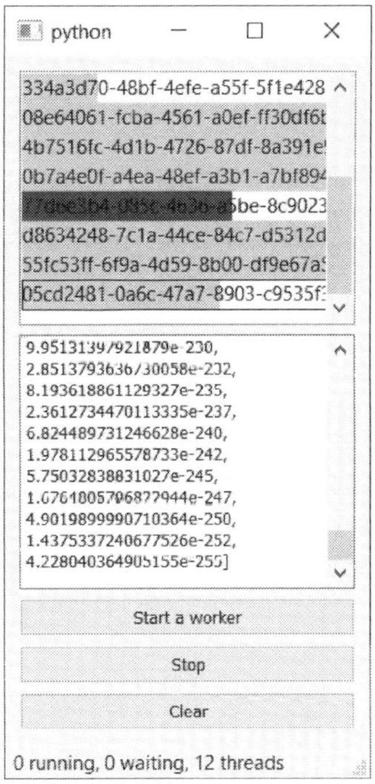

Figure 220. The manager, selecting a job allows you to stop it.

A sense of progress

When a user does something in your application, the consequences of that action should be immediately apparent—either through the result of the action itself, or through an indication that *something* is being done that will provide the result. This is particularly important for long-running tasks, such as calculations or network requests, where a lack of feedback could prompt the user to repeatedly mash buttons and seeing nothing in return.

One simple approach is to disable buttons once an operation has been triggered. But with no other indicator this looks a lot like "broken". A better alternative is to update the button with a "Working" message and an active progress indicator nearby. Progress bars are a common way to address this by informing the user of what is going on. But don't fall into the trap of thinking progress bars are always useful. They should always present a linear progress towards a task, if they don't they can be worse than no information ---

Progress bars are not helpful if -

- they go backwards and forward
- they don't increase linearly with the task progress
- they complete too quickly

Any of these behaviors can give users the sense that *something isn't right* whether "it's getting worse" to "what was that dialog I missed?" Your users must always *feel* in control.

✔ DO

- Provide progress bars for long-running tasks.
- Provide granular detail of sub-tasks where appropriate.
- Estimate how long something will take, when you can.

✖ DON'T

- Assume your users know what tasks are long- and short-running.
- Use progress bars when you have no idea of progress.
- Use progress bars that go up and down.

34. Running external commands & processes

So far we've looked at how to run things in separate threads, including external programs using Python `subprocess`. But in PyQt5 we can also make use of a Qt-based system for running external programs, `QProcess`. Creating and executing a job with `QProcess` is relatively straightforward.

The simplest possible example is shown below—we create a `QProcess` object and then call `.start` passing in the command to execute and a `list` of string arguments. In this case we're running our custom demo script, with Python `python dummy_script.py`.

```
p = QProcess()
p.start("python", ["dummy_script.py"])
```

Depending on your environment, you may need to specify `python3` instead of `python`.

You need to keep a reference to the created `QProcess` instance, either on `self` or elsewhere, while it is running.

The simple example is enough if you just want to *run* a program and don't care what happens to it. However, if you want to know more about what a program is doing, `QProcess` provides a number of signals which can be used to track the progress and state of processes.

One of the most useful is the are the `.readyReadStandardOutput` and `.readyReadStandardError` which fire whenever there is *standard output* and *standard error* ready to be read from the process. All running processes have two streams of output—*standard out* and *standard error*. The standard output returns the actual result of the execution (if any) while standard error returns any error *or* logging information.

```
p = QProcess()
p.readyReadStandardOutput.connect(self.handle_stdout)
p.readyReadStandardError.connect(self.handle_stderr)
p.stateChanged.connect(self.handle_state)
p.finished.connect(self.cleanup)
p.start("python", ["dummy_script.py"])
```

Additionally, there is a `.finished` signal which is fired when the process completes, and a `.stateChanged` signal which fires when the process status changes. Valid values—defined in the `QProcess.ProcessState` enum— are shown below.

Constant	Value	Description
QProcess.NotRunning	0	The process is not running.
QProcess.Starting	1	The process is starting, but the program has not yet been invoked.
QProcess.Running	2	The process is running and is ready for reading and writing.

In the following example we extend this basic `QProcess` setup to add handlers for the *standard out* and *standard err*. The signals notifying of available data connect to these handlers and trigger a request of the data from the process, using `.readAllStandardError()` and `.readAllStandardOutput()`.

The methods output raw `bytes`, so you need to decode it first.

In this example, our demo script `dummy_script.py` return a series of strings, which are parsed to provide progress information and structured data. The state of the process is also displayed on the statusbar.

The full code is shown below—

Listing 185. concurrent/qprocess.py

```python
import re
import sys

from PyQt5.QtCore import (
    QObject,
    QProcess,
    QRunnable,
    Qt,
    QThreadPool,
    QTimer,
    pyqtSignal,
    pyqtSlot,
)
from PyQt5.QtWidgets import (
    QApplication,
    QMainWindow,
    QPlainTextEdit,
    QProgressBar,
    QPushButton,
    QVBoxLayout,
    QWidget,
)

STATES = {
    QProcess.NotRunning: "Not running",
    QProcess.Starting: "Starting...",
    QProcess.Running: "Running...",
}

progress_re = re.compile("Total complete: (\d+)%")


def simple_percent_parser(output):
    """
    Matches lines using the progress_re regex,
    returning a single integer for the % progress.
    """
    m = progress_re.search(output)
    if m:
        pc_complete = m.group(1)
        return int(pc_complete)
```

```python
def extract_vars(l):
    """
    Extracts variables from lines, looking for lines
    containing an equals, and splitting into key=value.
    """
    data = {}
    for s in l.splitlines():
        if "=" in s:
            name, value = s.split("=")
            data[name] = value
    return data


class MainWindow(QMainWindow):
    def __init__(self):
        super().__init__()

        # Hold process reference.
        self.p = None

        layout = QVBoxLayout()

        self.text = QPlainTextEdit()
        layout.addWidget(self.text)

        self.progress = QProgressBar()
        layout.addWidget(self.progress)

        btn_run = QPushButton("Execute")
        btn_run.clicked.connect(self.start)

        layout.addWidget(btn_run)

        w = QWidget()
        w.setLayout(layout)
        self.setCentralWidget(w)

        self.show()

    def start(self):
        if self.p is not None:
            return
```

```
        self.p = QProcess()
        self.p.readyReadStandardOutput.connect(self.handle_stdout)
        self.p.readyReadStandardError.connect(self.handle_stderr)
        self.p.stateChanged.connect(self.handle_state)
        self.p.finished.connect(self.cleanup)
        self.p.start("python", ["dummy_script.py"])

    def handle_stderr(self):
        result = bytes(self.p.readAllStandardError()).decode("utf8")
        progress = simple_percent_parser(result)

        self.progress.setValue(progress)

    def handle_stdout(self):
        result = bytes(self.p.readAllStandardOutput()).decode("utf8")
        data = extract_vars(result)

        self.text.appendPlainText(str(data))

    def handle_state(self, state):
        self.statusBar().showMessage(STATES[state])

    def cleanup(self):
        self.p = None


app = QApplication(sys.argv)
w = MainWindow()
app.exec_()
```

In this example we store a reference to the process in `self.p`, meaning we can only run a single process at once. But you are free to run as many processes as you like alongside your application. If you don't need to track information from them, you can simply store references to the processes in a `list`.

However, if you want to track progress and parse output from workers individually, you may want to consider creating a manager class to handle and track all your processes. There is an example of this in the source files with the book, named `qprocess_manager.py`.

The full source code for the example is available in the source code for the book, but below we'll look at the JobManager class itself.

Listing 186. concurrent/qprocess_manager.py

```
class JobManager(QAbstractListModel):
    """
    Manager to handle active jobs and stdout, stderr
    and progress parsers.
    Also functions as a Qt data model for a view
    displaying progress for each process.
    """

    _jobs = {}
    _state = {}
    _parsers = {}

    status = pyqtSignal(str)
    result = pyqtSignal(str, object)

    def __init__(self):
        super().__init__()

        self.status_timer = QTimer()
        self.status_timer.setInterval(100)
        self.status_timer.timeout.connect(self.notify_status)
        self.status_timer.start()

    def notify_status(self):
        n_jobs = len(self._jobs)
        self.status.emit("{} jobs".format(n_jobs))

    def execute(self, command, arguments, parsers=no_parsers):
        """
        Execute a command by starting a new process.
        """

        job_id = uuid.uuid4().hex

        # By default, the signals do not have access to any
information about
        # the process that sent it. So we use this constructor to
annotate
```

```
        #  each signal with a job_id.

        def fwd_signal(target):
            return lambda *args: target(job_id, *args)

        self._parsers[job_id] = parsers

        # Set default status to waiting, 0 progress.
        self._state[job_id] = DEFAULT_STATE.copy()

        p = QProcess()
        p.readyReadStandardOutput.connect(fwd_signal(self
.handle_output))
        p.readyReadStandardError.connect(fwd_signal(self
.handle_output))
        p.stateChanged.connect(fwd_signal(self.handle_state))
        p.finished.connect(fwd_signal(self.done))

        self._jobs[job_id] = p

        p.start(command, arguments)

        self.layoutChanged.emit()

    def handle_output(self, job_id):
        p = self._jobs[job_id]
        stderr = bytes(p.readAllStandardError()).decode("utf8")
        stdout = bytes(p.readAllStandardOutput()).decode("utf8")
        output = stderr + stdout

        parser = self._parsers.get(job_id)

        if parser.progress:
            progress = parser.progress(output)
            if progress:
                self._state[job_id]["progress"] = progress
                self.layoutChanged.emit()

        if parser.data:
            data = parser.data(output)
            if data:
                self.result.emit(job_id, data)
```

```python
    def handle_state(self, job_id, state):
        self._state[job_id]["status"] = state
        self.layoutChanged.emit()

    def done(self, job_id, exit_code, exit_status):
        """
        Task/worker complete. Remove it from the active workers
        dictionary. We leave it in worker_state, as this is used to
        to display past/complete workers too.
        """
        del self._jobs[job_id]
        self.layoutChanged.emit()

    def cleanup(self):
        """
        Remove any complete/failed workers from worker_state.
        """
        for job_id, s in list(self._state.items()):
            if s["status"] == QProcess.NotRunning:
                del self._state[job_id]
        self.layoutChanged.emit()

    # Model interface
    def data(self, index, role):
        if role == Qt.DisplayRole:
            # See below for the data structure.
            job_ids = list(self._state.keys())
            job_id = job_ids[index.row()]
            return job_id, self._state[job_id]

    def rowCount(self, index):
        return len(self._state)
```

This class provides a model view interface allowing it to be used as the basis for a `QListView`. The custom delegate `ProgressBarDelegate` delegate draws a progress bar for each item, along with the job identifier. The color of the progress bar is determined by the status of the process — dark green if active, or light green if complete.

Parsing of progress information from workers is tricky in this setup, because the `.readyReadStandardError` and `.readyReadStandardOutput` signals do not pass the data, or information about the job that is ready. To work around this we define our custom `job_id` and intercept the signals to add this data to them.

Parsers for the jobs are passed in when executing the command and stored in `_parsers`. Output received from each job is passed through the respective parser and used to emit the data, or update the job's progress.

Listing 187. concurrent/qprocess_manager.py

```
def simple_percent_parser(output):
    """
    Matches lines using the progress_re regex,
    returning a single integer for the % progress.
    """
    m = progress_re.search(output)
    if m:
        pc_complete = m.group(1)
        return int(pc_complete)


def extract_vars(l):
    """
    Extracts variables from lines, looking for lines
    containing an equals, and splitting into key=value.
    """
    data = {}
    for s in l.splitlines():
        if "=" in s:
            name, value = s.split("=")
            data[name] = value
    return data
```

You can start multiple jobs, and watch them complete, updating their current progress as they go. Experiment with adding additional commands and parsers for your own jobs.

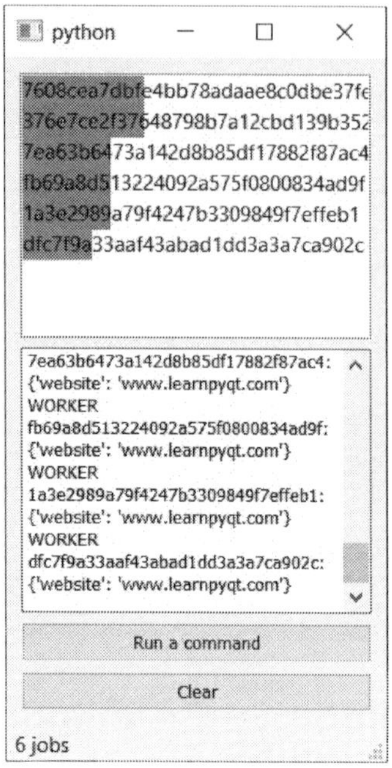

Figure 221. The process manager, showing active processes and progress.

Plotting

One of the major strengths of Python is in data science and visualization, using tools such as *Pandas*, *numpy* and *sklearn* for data analysis. Buiding GUI applications with PyQt5 gives you access to all these Python tools directly from within your app, allowing you to build complex data-driven apps and interactive dashboards. We've already covered the model views, which allow us to show data in lists and tables. In this chapter we'll look at the final piece of that puzzle — plotting data.

When building apps with PyQt5 you have two main choices — matplotlib (which also gives access to Pandas plots) and PyQtGraph, which creates plots with Qt-native graphics. In this chapter we'll look at how you can use these libraries to visualize data in your applications.

35. Plotting with PyQtGraph

While it is possible to embed `matplotlib` plots in PyQt5 the experience does not feel entirely *native*. For simple and highly interactive plots you may want to consider using PyQtGraph instead. PyQtGraph is built on top of PyQt5 native `QGraphicsScene` giving better drawing performance, particularly for live data, as well as providing interactivity and the ability to easily customize plots with Qt graphics widgets.

In this chapter we'll walk through the first steps of creating a plot widget with PyQtGraph and then demonstrate plot customization using line colors, line type, axis labels, background color and plotting multiple lines.

Getting started

To be able to use PyQtGraph with PyQt5 you first need to install the package to your Python environment. You can do this as normal using `pip`.

```
pip install pyqtgraph
```

Once the installation is complete you should be able to import the module as normal.

Creating a PyQtGraph widget

In PyQtGraph all plots are created using the `PlotWidget` widget. This widget provides a contained *canvas* on which plots of any type can be added and configured. Under the hood, this plot widget uses Qt native `QGraphicsScene` meaning it fast and efficient yet simple to integrate with the rest of your app. You can create a `PlotWidget` as for any other widget.

The basic template app, with a single `PlotWidget` in a `QMainWindow` is shown below.

In the following examples we'll create the PyQtGraph widget in code. However, you can also embed PyQtGraph widgets from Qt Designer.

Listing 188. plotting/pyqtgraph_1.py

```
import sys

from PyQt5 import QtWidgets  # import PyQt5 before PyQtGraph
import pyqtgraph as pg
from pyqtgraph import PlotWidget, plot


class MainWindow(QtWidgets.QMainWindow):
    def __init__(self):
        super().__init__()

        self.graphWidget = pg.PlotWidget()
        self.setCentralWidget(self.graphWidget)

        hour = [1, 2, 3, 4, 5, 6, 7, 8, 9, 10]
        temperature = [30, 32, 34, 32, 33, 31, 29, 32, 35, 45]

        # plot data: x, y values
        self.graphWidget.plot(hour, temperature)


app = QtWidgets.QApplication(sys.argv)
main = MainWindow()
main.show()
app.exec_()
```

In all our examples below we import PyQtGraph using import pyqtgraph as pg. This is a common convention in PyQtGraph examples to keep things tidy & reduce typing. You can import as `import pyqtgraph` if you prefer.

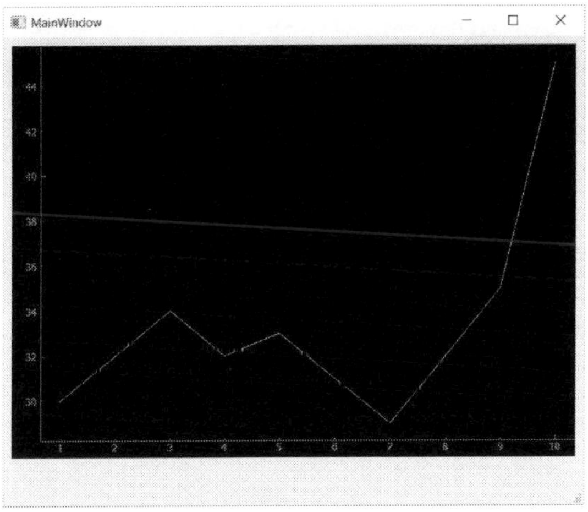

Figure 222. The custom PyQtGraph widget showing dummy data.

The default plot style of PyQtGraph is quite bare - a black background with a thin (barely visible) white line. In the next section we'll look at what options we have available to us in PyQtGraph to improve the appearance and usability of our plots.

Styling plots

PyQtGraph uses Qt's `QGraphicsScene` to render the graphs. This gives us access to all the standard Qt line and shape styling options for use in plots. However, PyQtGraph provides an API for using these to draw plots and manage the plot canvas.

Below we'll go through the most common styling features you'll need to create and customize your own plots.

Background Color

Beginning with the app skeleton above, we can change the background color by calling `.setBackground` on our `PlotWidget` instance (in `self.graphWidget`). The code below will set the background to white, by passing in the string 'w'.

```
self.graphWidget.setBackground('w')
```

You can set (and update) the background color of the plot at any time.

Listing 189. plotting/pyqtgraph_2.py

```
import sys

from PyQt5 import QtWidgets # import PyQt5 before PyQtGraph
import pyqtgraph as pg
from pyqtgraph import PlotWidget, plot


class MainWindow(QtWidgets.QMainWindow):
    def __init__(self):
        super().__init__()

        self.graphWidget = pg.PlotWidget()
        self.setCentralWidget(self.graphWidget)

        hour = [1, 2, 3, 4, 5, 6, 7, 8, 9, 10]
        temperature = [30, 32, 34, 32, 33, 31, 29, 32, 35, 45]

        self.graphWidget.setBackground("w")
        self.graphWidget.plot(hour, temperature)


app = QtWidgets.QApplication(sys.argv)
main = MainWindow()
main.show()
app.exec_()
```

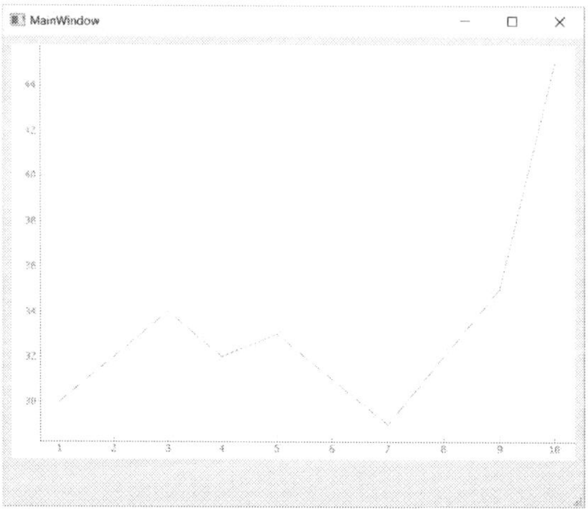

Figure 223. Changed PyQtGraph Plot Background to White.

There are a number of simple colors available using single letters, based on the standard colors used in `matplotlib`. They're pretty unsurprising, except that 'k' is used for black.

Table 13. Common color codes

Color	Letter code
blue	b
green	g
red	r
cyan (bright blue-green)	c
magenta (bright pink)	m
yellow	y
black	k
white	w

In addition to these single letter codes, you can also set colors using hex notation eg. `#672922` as a string.

```
self.graphWidget.setBackground('#bbccaa')         # hex
```

RGB and RGBA values can be passed in as a 3-tuple or 4-tuple respectively, using values 0-255.

```
self.graphWidget.setBackground((100,50,255))      # RGB each 0-255
self.graphWidget.setBackground((100,50,255,25))   # RGBA (A = alpha
opacity)
```

Lastly, you can also specify colors using Qt's `QColor` type directly.

```
self.graphWidget.setBackground(QtGui.QColor(100,50,254,25))
```

This can be useful if you're using specific `QColor` objects elsewhere in your application, or to set your plot background to the default GUI background color.

```
color = self.palette().color(QtGui.QPalette.Window)  # Get the
default window background,
self.graphWidget.setBackground(color)
```

Line Color, Width & Style

Lines in PyQtGraph are drawn using standard Qt `QPen` types. This gives you the same full control over line drawing as you would have in any other `QGraphicsScene` drawing. To use a pen to plot a line, you simply create a new `QPen` instance and pass it into the `plot` method.

Below we create a `QPen` object, passing in a 3-tuple of `int` values specifying an RGB value (of full red). We could also define this by passing 'r', or a `QColor` object. Then we pass this into `plot` with the *pen* parameter.

```
pen = pg.mkPen(color=(255, 0, 0))
self.graphWidget.plot(hour, temperature, pen=pen)
```

The complete code is shown below.

Listing 190. plotting/pyqtgraph_3.py

```
import sys

from PyQt5 import QtWidgets # import PyQt5 before PyQtGraph
import pyqtgraph as pg
from pyqtgraph import PlotWidget, plot


class MainWindow(QtWidgets.QMainWindow):
    def __init__(self):
        super().__init__()

        self.graphWidget = pg.PlotWidget()
        self.setCentralWidget(self.graphWidget)

        hour = [1, 2, 3, 4, 5, 6, 7, 8, 9, 10]
        temperature = [30, 32, 34, 32, 33, 31, 29, 32, 35, 45]

        self.graphWidget.setBackground("w")

        pen = pg.mkPen(color=(255, 0, 0))
        self.graphWidget.plot(hour, temperature, pen=pen)


app = QtWidgets.QApplication(sys.argv)
main = MainWindow()
main.show()
app.exec_()
```

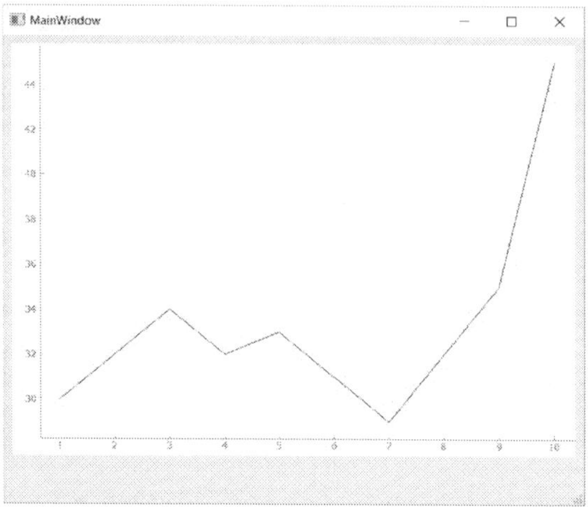

Figure 224. Changing Line Color.

By changing the QPen object we can change the appearance of the line, including both line width in pixels and style (dashed, dotted, etc.) using standard Qt line styles. For example, the following example creates a 15px width dashed line in red.

```
pen = pg.mkPen(color=(255, 0, 0), width=15, style=QtCore.Qt.DashLine)
```

The result is shown below, giving a 15px dashed red line.

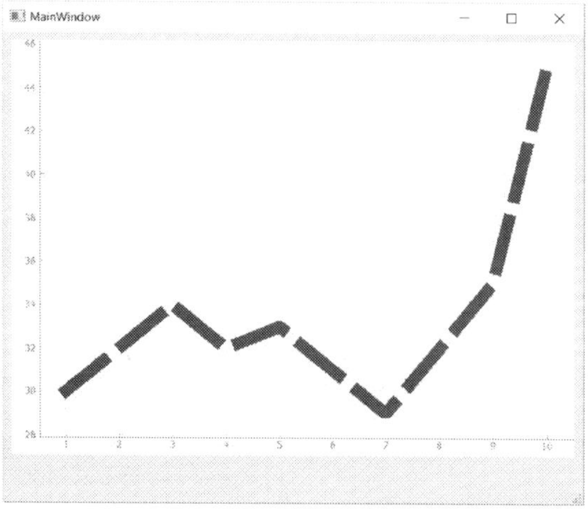

Figure 225. Changing Line Width and Style.

The standard Qt line styles can all be used, including Qt.SolidLine, Qt.DashLine, Qt.DotLine, Qt.DashDotLine and Qt.DashDotDotLine. Examples of each of these lines are shown in the image below, and you can read more in the Qt

Documentation [https://doc.qt.io/qt-5/qpen.html#pen-style].

Line Markers

For many plots it can be helpful to place markers in addition or instead of lines on the plot. To draw a marker on the plot, pass the symbol to use as a marker when calling `.plot` as shown below.

```
self.graphWidget.plot(hour, temperature, symbol='+')
```

In addition to `symbol` you can also pass in `symbolSize`, `symbolBrush` and `symbolPen` parameters. The value passed as `symbolBrush` can be any color, or `QBrush` type, while `symbolPen` can be passed any color or a `QPen` instance. The *pen* is used to draw the outline of the shape, while **brush** is used for the fill.

For example the below code will give a blue cross marker of size 30, on a thick red line.

```
pen = pg.mkPen(color=(255, 0, 0), width=15, style=QtCore.Qt.DashLine)
self.graphWidget.plot(hour, temperature, pen=pen, symbol='+',
symbolSize=30, symbolBrush=('b'))
```

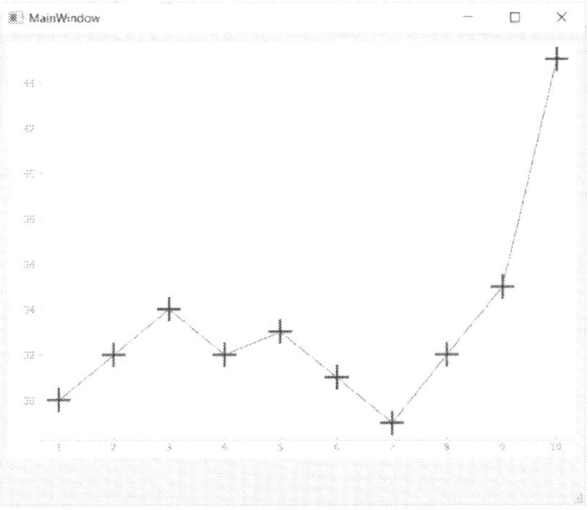

Figure 226. Symbols are shown at each data point on the line.

In addition to the + plot marker, PyQtGraph supports the following standard markers shown in the table below. These can all be used in the same way.

Variable	Marker Type
o	Circular
s	Square
t	Triangular
d	Diamond
+	Cross

> If you have more complex requirements you can also pass in any QPainterPath object, allowing you to draw completely custom marker shapes.

Plot Titles

Chart titles are important to provide context to what is shown on a given chart. In PyQtGraph you can add a main plot title using the `setTitle()` method on the `PlotWidget`, passing in your title string.

```
self.graphWidget.setTitle("Your Title Here")
```

You can apply text styles, including colors, font sizes and weights to your titles (and any other labels in PyQtGraph) by passing additional arguments. The available syle arguments are shown below.

Style	Type
color	(`str`) e.g. 'CCFF00'
size	(`str`) e.g. '8pt'
bold	(`bool`) `True` or `False`
italic	(`bool`) `True` or `False`

The code below sets the color to blue with a font size of 30pt.

```
self.graphWidget.setTitle("Your Title Here", color="b", size="30pt")
```

You can also style your headers with HTML tag syntax if you prefer, although it's less readable.

```
self.graphWidget.setTitle("<span style=\"color:blue;font-size:30pt
\">Your Title Here</span>")
```

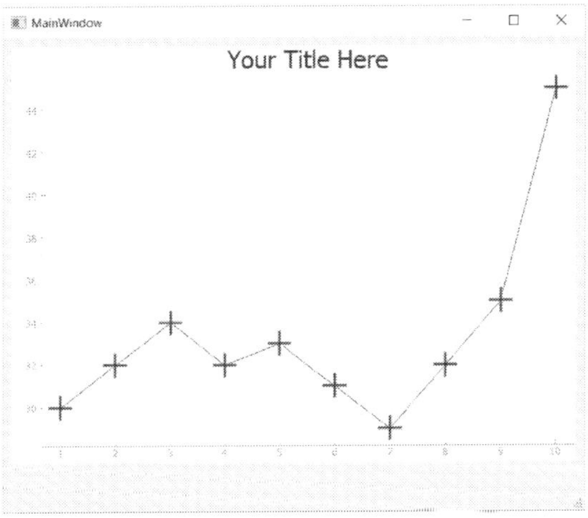

Figure 227. Plot with a styled title.

Axis Labels

Similar to titles, we can use the `setLabel()` method to create our axis titles. This requires two parameters, *position* and *text*. The *position* can be any one of `'left,'right','top','bottom'` which describe the position of the axis on which the text is placed. The 2nd parameter *text* is the text you want to use for the label.

You can pass additional style parameters into the method. These differ slightly than for the title, in that they need to be valid CSS name-value pairs. For example, the size is now `font-size`. Because the name `font-size` has a hyphen in it, you cannot pass it directly as a parameter, but must use the `**dictionary` method.

```
styles = {'color':'r', 'font-size':'30pt'}
self.graphWidget.setLabel('left', 'Temperature (°C)', **styles)
self.graphWidget.setLabel('bottom', 'Hour (H)', **styles)
```

These also support HTML syntax if you prefer.

```
self.graphWidget.setLabel('left', "<span style=\"color:red;font-
size:30px\">Temperature (°C)</span>")
self.graphWidget.setLabel('bottom', "<span style=\"color:red;font-
size:30px\">Hour (H)</span>")
```

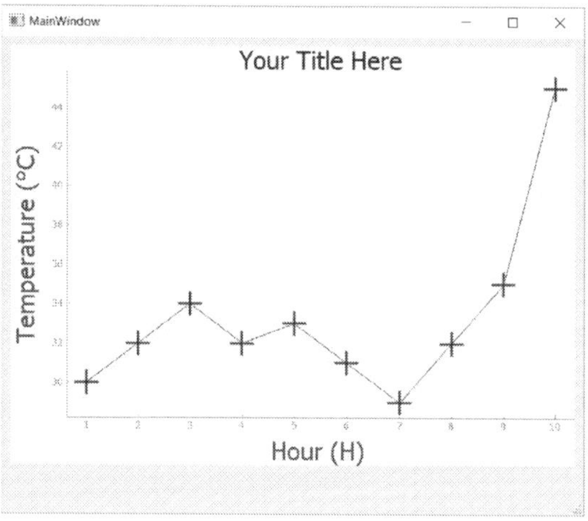

Figure 228. Axis labels with a custom style.

Legends

In addition to the axis and plot titles you will often want to show a legend identifying what a given line represents. This is particularly important when you start adding multiple lines to a plot. Adding a legend to a plot can be accomplished by calling `.addLegend` on the `PlotWidget`, however before this will work you need to provide a name for each line when calling `.plot()`.

The example below assigns a name "Sensor 1" to the line we are plotting with `.plot()`. This name will be used to identify the line in the legend.

```
self.graphWidget.plot(hour, temperature, name = "Sensor 1",  pen =
NewPen, symbol='+', symbolSize=30, symbolBrush=('b'))
self.graphWidget.addLegend()
```

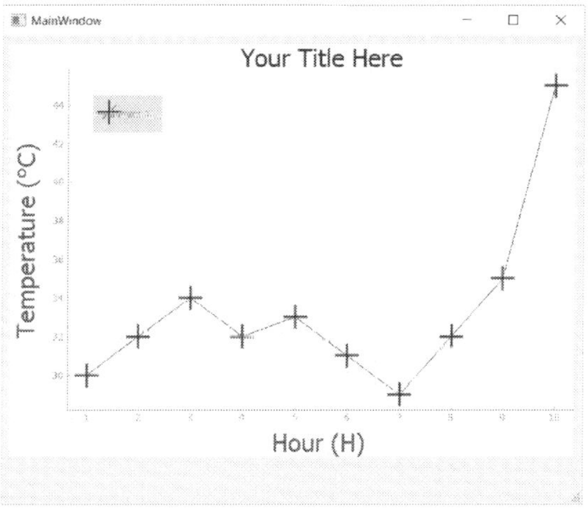

Figure 229. The plot with the legend, showing a single item.

> The legend appears in the top left by default. If you would like to move it, you can easily drag and drop the legend elsewhere. You can also specify a default offset by passing a 2-tuple to the *offset* parameter when creating the legend.

Background Grid

Adding a background grid can make your plots easier to read, particularly when trying to compare relative x & y values against each other. You can turn on a background grid for your plot by calling `.showGrid` on your `PlotWidget`. You can toggle x and y grids independently.

The following with create the grid for both the X and Y axis.

```
self.graphWidget.showGrid(x=True, y=True)
```

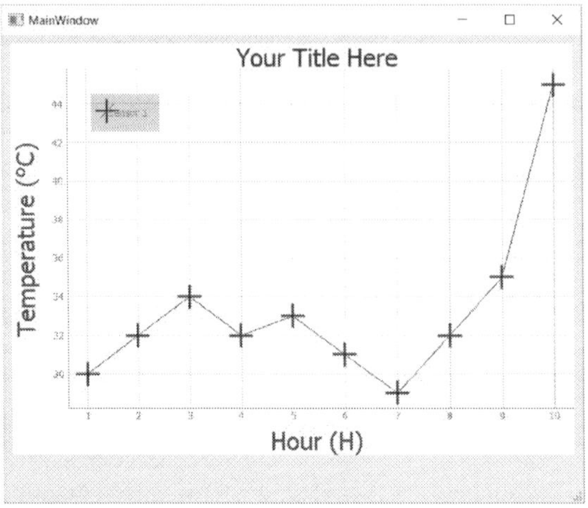

Figure 230. The plot grid.

Setting Axis Limits

Sometimes it can be useful to restrict the range of data which is visible on the plot, or to lock the axis to a consistent range regardless of the data input (e.g. a known min-max range). In PyQtGraph this can be done using the `.setXRange()` and `.setYRange()` methods. These force the plot to only show data within the specified ranges on each axis.

Below we set two ranges, one on each axis. The 1st argument is the minimum value and the 2nd is the maximum.

```
self.graphWidget.setXRange(5, 20, padding=0)
self.graphWidget.setYRange(30, 40, padding=0)
```

A optional padding argument causes the range to be set larger than specified by the specified fraction (this between 0.02 and 0.1 by default, depending on the size of the ViewBox). If you want to remove this padding entirely, pass 0.

```
self.graphWidget.setXRange(5, 20, padding=0)
self.graphWidget.setYRange(30, 40, padding=0)
```

The complete code so far is shown below:

Listing 191. plotting/pyqtgraph_4.py

```
import sys

from PyQt5 import QtWidgets # import PyQt5 before PyQtGraph
import pyqtgraph as pg
from pyqtgraph import PlotWidget, plot


class MainWindow(QtWidgets.QMainWindow):
    def __init__(self):
        super().__init__()

        self.graphWidget = pg.PlotWidget()
        self.setCentralWidget(self.graphWidget)

        hour = [1, 2, 3, 4, 5, 6, 7, 8, 9, 10]
        temperature = [30, 32, 34, 32, 33, 31, 29, 32, 35, 45]

        # Add Background color to white
        self.graphWidget.setBackground("w")
        # Add Title
        self.graphWidget.setTitle("Your Title Here", color="b", size
="30pt")
        # Add Axis Labels
        styles = {"color": "#f00", "font-size": "20px"}
        self.graphWidget.setLabel("left", "Temperature (°C)",
**styles)
        self.graphWidget.setLabel("bottom", "Hour (H)", **styles)
        # Add legend
        self.graphWidget.addLegend()
        # Add grid
        self.graphWidget.showGrid(x=True, y=True)
        # Set Range
        self.graphWidget.setXRange(0, 10, padding=0)
        self.graphWidget.setYRange(20, 55, padding=0)

        pen = pg.mkPen(color=(255, 0, 0))
        self.graphWidget.plot(
            hour,
            temperature,
            name="Sensor 1",
            pen=pen,
```

```
                symbol="+",
                symbolSize=30,
                symbolBrush=("b"),
            )


app = QtWidgets.QApplication(sys.argv)
main = MainWindow()
main.show()
app.exec_()
```

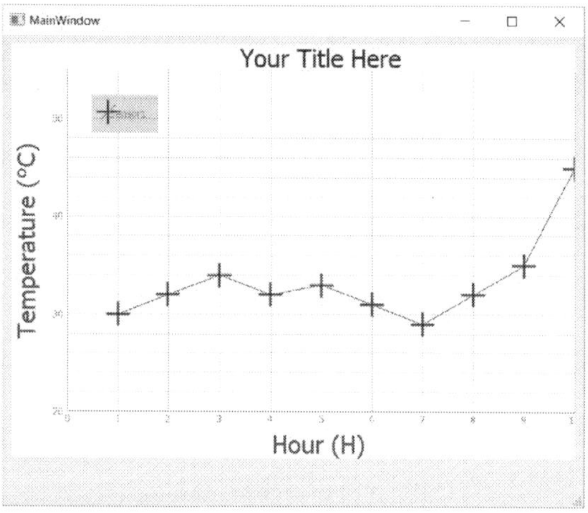

Figure 231. Limiting the range of the axis.

Plotting multiple lines

It is common for plots to involve more than one line. In PyQtGraph this is as simple as calling `.plot()` multiple times on the same `PlotWidget`. In the following example we're going to plot two lines of similar data, using the same line styles, thicknesses etc. for each, but changing the line color.

To simplify this we can create our own custom `plot` method on our `MainWindow`. This accepts `x` and `y` parameters to plot, the name of the line (for the legend) and a color. We use the color for both the line and marker color.

```
    def plot(self, x, y, plotname, color):
        pen = pg.mkPen(color=color)
        self.graphWidget.plot(x, y, name=plotname, pen=pen, symbol
='+', symbolSize=30, symbolBrush=(color))
```

To plot separate lines we'll create a new array called `temperature_2` and populate it with random numbers similar to `temperature` (now `temperature_1`). Plotting these alongside each other allows us to compare them together. Now, you can call plot function twice and this will generate 2 lines on the plot.

```
self.plot(hour, temperature_1, "Sensor1", 'r')
self.plot(hour, temperature_2, "Sensor2", 'b')
```

Listing 192. plotting/pyqtgraph_5.py

```
import sys

from PyQt5 import QtWidgets # import PyQt5 before PyQtGraph
import pyqtgraph as pg
from pyqtgraph import PlotWidget, plot


class MainWindow(QtWidgets.QMainWindow):
    def __init__(self):
        super().__init__()

        self.graphWidget = pg.PlotWidget()
        self.setCentralWidget(self.graphWidget)

        hour = [1, 2, 3, 4, 5, 6, 7, 8, 9, 10]
        temperature_1 = [30, 32, 34, 32, 33, 31, 29, 32, 35, 45]
        temperature_2 = [50, 35, 44, 22, 38, 32, 27, 38, 32, 44]

        # Add Background color to white
        self.graphWidget.setBackground("w")
        # Add Title
        self.graphWidget.setTitle("Your Title Here", color="b", size
="30pt")
```

```
        # Add Axis Labels
        styles = {"color": "#f00", "font-size": "20px"}
        self.graphWidget.setLabel("left", "Temperature (°C)",
**styles)
        self.graphWidget.setLabel("bottom", "Hour (H)", **styles)
        # Add legend
        self.graphWidget.addLegend()
        # Add grid
        self.graphWidget.showGrid(x=True, y=True)
        # Set Range
        self.graphWidget.setXRange(0, 10, padding=0)
        self.graphWidget.setYRange(20, 55, padding=0)

        self.plot(hour, temperature_1, "Sensor1", "r")
        self.plot(hour, temperature_2, "Sensor2", "b")

    def plot(self, x, y, plotname, color):
        pen = pg.mkPen(color=color)
        self.graphWidget.plot(
            x, y, name=plotname, pen=pen, symbol="+", symbolSize=30,
symbolBrush=(color)
        )


app = QtWidgets.QApplication(sys.argv)
main = MainWindow()
main.show()
app.exec_()
```

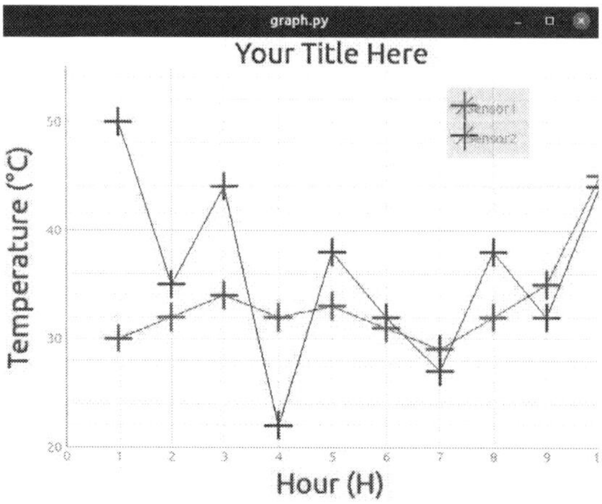

Figure 232. A plot with two lines.

Play around with this function, customizing your markers, line widths, colors and other parameters.

Clearing the plot

Finally, sometimes you might want to clear and refresh the plot periodically. You can easily do that by calling `.clear()`.

```
self.graphWidget.clear()
```

This will remove the lines from the plot but keep all other attributes the same.

Updating the plot

While you *can* simply clear the plot and redraw all your elements again, this means Qt has to destroy and recreate all your `QGraphicsScene` objects. For small or simple plots this is probably not noticeable, but if you want to create high-peformance streaming plots it is much better to update the data in place. PyQtGraph takes the new data and updates the plotted line to match without affecting any other elements in the plot.

To update a line we need a reference to the line object. This reference is returned when first creating the line using `.plot` and we can simply store this in a variable. Note that this is a reference to the *line* not to the plot.

```
my_line_ref = graphWidget.plot(x, y)
```

Once we have the reference, updating the plot is simply a case of calling `.setData` on the reference to apply the new data.

Listing 193. plotting/pyqtgraph_6.py

```
import os
import sys  # We need sys so that we can pass argv to QApplication
```

```
from random import randint

from PyQt5 import QtWidgets, QtCore # import PyQt5 before PyQtGraph
import pyqtgraph as pg
from pyqtgraph import PlotWidget, plot


class MainWindow(QtWidgets.QMainWindow):
    def __init__(self):
        super().__init__()

        self.graphWidget = pg.PlotWidget()
        self.setCentralWidget(self.graphWidget)

        self.x = list(range(100))  # 100 time points
        self.y = [randint(0, 100) for _ in range(100)]  # 100 data
points

        self.graphWidget.setBackground("w")

        pen = pg.mkPen(color=(255, 0, 0))
        self.data_line = self.graphWidget.plot(self.x, self.y, pen
=pen)  ①

        self.timer = QtCore.QTimer()
        self.timer.setInterval(50)
        self.timer.timeout.connect(self.update_plot_data)
        self.timer.start()

    def update_plot_data(self):

        self.x = self.x[1:]  # Remove the first y element.
        self.x.append(self.x[-1] + 1)  # Add a new value 1 higher
than the last.

        self.y = self.y[1:]  # Remove the first
        self.y.append(randint(0, 100))  # Add a new random value.

        self.data_line.setData(self.x, self.y)  # Update the data.


app = QtWidgets.QApplication(sys.argv)
w = MainWindow()
```

```
w.show()
app.exec_()
```

① Here we take a reference to the line we plotted, storing it as `self.data_line`.

We use a `QTimer` to update the data every 50ms, setting the trigger to call a custom slot method `update_plot_data` where we'll change the data. We define this timer in the `__init__` block so it is automatically started.

If you run the app you will see a plot with random data scrolling rapidly to the left, with the X values also updating and scrolling in time, as if streaming data. You can replace the random data with your own real data, taken for example from a live sensor readout or API. PyQtGraph is performant enough to support multiple plots using this method.

Conclusion

In this chapter we've discovered how to draw simple plots with PyQtGraph and customize lines, markers and labels. For a complete overview of PyQtGraph methods and capabilities see the PyQtGraph Documentation & API Reference [http://www.pyqtgraph.org/documentation/]. The PyQtGraph repository on Github [https://github.com/pyqtgraph/pyqtgraph] also has complete set of more complex example plots in Plotting.py (shown below).

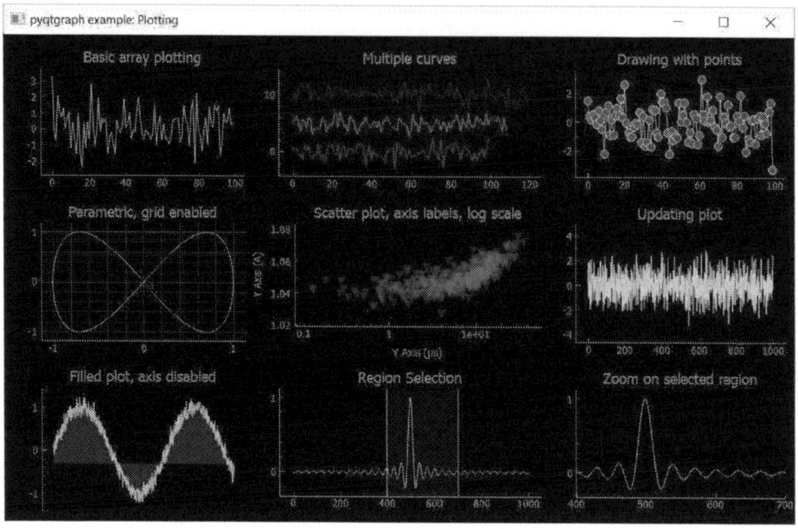

Figure 233. Example plots taken from the PyQtGraph documentation.

36. Plotting with Matplotlib

In the previous part we covered plotting in PyQt5 using PyQtGraph. That library uses the Qt vector-based QGraphicsScene to draw plots and provides a great interface for interactive and high performance plotting.

However, there is another plotting library for Python which is used far more widely, and which offers a richer assortment of plots — Matplotlib [https://www.matplotlib.org]. If you're migrating an existing data analysis tool to a PyQt5 GUI, or if you simply want to have access to the array of plot abilities that Matplotlib offers, then you'll want to know how to include Matplotlib plots within your application.

In this chapter we'll cover how to embed Matplotlib plots in your PyQt5 applications

> Many other Python libraries — such as seaborn [https://github.com/mwaskom/seaborn] and pandas [https://pandas.pydata.org/pandas docs/version/0.13/visualization.html] — make use of Matplotlib for plotting. These plots can be embedded in PyQt5 in the same way shown here, and the reference to the axes passed when plotting. There is a pandas example at the end of this chapter.

Installing Matplotlib

The following examples assume you have Matplotlib installed. If not you can install it as normal using `pip`, with the following —

```
pip install matplotlib
```

A simple example

The following minimal example sets up a Matplotlib canvas `FigureCanvasQTAgg` which creates the `Figure` and adds a single set of axes to it. This canvas object is also a QWidget and so can be embedded straight into an application as any other Qt widget.

Listing 194. plotting/matplotlib_1.py

```
import sys

from PyQt5 import QtWidgets # import PyQt5 before matplotlib

import matplotlib
from matplotlib.backends.backend_qt5agg import FigureCanvasQTAgg
from matplotlib.figure import Figure

matplotlib.use("Qt5Agg")


class MplCanvas(FigureCanvasQTAgg):
    def __init__(self, parent=None, width=5, height=4, dpi=100):
        fig = Figure(figsize=(width, height), dpi=dpi)
        self.axes = fig.add_subplot(111)
        super().__init__(fig)


class MainWindow(QtWidgets.QMainWindow):
    def __init__(self):
        super().__init__()

        # Create the maptlotlib FigureCanvas object,
        # which defines a single set of axes as self.axes.
        sc = MplCanvas(self, width=5, height=4, dpi=100)
        sc.axes.plot([0, 1, 2, 3, 4], [10, 1, 20, 3, 40])
        self.setCentralWidget(sc)

        self.show()


app = QtWidgets.QApplication(sys.argv)
w = MainWindow()
app.exec_()
```

In this case we're adding our MplCanvas widget as the central widget on the window with .setCentralWidget(). This means it will take up the entirety of the window and resize together with it. The plotted data `[0,1,2,3,4]`, `[10,1,20,3,40]` is provided as two lists of numbers (x and y respectively) as required by the `.plot` method.

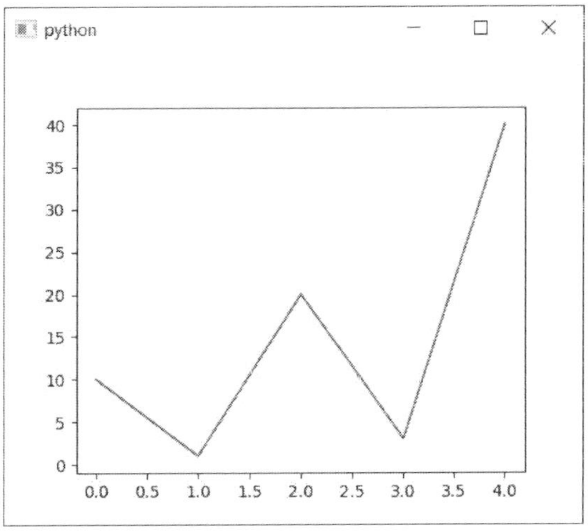

Figure 234. A simple plot.

Plot controls

Plots from Matplotlib displayed in PyQt5 are actually rendered as simple (bitmap) images by the *Agg* backend. The `FigureCanvasQTAgg` class wraps this backend and displays the resulting image on a Qt widget. The effect of this architecture is that Qt is unaware of the positions of lines and other plot elements — only the x, y coordinates of any clicks and mouse movements over the widget.

However, support for handling Qt mouse events and transforming them into interactions on the plot is built into Matplotlib. This can be controlled through a custom toolbar which can be added to your applications alongside the plot. In this section we'll look at adding these controls so we can zoom, pan and get data from embedded Matplotlib plots.

The complete code, importing the toolbar widget `NavigationToolbar2QT` and adding it to the interface within a `QVBoxLayout`, is shown below —

Listing 195. plotting/matplotlib_2.py

```
import sys
```

```
from PyQt5 import QtWidgets  # import PyQt5 before matplotlib

import matplotlib
from matplotlib.backends.backend_qt5agg import FigureCanvasQTAgg
from matplotlib.backends.backend_qt5agg import NavigationToolbar2QT
as NavigationToolbar
from matplotlib.figure import Figure


matplotlib.use("Qt5Agg")


class MplCanvas(FigureCanvasQTAgg):
    def __init__(self, parent=None, width=5, height=4, dpi=100):
        fig = Figure(figsize=(width, height), dpi=dpi)
        self.axes = fig.add_subplot(111)
        super().__init__(fig)


class MainWindow(QtWidgets.QMainWindow):
    def __init__(self):
        super().__init__()

        sc = MplCanvas(self, width=5, height=4, dpi=100)
        sc.axes.plot([0, 1, 2, 3, 4], [10, 1, 20, 3, 40])

        # Create toolbar, passing canvas as first parament, parent
(self, the MainWindow) as second.
        toolbar = NavigationToolbar(sc, self)

        layout = QtWidgets.QVBoxLayout()
        layout.addWidget(toolbar)
        layout.addWidget(sc)

        # Create a placeholder widget to hold our toolbar and canvas.
        widget = QtWidgets.QWidget()
        widget.setLayout(layout)
        self.setCentralWidget(widget)

        self.show()
```

```
app = QtWidgets.QApplication(sys.argv)
w = MainWindow()
app.exec_()
```

We'll step through the changes.

First we import the toolbar widget from `matplotlib.backends.backend_qt5agg.NavigationToolbar2QT` renaming it with the simpler name `NavigationToolbar`. We create an instance of the toolbar by calling `NavigationToolbar` with two parameters, first the canvas object `sc` and then the parent for the toolbar, in this case our `MainWindow` object `self`. Passing in the canvas links the created toolbar to it, allowing it to be controlled. The resulting toolbar object is stored in the variable `toolbar`.

We need to add two widgets to the window, one above the other, so we use a `QVBoxLayout`. First we add our toolbar widget `toolbar` and then the canvas widget `sc` to this layout. Finally, we set this layout onto our simple `widget` layout container which is set as the central widget for the window.

Running the above code will produce the following window layout, showing the plot at the bottom and the controls on top as a toolbar.

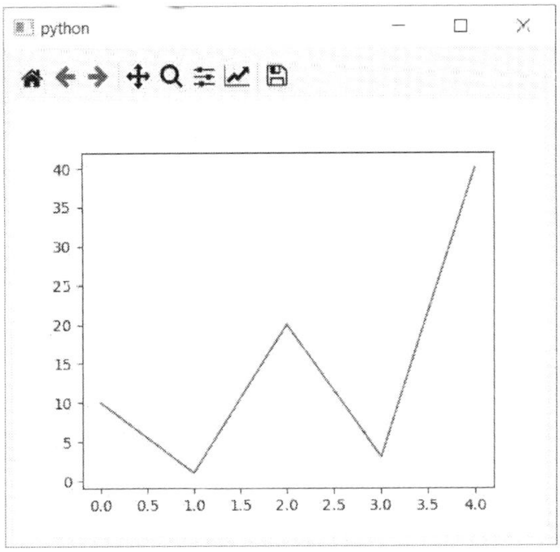

Figure 235. Matplotlib canvas with toolbar.

The buttons provided by `NavigationToolbar2QT` allow for control of the following actions —

- Home, Back/Forward, Pan & Zoom which are used to navigate through the plots. The Back/Forward buttons can step backwards and forwards through navigation steps, for example zooming in and then clicking Back will return to the previous zoom. Home returns to the initial state of the plot.
- Plot margin/position configuration which can adjust the plot within the window.
- Axis/curve style editor, where you can modify plot titles and axes scales, along with setting plot line colors and line styles. The color selection uses the platform-default color picker, allowing any available colors to be selected.
- Save, to save the resulting figure as an image (all Matplotlib supported formats).

A few of these configuration settings are shown below.

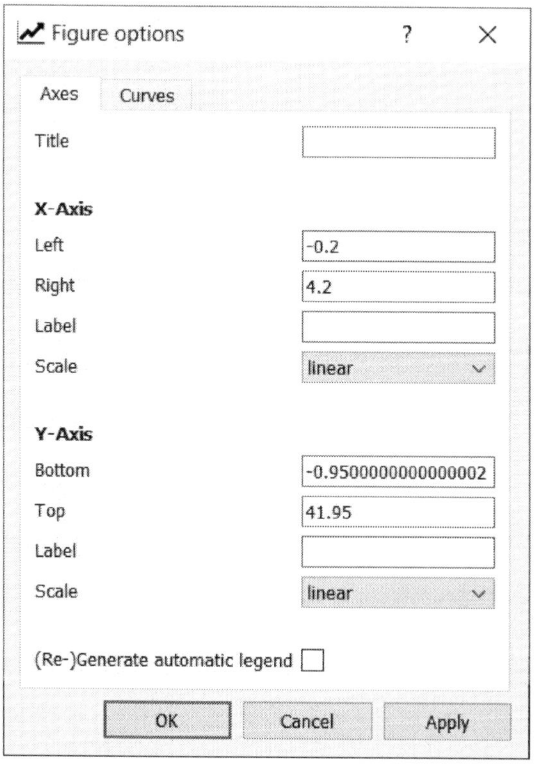

Figure 236. Matplotlib figure options.

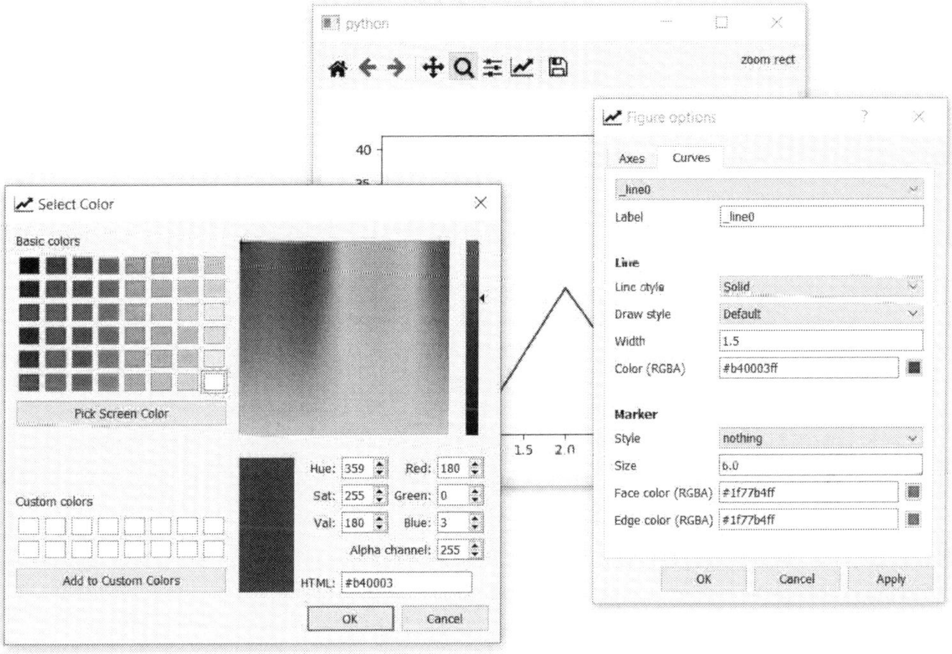

Figure 237. Matplotlib curve options.

For more information on navigating and configuring Matplotlib plots, take a look at the official Matplotlib toolbar documentation [https://matplotlib.org/3.1.1/users/navigation_toolbar.html].

Updating plots

Quite often in applications you'll want to update the data shown in plots, whether in response to input from the user or updated data from an API. There are two ways to update plots in Matplotlib, either

1. clearing and redrawing the canvas (simpler, but slower) or,
2. by keeping a reference to the plotted line and updating the data.

If performance is important to your app it is recommended you do the latter, but the first is simpler. We start with the simple clear-and-redraw method first below —

Clear and redraw

Listing 196. plotting/matplotlib_3.py

```
import random
import sys

from PyQt5 import QtCore, QtWidgets  # import PyQt5 before matplotlib

import matplotlib
from matplotlib.backends.backend_qt5agg import FigureCanvasQTAgg as
FigureCanvas
from matplotlib.figure import Figure


matplotlib.use("Qt5Agg")


class MplCanvas(FigureCanvas):
    def __init__(self, parent=None, width=5, height=4, dpi=100):
        fig = Figure(figsize=(width, height), dpi=dpi)
        self.axes = fig.add_subplot(111)
        super().__init__(fig)


class MainWindow(QtWidgets.QMainWindow):
    def __init__(self):
        super().__init__()

        self.canvas = MplCanvas(self, width=5, height=4, dpi=100)
        self.setCentralWidget(self.canvas)

        n_data = 50
        self.xdata = list(range(n_data))
        self.ydata = [random.randint(0, 10) for i in range(n_data)]
        self.update_plot()

        self.show()

        # Setup a timer to trigger the redraw by calling update_plot.
        self.timer = QtCore.QTimer()
        self.timer.setInterval(100)
        self.timer.timeout.connect(self.update_plot)
```

```
        self.timer.start()

    def update_plot(self):
        # Drop off the first y element, append a new one.
        self.ydata = self.ydata[1:] + [random.randint(0, 10)]
        self.canvas.axes.cla()  # Clear the canvas.
        self.canvas.axes.plot(self.xdata, self.ydata, "r")
        # Trigger the canvas to update and redraw.
        self.canvas.draw()


app = QtWidgets.QApplication(sys.argv)
w = MainWindow()
app.exec_()
```

In this example we've moved the plotting to a update_plot method to keep it self-contained. In this method we take our ydata array and drop off the first value with [1:] then append a new random integer between 0 and 10. This has the effect of scrolling the data to the left.

To redraw we simply call axes.cla() to clear the axes (the entire canvas) and the axes.plot(…) to re-plot the data, including the updated values. The resulting canvas is then redrawn to the widget by calling canvas.draw().

The update_plot method is called every 100 *msec* using a QTimer. The clear-and-refresh method is fast enough to keep a plot updated at this rate, but as we'll see shortly, falters as the speed increases.

In-place redraw

The changes required to update the plotted lines in-place are fairly minimal, requiring only an addition variable to store and retrieve the reference to the plotted line. The updated MainWindow code is shown below.

Listing 197. plotting/matplotlib_4.py

```
class MainWindow(QtWidgets.QMainWindow):
    def __init__(self):
        super().__init__()
```

```
        self.canvas = MplCanvas(self, width=5, height=4, dpi=100)
        self.setCentralWidget(self.canvas)

        n_data = 50
        self.xdata = list(range(n_data))
        self.ydata = [random.randint(0, 10) for i in range(n_data)]

        # We need to store a reference to the plotted line
        # somewhere, so we can apply the new data to it.
        self._plot_ref = None
        self.update_plot()

        self.show()

        # Setup a timer to trigger the redraw by calling update_plot.
        self.timer = QtCore.QTimer()
        self.timer.setInterval(100)
        self.timer.timeout.connect(self.update_plot)
        self.timer.start()

    def update_plot(self):
        # Drop off the first y element, append a new one.
        self.ydata = self.ydata[1:] + [random.randint(0, 10)]

        # Note: we no longer need to clear the axis.
        if self._plot_ref is None:
            # First time we have no plot reference, so do a normal
plot.
            # .plot returns a list of line <reference>s, as we're
            # only getting one we can take the first element.
            plot_refs = self.canvas.axes.plot(self.xdata, self.ydata,
"r")
            self._plot_ref = plot_refs[0]
        else:
            # We have a reference, we can use it to update the data
for that line.
            self._plot_ref.set_ydata(self.ydata)

        # Trigger the canvas to update and redraw.
        self.canvas.draw()
```

First, we need a variable to hold a reference to the plotted line we want to update, which here we're calling `_plot_ref`. We initialize `self._plot_ref` with `None` so we can check its value later to determine if the line has already been drawn — if the value is still `None` we have not yet drawn the line.

> If you were drawing multiple lines you would probably want to use a `list` or `dict` data structure to store the multiple references and keep track of which is which.

Finally, we update the `ydata` data as we did before, rotating it to the left and appending a new random value. Then we either —

1. if `self._plotref` is `None` (i.e. we have not yet drawn the line) draw the line and store the reference in `self._plot_ref`, or
2. update the line in place by calling `self._plot_ref.set_ydata(self.ydata)`

We obtain a reference to the plotted line when calling `.plot`. However `.plot` returns a list (to support cases where a single `.plot` call can draw more than one line). In our case we're only plotting a single line, so we simply want the first element in that list – a single `Line2D` object. To get this single value into our variable we can assign to a temporary variable `plot_refs` and then assign the first element to our `self._plot_ref` variable.

```
plot_refs = self.canvas.axes.plot(self.xdata, self.ydata, 'r')
self._plot_ref = plot_refs[0]
```

You could also use tuple-unpacking, picking off the first (and only) element in the list with —

```
self._plot_ref, = self.canvas.axes.plot(self.xdata, self.ydata, 'r')
```

If you run the resulting code, there will be no noticeable difference in performance between this and the previous method at this speed. However if you attempt to update the plot faster (e.g. down to every 10 *msec*) you'll start to notice that clearing the plot and re-drawing takes longer, and the updates do not keep up with the timer. Whether this performance difference is enough to matter in your application depends on what you're building, and should be weighed against the added complication of keeping and managing the references to plotted lines.

Embedding plots from Pandas

Pandas is a Python package focused on working with table (data frames) and series data structures, which is particularly useful for data analysis workflows. It comes with built-in support for plotting with Matplotlib and here we'll take a quick look at how to embed these plots into PyQt5. With this you will be able to start building PyQt5 data-analysis applications built around Pandas.

Pandas plotting functions are directly accessible from the `DataFrame` objects. The function signature is quite complex, giving a lot of options to control how the plots will be drawn.

```
DataFrame.plot(
    x=None, y=None, kind='line', ax=None, subplots=False,
    sharex=None, sharey=False, layout=None, figsize=None,
    use_index=True, title=None, grid=None, legend=True, style=None,
    logx=False, logy=False, loglog=False, xticks=None, yticks=None,
    xlim=None, ylim=None, rot=None, fontsize=None, colormap=None,
    table=False, yerr=None, xerr=None, secondary_y=False,
    sort_columns=False, **kwargs
)
```

The parameter we're most interested in is `ax` which allows us to pass in our own `matplotlib.Axes` instance on which Pandas will plot the `DataFrame`.

Listing 198. plotting/matplotlib_5.py

```python
import sys

from PyQt5 import QtCore, QtWidgets  # import PyQt5 before matplotlib

import matplotlib
import pandas as pd
```

```
from matplotlib.backends.backend_qt5agg import FigureCanvasQTAgg
from matplotlib.figure import Figure


matplotlib.use("Qt5Agg")


class MplCanvas(FigureCanvasQTAgg):
    def __init__(self, parent=None, width=5, height=4, dpi=100):
        fig = Figure(figsize=(width, height), dpi=dpi)
        self.axes = fig.add_subplot(111)
        super().__init__(fig)


class MainWindow(QtWidgets.QMainWindow):
    def __init__(self):
        super().__init__()

        # Create the maptlotlib FigureCanvas object,
        # which defines a single set of axes as self.axes.
        sc = MplCanvas(self, width=5, height=4, dpi=100)

        # Create our pandas DataFrame with some simple
        # data and headers.
        df = pd.DataFrame(
            [[0, 10], [5, 15], [2, 20], [15, 25], [4, 10],], columns
=["A", "B"]
        )

        # plot the pandas DataFrame, passing in the
        # matplotlib Canvas axes.
        df.plot(ax=sc.axes)

        self.setCentralWidget(sc)
        self.show()


app = QtWidgets.QApplication(sys.argv)
w = MainWindow()
app.exec_()
```

The key step here is passing the canvas axes in when calling the plot method on the DataFrame `on the line `df.plot(ax=sc.axes). You can use this same pattern to update the plot any time, although bear in mind that Pandas clears and redraws the entire canvas, meaning that it is not ideal for high performance plotting.

The resulting plot generated through Pandas is shown below —

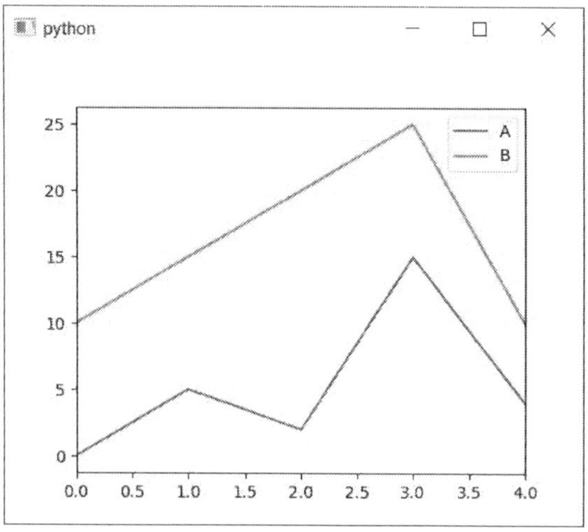

Figure 238. Pandas generated plot, in matplotlib Canvas.

Just as before, you can add the Matplotlib toolbar and control support to plots generated using Pandas, allowing you to zoom/pan and modify them live. The following code combines our earlier toolbar example with the Pandas example.

Listing 199. plotting/matplotlib_6.py

```
import sys

from PyQt5 import QtCore, QtWidgets  # import PyQt5 before matplotlib

import matplotlib
import pandas as pd
from matplotlib.backends.backend_qt5agg import FigureCanvasQTAgg
from matplotlib.backends.backend_qt5agg import NavigationToolbar2QT
as NavigationToolbar
from matplotlib.figure import Figure


matplotlib.use("Qt5Agg")
```

```
class MplCanvas(FigureCanvasQTAgg):
    def __init__(self, parent=None, width=5, height=4, dpi=100):
        fig = Figure(figsize=(width, height), dpi=dpi)
        self.axes = fig.add_subplot(111)
        super().__init__(fig)


class MainWindow(QtWidgets.QMainWindow):
    def __init__(self):
        super().__init__()

        # Create the maptlotlib FigureCanvas object,
        # which defines a single set of axes as self.axes.
        sc = MplCanvas(self, width=5, height=4, dpi=100)

        # Create our pandas DataFrame with some simple
        # data and headers.
        df = pd.DataFrame(
            [[0, 10], [5, 15], [2, 20], [15, 25], [4, 10],], columns
=["A", "B"]
        )

        # plot the pandas DataFrame, passing in the
        # matplotlib Canvas axes.
        df.plot(ax=sc.axes)

        # Create toolbar, passing canvas as first parament, parent
(self, the MainWindow) as second.
        toolbar = NavigationToolbar(sc, self)

        layout = QtWidgets.QVBoxLayout()
        layout.addWidget(toolbar)
        layout.addWidget(sc)

        # Create a placeholder widget to hold our toolbar and canvas.
        widget = QtWidgets.QWidget()
        widget.setLayout(layout)
        self.setCentralWidget(widget)
        self.show()
```

```
app = QtWidgets.QApplication(sys.argv)
w = MainWindow()
app.exec_()
```

Running this you should see the following window, showing a Pandas plot embedded in PyQt5 alongside the Matplotlib toolbar.

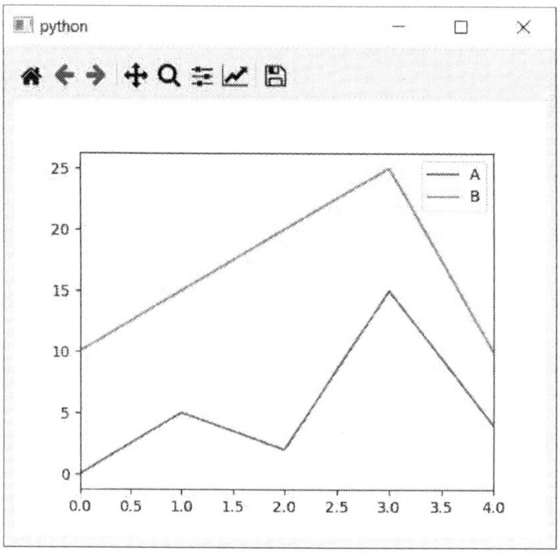

Figure 239. Pandas plot with matplotlib toolbar.

What's next

In this chapter we looked at how you can embed Matplotlib plots in your PyQt5 applications. Being able to use Matplotlib plots in your applications allows you to create custom data analysis and visualization tools from Python.

Matplotlib is a *huge* library and too big to cover in detail. If you're not familiar with Matplotlib plotting and want to give it a try, take a look at the documentation [https://matplotlib.org/] and example plots [https://matplotlib.org/3.1.1/gallery/index.html] to see what is possible.

Packaging & Distribution

> Design isn't finished until somebody is using it.
>
> — Brenda Laurel, PhD

There is not much fun in creating your own application if you can't share it with other people—whether that means publishing it commercially, sharing it online or just giving it to someone you know. Sharing your apps allows other people to benefit from your hard work!

Packaging Python applications for distribution has typically been a little tricky, particularly when targeting multiple platforms (Windows, macOS and Linux). This is in part because of the need to bundle the source, data files, the Python runtime and all associated libraries in a way that will work reliably on the target system.

In this chapter we'll look at one of the simpler options you have for packaging PyQt5 packages for distribution—*fbs*.

37. Packaging with fbs

fbs is a cross-platform PyQt5 packaging system which supports building desktop applications for Windows, macOS and Linux (Ubuntu, Fedora and Arch). Built on top of *PyInstaller* it wraps some of the rough edges and defines a standard project structure which allows the build process to be entirely automated. The included resource API is particularly useful, simplifying the handling of external data files, images or third-party libraries — a common pain point when bundling apps.

> *fbs* is licensed under the GPL. This means you can use the *fbs* system for free in open-source packages distributed with the GPL. For commercial (or non-GPL) packages you must buy a commercial license. See the fbs licensing page [https://build-system.fman.io/#licensing] for up-to-date information.
>
> If you're unable to use *fbs* take a look at PyInstaller [https://www.pyinstaller.org/] itself.

If you're impatient, you can grab the Moonsweeper installers directly for Windows [http://download.mfitzp.com/MoonsweeperSetup.exe], macOS [http://download.mfitzp.com/Moonsweeper.dmg] or Linux (Ubuntu) [http://download.mfitzp.com/Moonsweeper.deb].

Requirements

fbs works out of the box with PyQt5. The only other requirement is `PyInstaller` which handles the packaging itself. You can install these in a virtual environment (or your applications virtual environment) to keep your environment clean.

> *fbs* only supports Python versions 3.5 and 3.6

```
python3 -m venv fbsenv
```

Once created, activate the virtual environment by running from the command line —

```
# On macOS/Linux:
source fbsenv/bin/activate

# On Windows:
call fbsenv\scripts\activate.bat
```

Finally, install the required libraries —

```
pip3 install fbs PyQt5 PyInstaller==3.4
```

fbs installs a command line tool fbs into your path which provides access to all *fbs* management commands. To see the complete list of commands available run fbs.

```
martin@Martins-Laptop testapp $ fbs
usage: fbs [-h]

positional arguments:
    startproject        Start a new project in the current directory
    run                 Run your app from source
    freeze              Compile your code to a standalone executable
    installer           Create an installer for your app
    sign_installer      Sign installer, so the user\'s OS trusts it
    repo                Generate files for automatic updates
    upload              Upload installer and repository to fbs.sh
    release             Bump version and run clean,freeze,...,upload
    test                Execute your automated tests
    clean               Remove previous build outputs
    buildvm             Build a Linux VM. Eg.: buildvm ubuntu
    runvm               Run a Linux VM. Eg.: runvm ubuntu
    gengpgkey           Generate a GPG key for Linux code signing
    register            Create an account for uploading your files
    login               Save your account details to secret.json
    init_licensing      Generate public/private keys for licensing

optional arguments:
  -h, --help            show this help message and exit
```

Starting an app

If you're starting a PyQt5 application from scratch, you can use the `fbs startproject` management command to create a complete, working and packageable application stub in the current folder. This has the benefit of allowing you to test (and continue to test) the packageability of your application as you develop it, rather than leaving it to the end.

```
fbs startproject
```

The command walks you through a few questions, allowing you to fill in details of your application. These values will be written into your app source and configuration. The bare-bones app will be created under the `src/` folder in the current directory.

```
martin@Martins-Laptop ~ $ fbs startproject
App name [MyApp] : HelloWorld
Author [Martin] : Martin Fitzpatrick
Mac bundle identifier (eg. com.martin.helloworld, optional):
```

> If you already have your own working PyQt5 app you will need to either a) use the generated app as a guideline for converting yours to the same structure, or b) create a new app using `startproject` and migrate the code over.

Running your new project

You can run this new application using the following *fbs* command in the same folder you ran `startproject` from.

```
fbs run
```

If everything is working this should show you a small empty window with your apps' title — exciting eh?

Figure 240. HelloWorld on Windows, macOS and Linux (Ubuntu)

The application structure

The `startproject` command generates the required folder structure for a *fbs* PyQt5 application. This includes a `src/build` which contains the build settings for your package, `main/icons` which contains the application icons, and src/python for the source.

```
.
└── src
    ├── build
    │   └── settings
    │       ├── base.json
    │       ├── linux.json
    │       └── mac.json
    └── main
        ├── icons
        │   ├── Icon.ico
        │   ├── README.md
        │   ├── base
        │   │   ├── 16.png
        │   │   ├── 24.png
        │   │   ├── 32.png
        │   │   ├── 48.png
        │   │   └── 64.png
        │   ├── linux
        │   │   ├── 1024.png
        │   │   ├── 128.png
        │   │   ├── 256.png
        │   │   └── 512.png
        │   └── mac
        │       ├── 1024.png
        │       ├── 128.png
        │       ├── 256.png
        │       └── 512.png
        └── python
            └── main.py
```

Your bare-bones PyQt5 application is generated in src/main/python/main.py and is a complete working example you can use to base your own code on.

```python
import sys

from fbs_runtime.application_context import ApplicationContext
from PyQt5.QtWidgets import QMainWindow


class AppContext(ApplicationContext):  # 1. Subclass
ApplicationContext
    def run(self):  # 2. Implement run()
        window = QMainWindow()
        version = self.build_settings["version"]
        window.setWindowTitle("HelloWorld v" + version)
        window.resize(250, 150)
        window.show()
        return self.app.exec_()  # 3. End run() with this line


if __name__ == "__main__":
    appctxt = AppContext()  # 4. Instantiate the subclass
    exit_code = appctxt.run()  # 5. Invoke run()
    sys.exit(exit_code)
```

If you've built PyQt5 applications before you'll notice that building an application with *fbs* introduces a new concept — the `ApplicationContext`.

The `ApplicationContext`

When building PyQt5 applications there are typically a number of components or resources that are used throughout your app. These are commonly stored in the `QMainWindow` or as global vars which can get a bit messy as your application grows. The `ApplicationContext` provides a central location for initialising and storing these components, as well as providing access to some core *fbs* features.

The `ApplicationContext` object also creates and holds a reference to a global `QApplication` object — available under `ApplicationContext.app`. Every Qt application must have one (and only one) `QApplication` to hold the event loop and core settings. Without *fbs* you would usually define this at the base of your script, and call `.exec()` to start the event loop.

Without *fbs* this would look something like this —

```
app = QApplication()
w = MyCustomWindow()
app.exec_()
```

The equivalent with *fbs* would be —

```
ctx = ApplicationContext()
w = MyCustomWindow()
ctx.app.exec_()
```

> If you want to create your own custom `QApplication` initialization you can overwrite the `.app` property on your `ApplicationContext` subclass using `cached_property` (see below).

This basic example is clear to follow. However, once you start adding custom styles and translations to your application the initialization can grow quite a bit. To keep things nicely structured *fbs* recommends creating a `.run` method on your `ApplicationContext`.

This method should handle the setup of your application, such as creating and showing a window, finally starting up the event loop on the `.app` object. This final step is performed by calling `self.app.exec_()` at the end of the method.

```
class AppContext(ApplicationContext):
    def run(self):
        ...
        return self.app.exec_()
```

As your initialization gets more complicated you can break out subsections into separate methods for clarity, for example —

```python
class AppContext(ApplicationContext):
    def run(self):
        self.setup_fonts()
        self.setup_styles()
        self.setup_translations()
        return self.app.exec_()

    def setup_fonts(self):
        # ...do something ...

    def setup_styles(self):
        # ...do something ...

    def setup_translations(self):
        # ...do something ...
```

On execution the `.run()` method will be called and your event loop started. Execution continues in this event loop until the application is exited, at which point your `.run()` method will return (with the appropriate exit code).

Building a real application

The bare-bones application doesn't do very much, so below we'll look at something more complete — the *Moonsweeper* application from the previous chapter. The modified source code is available to download here [http://download.mfitzp.com/moonsweeper-fbs-src.zip].

Only the changes required to convert *Moonsweeper* over to *fbs* are covered here. If you want to see how *Moonsweeper* itself works, see the previous chapter. The custom application icons were created using icon art by Freepik [https://www.flaticon.com/authors/freepik/].

The project follows the same basic structure as for the stub application we created above.

```
.
├── README.md
├── requirements.txt
├── screenshot-minesweeper1.jpg
├── screenshot-minesweeper2.jpg
└── src
    ├── build
    │   └── settings
    │       ├── base.json
    │       ├── linux.json
    │       └── mac.json
    └── main
        ├── Installer.nsi
        ├── icons
        │   ├── Icon.ico
        │   ├── README.md
        │   ├── base
        │   │   ├── 16.png
        │   │   ├── 24.png
        │   │   ├── 32.png
        │   │   ├── 48.png
        │   │   └── 64.png
        │   ├── linux
        │   │   ├── 1024.png
        │   │   ├── 128.png
        │   │   ├── 256.png
        │   │   └── 512.png
        │   └── mac
        │       ├── 1024.png
        │       ├── 128.png
        │       ├── 256.png
        │       └── 512.png
        ├── python
        │   ├── __init__.py
        │   └── main.py
        └── resources
            ├── base
            │   └── images
            │       ├── bomb.png
            │       ├── bug.png
            │       ├── clock-select.png
            │       ├── cross.png
            │       ├── flag.png
```

```
│           ├── plus.png
│           ├── rocket.png
│           ├── smiley-lol.png
│           └── smiley.png
└── mac
    └── Contents
        └── Info.plist
```

The src/build/settings/base.json stores the basic details about the application, including the entry point to run the app with fbs run or once packaged.

```
{
    "app_name": "Moonsweeper",
    "author": "Martin Fitzpatrick",
    "main_module": "src/main/python/main.py",
    "version": "0.0.0"
}
```

The script *entry point* is at the base of src/main/python/main.py. This creates the AppContext object and calls the .run() method to start up the app.

```
if __name__ == '__main__':
    appctxt = AppContext()
    exit_code = appctxt.run()
    sys.exit(exit_code)
```

The ApplicationContext defines a .run() method to handle initialization. In this case that consists of creating and showing the main window, then starting up the event loop.

```python
from fbs_runtime.application_context import ApplicationContext, \
    cached_property


class AppContext(ApplicationContext):
    def run(self):
        self.main_window.show()
        return self.app.exec_()

    @cached_property
    def main_window(self):
        return MainWindow(self)  # Pass context to the window.

    # ... snip ...
```

The cached_property decorator

The `.run()` method accesses `self.main_window`. You'll notice that this method is wrapped in an *fbs* `@cached_property` decorator. This decorator turns the method into a property (like the Python `@property` decorator) and caches the return value.

The first time the property is accessed the method is executed and the return value cached. On subsequent calls, the cached value is returned directly without executing anything. This also has the side-effect of postponing creation of these objects until they are needed.

You can use `@cached_property` to define each application component (a window, a toolbar, a database connection or other resources). However, you don't *have* to use the `@cached_property` — you could alternatively declare all properties in your `ApplicationContext.init` block as shown below.

```python
from fbs_runtime.application_context import ApplicationContext

class AppContext(ApplicationContext):

    def __init__(self, *args, _kwargs):
        super(AppContent, self).__init__(*args, _kwargs)

        self.window = Window()

    def run(self):
        self.window.show()
        return self.app.exec_()
```

Accessing resources with `.get_resource`

Applications usually require additional data files beyond the source code — for example files icons, images, styles (Qt's `.qss` files) or documentation. You may also want to bundle platform-specific libraries or binaries. To simplify this *fbs* defines a folder structure and access method which work seamlessly across development and distributed versions.

The top level folder `resources/` should contain a folder `base` plus any combination of the other folders shown below. The `base` folder contains files common to all platforms, while the platform-specific folders can be used for any files specific to a given OS.

```
base/      # for files required on all OSs
windows/   # for files only required on Windows
mac/       # "   "       "     "         "  macOS
linux/     # "   "       "     "         "  Linux
arch/      # "   "       "     "         "  Arch Linux
fedora/    # "   "       "     "         "  Debian Linux
ubuntu/    # "   "       "     "         "  Ubuntu Linux
```

Getting files into the right place to load from a distributed app across all platforms is usually one of the faffiest bits of distributing PyQt5 applications. It's really handy that *fbs* handles this for you.

To simplify the loading of resources from your `resources/` folder in your applications *fbs* provides the `ApplicationContext\.get_resource()` method. This method takes the name of a file which can be found somewhere in the `resources/` folder and returns the absolute path to that file. You can use this returned absolute path to open the file as normal.

```
from fbs_runtime.application_context import ApplicationContext,
cached_property


class AppContext(ApplicationContext):

    # ... snip ...

    @cached_property
    def img_bomb(self):
        return QImage(self.get_resource('images/bug.png'))

    @cached_property
    def img_flag(self):
        return QImage(self.get_resource('images/flag.png'))

    @cached_property
    def img_start(self):
        return QImage(self.get_resource('images/rocket.png'))

    @cached_property
    def img_clock(self):
        return QImage(self.get_resource('images/clock-select.png'))

    @cached_property
    def status_icons(self):
        return {
            STATUS_READY: QIcon(self.get_resource(
"images/plus.png")),
            STATUS_PLAYING: QIcon(self.get_resource
("images/smiley.png")),
            STATUS_FAILED: QIcon(self.get_resource(
"images/cross.png")),
            STATUS_SUCCESS: QIcon(self.get_resource("images/smiley-
lol.png"))
        }

    # ... snip ...
```

In our *Moonsweeper* application above, we have a *bomb* image file available at `src/main/resources/base/images/bug.jpg`. By calling ctx.get_resource('images/bug.png') we get the absolute path to that image file on the filesystem, allowing us to open the file within our app.

> If the file does not exist FileNotFoundError will be raised instead.

The handy thing about this method is that it transparently handles the platform folders under src/main/resources giving OS-specific files precedence. For example, if the same file was also present under src/main/resources/mac/images/bug.jpg and we called ctx.get_resource('images/bug.jpg') we would get the macOS version of the file.

Additionally get_resource works both when running from source and when running a frozen or installed version of your application. If your resources/ load correctly locally you can be confident they will load correctly in your distributed applications.

Using the ApplicationContext from app

As shown above, our ApplicationContext object has cached properties to load and return the resources. To allow us to access these from our QMainWindow we can pass the context in and store a reference to it in our window __init__.

```
class MainWindow(QMainWindow):
    def __init__(self, ctx):
        super(MainWindow, self).__init__()

        self.ctx = ctx  # Store a reference to the context for
resources, etc.

# ... snip ...
```

Now that we have access to the context via self.ctx we can use it this in any place we want to reference these external resources.

```
        l = QLabel()
        l.setPixmap(QPixmap.fromImage(self.ctx.img_bomb))
        l.setAlignment(Qt.AlignRight | Qt.AlignVCenter)
        hb.addWidget(l)

# ... snip ...

        l = QLabel()
        l.setPixmap(QPixmap.fromImage(self.ctx.img_clock))
        l.setAlignment(Qt.AlignLeft | Qt.AlignVCenter)
        hb.addWidget(l)
```

The first time we access `self.ctx.img_bomb` the file will be loaded, the `QImage` created and returned. On subsequent calls, we'll get the image from the cache.

```
    def init_map(self):
        # Add positions to the map
        for x in range(0, self.b_size):
            for y in range(0, self.b_size):
                w = Pos(x, y, self.ctx.img_flag, self.ctx.img_start,
self.ctx.img_bomb)
                self.grid.addWidget(w, y, x)
                # Connect signal to handle expansion.
                w.clicked.connect(self.trigger_start)
                w.expandable.connect(self.expand_reveal)
                w.ohno.connect(self.game_over)

# ... snip ...

        self.button.setIcon(self.ctx.status_icons[STATUS_PLAYING])

# ... snip ...

    def update_status(self, status):
        self.status = status
        self.button.setIcon(self.ctx.status_icons[self.status])
```

Those are all the changes needed to get the *Moonsweeper* app packageable with *fbs*. If you open up the source folder you should be able to start it up as before.

```
fbs run
```

If that's working, you're ready to move onto freezing and building in the installer.

Freezing the app

Freezing is the process of turning a Python application into a standalone executable that can run on another user's computer. Use the following command to turn the app's source code into a standalone executable:

```
fbs freeze
```

The resulting executable depends on the platform you *freeze* on — the executable will only work on the OS you built it on (e.g. an executable built on Windows will run on another Windows computer, but not on a Mac).

- Windows will create an `.exe` executable in the folder `target/<AppName>`
- macOS will create an `.app` application bundle in `target/<AppName>.app`
- Linux will create an executable in the folder `target/<AppName>`

> On Windows you may need to install the Windows 10 SDK [https://dev.windows.com/en-us/downloads/windows-10-sdk], although *fbs* will prompt you if this is the case.

Creating an installer

While you can share the executable files with users, desktop applications are normally distributed with *installers* which handle the process of putting the executable (and any other files) in the correct place. See the following sections for platform-specific notes before creating

You must *freeze* your app first *then* create the installer.

Windows installer

The Windows installer allows your users to pick the installation directory for the executable and adds your app to the user's Start Menu. The app is also added to installed programs, allowing it to be uninstalled by your users.

Before you create installers on Windows you will need to install NSIS [http://nsis.sourceforge.net/Main_Page] and ensure its installation directory is in your PATH. You can then build an installer using —

```
fbs installer
```

The Windows installer will be created at `target/<AppName>Setup.exe`.

Figure 241. The Windows NSIS installer.

Download the *MoonsweeperSetup* .exe [http://download.mfitzp.com/MoonsweeperSetup.exe]

macOS installer

There are no additional steps to create a macOS installer. Just run the *fbs* command —

```
fbs installer
```

On macOS the command will generate a disk image at `target/<AppName>.dmg`. This disk image will contain the app bundle and a shortcut to the Applications folder. When your users open it they can drag the app to the Applications folder to install it.

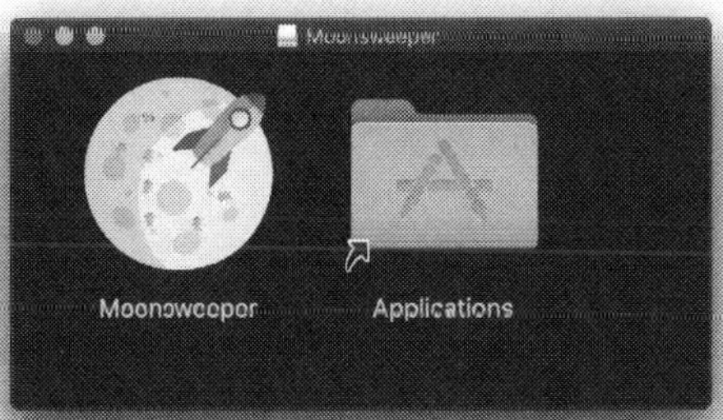

Figure 242. The .dmg installer on macOS.

Download the *Moonsweeper* .dmg bundle [http://download.mfitzp.com/Moonsweeper.dmg]

Linux installer

To build installers on Linux you need to install the Ruby tool Effing package management! [https://github.com/jordansissel/fpm] — use the installation guide [https://fpm.readthedocs.io/en/latest/installing.html] to get it set up. Once that is in place you can use the standard command to create the Linux package file.

```
fbs installer
```

The resulting package will be created under the `target/` folder. Depending on your platform the package file will be named `<AppName>.deb`, `<AppName>.pkg.tar.xz` or `<AppName>.rpm`. Your users can install this file with their package manager.

Download the *Moonsweeper* .deb file [http://download.mfitzp.com/Moonsweeper.deb]

Find out more about fbs

More information about how the *fbs* packaging system works can be found in the manual [https://build-system.fman.io/manual/] which also introduces more advanced features should as distributing releases of Linux apps [https://build-system.fman.io/manual/#releasing], reporting errors to the Sentry error logging platform [https://build-system.fman.io/manual/#error-tracking] and adding license keys [https://build-system.fman.io/manual/#license-keys] to your software.

Example applications

By now you should have a firm grasp of how to go about building simple applications with PyQt5. To show how you can put what you've learnt into practice, I've included a couple of example applications in this chapter. These applications are functional, simple and in some ways *incomplete*. Use them for inspiration, to pull apart and as an opportunity to improve. Read on for a walkthrough of each app's most interesting parts.

The full source for both applications is available for download, along with 13 other applications in my 15 Minute Apps [https://github.com/learnpyqt/15-minute-apps] repository on Github. Have fun!

There are also other examples of miniature apps throughout this book—for example the *Paint* and *Todo* apps—I encourage you to extend these too, it's the best way to learn.

38. Mozzarella Ashbadger

Mozzarella Ashbadger is the latest revolution in web browsing! Go back and forward! Print! Save files! Get help! (you'll need it). Any similarity to other browsers is entirely coincidental.

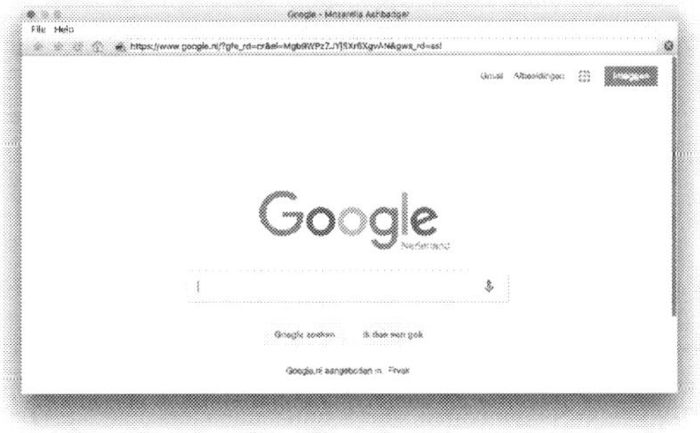

Figure 243. Mozzarella Ashbadger.

> This application makes use of features covered in Signals & Slots, Extending Signals and Widgets.

The source code for Mozzarella Ashbadger is provided in two forms, one with tabbed browsing and one without. Adding tabs complicates the signal handling a little bit, so the tab-less version is covered first.

To create the browser we need to install an additional PyQt5 component—*PyQtWebEngine*. You can do this with `pip` from the command line as follows.

```
pip3 install PyQtWebEngine
```

Source code

The full source for the tab-less browser is included in the downloads for this book. The browser code has the name `browser.py`.

```
python3 browser.py
```

🚀 **Run it!** Explore the *Mozzarella Ashbadger* interface and features before moving onto the code.

The browser widget

The core of our browser is the `QWebEngineView` which we import from `QtWebEngineWidgets`. This provides a complete browser window, which handles the rendering of the downloaded pages.

Below is the bare-minimum of code required to use web browser widget in PyQt5.

Listing 200. app/browser_skeleton.py

```python
import sys

from PyQt5.QtCore import QUrl
from PyQt5.QtWebEngineWidgets import QWebEngineView
from PyQt5.QtWidgets import QApplication, QMainWindow


class MainWindow(QMainWindow):
    def __init__(self):
        super().__init__()

        self.browser = QWebEngineView()
        self.browser.setUrl(QUrl("https://www.google.com"))

        self.setCentralWidget(self.browser)

        self.show()


app = QApplication(sys.argv)
window = MainWindow()

app.exec_()
```

If you click around a bit you'll discover that the browser behaves as expected—links work correctly, and you can interact with the pages. However, you'll also notice things you take for granted are missing—like an URL bar, controls or any sort of interface whatsoever. This makes it a little tricky to use.

Navigation

To convert this bare-bones browser into something usable we add some controls, as a series of QActions on a QToolbar. We add these definitions to the __init__ block of the QMainWindow.

Listing 201. app/browser.py

```
        navtb = QToolBar("Navigation")
        navtb.setIconSize(QSize(16, 16))
        self.addToolBar(navtb)

        back_btn = QAction(QIcon(os.path.join("icons", "arrow-
180.png")), "Back", self)
        back_btn.setStatusTip("Back to previous page")
        back_btn.triggered.connect(self.browser.back)
        navtb.addAction(back_btn)
```

The QWebEngineView includes slots for forward, back and reload navigation, which we can connect to directly to our action's .triggered signals.

We use the same QAction structure for the remaining controls.

Listing 202. app/browser.py

```
        next_btn = QAction(
            QIcon(os.path.join("icons", "arrow-000.png")), "Forward",
self
        )
        next_btn.setStatusTip("Forward to next page")
        next_btn.triggered.connect(self.browser.forward)
        navtb.addAction(next_btn)

        reload_btn = QAction(
            QIcon(os.path.join("icons", "arrow-circle-315.png")),
"Reload", self
        )
        reload_btn.setStatusTip("Reload page")
        reload_btn.triggered.connect(self.browser.reload)
        navtb.addAction(reload_btn)

        home_btn = QAction(QIcon(os.path.join("icons", "home.png")),
"Home", self)
        home_btn.setStatusTip("Go home")
        home_btn.triggered.connect(self.navigate_home)
        navtb.addAction(home_btn)
```

Notice that while forward, back and reload can use built-in slots, the navigate home button requires a custom slot function. The slot function is defined on our `QMainWindow` class, and simply sets the URL of the browser to the Google homepage. Note that the URL must be passed as a `QUrl` object.

Listing 203. app/browser.py

```
    def navigate_home(self):
        self.browser.setUrl(QUrl("http://www.google.com"))
```

> *Challenge*
>
> Try making the home navigation location configurable. You could create a Preferences `QDialog` with an input field.

Any decent web browser also needs an URL bar, and some way to stop the navigation—either when it's by mistake, or the page is taking too long.

Listing 204. app/browser.py

```
        self.httpsicon = QLabel()  # Yes, really!
        self.httpsicon.setPixmap(QPixmap(os.path.join("icons", "lock-
nossl.png")))
        navtb.addWidget(self.httpsicon)

        self.urlbar = QLineEdit()
        self.urlbar.returnPressed.connect(self.navigate_to_url)
        navtb.addWidget(self.urlbar)

        stop_btn = QAction(
            QIcon(os.path.join("icons", "cross-circle.png")), "Stop",
self
        )
        stop_btn.setStatusTip("Stop loading current page")
        stop_btn.triggered.connect(self.browser.stop)
        navtb.addAction(stop_btn)
```

As before the 'stop' functionality is available on the `QWebEngineView`, and we can simply connect the `.triggered` signal from the stop button to the existing slot. However, other features of the URL bar we must handle independently.

First we add a `QLabel` to hold our SSL or non SSL icon to indicate whether the page is secure. Next, we add the URL bar which is simply a `QLineEdit`. To trigger the loading of the URL in the bar when entered (return key pressed) we connect to the `.returnPressed` signal on the widget to drive a custom slot function to trigger navigation to the specified URL.

Listing 205. app/browser.py

```
    def navigate_to_url(self):  # Does not receive the Url
        q = QUrl(self.urlbar.text())
        if q.scheme() == "":
            q.setScheme("http")

        self.browser.setUrl(q)
```

We also want the URL bar to update in response to page changes. To do this we can use the .urlChanged and .loadFinished signals from the QWebEngineView. We set up the connections from the signals in the __init__ block as follows:

Listing 206. app/browser.py

```
        self.browser.urlChanged.connect(self.update_urlbar)
        self.browser.loadFinished.connect(self.update_title)
```

Then we define the target slot functions which for these signals. The first, to update the URL bar accepts a QUrl object and determines whether this is a http or https URL, using this to set the SSL icon.

> This is a terrible way to test if a connection is 'secure'. To be correct we should perform a certificate validation.

The QUrl is converted to a string and the URL bar is updated with the value. Note that we also set the cursor position back to the beginning of the line to prevent the QLineEdit widget scrolling to the end.

Listing 207. app/browser.py

```
    def update_urlbar(self, q):

        if q.scheme() == "https":
            # Secure padlock icon
            self.httpsicon.setPixmap(QPixmap(os.path.join("icons",
"lock-ssl.png")))

        else:
            # Insecure padlock icon
            self.httpsicon.setPixmap(QPixmap(os.path.join("icons",
"lock-nossl.png")))

        self.urlbar.setText(q.toString())
        self.urlbar.setCursorPosition(0)
```

It's also a nice touch to update the title of the application window with the title of the current page. We can get this via browser.page().title() which returns the contents of the <title></title> tag in the currently loaded web page.

Listing 208. app/browser.py

```
    def update_title(self):
        title = self.browser.page().title()
        self.setWindowTitle("%s - Mozzarella Ashbadger" % title)
```

File operations

A standard File menu with `self.menuBar().addMenu("&File")` is created assigning the F key as a Alt-shortcut (as normal). Once we have the menu object, we can can assign `QAction` objects to create the entries. We create two basic entries here, for opening and saving HTML files (from a local disk). These both require custom slot functions.

Listing 209. app/browser.py

```
        file_menu = self.menuBar().addMenu("&File")

        open_file_action = QAction(
            QIcon(os.path.join("icons", "disk--arrow.png")), "Open
file...", self
        )
        open_file_action.setStatusTip("Open from file")
        open_file_action.triggered.connect(self.open_file)
        file_menu.addAction(open_file_action)

        save_file_action = QAction(
            QIcon(os.path.join("icons", "disk--pencil.png")), "Save
Page As...", self
        )
        save_file_action.setStatusTip("Save current page to file")
        save_file_action.triggered.connect(self.save_file)
        file_menu.addAction(save_file_action)
```

The slot function for opening a file uses the built-in `QFileDialog.getOpenFileName()` function to create a file-open dialog and get a name. We restrict the names by default to files matching `*.htm` or `*.html`.

We read the file into a variable `html` using standard Python functions, then use `.setHtml()` to load the HTML into the browser.

Listing 210. app/browser.py

```
    def open_file(self):
        filename, _ = QFileDialog.getOpenFileName(
            self,
            "Open file",
            "",
            "Hypertext Markup Language (*.htm *.html);;" "All files
(*.*)",
        )

        if filename:
            with open(filename, "r") as f:
                html = f.read()

            self.browser.setHtml(html)
            self.urlbar.setText(filename)
```

Similarly to save the HTML from the current page, we use the built-in `QFileDialog.getSaveFileName()` to get a filename. However, this time we get the HTML using `self.browser.page().toHtml()`.

This is an *asynchronous* method, meaning that we do not receive the HTML immediately. Instead we must pass in a *callback* method which will receive the HTML once it is prepared. Here we create a simple `writer` function that handles it for us, using the filename from the local scope.

Listing 211. app/browser.py

```
    def save_file(self):
        filename, _ = QFileDialog.getSaveFileName(
            self,
            "Save Page As",
            "",
            "Hypertext Markup Language (*.htm *html);;" "All files
(*.*)",
        )

        if filename:
            # Define callback method to handle the write.
            def writer(html):
                with open(filename, "w") as f:
                    f.write(html)

            self.browser.page().toHtml(writer)
```

Printing

We can add a print option to the File menu using the same approach we used earlier. Again this needs a custom slot function to perform the print action.

Listing 212. app/browser.py

```
        print_action = QAction(
            QIcon(os.path.join("icons", "printer.png")), "Print...",
self
        )
        print_action.setStatusTip("Print current page")
        print_action.triggered.connect(self.print_page)
        file_menu.addAction(print_action)

        # Create our system printer instance.
        self.printer = QPrinter()
```

Qt provides a complete print framework which is based around `QPrinter` objects, on which you *paint* the pages to be printed. To start the process we open a `QPrintDialog` for the user. This allows them to choose the target printer and configure the print.

We created the `QPrinter` object in our `__init__` and stored it as `self.printer`. In our print handler method we pass this printer to the `QPrintDialog` so it can be configured. If the dialog is accepted we pass the (now configured) printer object to `self.browser.page().print` to trigger the print.

Listing 213. app/browser.py

```
    def print_page(self):
        page = self.browser.page()

        def callback(*args):
            pass

        dlg = QPrintDialog(self.printer)
        dlg.accepted.connect(callback)
        if dlg.exec_() == QDialog.Accepted:
            page.print(self.printer, callback)
```

Notice that `.print` also accepts a second parameter—a callback function which receives the result of the print. This allows you to show a notification that the print has completed, but here we're just swallowing the callback silently.

Help

Finally, to complete the standard interface we can add a Help menu. This is defined as before, two two custom slot functions to handle the display of a About dialog, and to load the 'browser page' with more information.

Listing 214. app/browser.py

```
        help_menu = self.menuBar().addMenu("&Help")

        about_action = QAction(
            QIcon(os.path.join("icons", "question.png")),
            "About Mozzarella Ashbadger",
            self,
        )
        about_action.setStatusTip("Find out more about Mozzarella
Ashbadger")  # Hungry!
        about_action.triggered.connect(self.about)
        help_menu.addAction(about_action)

        navigate_mozzarella_action = QAction(
            QIcon(os.path.join("icons", "lifebuoy.png")),
            "Mozzarella Ashbadger Homepage",
            self,
        )
        navigate_mozzarella_action.setStatusTip("Go to Mozzarella
Ashbadger Homepage")
        navigate_mozzarella_action.triggered.connect(self
.navigate_mozzarella)
        help_menu.addAction(navigate_mozzarella_action)
```

We define two methods to be used as slots for the Help menu signals. The first `navigate_mozzarella` opens up a page with more information on the browser (or in this case, this book). The second creates and executes a custom `QDialog` class `AboutDialog` which we will define next.

Listing 215. app/browser.py

```
    def navigate_mozzarella(self):
        self.browser.setUrl(QUrl("https://www.learnpyqt.com/"))

    def about(self):
        dlg = AboutDialog()
        dlg.exec_()
```

The definition for the about dialog is given below. The structure follows that seen earlier in the book, with a `QDialogButtonBox` and associated signals to handle user input, and a series of `QLabels` to display the application information and a logo.

The only trick here is adding all the elements to the layout, then iterate over them to set the alignment to the center in a single loop. This saves duplication for the individual sections.

Listing 216. app/browser.py

```
class AboutDialog(QDialog):
    def __init__(self):
        super().__init__()

        QBtn = QDialogButtonBox.Ok  # No cancel
        self.buttonBox = QDialogButtonBox(QBtn)
        self.buttonBox.accepted.connect(self.accept)
        self.buttonBox.rejected.connect(self.reject)

        layout = QVBoxLayout()

        title = QLabel("Mozzarella Ashbadger")
        font = title.font()
        font.setPointSize(20)
        title.setFont(font)

        layout.addWidget(title)

        logo = QLabel()
        logo.setPixmap(QPixmap(os.path.join("icons", "ma-icon-
128.png")))
        layout.addWidget(logo)

        layout.addWidget(QLabel("Version 23.35.211.233232"))
        layout.addWidget(QLabel("Copyright 2015 Mozzarella Inc."))

        for i in range(0, layout.count()):
            layout.itemAt(i).setAlignment(Qt.AlignHCenter)

        layout.addWidget(self.buttonBox)

        self.setLayout(layout)
```

Tabbed Browsing

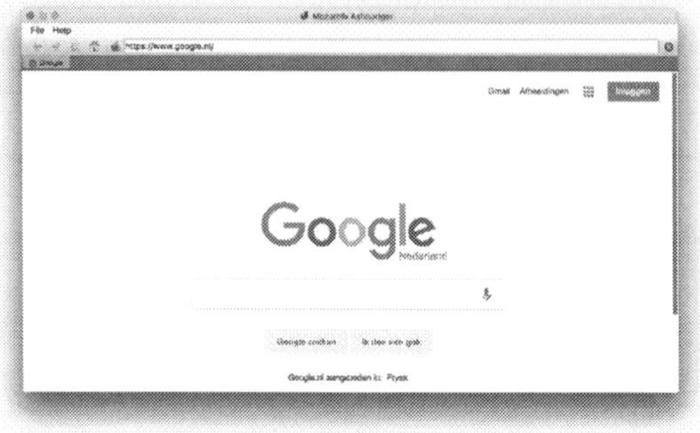

Figure 244. Mozzarella Ashbadger (Tabbed).

Source code

The full source for the tabbed browser is included in the downloads for this book. The browser code has the name `browser_tabs.py`.

> 🚀 **Run it!** Explore the Mozzarella Ashbadger *Tabbed Edition* before moving onto the code.

Creating a `QTabWidget`

Adding a tabbed interface to our browser is simple using a `QTabWidget`. This provides a simple container for multiple widgets (in our case `QWebEngineView` widgets) with a built-in tabbed interface for switching between them.

Two customizations we use here are `.setDocumentMode(True)` which provides a Safari-like interface on macOS, and `.setTabsClosable(True)` which allows the user to close the tabs in the application.

We also connect `QTabWidget` signals `tabBarDoubleClicked`, `currentChanged` and `tabCloseRequested` to custom slot methods to handle these behaviors.

Listing 217. app/browser_tabs.py

```
        self.tabs = QTabWidget()
        self.tabs.setDocumentMode(True)
        self.tabs.tabBarDoubleClicked.connect(self
.tab_open_doubleclick)
        self.tabs.currentChanged.connect(self.current_tab_changed)
        self.tabs.setTabsClosable(True)
        self.tabs.tabCloseRequested.connect(self.close_current_tab)

        self.setCentralWidget(self.tabs)
```

The three slot methods accept an `i` (index) parameter which indicates which tab the signal resulted from (in order).

We use a double-click on an empty space in the tab bar (represented by an index of -1 to trigger creation of a new tab. For removing a tab, we use the index directly to remove the widget (and so the tab), with a simple check to ensure there are at least 2 tabs—closing the last tab would leave you unable to open a new one.

The `current_tab_changed` handler uses a `self.tabs.currentWidget()` construct to access the widget (`QWebEngineView` browser) of the currently active tab, and then uses this to get the URL of the current page. This same construct is used throughout the source for the tabbed browser, as a simple way to interact with the current browser view.

Listing 218. app/browser_tabs.py

```
    def tab_open_doubleclick(self, i):
        if i == -1:  # No tab under the click
            self.add_new_tab()

    def current_tab_changed(self, i):
        qurl = self.tabs.currentWidget().url()
        self.update_urlbar(qurl, self.tabs.currentWidget())
        self.update_title(self.tabs.currentWidget())

    def close_current_tab(self, i):
        if self.tabs.count() < 2:
            return

        self.tabs.removeTab(i)
```

Listing 219. app/browser_tabs.py

```
    def add_new_tab(self, qurl=None, label="Blank"):

        if qurl is None:
            qurl = QUrl("")

        browser = QWebEngineView()
        browser.setUrl(qurl)
        i = self.tabs.addTab(browser, label)

        self.tabs.setCurrentIndex(i)
```

Signal & Slot changes

While the setup of the `QTabWidget` and associated signals is simple, things get a little trickier in the browser slot methods.

Whereas before we had a single `QWebEngineView` now there are multiple views, all with their own signals. If signals for hidden tabs are handled things will get all mixed up. For example, the slot handling a `loadCompleted` signal must check that the source view is in a visible tab.

We can do this using our trick for sending additional data with signals. In the tabbed browser we're using the `lambda` style syntax to do this.

Below is an example of doing this when creating a new `QWebEngineView` in the `add_new_tab` function.

Listing 220. app/browser_tabs.py

```
        # More difficult! We only want to update the url when it's
from the
        # correct tab
        browser.urlChanged.connect(
            lambda qurl, browser=browser: self.update_urlbar(qurl,
browser)
        )

        browser.loadFinished.connect(
            lambda _, i=i, browser=browser: self.tabs.setTabText(
                i, browser.page().title()
            )
        )
```

As you can see, we set a `lambda` as the slot for the `urlChanged` signal, accepting the `qurl` parameter that is sent by this signal. We add the recently created `browser` object to pass into the `update_urlbar` function.

The result is, whenever this `urlChanged` signal fires `update_urlbar` will receive both the new URL and the browser it came from. In the slot method we can then check to ensure that the source of the signal matches the currently visible browser — if not, we simply discard the signal.

Listing 221. app/browser_tabs.py

```
    def update_urlbar(self, q, browser=None):

        if browser != self.tabs.currentWidget():
            # If this signal is not from the current tab, ignore
            return

        if q.scheme() == "https":
            # Secure padlock icon
            self.httpsicon.setPixmap(QPixmap(os.path.join("icons",
"lock-ssl.png")))

        else:
            # Insecure padlock icon
            self.httpsicon.setPixmap(QPixmap(os.path.join("icons",
"lock-nossl.png")))

        self.urlbar.setText(q.toString())
        self.urlbar.setCursorPosition(0)
```

Going further

Explore the rest of the source code for the tabbed version of the browser paying particular attention to the user of `self.tabs.currentWidget()` and passing additional data with signals. This a good practical use case for what you've learnt, so experiment and see if you can break/improve it in interesting ways.

Challenges

You might like to try adding some additional features—

- Bookmarks (or Favorites)—you could store these in a simple text file, and show them in a menu.
- Favicons -- those little website icons, would look great on the tabs.
- View source code -- add a menu option to see the source code for the page.
- Open in New Tab—add a right-click context menu, or keyboard shortcut, to open a link in a new tab.

39. Moonsweeper

Explore the mysterious moon of Q'tee without getting too close to the alien natives!

Moonsweeper is a single-player puzzle video game. The objective of the game is to explore the area around your landed space rocket, without coming too close to the deadly B'ug aliens. Your trusty tricounter will tell you the number of B'ugs in the vicinity.

> *Suggested reading*
>
> This application makes use of features covered in Signals & Slots, and Events.

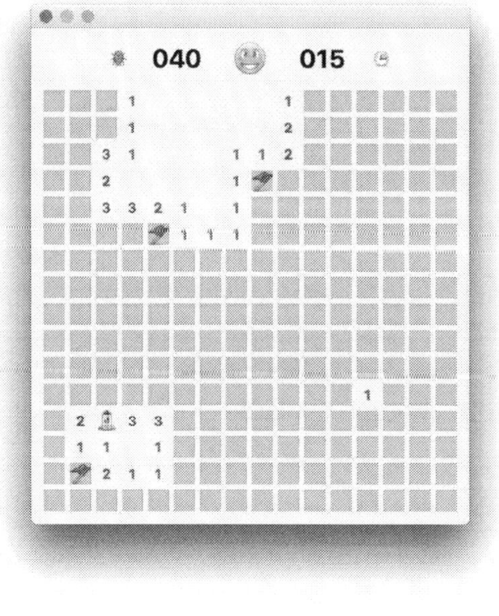

Figure 245. Moonsweeper.

This a simple single-player exploration game modelled on *Minesweeper* where you must reveal all the tiles without hitting hidden mines. This implementation uses custom `QWidget` objects for the tiles, which individually hold their state as mines, status and the adjacent count of mines. In this version, the mines are replaced with alien bugs (B'ug) but they could just as easily be anything else.

In many **Minesweeper** variants the initial turn is considered a free go -- if you hit a mine on the first click, it is moved somewhere else. Here we cheat a little bit by taking the first go for the player, ensuring that it is on a non-mine spot. This allows us not to worry about the bad first move which would require us to recalculate the adjacencies. We can explain this away as the "initial exploration around the rocket" and make it sound completely sensible.

> *Challenge!*
>
> If you want to implement this, you can catch the first click on a position and at that point generate mines/adjacencies, excluding your location, before handling the click. You will need to give your custom widgets access to the parent window object.

Source code

The full source for the *Moonsweeper* game is included in the downloads for this book. The game file is saved with the name `minesweeper.py`.

```
python3 minesweeper.py
```

Playing Field

The playing area for Moonsweeper is a NxN grid, containing a set number of mines. The dimensions and mine counts we'll used are taken from the default values for the Windows version of Minesweeper. The values used are shown in the table below:

Table 14. Table Dimensions and mine counts

Level	Dimensions	Number of Mines
Easy	8 x 8	10
Medium	16 x 16	40

Hard	24 x 24	99

We store these values as a constant `LEVELS` defined at the top of the file. Since all the playing fields are square we only need to store the value once (8, 16 or 24).

Listing 222. app/minesweeper.py

```
LEVELS = [("Easy", 8, 10), ("Medium", 16, 40), ("Hard", 24, 99)]
```

The playing grid could be represented in a number of ways, including for example a 2D 'list of lists' representing the different states of the playing positions (mine, revealed, flagged).

However, in our implementation we'll be using an object-orientated approach, where individual positions on the map hold all relevant data about themselves. Taking this a step further, we can make these objects individually responsible for drawing themselves. In Qt we can do this simply by subclassing from `QWidget` and then implementing a custom paint function.

We'll cover the construction and behavior of these custom widgets before moving onto it's appearance. Since our tile objects are subclassing from `QWidget` we can lay them out like any other widget. We do this, by setting up a `QGridLayout`.

Listing 223. app/minesweeper.py

```
        self.grid = QGridLayout()
        self.grid.setSpacing(5)
        self.grid.setSizeConstraint(QLayout.SetFixedSize)
```

Next we need to set up the playing field, creating our position tile widgets and adding them our grid. The initial setup for the level is defined in custom method, which reads from `LEVELS` and assigns a number of variables to the window. The window title and mine counter are updated, and then the setup of the grid is begun.

Listing 224. app/minesweeper.py

```
    def set_level(self, level):
        self.level_name, self.b_size, self.n_mines = LEVELS[level]

        self.setWindowTitle("Moonsweeper - %s" % (self.level_name))
        self.mines.setText("%03d" % self.n_mines)

        self.clear_map()
        self.init_map()
        self.reset_map()
```

The setup functions will be covered next.

We're using a custom Pos class here, which we'll look at in detail later. For now you just need to know that this holds all the relevant information for the relevant position in the map—including, for example, whether it's a mine, revealed, flagged and the number of mines in the immediate vicinity.

Each Pos object also has 3 custom signals *clicked*, *revealed* and *expandable* which we connect to custom slot methods. Finally, we call resize to adjust the size of the window to the new contents. Note that this is actually only necessary when the window *shrinks*—it will grow automatically.

Listing 225. app/minesweeper.py

```
    def init_map(self):
        # Add positions to the map
        for x in range(0, self.b_size):
            for y in range(0, self.b_size):
                w = Pos(x, y)
                self.grid.addWidget(w, y, x)
                # Connect signal to handle expansion.
                w.clicked.connect(self.trigger_start)
                w.revealed.connect(self.on_reveal)
                w.expandable.connect(self.expand_reveal)

        # Place resize on the event queue, giving control back to Qt
before.
        QTimer.singleShot(0, lambda: self.resize(1, 1)) ①
```

① The `singleShot` timer is required to ensure the resize runs after Qt is aware of the new contents. By using a timer we guarantee control will return to Qt *before* the resize occurs.

We also need to implement the inverse of the `init_map` function to remove tile objects from the map. Removing tiles will be necessary when moving from a higher to a lower level. It would be possible to be a little smarter here and adding/removing only those tiles that are necessary to get to the correct size. But, since we already have the function to add all up to the right size, we can cheat a bit.

> *Challenge*
>
> Update this code to add/remove the neccessary tiles to size the new level dimensions.

Notice that we both remove the item from the grid with `self.grid.removeItem(c)` and clear the parent `c.widget().setParent(None)`. This second step is necessary, since adding the items assigning them the parent window as a parent. Just removing them leaves them floating in the window outside the layout.

Listing 226. app/minesweeper.py

```
    def clear_map(self):
        # Remove all positions from the map, up to maximum size.
        for x in range(0, LEVELS[-1][1]):  ①
            for y in range(0, LEVELS[-1][1]):
                c = self.grid.itemAtPosition(y, x)
                if c: ②
                    c.widget().close()
                    self.grid.removeItem(c)
```

① To ensure we clear all sizes of maps we take the dimension of the highest level.

② If there isn't anything in the grid at this location, we can skip it.

Now we have our grid of positional tile objects in place, we can begin creating the initial conditions of the playing board. This process is rather complex, so it's broken down into a number of functions. We name them `_reset` (the leading underscore is a convention to indicate a private function, not intended for external use). The main function `reset_map` calls these functions in turn to set it up.

The process is as follows—

1. Remove all mines (and reset data) from the field.
2. Add new mines to the field.
3. Calculate the number of mines adjacent to each position.
4. Add a starting marker (the rocket) and trigger initial exploration.
5. Reset the timer.

Listing 227. app/minesweeper.py

```
    def reset_map(self):
        self._reset_position_data()
        self._reset_add_mines()
        self._reset_calculate_adjacency()
        self._reset_add_starting_marker()
        self.update_timer()
```

The separate steps from 1-5 are described in detail in turn below, with the code for each step.

The first step is to reset the data for each position on the map. We iterate through every position on the board, calling `.reset()` on the widget at each point. The code for the `.reset()` function is defined on our custom `Pos` class, we'll explore in detail later. For now it's enough to know it clears mines, flags and sets the position back to being unrevealed.

Listing 228. app/minesweeper.py

```
    def _reset_position_data(self):
        # Clear all mine positions
        for x in range(0, self.b_size):
            for y in range(0, self.b_size):
                w = self.grid.itemAtPosition(y, x).widget()
                w.reset()
```

Now all the positions are blank, we can begin the process of adding mines to the map. The maximum number of mines `n_mines` is defined by the level settings, described earlier.

Listing 229. app/minesweeper.py

```
    def _reset_add_mines(self):
        # Add mine positions
        positions = []
        while len(positions) < self.n_mines:
            x, y = (
                random.randint(0, self.b_size - 1),
                random.randint(0, self.b_size - 1),
            )
            if (x, y) not in positions:
                w = self.grid.itemAtPosition(y, x).widget()
                w.is_mine = True
                positions.append((x, y))

        # Calculate end-game condition
        self.end_game_n = (self.b_size * self.b_size) - (self.n_mines
+ 1)
        return positions
```

With mines in position, we can now calculate the 'adjacency' number for each position -- simply the number of mines in the immediate vicinity, using a 3x3 grid around the given point. The custom function `get_surrounding` simply returns those positions around a given `x` and `y` location. We count the number of these that is a mine `is_mine == True` and store.

> *Pre-calculation*
>
> Pre-calculating the adjacent counts in this way helps simplify the reveal logic later.

Listing 230. app/minesweeper.py

```python
    def _reset_calculate_adjacency(self):
        def get_adjacency_n(x, y):
            positions = self.get_surrounding(x, y)
            return sum(1 for w in positions if w.is_mine)

        # Add adjacencies to the positions
        for x in range(0, self.b_size):
            for y in range(0, self.b_size):
                w = self.grid.itemAtPosition(y, x).widget()
                w.adjacent_n = get_adjacency_n(x, y)
```

A starting marker is used to ensure that the first move is *always* valid. This is implemented as a *brute force* search through the grid space, effectively trying random positions until we find a position which is not a mine. Since we don't know how many attempts this will take, we need to wrap it in an continuous loop.

Once that location is found, we mark it as the start location and then trigger the exploration of all surrounding positions. We break out of the loop, and reset the ready status.

Listing 231. app/minesweeper.py

```
    def _reset_add_starting_marker(self):
        # Place starting marker.

        # Set initial status (needed for .click to function)
        self.update_status(STATUS_READY)

        while True:
            x, y = (
                random.randint(0, self.b_size - 1),
                random.randint(0, self.b_size - 1),
            )
            w = self.grid.itemAtPosition(y, x).widget()
            # We don't want to start on a mine.
            if not w.is_mine:
                w.is_start = True
                w.is_revealed = True
                w.update()

                # Reveal all positions around this, if they are not
mines either.
                for w in self.get_surrounding(x, y):
                    if not w.is_mine:
                        w.click()
                break

        # Reset status to ready following initial clicks.
        self.update_status(STATUS_READY)
```

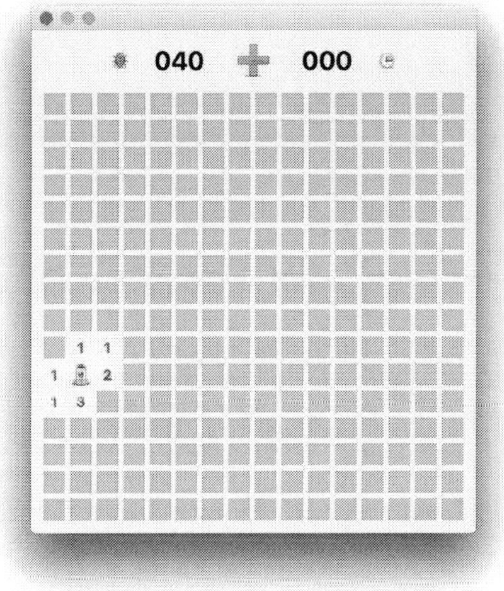

Figure 246. Initial exploration around rocket.

Position Tiles

As previously described, we've structured the game so that individual tile positions hold their own state information. This means that Pos objects are ideally positioned to handle game logic which reacts to to interactions that relate to their own state—in other words, this is where the magic is.

Since the Pos class is relatively complex, it is broken down here in to main themes, which are discussed in turn. The initial setup `__init__` block is simple, accepting an x and y position and storing it on the object. Pos positions never change once created.

To complete setup the `.reset()` function is called which resets all object attributes back to default, zero values. This flags the mine as *not the start position*, *not a mine*, *not revealed* and *not flagged*. We also reset the adjacent count.

Listing 232. app/minesweeper.py

```
class Pos(QWidget):

    expandable = pyqtSignal(int, int)
    revealed = pyqtSignal(object)
    clicked = pyqtSignal()

    def __init__(self, x, y):
        super().__init__()

        self.setFixedSize(QSize(20, 20))
        self.x = x
        self.y = y
        self.reset()

    def reset(self):
        self.is_start = False
        self.is_mine = False
        self.adjacent_n = 0
        self.is_revealed = False
        self.is_flagged = False

        self.update()
```

Gameplay is centered around mouse interactions with the tiles in the playfield, so detecting and reacting to mouse clicks is central. In Qt we catch mouse clicks by detecting the `mouseReleaseEvent`. To do this for our custom `Pos` widget we define a handler on the class. This receives `QMouseEvent` with the information containing what happened. In this case we are only interested in whether the mouse release occurred from the left or the right mouse button.

For a left mouse click we check whether the tile is flagged or already revealed. If it is either, we ignore the click—making flagged tiles 'safe', unable to be click by accident. If the tile is not flagged we simply initiation the `.click()` method (see later).

For a right mouse click, on tiles which are *not* revealed, we call our `.toggle_flag()` method to toggle a flag on and off.

Listing 233. app/minesweeper.py

```
    def mouseReleaseEvent(self, e):

        if e.button() == Qt.RightButton and not self.is_revealed:
            self.toggle_flag()

        elif e.button() == Qt.LeftButton:
            # Block clicking on flagged mines.
            if not self.is_flagged and not self.is_revealed:
                self.click()
```

The methods called by the `mouseReleaseEvent` handler are defined below.

The `.toggle_flag` handler simply sets `.is_flagged` to the inverse of itself (`True` becomes `False`, `False` becomes `True`) having the effect of toggling it on and off. Note that we have to call `.update()` to force a redraw having changed the state. We also emit our custom `.clicked` signal, which is used to start the timer -- because placing a flag should also count as starting, not just revealing a square.

The `.click()` method handles a left mouse click, and in turn triggers the reveal of the square. If the number of adjacent mines to this `Pos` is zero, we trigger the `.expandable` signal to begin the process of auto-expanding the region explored (see later). Finally, we again emit `.clicked` to signal the start of the game.

Finally, the `.reveal()` method checks whether the tile is already revealed, and if not sets `.is_revealed` to `True`. Again we call `.update()` to trigger a repaint of the widget.

The optional emit of the `.revealed` signal is used only for the endgame full-map reveal. Because each reveal triggers a further lookup to find what tiles are also revealable, revealing the entire map would create a large number of redundant callbacks. By suppressing the signal here we avoid that.

Listing 234. app/minesweeper.py

```
    def toggle_flag(self):
        self.is_flagged = not self.is_flagged
        self.update()

        self.clicked.emit()

    def click(self):
        self.reveal()
        if self.adjacent_n == 0:
            self.expandable.emit(self.x, self.y)

        self.clicked.emit()

    def reveal(self, emit=True):
        if not self.is_revealed:
            self.is_revealed = True
            self.update()

            if emit:
                self.revealed.emit(self)
```

Finally, we define a custom `paintEvent` method for our `Pos` widget to handle the display of the current position state. As described in [chapter] to perform custom paint over a widget canvas we take a `QPainter` and the `event.rect()` which provides the boundaries in which we are to draw -- in this case the outer border of the `Pos` widget.

Revealed tiles are drawn differently depending on whether the tile is a *start position*, *bomb* or *empty space*. The first two are represented by icons of a rocket and bomb respectively. These are drawn into the tile `QRect` using `.drawPixmap`. Note we need to convert the `QImage` constants to pixmaps, by passing through `QPixmap` by passing.

QPixmap vs. QImages

You might think "why not just store these as `QPixmap` objects since that's what we're using? We can't do this and store them in constants because you can't create `QPixmap` objects before your `QApplication` is up and running.

For empty positions (not rockets, not bombs) we optionally show the adjacency number if it is larger than zero. To draw text onto our `QPainter` we use `.drawText()` passing in the `QRect`, alignment flags and the number to draw as a string. We've defined a standard color for each number (stored in `NUM_COLORS`) for usability.

For tiles that are *not* revealed we draw a tile, by filling a rectangle with light gray and draw a 1 pixel border of darker grey. If `.is_flagged` is set, we also draw a flag icon over the top of the tile using `drawPixmap` and the tile `QRect`.

Listing 235. app/minesweeper.py

```
    def paintEvent(self, event):
        p = QPainter(self)
        p.setRenderHint(QPainter.Antialiasing)

        r = event.rect()

        if self.is_revealed:
            if self.is_start:
                p.drawPixmap(r, QPixmap(IMG_START))

            elif self.is_mine:
                p.drawPixmap(r, QPixmap(IMG_BOMB))

            elif self.adjacent_n > 0:
                pen = QPen(NUM_COLORS[self.adjacent_n])
                p.setPen(pen)
                f = p.font()
                f.setBold(True)
                p.setFont(f)
                p.drawText(r, Qt.AlignHCenter | Qt.AlignVCenter, str
(self.adjacent_n))

        else:
            p.fillRect(r, QBrush(Qt.lightGray))
            pen = QPen(Qt.gray)
            pen.setWidth(1)
            p.setPen(pen)
            p.drawRect(r)

            if self.is_flagged:
                p.drawPixmap(r, QPixmap(IMG_FLAG))
```

Mechanics

We commonly need to get all tiles surrounding a given point, so we have a custom function for that purpose. It simple iterates across a 3x3 grid around the point, with a check to ensure we do not go out of bounds on the grid edges (`0 ≥ x ≤ self.b_size`). The returned list contains a `Pos` widget from each surrounding location.

Listing 236. app/minesweeper.py

```
    def get_surrounding(self, x, y):
        positions = []

        for xi in range(max(0, x - 1), min(x + 2, self.b_size)):
            for yi in range(max(0, y - 1), min(y + 2, self.b_size)):
                if not (xi == x and yi == y):
                    positions.append(self.grid.itemAtPosition(yi,
xi).widget())

        return positions
```

The `expand_reveal` method is triggered in response to a click on a tile with zero adjacent mines. In this case we want to expand the area around the click to any spaces which also have zero adjacent mines, and also reveal any squares around the border of that expanded area (which aren't mines).

This *can* be achieved by looking at all squares around the clicked square, and triggering a `.click()` on any that do not have `.n_adjacent == 0`. The normal game logic takes over and expands the area automatically. However, this is a bit inefficient, resulting in a large number of redundant signals (each square triggers up to 9 signals for each surrounding square).

Instead we use a self-contained method to determine the area to be revealed, and then trigger the reveal (using `.reveal()` to avoid the `.clicked` signals.

We start with a list `to_expand` containing the positions to check on the next iteration, a list `to_reveal` containing the tile widgets to reveal, and a flag `any_added` to determine when to exit the loop. The loop stops the first time no new widgets are added to `to_reveal`.

Inside the loop we reset `any_added` to `False`, and empty the `to_expand` list, keeping a temporary store in `l` for iterating over.

For each `x` and `y` location we get the 8 surrounding widgets. If any of these widgets is not a mine, and is not already in the `to_reveal` list we add it. This ensures that the edges of the expanded area are all revealed. If the position has no adjacent mines, we append the coordinates onto `to_expand` to be checked on the next iteration.

By adding any non-mine tiles to `to_reveal`, and only expanding tiles that are not already in `to_reveal`, we ensure that we won't visit a tile more than once.

Listing 237. app/minesweeper.py

```python
    def expand_reveal(self, x, y):
        """
        Iterate outwards from the initial point, adding new locations
to the
        queue. This allows us to expand all in a single go, rather
than
        relying on multiple callbacks.
        """
        to_expand = [(x, y)]
        to_reveal = []
        any_added = True

        while any_added:
            any_added = False
            to_expand, l = [], to_expand

            for x, y in l:
                positions = self.get_surrounding(x, y)
                for w in positions:
                    if not w.is_mine and w not in to_reveal:
                        to_reveal.append(w)
                        if w.adjacent_n == 0:
                            to_expand.append((w.x, w.y))
                            any_added = True

        # Iterate an reveal all the positions we have found.
        for w in to_reveal:
            w.reveal()
```

Endgames

Endgame states are detected during the reveal process following a click on a title. There are two possible outcomes --

1. Tile is a mine, game over.
2. Tile is not a mine, decrement the `self.end_game_n`.

This continues until `self.end_game_n` reaches zero, which triggers the win game process by calling either `game_over` or `game_won`. Success/failure is triggered by revealing the map and setting the relevant status, in both cases.

Listing 238. app/minesweeper.py

```
    def on_reveal(self, w):
        if w.is_mine:
            self.game_over()

        else:
            self.end_game_n -= 1  # decrement remaining empty spaces

            if self.end_game_n == 0:
                self.game_won()

    def game_over(self):
        self.reveal_map()
        self.update_status(STATUS_FAILED)

    def game_won(self):
        self.reveal_map()
        self.update_status(STATUS_SUCCESS)
```

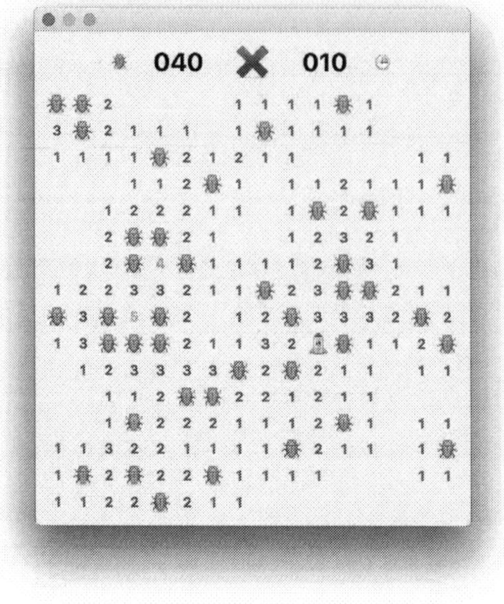

Figure 247. Oh no. Eaten by a B'ug.

Status

The user interface for Moonsweeper is pretty simple: one display showing the number of mines, one showing the amount of time elapsed, and a button to start/restart the game.

Both the labels are defined as `QLabel` objects with the with the same `QFont` size and color. These are defined on the `QMainWindow` object so we can access and update them at a later time. Two additional icons (a clock and a mine) are also defined as `QLabel` objects.

The button is a `QPushButton` with a defined icon, which is updated in `set_status` in response to status changes. The `.pressed` signal is connected to a custom slot method `button_pressed` which handles the signal differently depending on the game state.

Listing 239. app/minesweeper.py

```python
        self.mines = QLabel()
        self.mines.setAlignment(Qt.AlignHCenter | Qt.AlignVCenter)

        self.clock = QLabel()
        self.clock.setAlignment(Qt.AlignHCenter | Qt.AlignVCenter)

        f = self.mines.font()
        f.setPointSize(24)
        f.setWeight(75)
        self.mines.setFont(f)
        self.clock.setFont(f)

        self.clock.setText("000")

        self.button = QPushButton()
        self.button.setFixedSize(QSize(32, 32))
        self.button.setIconSize(QSize(32, 32))
        self.button.setIcon(QIcon("./icons/smiley.png"))
        self.button.setFlat(True)

        self.button.pressed.connect(self.button_pressed)

        self.statusBar()

        l = QLabel()
        l.setPixmap(QPixmap.fromImage(IMG_BOMB))
        l.setAlignment(Qt.AlignRight | Qt.AlignVCenter)
        hb.addWidget(l)

        hb.addWidget(self.mines)
        hb.addWidget(self.button)
        hb.addWidget(self.clock)

        l = QLabel()
        l.setPixmap(QPixmap.fromImage(IMG_CLOCK))
        l.setAlignment(Qt.AlignLeft | Qt.AlignVCenter)
        hb.addWidget(l)

        vb = QVBoxLayout()
        vb.setSizeConstraint(QLayout.SetFixedSize)
        vb.addLayout(hb)
```

If the game is currently in progress `self.status == STATUS_PLAYING` a button press is interpreted as "I give up" and the game_over state is triggered.

If the game is currently won `self.status == STATUS_SUCCESS` or lost `self.status == STATUS_FAILED` the press is taken to mean "Try again" and the game map is reset.

Listing 240. app/minesweeper.py

```
    def button_pressed(self):
        if self.status == STATUS_PLAYING:
            self.game_over()

        elif self.status == STATUS_FAILED or self.status ==
STATUS_SUCCESS:
            self.reset_map()
```

Menus

There is only a single menu for Moonsweeper which holds the game controls. We create a `QMenu` by calling `.addMenu()` on the `QMainWindow.menuBar()` as normal.

The first menu item is a standard `QAction` for "New game" wit the `.triggered` action connected to the `.reset_map` function, which performs the entire map setup process. For new games we keep the existing board size & layout so do not need to re-init the map.

In addition we add a submenu "Levels" which contains a `QAction` for each level defined in `LEVELS`. The level name is taken from the same constant, and custom status message is built from the stored dimensions. We connect the action `.triggered` signal to `.set_level`, using the `lambda` method to discard the default signal data and instead pass along the level number.

Listing 241. app/minesweeper.py

```
        game_menu = self.menuBar().addMenu("&Game")

        new_game_action = QAction("New game", self)
        new_game_action.setStatusTip(
            "Start a new game (your current game will be lost)"
        )
        new_game_action.triggered.connect(self.reset_map)
        game_menu.addAction(new_game_action)

        levels = game_menu.addMenu("Levels")
        for n, level in enumerate(LEVELS):
            level_action = QAction(level[0], self)
            level_action.setStatusTip("{1}x{1} grid, with {2} mines"
.format(*level))
            level_action.triggered.connect(lambda checked=None, n=n:
self.set_level(n))
            levels.addAction(level_action)
```

Going further

Take a look through the rest of the source code we've not covered.

Challenge

You might like to try make the following changes—

- Try changing the graphics to make you're own themed version of Minesweeper.
- Add support for non-square playing fields. Rectangular? Try a circle!
- Change the timer to count down—explore the Moon against the clock!
- Add power-ups: squares give bonuses, extra time, invincibility.

Appendix A: Installing PyQt5

Before you start coding you will first need to have a working installation of PyQt5 on your system. If you don't have PyQt5 set up yet, the following sections will guide you through how to do this on Windows, macOS and Linux.

> Note that the following instructions are **only** for installation of the **GPL licensed** version of PyQt. If you need to use PyQt in a non-GPL project you will need to purchase an alternative license from Riverbank Computing [https://www.riverbankcomputing.com] to release your software.

Installation on Windows

PyQt5 for Windows can be installed as for any other application or library. As of Qt 5.6 installers are available to install via PyPi, the Python Package archive. To install PyQt5 from Python3 simply run—

```
pip3 install pyqt5
```

After install is finished, you should be able to run `python` and `import PyQt5`.

Note that if you want access to Qt Designer or Qt Creator you will need to download this from the Qt downloads site [https://qt.io/download].

Installation on macOS

If you already have a working installation of Python 3 on macOS, you can go ahead and install PyQt5 as for any other Python package, using the following—

```
pip3 install pyqt5
```

If you *don't* have an installation of Python 3, you will need to install one first. You can download macOS installers for Python 3 from the Python homepage [https://www.python.org/]. Once installed, you should be able to use the `pip3 install` command above to install PyQt5.

Another alternative is to use Homebrew [http://brew.sh/]. Homebrew is a package manager for command-line software on macOS. Homebrew has both Python 3 and PyQt5 available in their repositories.

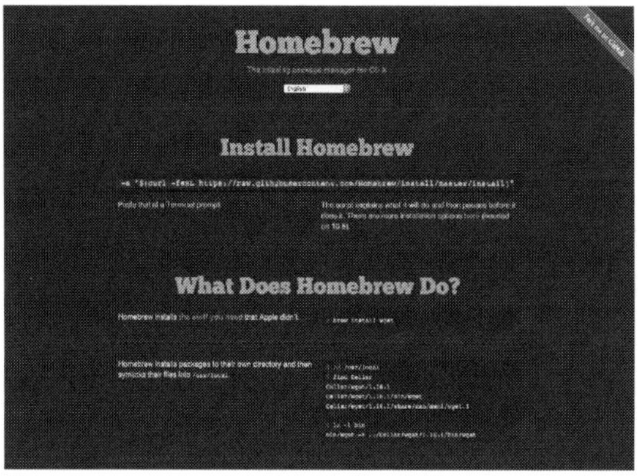

Figure 248. Homebrew—the missing package manager for macOS.

To install homebrew run the following from the command line—

```
ruby -e "$(curl -fsSL
https://raw.githubusercontent.com/Homebrew/install/master/install)"
```

> This is also available to copy and paste from the Homebrew homepage.

Once Homebrew is installed you can then install Python with—

```
brew install python3
```

With Python installed, you can then install PyQt5 as normal, using `pip3 install pyqt5`, or alternatively choose to install it using Homebrew with—

```
brew install pyqt5
```

Installation on Linux (Ubuntu & Debian)

Installation on Linux is very straightforward as packages for PyQt5 are available in the repositories of most distributions. In Ubuntu you can install either from the command line or via "Software Center". The package you are looking for is named `python3-pyqt5`.

You can also install these from the command line as follows—

```
apt-get install python3-pyqt5
```

Once the installation is finished, you should be able to run `python3` or `python` and `import PyQt5`.

Appendix B: Translating C++ Examples to Python

When writing applications with PyQt5 we are really writing applications with Qt.

PyQt5 acts as a wrapper around the Qt libraries, translating Python method calls to C++, handling type conversions and transparently creating Python objects to represent Qt objects in your applications. The result of all this cleverness is that you can use Qt from Python while writing *mostly* Pythonic code — if we ignore the *camelCase*.

While there is a lot of PyQt5 example code out there, there are far more Qt C++ examples. The core documentation is written for C++. The library is written in C++. This means that sometimes, when you're looking how to do something, the only resource you'll find is a C++ tutorial or some C++ code.

Can you use it? Yes! If you have no experience with C++ (or C-like languages) then the code can look like gibberish. But before you were familiar with Python, Python probably looked a bit like gibberish too. You don't need to be able to *write* C++ to be able to *read* it. Understanding and decoding is easier than writing.

With a little bit of effort you'll be able to take any C++ example code and translate it into fully-functional Python & PyQt5. In this chapter we'll take a snippet of Qt5 code and step-by-step convert it into fully-working Python code.

The example code

We'll start with the following example block of code creating a simple window with a `QPushButton` and a `QLineEdit`. Pressing on the button will clear the line edit. Pretty exciting stuff, but this includes a few key parts of translating Qt examples to PyQt5 — namely, widgets, layouts and signals.

```cpp
#include <QtWidgets>

int main(int argc, char *argv[])
{
    QApplication app(argc, argv);
    QWidget window;
    QLineEdit *lineEdit = new QLineEdit();
    QPushButton *button = new QPushButton("Clear");
    QHBoxLayout *layout = new QHBoxLayout();
    layout->addWidget(lineEdit);
    layout->addWidget(button);

    QObject::connect(&button,   &QPushButton::pressed,
                     &lineEdit, &QLineEdit::clear);

    window.setLayout(layout);
    window.setWindowTitle("Why?");
    window.show();
    return app.exec();
}
```

Remember that a Qt widget without a parent is always a separate window. Here we have a single window created as a `QWidget`.

Below we'll step through the process of converting this code to Python.

Imports

In C++ *imports* are called *includes*. They're found at the top of the file, just as in Python (though only by convention) and look like this—

```cpp
#include <QtWidgets>
```

In C-like languages the `#` indicates that `include` is a *pre-processor directive* not a comment. The value between <> is the name of the module to import. Note that unlike Python, importing a module makes all contents of that module available in the global namespace. This is the equivalent of doing the following in Python—

```
from PyQt5.QtWidgets import *
```

Global imports like this are generally frowned upon in Python, and you should instead either—

1. only import the objects you need, or
2. import the module itself and use it to reference it's children

```
from PyQt5.QtWidgets import QApplication, QWidget, QLineEdit,
QPushButton, QHBoxLayout
```

Or, alternatively...

```
from PyQt5 import QtWidgets
```

...and then reference as `QtWidgets.QApplication()`. Which you choose for your own code is entirely up to you, however in this example we're going to follow the first style. Applying that to the code gives us the following result so far.

```
from PyQt5.QtWidgets import (
    QApplication, QWidget, QLineEdit, QPushButton, QHBoxLayout
)

int main(int argc, char *argv[])
{
    QApplication app(argc, argv);
    QWidget window;
    QLineEdit *lineEdit = new QLineEdit();
    QPushButton *button = new QPushButton("Clear");
    QHBoxLayout *layout = new QHBoxLayout();
    layout->addWidget(lineEdit);
    layout->addWidget(button);

    QObject::connect(&button,   &QPushButton::pressed,
                     &lineEdit, &QLineEdit::clear);

    window.setLayout(layout);
    window.setWindowTitle("Why?");
    window.show();
    return app.exec();
}
```

Since we're making changes iteratively, the code won't work until the very end.

int main(int argc, char *argv[])

Every C++ program needs a `main(){}` block which contains the first code to be run when the application is executed. In Python *any* code at the top-level of the module (i.e. not indented inside a function, class or methods) will be run when the script is executed.

```
from PyQt5.QtWidgets import (
   QApplication, QWidget, QLineEdit, QPushButton, QHBoxLayout
)

QApplication app(argc, argv);
QWidget window;
QLineEdit *lineEdit = new QLineEdit();
QPushButton *button = new QPushButton("Clear");
QHBoxLayout *layout = new QHBoxLayout();
layout->addWidget(lineEdit);
layout->addWidget(button);

QObject::connect(&button,   &QPushButton::pressed,
                 &lineEdit, &QLineEdit::clear);

window.setLayout(layout);
window.setWindowTitle("Why?");
window.show();
app.exec();
```

You may have seen the following code block in Python application code, which is also often referred to as the `__main__` block.

```
if __name__ == '__main__':
   ...your code here...
```

However, this works in a subtly different way. While this block *will* be run when a script is executed, so would any code that is not indented. The purpose of this block is actually to *prevent* this code executing when the module is imported, rather than executed as a script.

You can nest your code inside this block if you wish, although unless your file is going to be imported as a module it isn't strictly necessary.

C++ types

Python is a *dynamically typed* language, meaning you can change the type of a variable after it has been defined. For example, the following is perfectly valid Python.

```
a = 1
a = 'my string'
a = [1,2,3]
```

Many other languages, C++ included, are *statically typed*, meaning that once you define the type of a variable it cannot be changed. For example, the following is very definitely *not* valid C++.

```
int a = 1;
a = 'my string';
```

The above highlights an immediate consequence of static typing in languages: you define the type of a variable *when you create it*.

In C++ this is done explicitly by providing a type decorator on the line when the variable is defined, above `int`.

In lines like the following the first name is the name of type (class) that is being created by the remainder of the line.

```
QApplication app(argc, argv);
QWidget window;

QLineEdit *lineEdit = new QLineEdit();
QPushButton *button = new QPushButton("Clear");
QHBoxLayout *layout = new QHBoxLayout();
```

In Python we do not need these type definitions, so we can just delete them.

```
lineEdit = new QLineEdit();
button = new QPushButton("Clear");
layout = new QHBoxLayout();
```

For `application` and `window` it's exactly the same principle. However, if you're not familiar with C++ it might not be obvious those lines are creating an variable at all.

There are differences between creating objects with `new` and without in C++ but you don't need to concern yourself with that in Python and can consider them both equivalent.

```
QWidget *window = new QWidget();
QWidget window;

QApplication *app = new QApplication(argc, argv);
QApplication app;
```

To convert to Python, take the class name (e.g. `QApplication`) from the left, and place it in front of open and closing brackets (), adding them if they aren't already there. Then move the name of the *variable* to the left, with an =. For `window` that gives us—

```
window = QWidget()
```

In Python `QApplication` only accepts a single parameter, a list of arguments from `sys.argv` (equivalent to `argv`). This gives us the code—

```
import sys

app = QApplication(sys.argv);
```

So far our complete code block is looking like the following.

```
from PyQt5.QtWidgets import (
    QApplication, QWidget, QLineEdit, QPushButton, QHBoxLayout
)

import sys

app = QApplication(argc, argv);
window = QWidget()
lineEdit = QLineEdit();
button = QPushButton("Clear");
layout = QHBoxLayout();
layout->addWidget(lineEdit);
layout->addWidget(button);

QObject::connect(&button,   &QPushButton::pressed,
                 &lineEdit, &QLineEdit::clear);

window.setLayout(layout);
window.setWindowTitle("Why?");
window.show();
app.exec();
```

Signals

Signals are key to making the example work, and unfortunately the C++ syntax for Qt signals is a little tricky. The example signal we're working with is shown below.

```
QObject::connect(&button,   &QPushButton::pressed,
                 &lineEdit, &QLineEdit::clear);
```

If you're not familiar with C++ this will be quite difficult to parse. But if we remove all the syntax it will get much clearer.

```
connect(button, QPushButton.pressed, lineEdit, QLineEdit.clear)
// or...
connect(<from object>, <from signal>, <to object>, <to slot>>)
```

Working from left to right we have, the *object* we're connecting from, the *signal* we're connecting from on that object, then the *object* we're connecting to, then finally the *slot* (or function) we're connecting to on that object. This is the equivalent of writing the following in PyQt5—

```
button.pressed.connect(lineedit.clear)
```

Making that change gives us the following in progress code.

```
from PyQt5.QtWidgets import (
    QApplication, QWidget, QLineEdit, QPushButton, QHBoxLayout
)

app = QApplication(sys.argv)
window = QWidget()
lineEdit = QLineEdit()
button = QPushButton("Clear")
layout = QHBoxLayout()
layout->addWidget(lineEdit);
layout->addWidget(button);

button.pressed.connect(lineEdit.clear)

window.setLayout(layout);
window.setWindowTitle("Why?");
window.show();
app.exec();
```

Syntax

By now we've converted all the really troublesome parts, so we can do a final syntax-correction pass. These are a simple search-replace.

First search for all instances of `->` or `::` and replace with `.`. You'll notice that the C++ code also uses `.` in some places—this comes back to how those variables were created earlier (`new` vs. not). Again, you can ignore that here and simply use `.` everywhere.

```
layout.addWidget(lineEdit);
layout.addWidget(button);
```

Finally, remove all line-ending semi-colon ; marks.

```
layout.addWidget(lineEdit)
layout.addWidget(button)
```

> You technically don't *have* to do this, as ; is a valid line-terminator in Python. It's just not necessary.

The following code is now working Python.

```
import sys

from PyQt5.QtWidgets import QApplication, QHBoxLayout, QLineEdit,
QPushButton, QWidget

app = QApplication(sys.argv)
window = QWidget()
lineEdit = QLineEdit()
button = QPushButton("Clear")
layout = QHBoxLayout()
layout.addWidget(lineEdit)
layout.addWidget(button)

button.pressed.connect(lineEdit.clear)

window.setLayout(layout)
window.setWindowTitle("Why?")
window.show()
app.exec_()
```

In Python code it is normal (though not *required*) to subclass the window class so the initialization code can be self-contained within the `__init__` block. The code below has been reworked into that structure, moving all except the creation of the window object (now `MyWindow`) and app, and app.exec() call into the __init__ block.

```
import sys

from PyQt5.QtWidgets import QApplication, QHBoxLayout, QLineEdit,
QPushButton, QWidget


class MyWindow(QWidget):
    def __init__(self, *args, **kwargs):
        super().__init__(*args, **kwargs)

        lineEdit = QLineEdit()
        button = QPushButton("Clear")
        layout = QHBoxLayout()
        layout.addWidget(lineEdit)
        layout.addWidget(button)

        button.pressed.connect(lineEdit.clear)

        self.setLayout(layout)
        self.setWindowTitle("Why?")
        self.show()


app = QApplication(sys.argv)
window = MyWindow()
app.exec_()
```

Applying the process to your own code

This is a very simple example, however if you follow the same process you can reliably convert any C++ Qt code over to it's Python equivalent. When converting your own sample of code try and stick to this stepwise approach to minimize the risk of missing something or inadvertently breaking it. If you end up with Python code that runs but is subtly different it can be hard to debug.

If you have a code example you would like help with translating, you can always get in touch and I'll try and help you out.

Appendix C: PyQt5 and PySide2 — What's the difference?

If you start building Python application with Qt5 you'll soon discover that there are in fact two packages which you can use to do this — PyQt5 and PySide2.

In this short chapter I'll run through why exactly this is, whether you need to care (spoiler: you really don't), what the (few) differences are and how to work around them. By the end you should be comfortable re-using code examples from both PyQt5 and PySide2 tutorials to build your apps, regardless of which package you're using yourself.

> If you bought a copy of this ebook you can have access to both PyQt5 and PySide2 versions of this book. Just let me know and I'll add them onto your account on www.learnpyqt.com [https://www.learnpyqt.com].

Background

Why are there two libraries?

PyQt is developed by Phil Thompson of Riverbank Computing Ltd. [https://www.riverbankcomputing.com/software/pyqt/intro] and has existed for a very long time — supporting versions of Qt going back to 2.x. In 2009 Nokia, who owned Qt toolkit at the time, wanted to make the Python bindings for Qt available in a more permissive LGPL license. Unable to come to agreement with Riverbank (who would lose money from this, so fair enough) they then released their own *bindings as _PySide*.

> It's called *PySide* because "side" is Finnish for "binder".

The two interfaces were basically equivalent, but over time development of PySide lagged behind PyQt. This was particularly noticeable following the release of Qt 5 — the Qt5 version of PyQt (PyQt5) has been available since mid-2016, while the first stable release of PySide2 was 2 years later.

With that in mind, it is unsurprising that many Qt5 on Python examples use PyQt5 — if only because it was *available*. However, the Qt project has recently adopted PySide as the official Qt for Python release [https://www.qt.io/qt-for-python] which should ensure its viability going forward.

	PyQt5	PySide2
First stable release	Apr 2016	Jul 2018
Developed by	Riverbank Computing Ltd.	Qt
License	GPL or commercial	LGPL
Platforms	Python 3	Python 3 and Python 2.7 (Linux and macOS only)

Which should you use? Well, honestly, it doesn't really matter.

Both packages are wrapping the same library — Qt5 — and so have 99.9% identical APIs (see below for the few differences). Code that is written for one can often be used as-is with other, simply changing the imports from `PyQt5` to `PySide2`. Anything you learn for one library will be easily applied to a project using the other.

Also, no matter with one you choose to use, it's worth familiarizing yourself with the other so you can make the best use of all available online resources — using PyQt5 tutorials to build your PySide2 applications for example, and *vice versa*.

In this short chapter I'll run through the few notable differences between the two packages and explain how to write code which works seamlessly with both. After reading this you should be able to take any PyQt5 example online and convert it to work with PySide2.

Licensing

The main notable difference between the two versions is licensing — with PyQt5 being available under a GPL or commercial license, and PySide2 under a LGPL license.

If you are planning to release your software itself under the GPL, or you are developing software which will not be *distributed*, the GPL requirement of PyQt5 is unlikely to be an issue. However, if you want to distribute your software but not share your source code you will need to purchase a commercial license from Riverbank for PyQt5 or use PySide2.

> Qt itself is available under a *Qt Commercial License*, GPL 2.0, GPL 3.0 and LGPL 3.0 licenses.

UI files

The only major difference between the two libraries is in their handling of loading `.ui` files exported from Qt Creator/Designer. PyQt5 provides the `uic` submodule which can be used to load UI files directly, to produce an object. This feels pretty Pythonic (if you ignore the camelCase).

```
import sys
from PyQt5 import QtWidgets, uic

app = QtWidgets.QApplication(sys.argv)

window = uic.loadUi("mainwindow.ui")
window.show()
app.exec()
```

The equivalent with PySide2 is one line longer, since you need to create a `QUILoader` object first. Unfortunately the API of these two interfaces is different too (`.load` vs `.loadUI`).

```
import sys
from PySide2 import QtCore, QtGui, QtWidgets
from PySide2.QtUiTools import QUiLoader

loader = QUiLoader()

app = QtWidgets.QApplication(sys.argv)
window = loader.load("mainwindow.ui", None)
window.show()
app.exec_()
```

To load a UI onto an existing object in PyQt5, for example in your `QMainWindow.init` you can call `uic.loadUI` passing in `self`(the existing widget) as the second parameter.

```
import sys
from PyQt5 import QtCore, QtGui, QtWidgets
from PyQt5 import uic


class MainWindow(QtWidgets.QMainWindow):

    def __init__(self, *args, **kwargs):
        super().__init__(*args, **kwargs)
        uic.loadUi("mainwindow.ui", self)


app = QtWidgets.QApplication(sys.argv)
window = MainWindow()
window.show()
app.exec_()
```

The PySide2 loader does not support this — the second parameter to `.load` is the *parent* widget of the widget you're creating. This prevents you adding custom code to the `__init__` block of the widget, but you can work around this with a separate function.

```
import sys
from PySide2 import QtWidgets
from PySide2.QtUiTools import QUiLoader

loader = QUiLoader()

def mainwindow_setup(w):
    w.setWindowTitle("MainWindow Title")

app = QtWidgets.QApplication(sys.argv)

window = loader.load("mainwindow.ui", None)
mainwindow_setup(window)
window.show()
app.exec()
```

Converting UI files to Python

Both libraries provide identical scripts to generate Python importable modules from Qt Designer `.ui` files. For PyQt5 the script is named `pyuic5` —

```
pyuic5 mainwindow.ui -o MainWindow.py
```

You can then import the `UI_MainWindow` object, subclass using multiple inheritance from the base class you're using (e.g. `QMainWIndow`) and then call `self.setupUI(self)` to set the UI up.

```python
import sys
from PyQt5 import QtWidgets
from MainWindow import Ui_MainWindow

class MainWindow(QtWidgets.QMainWindow, Ui_MainWindow):

    def __init__(self, *args, **kwargs):
        super().__init__(*args, **kwargs)
        self.setupUi(self)


app = QtWidgets.QApplication(sys.argv)
window = MainWindow()
window.show()
app.exec()
```

For PySide2 it is named `pyside2-uic` —

```
pyside2-uic mainwindow.ui -o MainWindow.py
```

The subsequent setup is identical.

```python
import sys
from PySide2 import QtWidgets
from MainWindow import Ui_MainWindow

class MainWindow(QtWidgets.QMainWindow, Ui_MainWindow):

    def __init__(self, *args, **kwargs):
        super().__init__(*args, **kwargs)
        self.setupUi(self)


app = QtWidgets.QApplication(sys.argv)
window = MainWindow()
window.show()
app.exec_()
```

For more information in using Qt Designer with either PyQt5 or PySide2 see the Qt Creator chapter.

exec() or exec_()

The `.exec()` method is used in Qt to start the event loop of your `QApplication` or dialog boxes. In Python 2.7 `exec` was a keyword, meaning it could not be used for variable, function or method names. The solution used in both PyQt4 and PySide was to rename uses of `.exec` to `.exec_()` to avoid this conflict.

Python 3 removed the `exec` keyword, freeing the name up to be used. As PyQt5 targets only Python 3 it could remove the workaround, and `.exec()` calls are named just as in Qt itself. However, the `.exec_()` names are maintained for backwards compatibility.

PySide2 is available on both Python 3 and Python 2.7 and so still uses `.exec_()`. It is however only available for 64bit Linux and macOS.

If you're targeting both PySide2 and PyQt5 use `.exec_()`

Slots and Signals

Defining custom slots and signals uses slightly different syntax between the two libraries. PySide2 provides this interface under the names `Signal` and `Slot` while PyQt5 provides these as `pyqtSignal` and `pyqtSlot` respectively. The behavior of them both is identical for defining and slots and signals.

The following PyQt5 and PySide2 examples are identical —

```
my_custom_signal = pyqtSignal()  # PyQt5
my_custom_signal = Signal()  # PySide2

my_other_signal = pyqtSignal(int)  # PyQt5
my_other_signal = Signal(int)  # PySide2
```

Or for a slot —

```
@pyqtslot
def my_custom_slot():
    pass

@Slot
def my_custom_slot():
    pass
```

If you want to ensure consistency across PyQt5 and PySide2 you can use the following import pattern for PyQt5 to use the `Signal` and `@Slot` style there too.

```
from PyQt5.QtCore import pyqtSignal as Signal, pyqtSlot as Slot
```

You could of course do the reverse `from PySide2.QtCore import Signal as pyqtSignal, Slot as pyqtSlot` although that's a bit confusing.

Supporting both in libraries

You don't need to worry about this if you're writing a standalone app, just use whichever API you prefer.

If you're writing a library, widget or other tool you want to be compatible with both PyQt5 and PySide2 you can do so easily by adding both sets of imports.

```python
import sys

if 'PyQt5' in sys.modules:
    # PyQt5
    from PyQt5 import QtGui, QtWidgets, QtCore
    from PyQt5.QtCore import pyqtSignal as Signal, pyqtSlot as Slot

else:
    # PySide2
    from PySide2 import QtGui, QtWidgets, QtCore
    from PySide2.QtCore import Signal, Slot
```

This is the approach used in our custom widgets library, where we support for PyQt5 and PySide2 with a single library import. The only caveat is that you must ensure PyQt5 is imported before (as in on the line above or earlier) when importing this library, to ensure it is in `sys.modules`.

> An alternative would be to use an environment variable to switch between them — see QtPy later.

If you're doing this in multiple files it can get a bit cumbersome. A nice solution to this is to move the import logic to its own file, e.g. named `qt.py` in your project root. This module imports the Qt modules (`QtCore`, `QtGui`, `QtWidgets`, etc.) from one of the two libraries, and then you import into your application from there.

The contents of the `qt.py` are the same as we used earlier —

```python
import sys

if 'PyQt5' in sys.modules:
    # PyQt5
    from PyQt5 import QtGui, QtWidgets, QtCore
    from PyQt5.QtCore import pyqtSignal as Signal, pyqtSlot as Slot

else:
    # PySide2
    from PySide2 import QtGui, QtWidgets, QtCore
    from PySide2.QtCore import Signal, Slot
```

You must remember to add any other PyQt5 modules you use (browser, multimedia, etc.) in both branches of the if block. You can then import **Qt5** into your own application as follows —

```python
from .qt import QtGui, QtWidgets, QtCore
```

...and it will work seamlessly across either library.

QtPy

If you need to target more than just Qt5 support (e.g. including PyQt4 and PySide v1) take a look at QtPy [https://github.com/spyder-ide/qtpy]. This provides a standardized PySide2-like API for PyQt4, PySide, PyQt5 and PySide2. Using QtPy you can control which API to load from your application using the `QT_API` environment variable e.g.

```python
import os
os.environ['QT_API'] = 'pyside2'
from qtpy import QtGui, QtWidgets, QtCore  # imports PySide2.
```

That's really it

There's not much more to say — the two libraries really are that similar.

However, if you do stumble across any other PyQt5/PySide2 examples or features which you can't easily convert, drop me a note.

Appendix D: What next?

This book covers the key things you need to know to start creating GUI applications with Python. If you've made it here you should be well on your way to create your own apps!

But there is still a lot to discover while you build your applications. To help with this I post regular tips, tutorials and code snippets on the accompanying website [https://www.learnpyqt.com/]. Like this book all samples are MIT licensed and free to mix into your own apps.

You can also drop by the forum [https://forum.learnpyt.com] to ask questions and get help from me & fellow students. You may also be interested in my related video course [https://www.learnpyqt.com/purchase] which allows you to follow through and see the development of PyQt applications live.

Thanks for reading, and if you have any feedback or suggestions please let me know [mailto:martin@learnpyqt.com]!

Get access to updates

If you bought this book direct from me, you will have an account on LearnPyQt [https://www.learnpyqt.com/] where you will receive automatic updates to this book.

If you bought this book elsewhere, create an account at LearnPyQt [https://www.learnpyqt.com] and then email your receipt to me [mailto:martin@learnpyqt.com]. I'll add the books to your account for you right away.

Documentation

Resource
Qt5.10 Documentation [http://doc.qt.io/qt-5/]
PyQt5 Library documentation [http://pyqt.sourceforge.net/Docs/PyQt5/]

Resource
PySide "Qt for Python" Library documentation [https://doc.qt.io/qtforpython/]

Index

R

S

T

U

V

W

Printed in Great Britain
by Amazon

57716935R00407